THE BRITISH SHOW

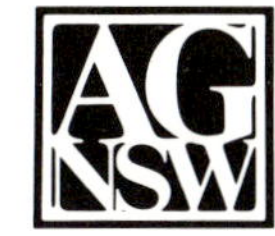

ART GALLERY OF NEW SOUTH WALES

DESIGNED, TYPESET AND PRINTED BY BEAVER PRESS
COVER: WORK, 1984, BY ANTHONY GORMLEY.

ITINERARY

Art Gallery of Western Australia
19 Feb — 24 March

Art Gallery of New South Wales
23 April — 9 June

Queensland Art Gallery
5 July — 11 August

CONTENTS Page

ESSAYS ON THE ARTISTS

INTRODUCTION TO THE TEMPORAL WORKS

'The British Show' has been arranged by the Art Gallery of New South Wales in association with The British Council with the assistance of the Department of Home Affairs and the Environment.

Indemnified by the British Government.

Published by the Art Gallery of New South Wales, Sydney.

ISBN 0 7305 1210 X

This exhibition has been realised with the most generous support of:

John Kaldor Fabricmaker Pty. Ltd. Australia
The British Council
The Visual Arts Board of the Australia Council

Editors: William Wright
             Anthony Bond

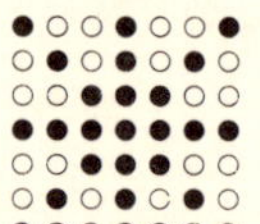

THE BRITISH COUNCIL

FOREWORD FOR THE BRITISH SHOW

This exhibition is the result of an exemplary co-operation between the British Council and the Art Gallery of New South Wales. In some respects it is unique among international exhibitions arranged for Australia. Two curators from Australia were invited by the British Council with the assistance of the Visual Arts Board of the Australia Council to make two extensive trips to Britain to determine the framework for an exhibition and to select specific works to ensure the very best representation of contemporary developments as they saw them. Thus from a profusion of options they were able to distil a coherent and positive selection.

Past experience of exhibitions selected by Australians overseas has shown that the works which actually arrived were not always those chosen. In avoiding such confusion in this case we must thank Brett Rogers of the British Council for her work in following up the loans requested by the curators and her tireless efforts to ensure strict adherence to the selected works.

While the exhibition covers a wide range of activity from painting to temporal works there is a strong nucleus of sculpture which represents the most visible recent development in British art. There is a strong interest in the future of three-dimensional work in Australia at present and this selection of new works representing many facets of the revitalised art form in England is, therefore, ideally timed.

We express particular thanks to the British Council for their very substantial contribution to and support of this exhibition, to John Kaldor Fabricmakers and to the Visual Arts Board of the Australia Council our appreciation for their most generous financial support. My own thanks also to William Wright (Assistant Director-Professional) and Tony Bond (Curator of Contemporary Art) from this Gallery for their wholehearted organisation of this project from its very beginning.

Edmund Capon (Director)

FOREWORD

As the present exhibition marks the first occasion in well over a decade a major exhibition of British contemporary art has toured Australia, it would seem appropriate to ask: why the need for a British show at this particular time? An answer to this question is perhaps best prefaced by some remarks on both the immediate and the more distant historical contexts within which this exhibition will take place.

It is hardly surprising that the character of Australian art during the first 100 years of its existence was largely shaped by the conventions of English art. Even the periods of pronounced nationalist fervour, particularly the late 19th century and again in the immediate post-war era of the 1940s and fifties may have quelled, but did not diminish the strangle-hold which the British academic tradition continued to exert, especially in art schools, well into the 1960s. Richard Francis' comments in his introductory essay on the nature of the British response to European modernism are important just because early modernism was brought to Australia by artists who had gained their experience of it through London, and only to a lesser extent through France.

With the emergence of International Abstraction in the fifties and sixties the relationship was changed but, surprisingly, not severed. Patrick McCaughey (Director, National Gallery of Victoria) has in fact gone so far as to say "The Englishness of Australian art is endemic and the new generation of the 1960s was no exception". Although the momentum for this new art derived from New York, it was the experience of it gained through London which proved most significant to Australian artists. Not only were many Australian artists drawn to live in London during the sixties, but conversely a number of British artists chose to bring a particular form of British abstraction to Australia at this time.

During the seventies, the absence of a predominant international art centre coincided with the growth of a regional impetus in contemporary art, which altered, as a matter of course, the relationship between the two communities. At the same time social and political forces at work within Australia forced a re-evaluation of the country's traditional allegiances.

It is nearly two decades since the last survey show of contemporary British art was shown in Australia. In the interim the British Council has toured several important exhibitions of works by contemporary artists such as Bridget Riley and Anthony Caro as well as a major survey of art from previous centuries, *British Painting 1600-1800.* During this period, several enterprising individuals have presented work of a younger generation of British artists, including Nigel Hall, Richard Long, Gilbert & George, John Hoyland and Michael Craig-Martin. Since its inception in 1973, the Biennale of Sydney has played a major role in the dissemination of information about recent developments in British art. Whilst all these avenues have provided some indication of current activity, they have been unable to reflect fully the range, energy and commitment which characterises contemporary British art. The current exhibition, in which the work of artists hitherto rarely shown outside Britian is seen in conjunction with that of established artists already well-known to an Australian audience, will, we trust, help to fill this gap.

Just as is customary for the Director of the Biennale of Sydney to select the British contingent for that event, we have elected on this occasion to invite two Australian curators to undertake the selection of what they consider to be the most vital and pertinent work being produced in Britain today. William Wright, Assistant Director of the Art Gallery of New South Wales, and Anthony Bond, its recently appointed Curator of Contemporary Art, have undertaken this formidable task with the advice and assistance of Richard Francis of the Tate Gallery, London. We thank all three of them for producing a selection which reflects much of the vitality and exuberance of British art at this particular time. In addition to 'New British Sculpture' which has received a great deal of international attention recently, time-based work and painting have been included. This juxtaposition should enable serious discussion and analysis of the close interaction between these different media in recent years.

We should like to express our warm thanks to all those lenders whose generous support has made this exhibition possible. Thanks are also due to the participating artists whose close co-operation and personal involvement throughout the preparation of the show has been invaluable. We must also extend our thanks to the many contributors to this catalogue who produced specially commissioned essays for the occasion. The Fine Arts Department is extremely grateful to the Visual Arts Board of the Australia Council and John Kaldor for the considerable financial support they have provided, and to the staff of both the Art Gallery of New South Wales, Sydney, and the British Council office, Sydney, for their advice and assistance throughout the planning of the exhibition. Our special thanks go to Patsy Zeppel, Peter Prescott (former Representative), Ray Newbuerry (Representative) from our Sydney office and to Edmund Capon and Jan Meek and Anna Waldman of the Art Gallery of New South Wales.

Julian Andrews & Brett Rogers

ACKNOWLEDGEMENTS

We would like to thank the many people who have contributed to this exhibition:

John Kaldor — has generously contributed the private sponsorship, which was necessary to allow the Show to occur, at a time when he was already deeply involved in his Art Project No. 7 'An Australian Accent'.

Julian Andrews — (Director of Fine Arts at the British Council in London) & **Nick Waterlow** — (previously Director of the Visual Arts Board at the Australia Council), whose early discussions seeded the exhibition.

Muriel Wilson Deputy Director British Council Fine Arts Department.

Patsy Zeppel, Peter Prescott and Ray Newbury of the British Council in Sydney who have made tireless efforts to achieve support from the corporate sector and to ensure the success of the Show in addition to providing substantial financial support.

Ross Wolfe and Seva Frangos of the Visual Arts Board staff, and **Betty Churcher, Chairperson**, who have patiently supported the efforts to realise the exhibition and its ancillary projects.

Richard Francis, Tate Gallery who listened and gave advice to the curators on their visits to London and whose contributions to the catalogue are beyond the call of duty. All the other notable contributors to the catalogue listed in the contents page.

The staff of the Art Gallery of NSW, including **Jan Meek** who worked hard at the unrewarding task of seeking sponsorship, and the more rewarding aspect of promoting the exhibition to the media.

Anna Waldmann who has helped at various stages in assembling material and summarising texts for the catalogue; **Rita Matthews** who typed and copied copious material and fielded hundreds of calls and telegrams, and the Education staff, in particular **Ursula Prunster** and **Brian Ladd**.

Above all, **Brett Rogers** of the British Council in London who set up the interviews and visits for the curators, arranged their needs and urgent requests, negotiated loans, confirmed the commissions of essays and delivered the catalogue material and finally arranged the shipping. All of this made the work of the curators in Australia as pleasant as possible and ensured that the exhibition and catalogue is what they intended.

Anthony Bond
William Wright

The organisers would like to express their thanks to the following individuals, galleries and institutions who have lent works to this exhibition.

Salvatore Ala, New York and Milan
Art Gallery of New South Wales, Sydney
Art Gallery of Western Australia, Perth
Arts Council of Great Britain
The British Council Collection, London
Mr and Mrs Brooks Barron, Detroit
Contemporary Art Society, London
Mr and Mrs Archibald Cox Jnr, London
Anthony D'Offay Gallery, London
Gimpel Fils, London
Fischer Fine Art, London
Janet and Michael Green, London
Nigel Greenwood Gallery, London
Nicola Jacobs Gallery, London
John Kaldor, Sydney
James Kirkman, London
Lisson Gallery, London
S.A. McLean, Ireland
Marlborough Fine Art (London) Ltd
Graeme Murray Gallery, Edinburgh
The Pace Gallery, New York
Private Collections, London
Private Collection, New York
Queensland Art Gallery, Brisbane
Richard Salmon Esq. London
The Saatchi Collection, London
Southampton Art Gallery, Southampton
Waddington Galleries, London
Ed Wolf, London
Museum of Modern Art, New York
National Gallery of Scotland Edinburgh

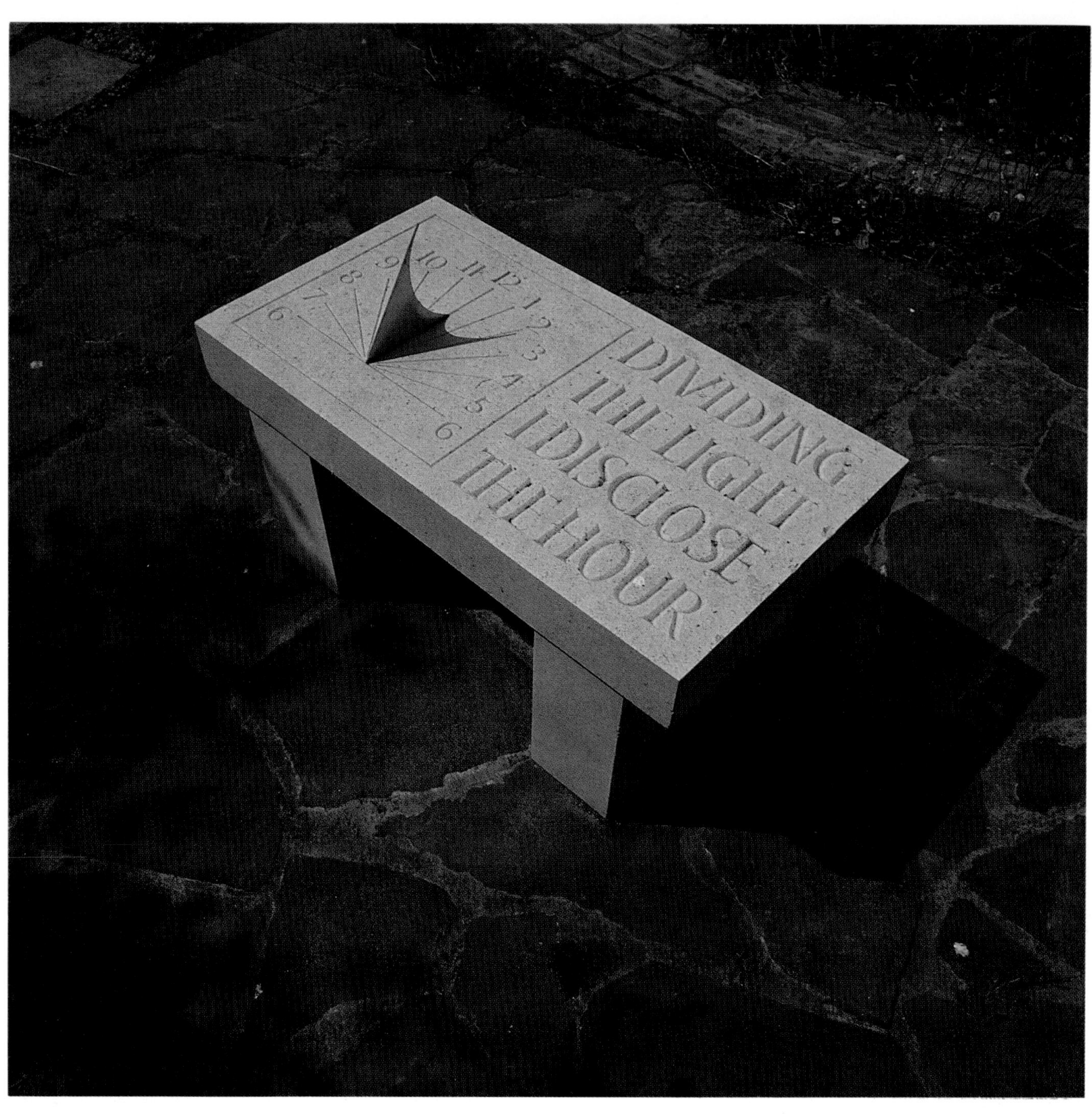

Sundial at Stonypath
by Ian Hamilton Finlay
photo by David Paterson, London

*"On a continent even in small countries on a continent,
the daily life is of course a daily life but it is not held in
within as it is on an island and that makes an
enormous difference, and I am quite certain that even if
you do not see it as the same anybody does see that
this if it is the truth is the truth".[1]*
Gertrude Stein.

INTRODUCTION

British art exists within a spiritual past, a history of place, of an order long since irretrievably lost to the new-world transplants — the Australians. To the generations of Moore, Nicholson, Hepworth, or Lanyon and Heron its *old-stones* are living reminders of cultural memory, a conditional presence within collective awareness. Avebury, Stonehenge or Men an Tol are more than familiar motifs, but their presence also exists in the mental environment of urban British artists. Such time-absorbed sites (and legends) and by extension those of other cultures, have recently gained renewed meaning as mnemonic touch-stones of a dislocated spiritual past, in the face of an imponderable post-industrial future.

While our cultural allegiance has been immutably transformed, Australian and British artists continue to share many common attitudes and values, and a similarly resistant "island" disposition: both experience, if in differing circumstance and degree, a parallel critical vantage due to physical and linguistic separation from the hegemony of Europe and America: hence an essentially provisionary mode of engagement in the international dynamics of art: reinforcing an understanding of identity as being determined by place other than events.

It is only 18 years since the last major exhibition of contemporary British art in Australia. In this period however both British and Australian art have undergone far-reaching transformations. There has also been an inevitable loosening of the ties of kinship which previously bound one to the other.

Until as late as the sixties most Australians were still predisposed, if residually, to a single-parent relationship with the nation of our earliest forebears; and exhibitions of British art had perhaps reinforced this filial predilection. Yet during the recent past, particularly since the culturally enlightened Whitlam period, Australians have come increasingly to embrace the dual realities of post-war multi-cultural immigration and of their Asian-Pacific global context, resulting in a consequent revitalisation of cultural priorities and objectives.

In concert with the social transformation towards multi-culturalism, the Australia Council, since its inception in 1972, has assisted in the cultural transition away from the old Anglocentricity by supporting an active, two-way international programme of exhibitions and forums. An increasing flow of artists and curators, in and out of Australia, has done much to alter the climate of cultural dependency. This current survey of innovative works from Britain will be accorded recognition for intrinsic value, as one vitally relevant contribution within a larger, continuing programme of international and Australian exhibitions.

Some of the best work of the present generation of British artists operates as a paradoxical re-investiture in nomadic tradition, but transposed into the urban landscape. Integration in so much recent British art of landscape, myth and language with the ironic expressions of sub-cultural style is centrally characteristic of the new developments in British art: its meaning is explicit as within an inter-connecting urban social attitude.

British art also exists, however sceptically, as part of an internationally fluid scheme of ideas and interventions. Having wavered in their trans-Atlantic affiliation during the past decade, in concert with the Europeans, and ourselves, there has been a recent concerted move towards realigning their broad artistic intentions with the more 'ethically' formulated 'poetics' of the old world. In this, British art is also part of a larger Eurocentric process of affirmation which is reflective of a loss of faith, a response as much to the application of power, as in the artistic realm, to the consequent prior dominance of prescriptive modes. This appears as a new variant of contention between the 'analytic/pragmatic, depoliticised and commercial' nature of American art, and the 'intuitive/idealistic, self-questioning and ethical modes ascribed as intrinsically European. A dichotomy which may appear less immediately convincing within an Australian perspective than a European one.

The recent widespread return to object-based practices is clearly not merely an expression of collective nostalgia for the sanctitude of an earlier traditionalism nor, as it has been asserted, the fabrication of art markets in the interest of the stagnant tastes of a decaying society, but represents the consolidating enrichment of many prior developments; substantiating a common desire to expand an experiential basis of artistic expression, hard-won during the preceding decades.

As part of this process we have seen the beginnings

of an attempt to review the role of sculptural works in the post-1970s context. Essentially this is centred on two developments, distinct from each other; the extension of recent German and Italian painting into hybrid sculptural image: Baselitz, Immendorff, Penck, Lupertz, Muller, Paladino, Cucchi, Chia and the more complex issue of the new British sculpture which encompasses a more diverse, and more individuated, field of ideas and processes. Flanagan, Gilbert and George, Woodrow, Cragg, Willats and the younger artists, Cox, Deacon, Gormley, Kapoor, Opie and Housiary.

While in its composition the British Show contradicts any short-circuiting of the modernist legacy, many of the sculptural works included will contribute substantially to a reconsideration of the role of the image in post-1970s deconstruction.

The influence of post-war British sculpture began with the work of Henry Moore and Barbara Hepworth and was later sustained by Anthony Caro and the international formalist movement, which, nurtured under his influence, established a level of continuing interest beyond that afforded other areas of British art in this century. It was not coincidental that one of the major areas of recent development in sculpture came into being at St. Martins School of Art in London, where for years Caro had been mentor to innumerable formalist sculptors and where the background of willing proselytism lent moral conviction to other more ambitious members of the student generation of the mid-sixties to early seventies. Artists now in mid-career who during their early development experienced the formative periods of pop art, environmental art, minimalism, conceptual art, earth, land and body art, they arrived at their early artistic formation at a period of greatest reaction against formalist tenets, a time of fundamental questioning about the ethical determination of art; in the process precursively contributing to the reformation of late modernism. This development has persisted in the independent British context in confluence with the emergence of a second revisionist generation of image sculptors who have benefitted additionally from the more recent periods of feminist and post-structuralist theories within a widening media context.

In accepting the British Council's invitation to organise and select an exhibition of recent British art we have opted to present several spheres of currently vital activity. Providing an exhibition of works which are of significant interest in the art context in Australia, and correspondingly pertinent in an international context, but which for the major part exist quite separate from the framework of ideas and developments in recent Australian art. In so doing we have not represented a unified ideological or stylistic path in British art, but have chosen, on the basis of individual preferences, a diverse array of works of a challenging cultural motivation; modalities connected more in spirit than content.

At a less specific level the selection has been informed by a desire to communicate the essence of what is a very particular and exceptionally developed artistic climate of activity at its time of present social and cultural catharsis. An equal priority, was to represent the selected artists essentially, and well, and we have chosen examples of work which are most irreducibly complete in representing each artist's strategic content and development.

In our intention to present an exhibition of the most challenging of recent developments, we were unusually fortunate in having ample time for planning, negotiations and studio visits, and especially in having been able to plan so well in advance of the many American, European and British exhibition organisers who, subsequent to our involvement, became interested in exhibiting many of the works selected for this exhibition.

William Wright
16.1.1985

1. Stein, Gertrude *Lectures in America*. Boston, Beacon Press, 1957.

INTRODUCTION: THE SELECTION

When research started on the exhibition it was to have been called 'British Art through Australian eyes'. Although this title was considered too unwieldly the concept has remained relevant. The exhibition contrasts with the British Art Show arranged by British curators to tour Britain in 1984-85 for the Arts Council. Our selection represents a particular point of view and is not an attempt to survey all that is excellent in Britain today. We have captured the essence of what we perceived to be significantly different about contemporary British art with a view to providing a relevant context for Australian audiences.

A network of association and common practices linked the works in this exhibition, although there is in no sense a mainstream or school of thought. Even within what is loosely termed 'The new Sculpture', there are highly diverse intentions and working strategies. The most obvious linking factor is the use of the image. Auerbach, Kossoff, Freud and Kiff have maintained a figurative stance in the face of savage opposition from abstraction throughout the fifties and sixties. For most of the younger artists there had to be a search for the image and for a viable methodology through which content and image could be re-incorporated conceptually without losing the essential gains of modernism in the 20th century.

While much of the newer work has an affinity with 'Pop' art it is the hard-won analytical and often ironic art of Hamilton rather than the instant-image value of American 'Pop'. Conceptual art has been a critical mediator in the process of rediscovery and as we see with the sculptors, minimalism has provided the crucial backbone.

In the case of the older generation of painters in the exhibition their enquiry into the hard-won possibilities of the figure run counter to the post-modern context in to which they are at times thrown. All the artists in this exhibition, including those most easily identified with post-modern recycling have succeeded, because they have taken the best of modernist theory, applied it in a changing world, and adapted it in full knowledge of the meaning of their adaptation. Contrary to superficial appearances, rummaging in 'trash cans' for material need not equate with the new 'imagist' tendency to rummage indiscriminately in the history of art.

A strong intuition was at work during the selection process, enabling a coherent structure to be developed without being seduced by too obvious categorisations and superficial appearances such as that of urban recycling. Since then the intuition has crystallised into a rather loose but useful aesthetic proposition. The following remarks cannot be applied uniformly or universally to the art in this exhibition, yet they do demonstrate an ethos of British art and help to characterise the context for our selection.

Peter Fuller has written about English psycho-analytical object theory in his book on Robert Natkin, the American abstract painter. In this book he identifies veils of colour with a psychological barrier which must be crossed by the weaning infant when self, as in some way separate from all-embracing mother, is first realised and, by implication, the 'otherness' of all objects in the world. In some form or other, a dichotomy between undifferentiated chaos and objectively ordered existence crops up in European thinking from the very earliest times to current psycho-analytical theory. One aspect of this dichotomy is the eternal desire to merge into the pre-social, pre-objective world. Lacan speaks of the desire to submerge individual identity in order to regain a sense of 'oneness' or zero-relationship. Identity separates us, while weaning leaves us slightly dissatisfied. Behind many undefined desires in the human psyche lies this craving for sublimation or re-integration. In the symposium Plato refers to the myth in which man is punished by Zeus by having his essential unity split. He therefore spends the remainder of his mortal life seeking re-integration through love.

Stuart Brisley, whose work is in the show, has suggested another aspect of this experience. He talks about a realm of primodial flux in which, the processes of entropy complete, man falls back to the pre-social condition of the animal world. He points to the chaos which lies just behind the surface of social organisation and the way in which ritual has traditionally provided access or release to this aspect of experience, and how performance art has re-invoked these rituals in an alienated individual form.

The artist has an interesting relationship to this ancient psychological dichotomy. He stands at the edge allowing passage and partial gratification of the urge for sublimation. He also holds the 'veil' which can be broken, to allow new objects to enter the world of objective appearance, fabricated from the primodial flux. Many artists have abdicated this responsibility and merely seek to make pictures of previously extant models, either from the world at large, or from the history of art. The artists in this exhibition not only provide evidence of an understanding of this role, they often directly invoke the metaphor in the process of production and the form of the work. It is in effect a reference to the very act of becoming.

Auerbach is quoted elsewhere in this catalogue as distinguishing paintings of things, of which there are already too many in the world, from the new objects which he wishes to bring into the world, created out of the surface of the paint.

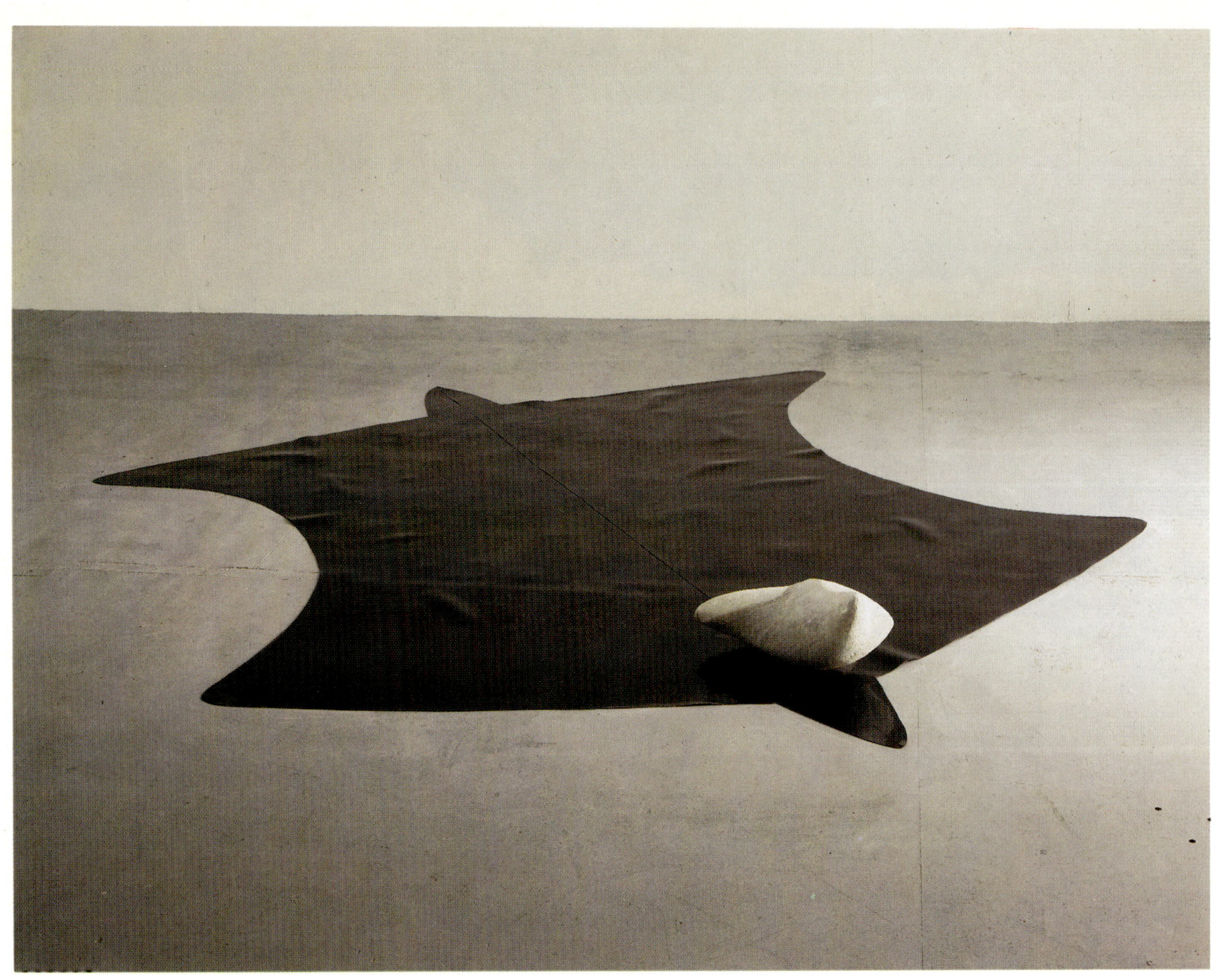

Alison Wilding
Dark Horse I
1983

portland stone & rubber
24 x 255 x 312.5cms
The Artist, courtesy Salvatore Ala gallery Milan & New York

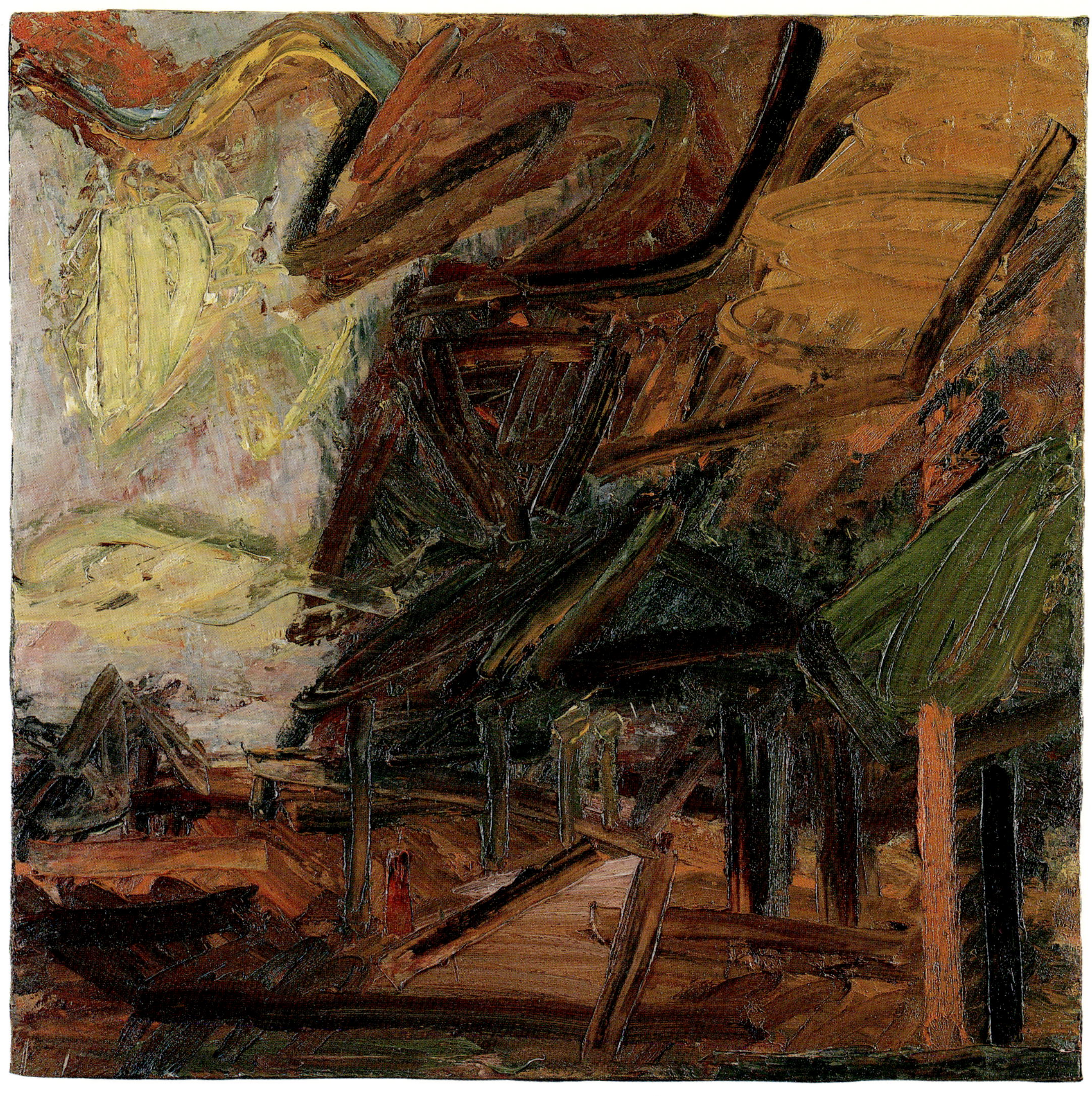

Frank Auerbach
Primrose Hill, Autumn
1984

oil on canvas
48 x 48ins
121.9 x 121.9cms
Marlborough Fine Art London

Kossoff paints figures which seem to be struggling into existence within a surface of paint which suggests the edge of primodial flux.

Woodrow uses the skin of discarded industrial objects and by a logical system of cuts turns them inside out to blossom into new forms.

Gormley makes his figures as vessels with apertures which occur at the classic points of entry and exit, where man and nature interact most emphatically. When he chooses to photograph his work on the seashore, the eternal symbol of the sea as universal unconscious, or homogeneous, chaos gives an added piquancy.

In Kapoor the pigmented surface somehow becomes the form suggesting energy rather than substantial matter.

Bob Law has made an art in which the absence becomes the point of concentration. His voids turn into mirrors of self-reflection for the viewer and his empty chairs provide a presence created in the imagination from beyond the void.

The work of Stephen Willats helps to illuminate the sculptural section by his articulation of the idea of transformation. In the 'Pat Purdy' piece which derived from a series in the 'Lurky Place' since 1977, he presents us with the extraordinary metamorphosis of an object as it passes between two cultural situations. In the determinist object-oriented housing estate, the glue can has a pragmatic constructive function. When it passes through a hole in the cyclone wire fence into the adjacent wastelands it becomes the focal point of an anarchic cult of destruction in the hands of the alienated youths who build their camps there (see Richard Francis' essay on Willats). The form of the work is four triptychs comprising one large panel of the estate, and one for the wasteland. These are separated by three smaller panels presenting the fence as a nodal point or pivot. On the smaller panel at the point of transformation he has attached an object retrieved from the sites. The fence has now become a psychological metaphor for the veil which divides chaos and determinism. For Willats the activity of the youths is a creative attempt at self-determination in the only way possible to them.

In Tony Cragg's 'New Stones Newton's Tones' 1978, the rectangle of coloured fragments from consumer waste creates an image which apes high formalist aesthetics while continuously reminding us of the transformation of plastic detritus into expensive art. As with Willats, the use of classic form of organisation is not only ironic but also gives the work its presence and its working ethic. The form of 'Pat Purdy' is an essential part of its metaphoric content. The form of 'New Stones Newton's Tones' by Cragg is a reference to Richard Long and Carl Andre without which the work would have no meaning. Subsequent developments of the image are contingent upon this step and involve deliberate contraventions of minimalist working ideals. The history of ideas takes many channels, but all of these artists have made calculated moves in relation to the past 20 years of visual arts enquiry. It is to be hoped that this exhibition will be of use to contemporary Australian artists in making the value of this historically-integrated attitude manifest.

Other strands that run through this exhibition are an ironic sense of humour and a well developed sense of the surreal. This should not be confused with whimsicality or with a lack of essential aesthetic commitment. The well orchestrated moment of surreal ambiguity is as hard-won as any monument to high tragedy. Richard Wentworth is a master of the tantalisingly juxtaposed object. Like Bob Law he opens up a space for the audience to join in the process of association. In the early sixties Ron Kitaj spoke of the need for all art to be 'allusive' while remaining 'illusive'. It is a political statement about the role of the artists and the viewer in relation to the imagination and that realm between chaos and order where art can open doors rather than close them. It is this attitude as much as anything else which sums up the meaning of this exhibition.

Anthony Bond

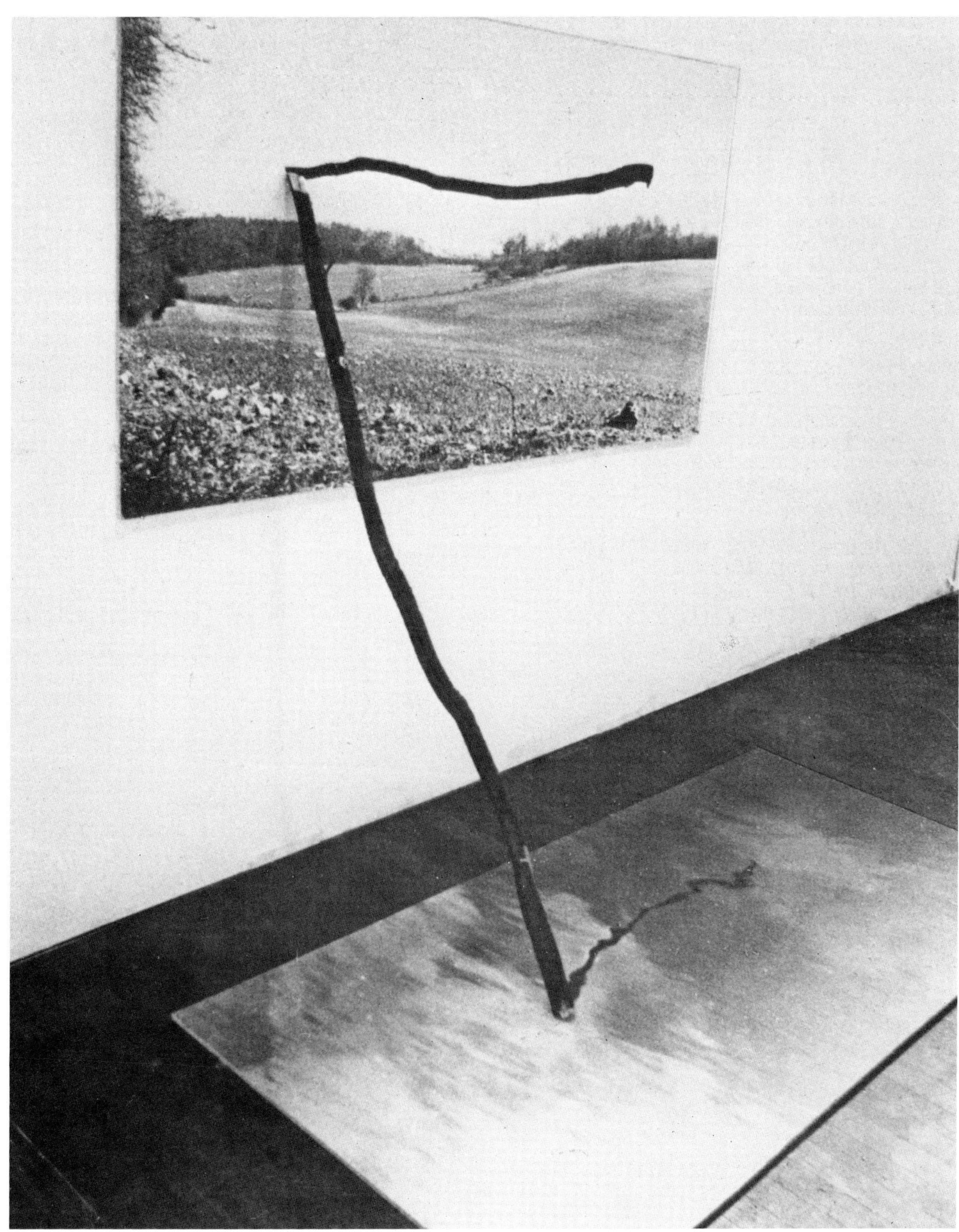

Bill Woodrow
Untitled
1970-71

photographic panels,
wooden stick
photo credit: Lisson Gallery, London

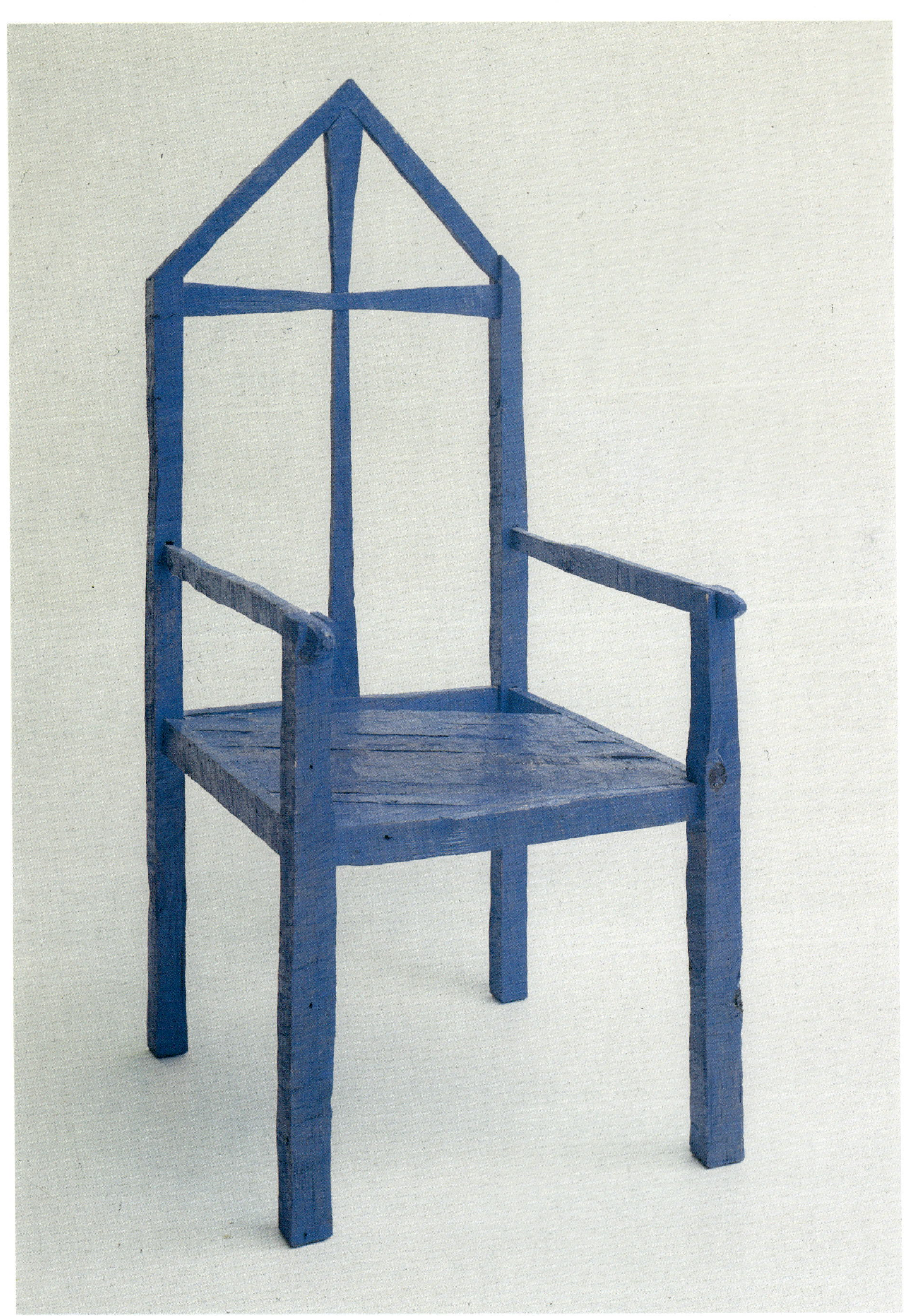

Bob Law
Christ Chair in Ultramarine
1984

painted wood
120.3 x 57.5 x 52cms
Lisson Gallery, London
photo credit: Rodney Todd White & Associates, London

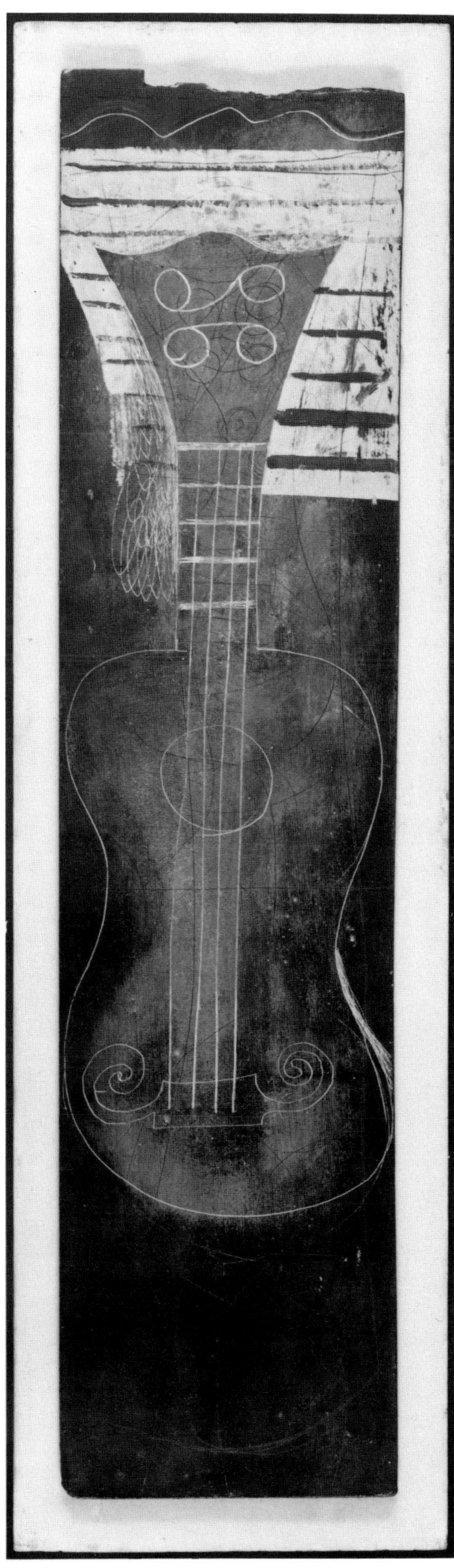

Ben Nicholson
Guitar
1933

Tate Gallery London
oil on wood
photo credit: The Tate Gallery, London

EVEN THE BRITISH . . .

Two ambitious exhibitions of current British art have recently been mustered — this and one for home consumption. The Arts Council of Great Britain's "The British Art Show" organised to tour Britain is an uncomfortably diffuse large-scale touring exhibition which opened in early November. Selected by three insider-outsiders, (that is people prominent in their own parts of the artworld but not regularly exposed to public inspection) from more than 1,000 studio visits, it presented 82 artists or groups under the subtitle *Old Allegiances and New Directions*.[1] In their persuasively bland preface, the Arts Council's officers attempted to reconcile not only the contradiction of a view that is at once 'personal' but also 'structured and argued' but one which would acknowledge the traditional roots of recent art and the demise of modernism as it affects current British art. In the event, the catalogue perhaps speaks more clearly than the exhibition.[2] Each of the selectors' introductory essays offers a view which encapsulates the prevailing mood. John Thompson, Director of Post-graduate studies at Goldsmith's College of Art in his essay "Reversing the Trans-atlantic drift" argues that American colonisation of the notions of Modernism and subsequent debasement of it to 'progress', materialism and an abstraction rooted in the sterile soil of presentation rather than representation — in short an art which had lost its morality in its crude attempts to be the dominant ideology — masked temporarily the great European liberal utopian idea of progress — towards goodness and the sublime. Thompson suggests that the re-discovery of strengths in European art which in current terms is pluralistic, poetic and incorporates traditional ideas has meant the demise of New York in favour of European, specifically German and Italian painting. He concludes by citing a New York siege mentality and a last-ditch stand on the part of some critics to recapture Modernism's ground. He writes "After all, the Teutonic hordes are at the gate; some are already within the citadel. The Italian carnival is parading in their streets and *even the British* are beginning to throw off the yoke of 25 years of cultural domination" (my italics)[3].

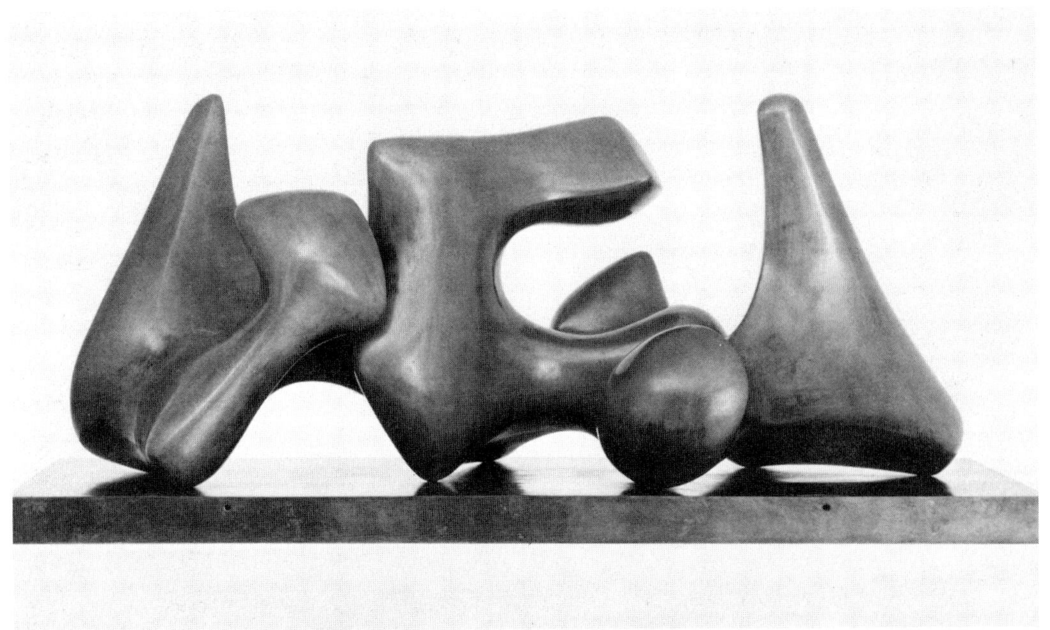

Henry Moore
Working Model for Three Piece No. 3.: Vertebrae

Tate Gallery London
2nd view
photo credit: The Tate Gallery, London

Within a week of opening the British Art Show, Lord Gowrie, Minister for the Arts, announced the winner of the first *Turner Prize*, a £10,000 award given anonymously by a Patron of New Art, a group created by the Director of Tate Gallery to promote interest in and collection of 'new art' in Britain. When the award 'for the greatest contribution to British Art in the past 12 months' was given to Malcolm Morley, who had left Britain in 1958 to live and work in New York, (but had retained his citizenship) it occasioned immediate surprise, subsequent outrage and was called the worst possible choice by the Guardian's critic. The jury which included Rudi Fuchs, the director of the Van Abbemuseum in Eindhoven (a keen supporter of the middle generation of British artists) and Nick Serota, director of Whitechapel, (the curator responsible for most of the contemporary European Art brought to England) had chosen Morley over indigenous and perhaps more "British" artists. Morley, in a telephone conversation with the BBC, said that he regarded himself as an "international" artist.

Old Directions...

During his Prize giving speech, Lord Gowrie not only praised the liveliness of current British Art but also paid "pious tribute" to three men "above all honour" — Francis Bacon, Henry Moore and Ben Nicholson. (Bacon is 75, Moore 86, Nicholson died in 1982, aged 88). Their work was brought together 50 years ago, in 1934, when the Mayor Gallery mounted an exhibition entitled *Art Now* to coincide with the publication of Herbert Read's book of the same title. Moore and Nicholson were acknowledged leaders, Bacon a relative newcomer who painted only sparingly in the decade that was to follow.

The centre of the argument surrounding that exhibition was expressed clearly in Adrian Stokes' review in the Spectator. Stokes wrote:—

"All modern visual art whatsoever, good or bad, 'advanced' or academic, is characterised by a self-conscious and literary approach. Art to us is manifestly a personal projection, a synthesis of experience...We may take it that the louder his protestation of purely visual values and the greater the abstraction that the true painter achieves, the more concentrated...perhaps the more unconscious and therefore the more pervasive is the literary content of his art."[4]

Stokes' review, with its insistence on experience over abstraction preceded statements by Moore and Nicholson in the *Circle* manifesto of 1937. That publication brought together European representatives of the 'modern movement' (not modernism), a process greatly encouraged by the flight of refugees from Germany and Holland, and gave some British Art a status equal with advanced European art. Nicholson wrote, concerning his own work and the nature of abstraction:—

"It must be understood that a good idea is exactly as good as it can be universally applied, that no idea can have a universal application which is not solved in its own terms... 'Realism' has been abandoned in the search for reality: the 'principle objective of abstract art is precisely this reality."[5]

and Moore

"I dislike the idea that contemporary art is an escape from life. Because a work does not aim at reproducing the natural appearance it is not therefore an escape from life — it may be a penetrating into reality...and expression of the significance of life, a stimulation to greater effort in living."[6]

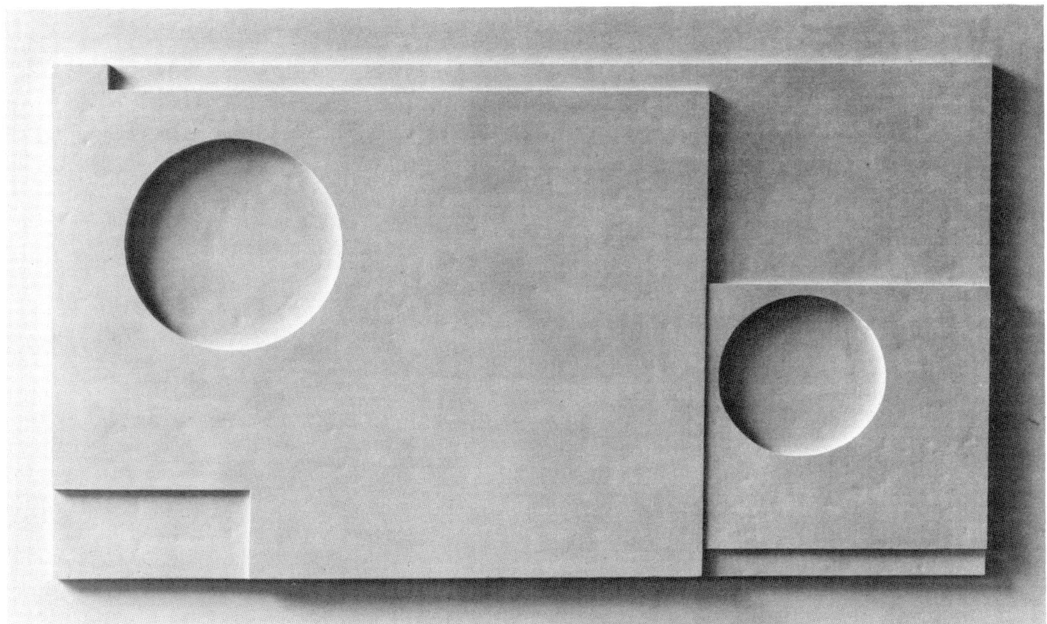

Ben Nicholson
White Relief
1935

Tate Gallery London
photo credit: The Tate Gallery, London

The contrast appears extreme — Nicholson striving to create universals which create a higher reality, an abstracted world, Moore blithely commonsensical, anxious that his reality should be informed by life outside. Moore had shown in the *International Surrealist Exhibition* in London in 1936, and in 1938 was cast as a 'surrealist' in the issue of the London Bulletin that published Nicholson as a 'constructivist'[7]. This merely confirmed the battle-lines that had been drawn up. But Moore would have none of this quarrel: he had written, in 1937, "All good art has contained both abstract and surrealist elements, just as it has contained both classical and romantic elements — order and surprise, intellect and imagination, conscious and unconscious."[8] and placed himself outside both the reductive idealising of the abstract artists and the expressive, neo-romantic camp. In one sense, Moore's proposed route, of pragmatism, sensibility and nature, the *via media* was conventionally British. The satisfactory compromise resulted perhaps in a less extreme and possibly more insular art.

Adrian Stokes' suspicion that Nicholson was as fully a 'literary' artist as any other was confirmed for him by a story he recounted in 1969. Talking of Nicholson's work as a "permeation of his approach to life", of his graceful ease among "surfaces and weights" and his predilection for spiritual rather than conceptual thought, Stokes writes:— "he would speak of the merits or demerits of a painting as its "thought", or, maybe, of a tool. He has told that his mother, herself an artist, distressed by high-flown talk, would find herself wanting to scrub the kitchen table."[9] Nicholson and Moore can be joined together by a non-conformist matter-of-factness, by their appraisal of spiritual or artistic, theoretical matters in terms, specifically, of materials. For the crux of Nicholson's case rests on the conjunction of "thought" and "tool": the literal surface represents the ideology of its making. English art was more likely to accede to this argument rather than the continental modern movement's ideas. The conventions of pragmatism, concern for surface and materials were perhaps more easily expressible.

The point that I am making is that English Art in the persons of Nicholson and Moore, appears to have taken on board only those parts of the modernist theoretical framework that suited them. David Sylvester wrote in 1978 that Moore "has always been more or less involved in reconciling certain modernist assumptions with the European tradition against which modernism has rebelled"[10]. He suggests that Moore's work is given a complexity of articulation, springing from a desire 'to relate and combine together several forms of varied sizes, sections and directions'. He noted that this was contrary to Moore's expressed preference for simple iconic images — those that would agree more easily with the modernist prescription. If this is clear in the work of the 20's and 30's, it is especially apparent in a series of works such as *Working Model for Three Piece No. 3: Vertebrae*, (1968) were the articulations are extreme in their diversity and direction. Nicholson too diverged from the purity of his 1930s work, and, by 1956, in a painting such as *Val d'Orcia August '56* (1956) was reworking some of the recognizable imagery of his early paintings. The work of the 1950s is baroque by comparison with *White Relief* (1935) and includes colours and forms that allude to European landscape and to emotional ideas. (Nicholson admired Mark Rothko greatly but their work could not look more different, the Englishman's being almost completely divorced from Rothko's "modernism", by then firmly defined by Greenberg and his followers.)

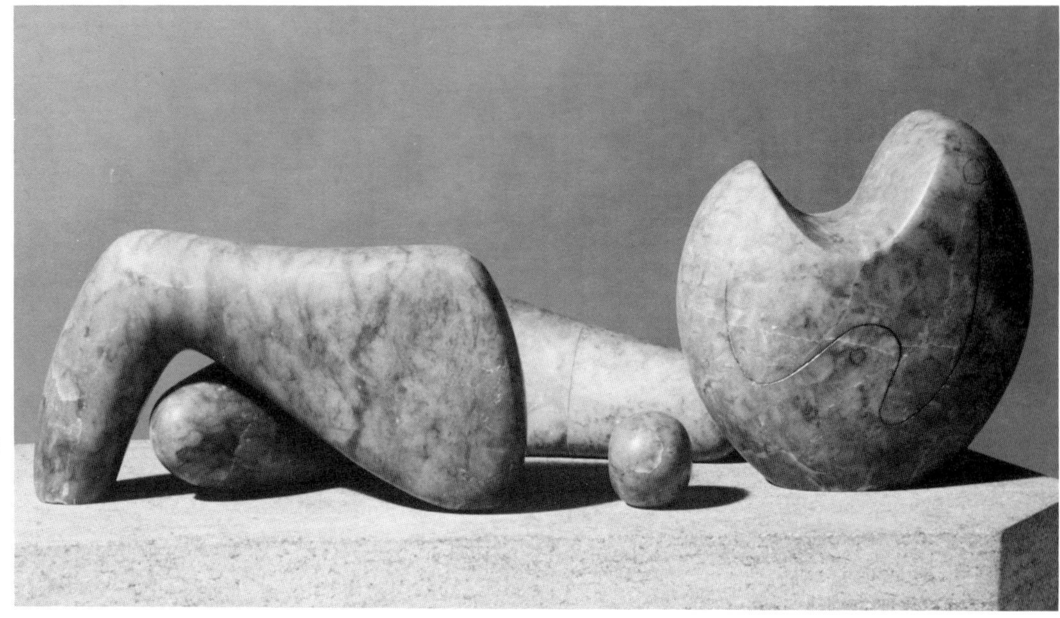

Henry Moore
Four-Piece Composition:
Reclining Figure
1934

Tate Gallery London
sculpture-stone
main view
photo credit: The Tate Gallery, London

Bacon has preferred always to regard himself as an outsider, not only outside the conventions of the English art world (not many of his friends are artists and he has refused honours) but outside modernist conventions. His early commentators assumed that he aspired to the *Grand Manner* rather than modernism.[11] Bacon has often made clear his dislike of abstract painting.

> "I believe that art is recording; I think it's reporting. And I think that in abstract art, as there's no report, there's nothing other than the aesthetic of the painter and his few sensations. There's never any tension in it . . . I think I can convey very watered-down lyrical feelings, because I think any shapes can. But I don't think it can easily convey feeling in the grand sense."[12]

Or, on another occasion

> "I think painting is a duality, and that abstract painting is an entirely aesthetic thing . . . We know that most people, especially artists, have large areas of undisciplined emotion, and I think that abstract artists believe that in these marks that they're making they are catching all these sorts of emotions."[13]

Donald Kuspit argues that Bacon is in one sense "the perfect modernist realist, for as the world has become more anonymous, feeling has had to become more acute to encompass it and find release within and through it."[14] Kuspit pursues this argument to suggest that Bacon's art is guided by false emotional drives, that, in effect, assume the very abstractness that he was seeking to avoid. (He cites solitude as a state of abstraction from the world to support his argument). Kuspit may be seen to incorporate Bacon within modernism primarily to preserve the hegemony of that argument, supported most strongly within the United States. He also ultimately denies Bacon's authority through his

perception of its falsehood.

Bacon prefers not to enter this sort of argument; he is concerned with a view that he cogently (and almost exclusively) puts forward through his own words, in interviews principally with David Sylvester. There, he discusses his own art in its own terms and the problems of modernist theory rarely impinge. He talks of "unlocking the valves of sensation" and of the artist's purpose being "to record one's own feelings about certain situations as closely to one's own nervous system as one possibly can" — of making the sensations construct the reality within the painted arena.

Strangely, when he talks in this way, he sounds closer to abstract expressionists than his English peers, both in this aspiration for the use of his "undisciplined emotions" and in his primary philosophical support, the Nietzschean "will to power". Bacon's view is mediated however through his regard for Picasso and the leaders of the European surrealist movement. (Subsequently, Kuspit suggests, Bacon's aesthetic becomes closer to the solitariness of Sartre's *choice of being*, to the European Existentialists.) Bacon has always aspired to the grand manner, not only in his painting but also in the books he reads. These are principally Aesychylus and Shakespeare, alongside Proust and Freud. They all have characteristics which differentiate them from the modernisms of those most often seen as like him, Joyce and Beckett. (Beckett, writing of Proust talks of "involuntary memory" — "there is only one real impression and one adequate mode of evocation. Over neither have we the least control." Beckett claims that Proust mastered "this deep source" and John Russell in his book on Bacon suggests that Joyce in *Ulysses* made a "many-jawed trap for sensation". We might conclude, however, that Joyce's construction is too full of the results of the play of voluntary memory to coincide with Bacon's method.) Bacon's work is *felt*

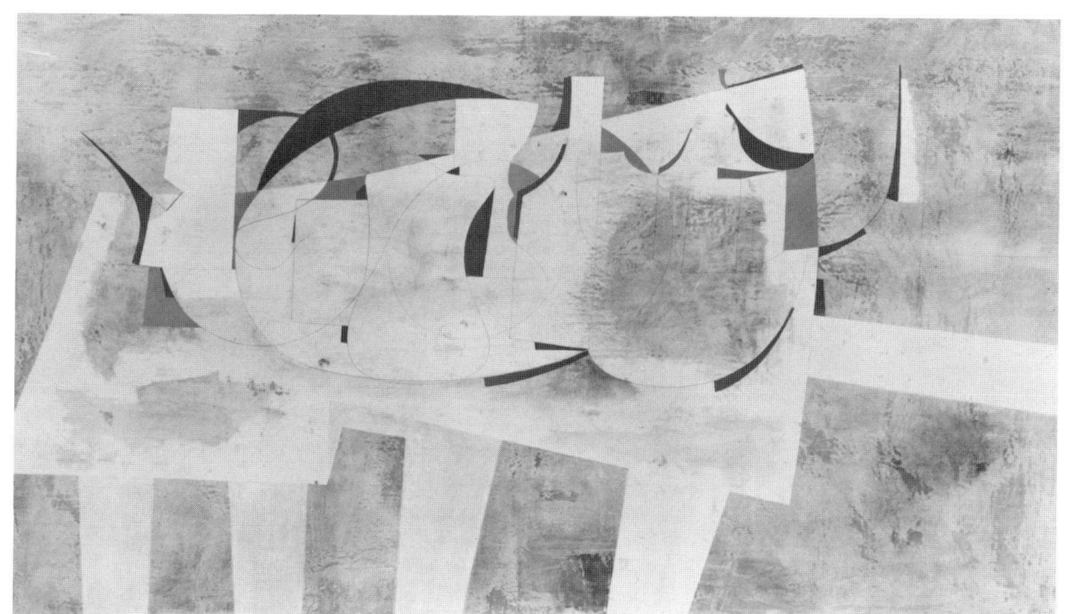

Ben Nicholson
Val d'Orcia
August 1956

Tate Gallery London
photo credit: The Tate Gallery, London

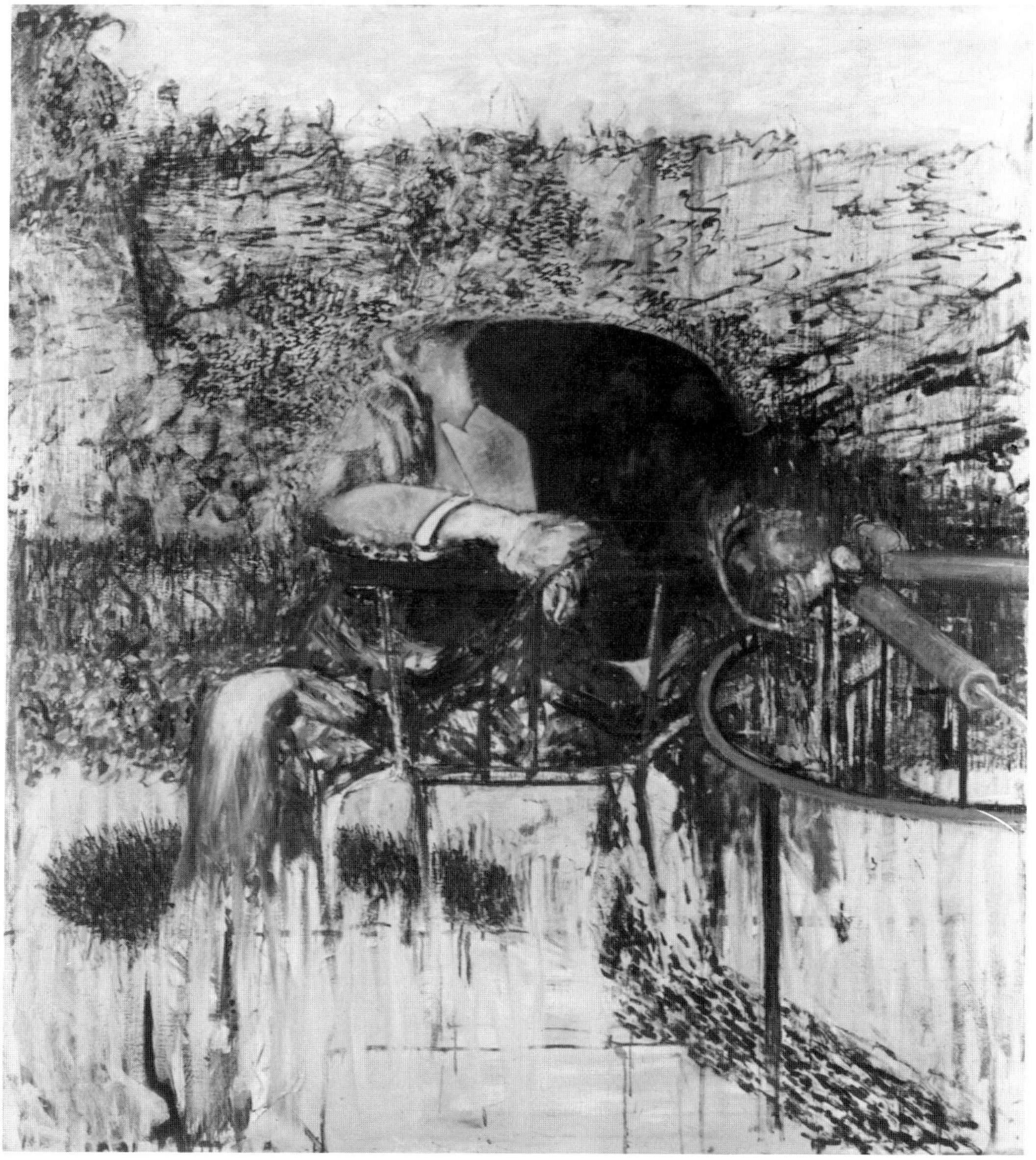

Francis Bacon
Figure in a Landscape
1945

Tate Gallery London
photo credit: The Tate Gallery, London

in a way that seems alien to Moore and Nicholson, often in a way that is distinctly not-English, and which separates him clearly from English art. There are few artists in England within Bacon's own tradition, who have taken up his project. Bacon's position is taken to be entirely distinct from that of artists represented here. (A partial conjunction with younger artists is imaginable since economic conditions are now closest to those of Bacon's formative decade, but art making is conditioned more often by intellectual ideas than market forces.)

...and New Allegiances

Imagine my surprise, when, in Francis Bacon's studio, I found, face-down on the table, a copy of Jacques Derrida's *Writing and Difference* which he was reading and annotating. He had marked a passage about absence and presence, about artists and writers who in Artaud's words wrote "in order to say that I could write nothing at all"[15]. It is not unexpected that Bacon should be reading such a book, only that he might be a follower of the deconstructionist argument. Perhaps artists only take for themselves what is most relevant to them: you can look through Bacon's published interviews and find he says almost the same thing. Nevertheless, the interweaving of intellectual thought with the idea of the primacy of individual creativity are central to his work.

Currently the debate about post-modernism concerns what we can find to replace the prescriptive morality of modernism itself. In this debate the critics appear to be less concerned with the new and more with the ideological apparatus that spawned modernism: they tend to use the deconstructionists' linguistic methods as their critical tools. (The debate currently undertaken by T J Clark, Buchloch and others about Greenberg's Marxist position is typical.)[16] The critical discourse is not new in any substantive way but the critical base has changed and, ironically, is more, rather than less, self-reflexive. The argument shows up most clearly in architecture where the theorists are also teachers and practitioners whose newly collaged or stitched-together monuments betray the sources of their appropriations and conjunctions only too clearly.

Artists do not work with those practical limitations, and Bacon ultimately denies the validity of anything other than the artist's personal actions: the creative act may be modified by an outside influence but it is essentially personal and irrational. This "irrationality" creates the "presence" of the works and the mystery, not only of the paint, but of the painted object. The most distinct rupture with this view occurs at the end of the American modernist phase, when a generation conceived and created the minimal and conceptual aesthetic. This generation was matched in Europe and Britain by its equivalent whose ambitions, perhaps for the first time, were international and *within* the avant garde. They eschewed the art object almost completely, denying specifically its "presence". Victor Burgin is an examplar of this generation, because of what he did before and after his "conceptual period". (I can imagine him complaining bitterly over my art-historical licence — "period" indeed). Born in 1941, Burgin trained as a painter at the Royal College of

Barry Flanagan
Plant 5
1971

hessian, resin
130 x 55 x 47cms

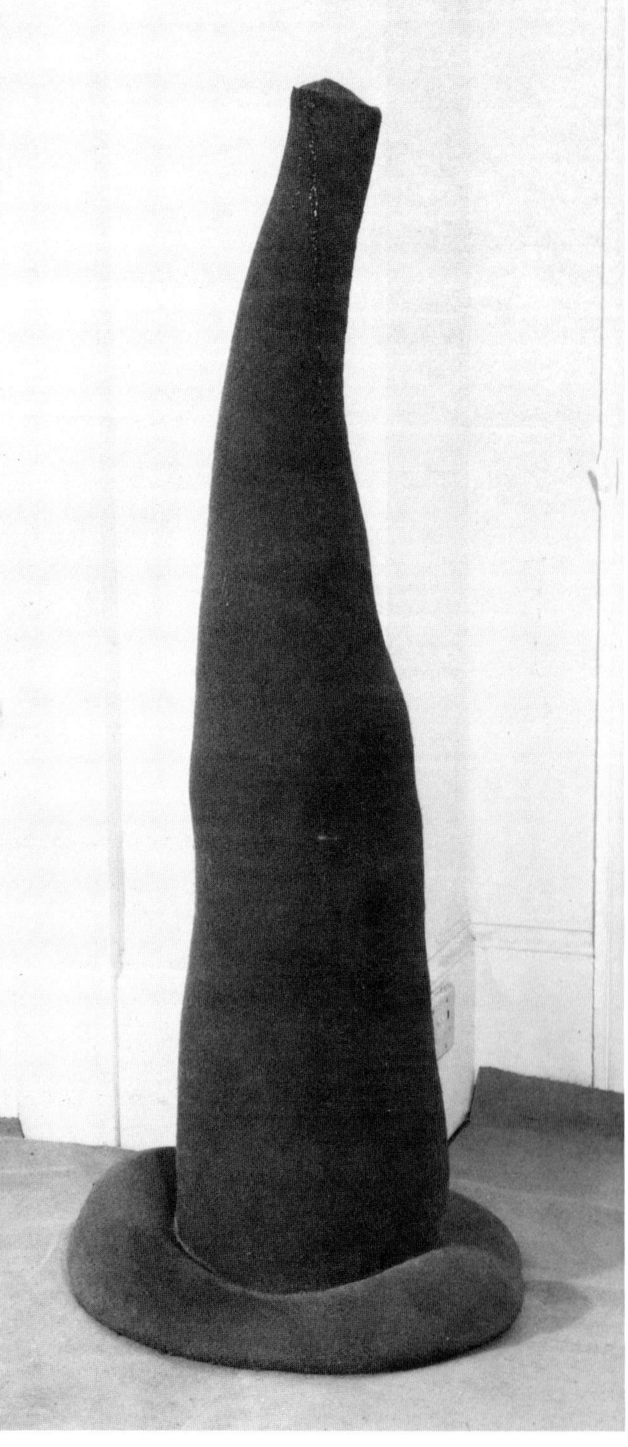

Art (1963-65) and then at Yale (under Josef Albers) between 1965 and 1967. It was there that his contacts with minimalism and the minimalist artists were made. He returned to England in 1967 and worked as an art teacher concentrating on photography and theories of photography and representation and the social position of art. (I am taking him as an example not to equate him with the old masters, but because he has displayed his aesthetic transparently, both in his art and his writings.) In 1970 he wrote

> "Perhaps it is time for a moratorium on things — a temporary withdrawal from real objects during which the object analogue formed in consciousness may be examined as the origin of a new generating system".[17]

Gradually he began to combine image and text and, over the last decade, these works have increased in subtlety and in the interplay of meanings. The most recent, for example, combines motifs and images from Alfred Hitchcock, Millais — the English PreRaphaelite and Freud, mediated through Burgin's own experience and sensibility. Burgin has stated his current position in an introduction to an exhibition of the middle generation of English sculptors, those who effectively overturned the prevailing Greenbergian canon.[18]

Burgin opposes what he calls the old fashioned "logocentric" Renaissance-based view of painting's "presence" with an art whose new "apparatus" (his term) includes the notion of the institution and psychology, and which uses the twentieth century's primary means of communication, photography (including cinema and television). The use of the despised medium, and a critique of the means of production led Burgin to cast conceptual art as a gesture not of denial but of opening up the institution of art to the world outside, letting other crucial disciplines in. These included semiological analysis, linguistics, political theory but above all psychoanalysis.[19]

Burgin's fear is that post-modernism, what he calls "rummaging through all this iconographic jumble of the past" is remaining resolutely a nineteenth century art — one that is locked up in its own history, its own fetishism. Without the tools of twentieth century thought it will reintegrate past and present and make them the same. Burgin concludes his essay:—

> "Psychoanalysis shows us how jealously, and with what skill, we guard our symptoms; they are not something we wish to give up for they speak our *desire*. But the same desire may find other symbolic forms . . . en route to a 'redistribution of capital' in the economy of desire. In the meantime, the consequence of modern art's disavowal of modern history remains its almost total failure to be about anything of consequence."[20]

I do not think it is stretching it too far to suggest that Bacon himself could be viewed as an examplar of Burgin's proposed scheme; Bacon's subject has always been *desire* and he has, it has been said, attempted to paint a History of Europe in his own time. (Bacon has not expressed his ambition in these terms; he talks of the primacy of figure painting. His critics are suggesting that his aims are those of History painting itself.) We cannot allow ourselves to conclude that Bacon's work and Burgin's are really similar: that would stretch theorising too far. It is not simply that Burgin's work looks 'of the moment' — its technics are contemporary — whilst Bacon's remains resolutely *painting* — its technics are, in Burgin's terms, redundant. There is a significant *difference*. Burgin is the analyst of his own desires, Bacon does not attempt analysis. The aspiration of Bacon's work is not to make a mediated simulacrum of the politics of desire but to approach as near to the reality of that desire as possible, to be in a complex and full way, "realistic". Neither Bacon nor Burgin is willing to be restricted by a debased modernism and both have a significant influence on the artists in this exhibition who are attempting in various ways to reconcile English art, modernism and what is so loosely called post-modernism.

Richard Francis

1. *The British Art Show*, an Arts Council touring exhibition, travelling to Birmingham, Edinburgh, Sheffield and Southampton, 1984-5, selected by Jon Thompson, Alexander Moffat and Marjorie Allthorp-Guyton.

2. *The British Art Show* Old allegiances and New directions, 1979-94, authors as selectors above, London 1984, pp144.

3. ibid., p.15 It is perhaps reasonable to point out that Buchloch is blowing the whistle on what, he as a German, sees as a regressive return to nationalism in recent art.

4. "Art Today" in Stokes, Adrian, *The Critical Writings of Adrian Stokes*, Vol 1, 1930-37, edited by Lawrence Gowing, London 1978, p.305.

5. From Ben Nicholson "Quotations" in *Circle* International Survey of Constructive Art, edited by J L Martin, Ben Nicholson and N Gabo, London 1937, p.75.

6. From Henry Moore "Quotations", ibid. p.118.

7. *London Bulletin*, Nos. 8-9, January-February 1939.

8. Quoted in David Sylvester, Introduction to *Henry Moore at the Serpentine*, Arts Council of Great Britain, 1978.

9. Quoted in Lawrence Gowing, Preface to *The Critical Writings of Adrian Stokes*, Vol. 1, p.10.

10. In the introduction to *Henry Moore at the Serpentine*.

11. The principal orchestrators of this opinion were Mark Roskill and Lawrence Alloway in the early 1960s.

12. Quoted in Kuspit, Donald "Francis Bacon: the authority of flesh", *Artforum*, Summer 1975 (vol. 13 no. 10), p.50.

13. ibid.

14. ibid., p.51.

15. Derrida, Jacques *Writing and Difference*, London 1978, p.10.

16. See *Modernism and Modernity*, Halifax 1984 for the most recent episodes in this debate.

17. Burgin, Victor in "Thanks for the Memory" *Architectural Design,* August 1970, quoted 1965 to 1972 — *When Attitudes became Form* Cambridge, Kettle's Yard Gallery 1974, p.22.

18. They included Richard Long, Bruce McLean, Gilbert & George, Barry Flanagan and Burgin himself.

19. Thus, the routes towards deconstructionist practice are revealed: the work of Barthes, Foucault, Lacan, Derrida and Kristeva is after all posited in the history of ideas developed post-Freud.

20. Burgin, Victor, The absence of presence: conceptualism and post-modernisms in 1965 to 1972 *When Attitudes became Form, Cambridge,* Kettle's Yard Gallery, 1984, p.24.

21. Victor Burgin was not included in the present show as a separate presentation of British photograph which has failed to eventuate, was planned to tour concurrently.

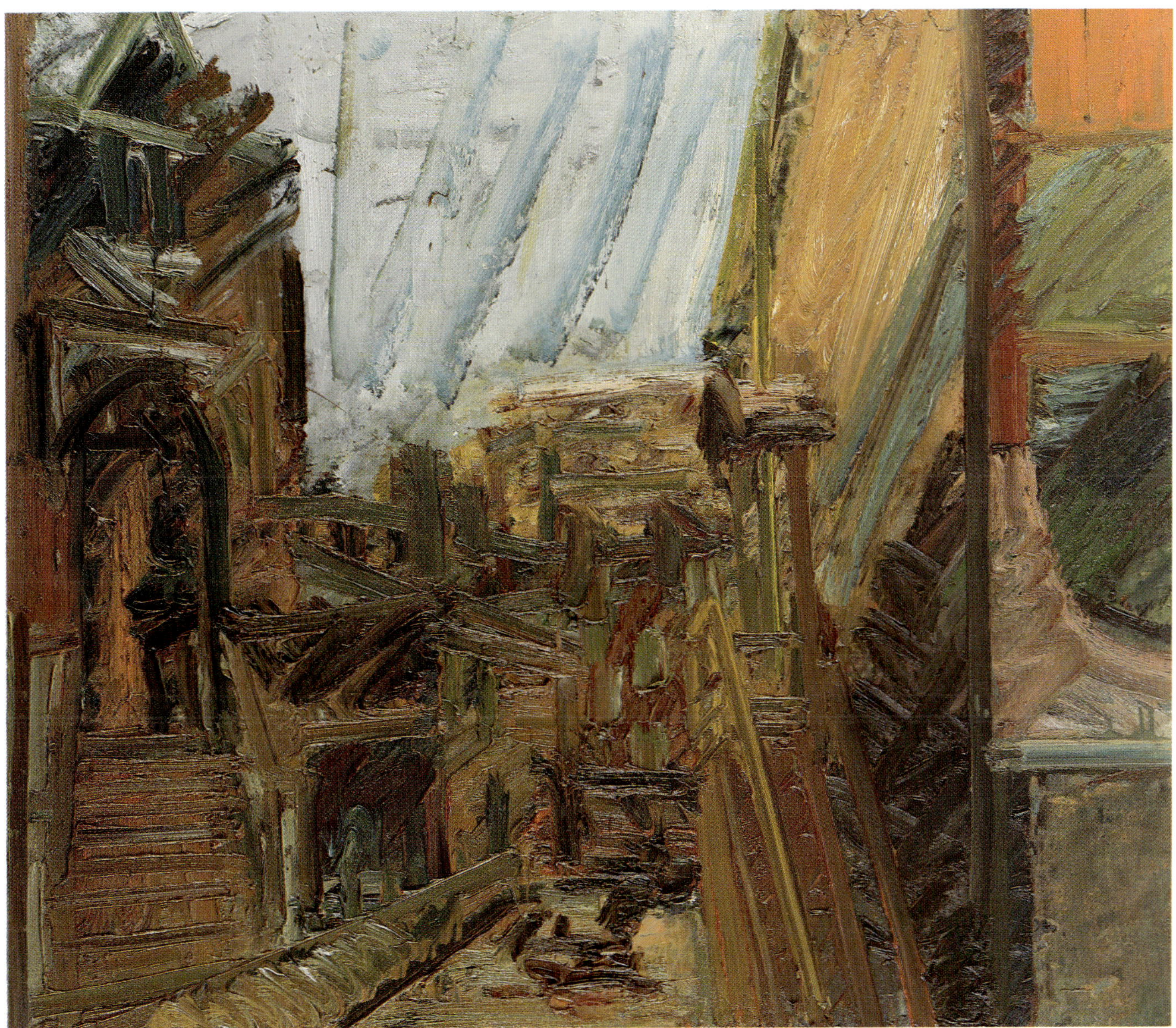

The following extract has been taken from an interview between Catherine Lampert and the artist, originally published in the Arts Council of Great Britain's catalogue 'Frank Auerbach' 1978. We are most grateful for permission to reuse a part of this text on this occasion.

To the Studios II
1982

oil on board
48 x 54ins
122 x 137.2cms
S.A. McLean Ireland

A conversation with Frank Auerbach

Catherine Lampert: *When you begin a painting what are you hoping to be able to put on the canvas?*

Frank Auerbach: What I'm not hoping to do is to paint another picture because there are enough pictures in the world. I'm hoping to make a new thing for the world that remains in the mind like a new species of living thing. It sounds very grandiloquent. The only way I know how to do it, or to try and do it, is to start with something that I know specifically, so that I have something to cling to beyond aesthetic feelings and my knowledge of other paintings. Ideally one should have more material than one can possibly cope with.

When I see the great pictures of the world paraded in my mind's eye they are great images which don't leak into other images, they are new things. I could name them, or could try to name 20 of them — the Kenwood Rembrandt is pretty close, the Picasso of the pre-Cubist period called *Head (Femme au nez en quart de Brie)* seems to me to be one of them. There's a blue cut-out late Matisse, *Acrobats*. There's the Dürer with the bent nose (*Conrad Vernell*), a Philips Koninck landscape, *View in Holland*. One hopes somehow to make something that has a similar degree of individuality, independence, fullness and perpetual motion to these pictures. But actually one hopes, although of course one won't achieve it, one actually hopes in one's heart of hearts to surpass them.

CL: *You've made the remark that the painter does the persistent thing and then something remarkable happens. Do you feel that each stage, every sitting contributes to the building of the total awareness of the subject?*

FA: I've often thought about that because of course it isn't only every sitting in the sense of every time the model comes, but actually every time the model has a rest and starts again the thing will be totally different if one's got any sensibility at all. The problem of painting is to see a unity within a multiplicity of pieces of evidence and the very slightest change of light, the very slightest, tiniest hairs-breadth inflection of the form creates a totally different visual synthesis. I actually more or less start again every time the model rests and gets up again, but my mind has travelled along certain paths and tried out certain possibilities and created certain hopes, so that I somehow digest some of the possibilities. When the conclusion occurs and I feel I've been lucky enough to find some sort of whole for this overwhelming and unmanageable heap of sensations and impressions, I think that the previous attempts have contributed. So there is a sort of rehearsal, there's a sort of build-up or an accruing of possibilities of how to behave, but when one finally does finish the painting I think one tends to contradict what's gone before.

I think all good painting looks as though the painting has escaped from the thicket of prepared positions and has entered some sort of freedom where it exists on its own, and by its own laws, and inexplicably has got free of all possible explanations. Possibly the explainers will catch up with it again, but never completely. There is always an element of the unclassifiable about great pictures so that when we're standing in front of them quite often our first reaction is that everything that everybody's said about this picture and this painter's all wrong. Everything everybody's said about Courbet is totally wrong. All I've heard about Courbet is that there was this sensual peasant painter with instincts who went beyond his intelligence and one goes along and one sees these poignant dream inventions by somebody who has made the most intelligent concoctions from art and photography and working in the studio and working outdoors and putting it all together to make these marvellous dream images.

CL: *You choose models that you know well and landscapes in your immediate vicinity. You've said that it was partly because you felt you could take more liberties with what you knew well. Do you always feel that you have a better chance of arriving at something incredible if you begin with something familiar?*

FA: I think so, simply because one knows more about them. The thing is after all done from the mind, and the accrued information enriches the content to an extraordinary degree, I mean, if one has a chance of seeing people apart from the time when one's painting them, one notices all sorts of things about them. If one sees them in movement, one realises all sorts of truths about them and one's infinitely less likely to be satisfied with a superficial statement. Those things that are particular to them to some small extent may lead to a particularity of image, because one thereby gets the confidence to make statements which one knows to be true which conform to no statement that already exists in painting. The same can be done simply by work. I don't suppose that Monet's lilypond was the thing that was the nearest to his heart, but he certainly went on long enough about it to be able to make statements about it which nobody else could possibly have made. It's just that familiarity with the subject and with the person is a sort of short-cut in that sphere of study.

CL: *Do you find that events in your personal life continue to provide stimulus, that they influence the way you treat a subject?*

FA: It has always been the same, always been difficult. My first consideration on getting up in the morning every day of my life has always been about painting and one can't expect other human beings to be subservient to one's ambition. There have been times when it's been more propitious, and times when it's been less so. I suppose the relationship is to some extent meaningful because one is trying to capture this poignant drama of the life that is going on outside, and that one's fighting off in order to be able to do the painting. You know people talk of travel and there seems to be some sort of image-connection between travel and what the artist does, and there is, but I don't think it's quite as it's been presented. The traveller is somebody who sits in a railway-carriage and doesn't change, or moves from country to country and doesn't change, and the scene around him changes. The traveller's the unchanging man. It's not a question of a protean adventurer — the traveller's unaltered and what he sees changes. Likewise the artist is the man in front of the writing-pad or in front of the easel, and things around him change and he doesn't change — that's the connection. So that if there wasn't any life there wouldn't be any point in painting, but in order to paint one has to put up a fairly consistent struggle against it.

CL: *Have you an awareness of the racing of time as well?*

FA: Yes, sure, absolutely. I think people who paint are poignantly aware of the passing of time, and what one tries to do is somehow to pin down an experience in its essential aspect before it disappears.

CL: *Do you have a specific feeling about oil paint, that it is direct, and mentally you are handling it with your mind and fingers as much as with the brush?*

FA: Well I do actually use my fingers quite a bit. But I don't have any particular attachment to oil paint, although there are two advantages to oil paint as opposed to, say, gouache or watercolour. One is its infinite workability and since I take ages, it's the only coloured material that I can think of that's infinitely workable. And the other thing is its comparative permanence. Hogarth's *Shrimp Girl* seems to me to be more of a frozen instant than any watercolour that I can think of. I have never tried to analyse why this should be except that perhaps oil paint remains liquid, the whole picture's liquid and stays where you put it, and I suppose it's bigger and fatter and it seems more miraculous that this sort of thing should have been an instant in time 200 years ago and still remain a tiny instant over the years.

CL: *Can you remember what you were taught in David Bomberg's classes? You said that Bomberg had a language of his own.*

FA: In the school where I went, art was taught by the scripture mistress and we didn't do good children's art or anything. But I read the books in the library and the thing that I knew was that one's teachers were going to be silly fools and that one was going to rebel against them. Then, I was 17 and I went to Bomberg's class where he said to me 'Oh so you think I'm a silly old idiot don't you?', or something like that, and I said in my 17-year-old arrogance, 'Yes I do'. He was delighted and I didn't realise that I had met with probably the most original, stubborn, radical intelligence that was to be found in art schools. It wasn't his phrases that made sense to me because my relationship to teaching was one of rejection and rebellion. I mean, by itself and whether I was consciously aware of it or not, the status of the discipline seemed to me to be a totally futile one. Bomberg had a phrase about the spirit of the mass, something to do with a very particular and specific expression of a particular conformation of matter. But at the time this seemed rhetorical to me, and it was his practical instruction rather than his maxims which registered.

J.Y.M. seated II
1981

oil on board
22 x 20ins
55.9 x 50.8cms
private collection, London

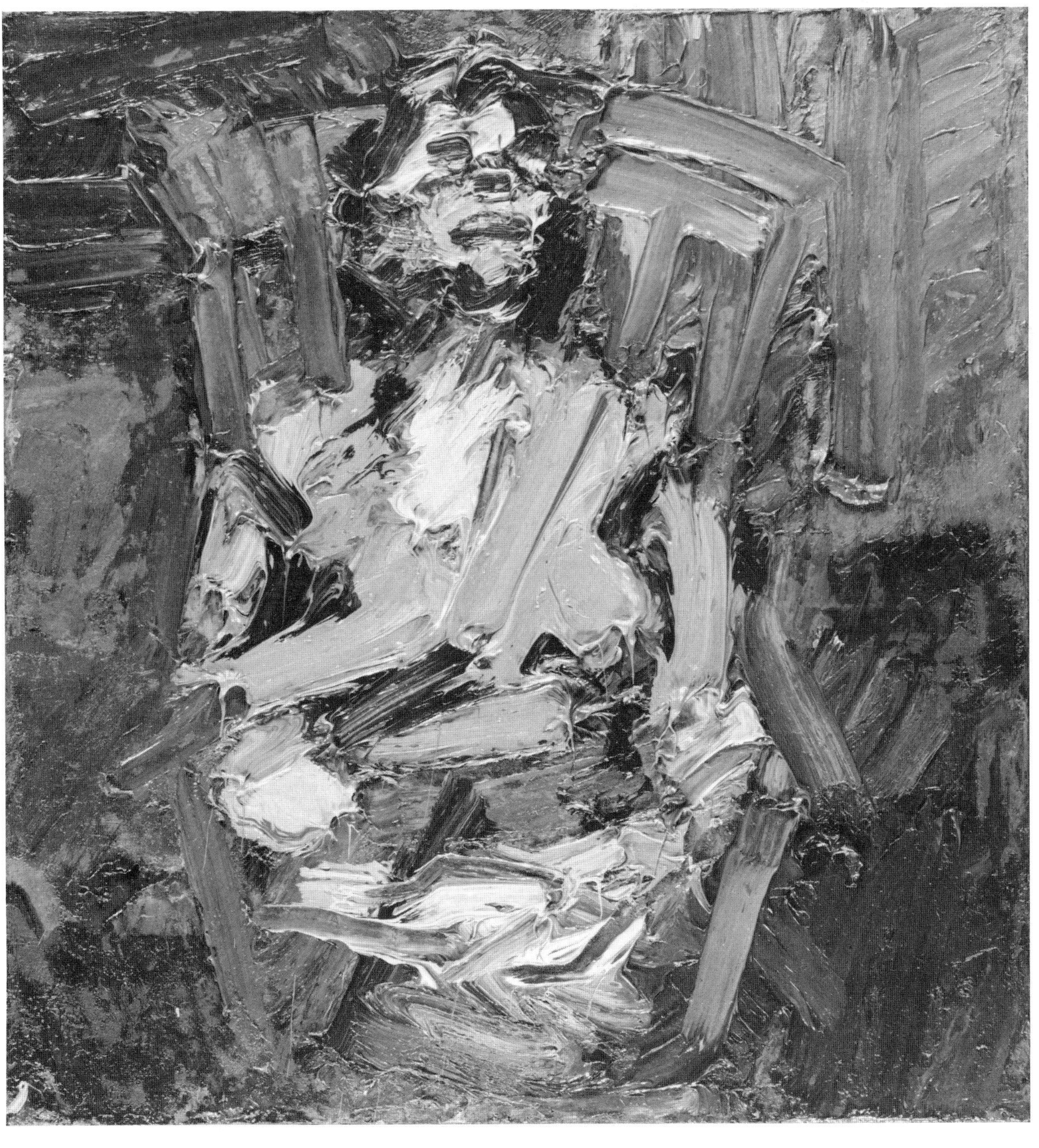

CL: *As for the work of your contemporaries at the Beaux Arts Gallery, did you respond to any? The early Jack Smith's or early Bratby's?*

FA: I felt that their ambitions and what they seemed to me to be aiming at in their picture was a sort of young artist's passionate illustration, and I was born old and I wanted to make a dignified perverse image, a formal image.

CL: *And were you less affected by the period itself, the hopes focused around the time of the Festival of Britain and so on because you weren't, you're not British?*

FA: Yes, that's absolutely right. It wasn't only because I wasn't British born, it was because I didn't have a family and I didn't have anything to anchor me to whatever was going on. I still haven't any interest in trends — television is a barbarous invention. I mean I think it's possible to show an early talent, but unless one has the sort of speculative imagination that makes one reinvent oneself, which is what really what reading a book does, I don't think one can last as a painter. Everybody I know, who paints, Lucian Freud or Leon Kossoff, or anybody who seems to me to have shown some sort of sustained level of artistic invention, has read books. I'm not at all certain that the reason that people have stopped coming up with any sort of authority since Hockney came up (and he also reads a great deal), is because they've simply stopped reading, and that sort of easy commerce of television perhaps is not conducive to an activity which has to do with somebody standing in a room and inventing something, for themselves.

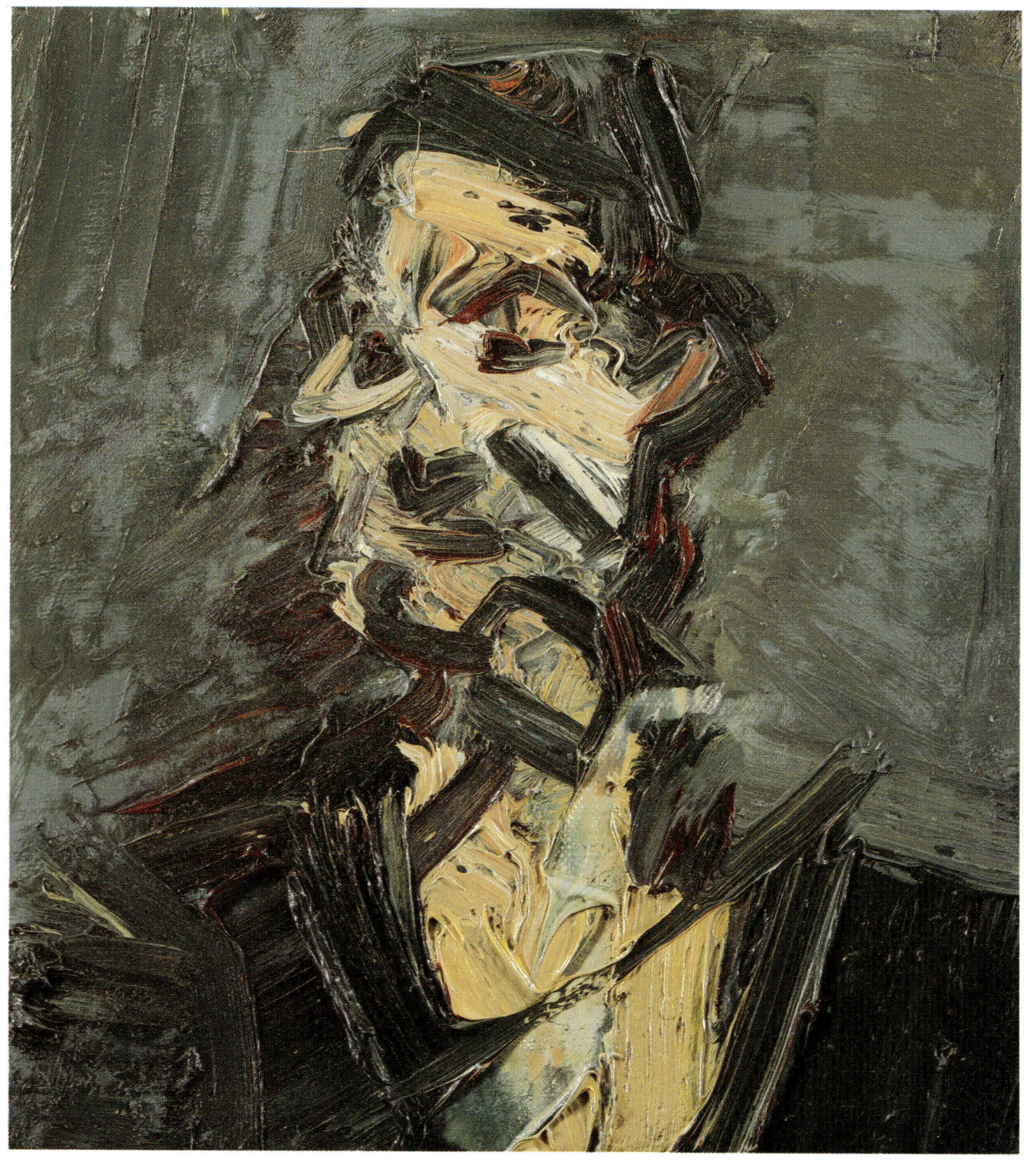

Head of
Debbie Ratcliff
1983/84

oil on canvas
18 x 16ins
45.7 x 40.6cms
Richard Salmon Ltd
London

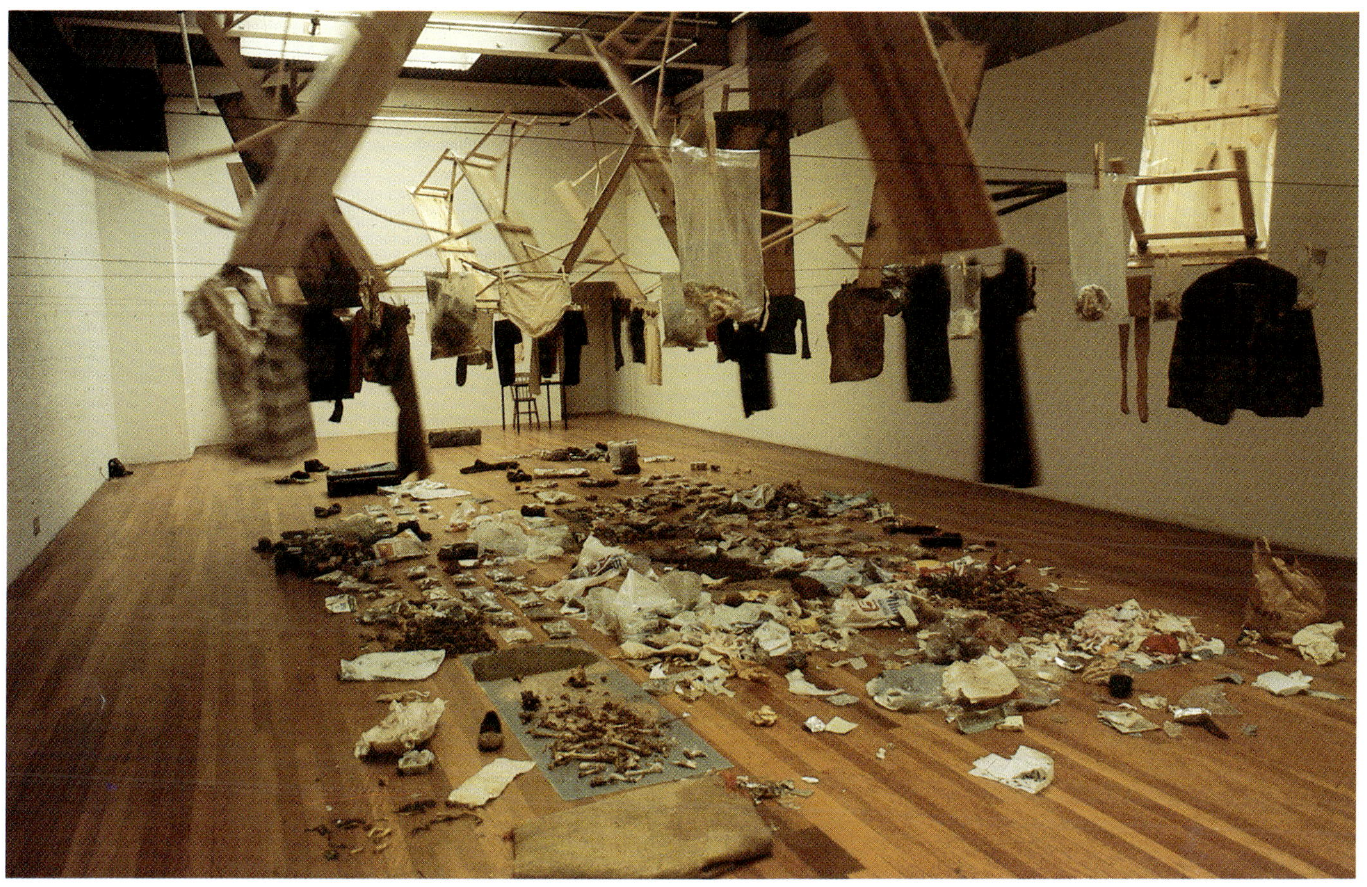

STUART BRISLEY

Leaching out at the intersection
1981

Institute of Contemporary Arts London
photo credit Janet Anderson

Marking Intervals in Time

One of the least discussed areas relating to performance is age. How do performers cope with arduous actions when they get older? Unlike actors performance artists do not get offered sedentary roles to see them quietly into their senescence. On the contrary they have to make their own roles, find new lines of attack, particularly if they are concerned to sustain any rigour in their work. Stuart Brisley's switch to other areas of activity (installation, sound tape, film) over the last few years has had much to do with the physical demands of his performance, which at its most visceral required great reserves of energy. Brisley is now in his early fifties. The days of the marathon performances are over.

However, it would be a mistake to attribute Brisley's change solely to age. The changing ideological climate has made the founding proclamations of performance as an interventionist activity today extremely vulnerable to mannerism; the decay of performance into artworld entertainment is now widely evident. The presentation of the body as a site of emancipatory force, a site of struggle beyond mediation to some imagined state of collective or spiritual redemption has long lost the context in which it found its most uncompromising forms: the counter-culture. Transcendence is not so easily won, power not so easily disposed of. Performance's representation of the body as an existential 'acting out' has become more a question of being 'acted upon', as, for example, in Laurie Anderson's work in which the function of the performer is reduced to that of a conduit through which other voices find their expression.

Now, although it is overly simplistic to identify Brisley with the gesturalism of the sixties (his performances were always as much about acting out as being acted upon) it is precisely this switch from the expressive unity of the body to its breakdown into parts which represents his move away from performance proper. The body has either become a disembodied voice or member, or completely formless as in some collective absent presence. The dynamic visualisation of power-relations has been exchanged for a more fragmentary analysis. However understood as an *extension* of content, this reduction of the body is less of a break than one would initially think; Brisley's performances were very much meetings between the self/alter-ego and some external structure and object: the new objects and voices are still part of that same symbolic order: the bourgeois categorisation of the world into binary opposites — useful/useless, strong/weak, clean/dirty.

In fact it has been the centrality of this binary vision which has given Brisley's work its salient political character: its sense of stasis, of waiting, of individuals being caught between the two fixed points, as if like Walter Benjamin's pile of "skyward debris", history is lining up behind us, dead and flat in its awful sameness. Brisley's switch from performer to 'script writer' has in a way reinforced this anomie, driven it right to his very door. Not only has he now become a rag-picker, an appropriate collator of the signs and symptoms of the dead, but a recorder of the flux and times of his local area, Camden in central London. In the recent sound tapes and installations, his own surroundings — which are a regular stalking ground of tramps and derelicts — are pressed into allegorical view. The characters and shadowy figures that move in and out of his life, that stop and ask him for money, that call on him, become the human 'debris' of Benjamin's tower, the ghostly presence of the other side of capitalism, its unseen 'exceptions'. If debris and detritus have always played a part in Brisley's work as evidence of a system in which exchange value stands in unequal relation to use-value then

I = 66,666
1983

Collection Arts Council of Great Britain
photo credit Janet Anderson

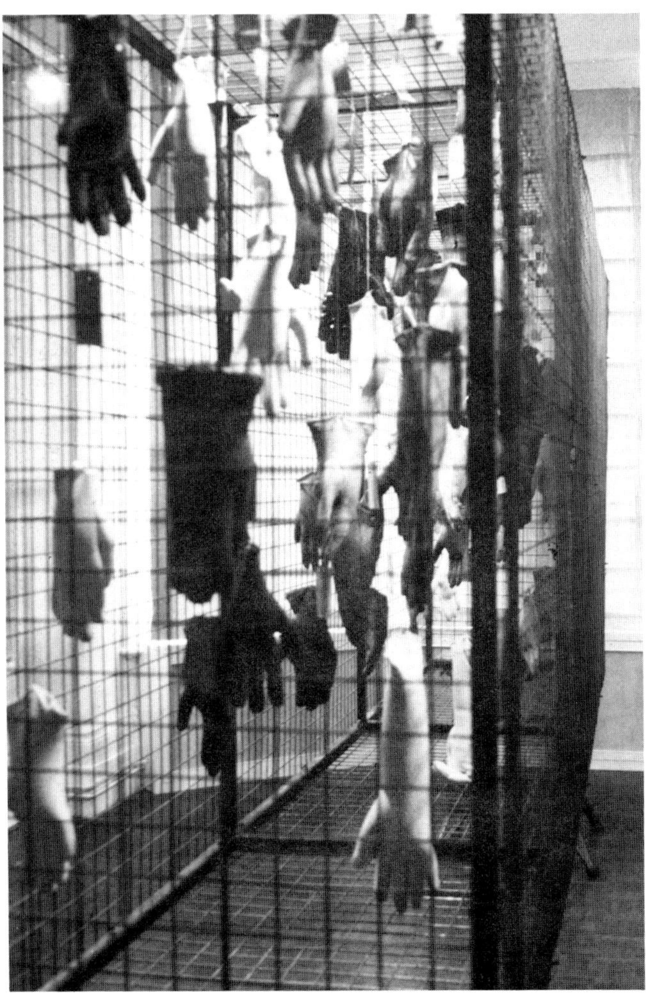

here these shifting human presences represent the same, if more brutalized, effects of this process.

These figures however are outside of production. Capitalism needs a certain amount of human wastage *within* production, if it is to reproduce itself. Marx called this surfeit of labour power a "disposable industrial reserve army". In a recent installation *I = 66, 666* (1983), Brisley uses this image as the basis for a piece which traduces the idea of *un*-employment as such. Inside a long steel cage, standing on two work benches, Brisley hung 66 gloves filled with plaster. Their occasional grotesque distortions (some are over-filled giving the leather or plastic the appearance of flesh bloated by water) create the disturbing image of the victims of some bizarre and horrific purge. However the cage does more than expose these hands: it defines them, gives each one its individual identity as something not just obsolete but dead, a specimen. Brisley's sculpture in effect throws into question the common assumption that 'work' and 'having a job' are the same thing. That without a 'job' you are out of 'work'. Under the present economic crisis — as in all economic crisis — such a homology serves a clear ideological function. If unemployment is inevitable then those in full time employment must be very lucky indeed; protectionism takes over from work-sharing, strengthening the hand of the employer and government alike. In this sense Brisley's imprisoned gloves signify not just an image of imprisoned capacities but the limitations of our understanding of work, time and leisure. How we see work, the distinction we make between wage-labour and freely chosen activities is perpetually reinforced by our desire to escape from the former into the latter. Unemployment therefore is not so much an economic fact but a means of defining what constitutes proper human activity. Non-wage labour is so called un-skilled (domestic labour for instance) and socially unproductive; to be unemployed is therefore to be unskilled and socially unproductive. Of course capitalism doesn't *say* as much but that's how ideology works. Brisley's cage then is the ideological framework which places individuals under the self-defining powers of the market economy.

As part of Brisley's ongoing work *The Georgiana Collection, 1 = 66, 666* is a work that fragments the body in order to say something about how human capacities under capitalism are fragmented. In an installation made for the Camden Arts Centre as part of their show '1984', the body is liquidated altogether, disappearing quite literally under a layer of discarded clothes. As in *1 = 66, 666* the sense of absence is to be understood as a purge, but here the crime is historic. As Brisley says *Nul Comma Nul*[1] is not *about* Stalinism in any specific sense, (one should avoid the temptation of reading the liquidation of the human body here as a liquidation of the Kulaks); nonetheless Brisley's construction of a place that is without escape or memory is Stalinist in intent and effect. Rather, *Nul Comma Nul* offers us a view of Stalinism as the enclosure of socialist teleology; the identification of socialism *as* Stalinism in the West by the enemies of socialism.

For this piece Brisley built a tall wedge compound which extended twenty feet into the gallery from the entrance. On the floor of the space were scattered numerous articles of old and found clothing. At the entrance Brisley left the gallery's iron-grill security gate closed. In front of this in the entrance hall was a partition on which was fixed a large mirror. At the end of the space, shining directly into the spectator's eyes, was a 500 watt bulb. Effectively a work of reduced horizons, the space folds in on itself. Our view is trapped, or rather uni-directional. We can only look back, a view which is itself closed off; the implication is clear: this is dead history, history that is beyond reclamation or resignification. Moreover this history is perpetually reflected back to us as we turn away from it. *Nul Comma Nul* stages the post-war space of reduced political options that we take for granted as the Cold War divide. For revolutionary socialism to reclaim Stalinism is incomprehensible and mendacious; for revolutionary socialism to denounce the USSR is to lose the very historical space in which it has come into being. Revolutionary socialism is quite literally at the thin end of the wedge. Benjamin's pile of debris is more prescient than imagined.

History, labour, politics were in a sense inscribed across Brisley's body in his earlier work. By placing himself under certain situations of constraint or by carrying out lengthy tasks, he placed himself in a position of functional instability. Physically de-

sensitised Brisley's aim was to reproduce the effects of the capitalist work process. By reducing the volition and freedom of the body Brisley became a manifestation of waste itself. In this respect the new work is no different. The reduction of human possibility in *Nul Comma Nul* and *1 = 66, 666*, or rather the distortion of human possibility into its opposite, is likewise a process of retardation. However, to subject the body to such tasks, to symbolize such degeneration is to create its opposite: resistance. Brisley's performances and installations may be bleak but only to the extent that by recognising this bleakness it may be possible to move out of its reach. But it is as if 'resistance' is what we are obliged to perform in order to improve capitalism's own performance; capitalism's 'stability' is inconceivable without democratic transformation. This is perfectly illustrated in Brisley's performance *Between* performed in Holland in 1979. *Between* could be best described as a model of capitalist progress.

Iain Robertson and Brisley in a state of uninterrupted agitation on a steep ramp they had constructed in the gallery, struggled for space and a semblance of relief on their repeated return to the top. An impression of achievement was continually countered by numerous falls and slumps. But to

Nul Comma Nul
1984

installation Camden Arts Centre
photo credit Janet Anderson

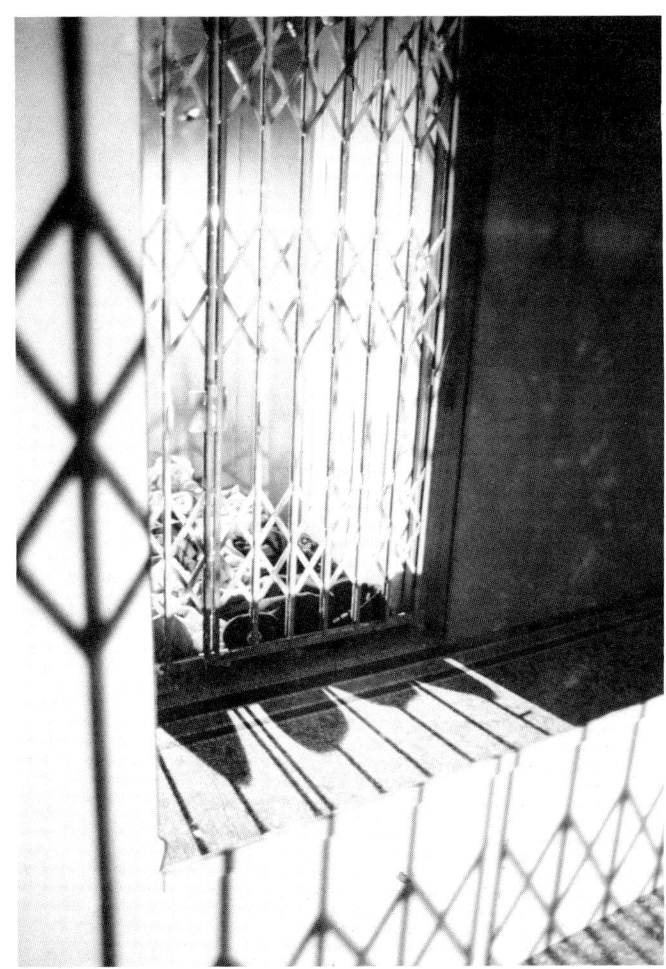

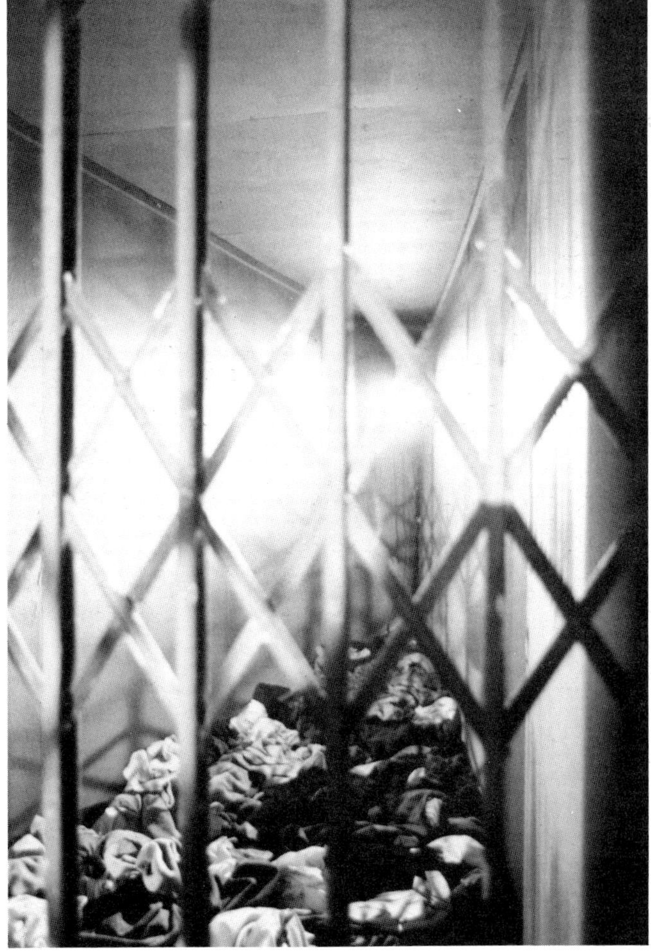

stay off the ramp was to be non-functional. Thus it was not so much that the space was confined, but that the freedom to operate in it had certain restrictions; there was a great deal of movement but within set limits. This is the key to an understanding of Brisley's use of spatial metaphor. We can only go so far: what we can't struggle for or imagine we have to wait for, as history disgorges its monsters.

This sense of dead-time, of waiting, is extended further in two recent sound pieces. Whilst a gallery wall or structure constrains the possibility of movement in the performances, here memory and the imagination are constrained by the 'factual'. In *Tanzen im Gehege* (*Dancing in the Paddock*) a sound tape with action performed by Janet Anderson in Dusseldorf in 1983, Brisley draws together observation, personal memory and fictional reconstruction into a chain of violent association. Opening with the reconstruction of a moment from the Nazi massacre of the inhabitants of the Czech village Lidice in 1943, a report of which Brisley

Between

a performance in collaboration with Iain Robertson at De Appel Foundation, Amsterdam 1979.
photo credit Brisley/Robertson

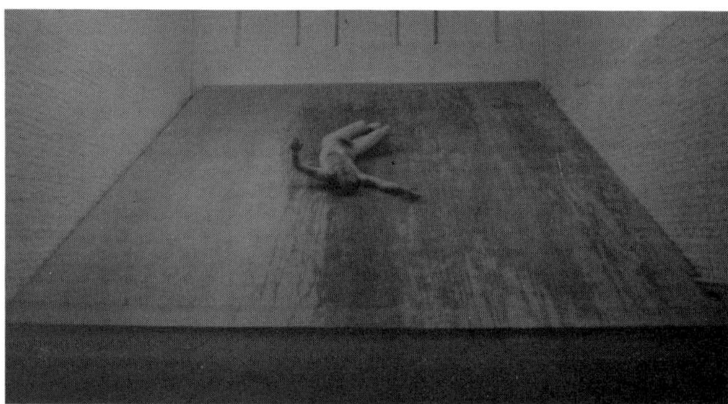

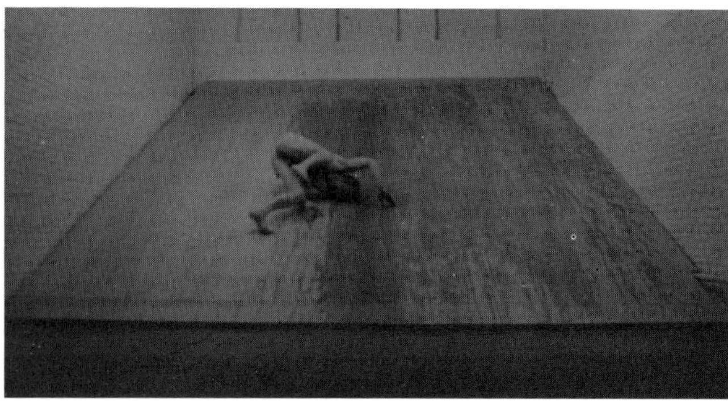

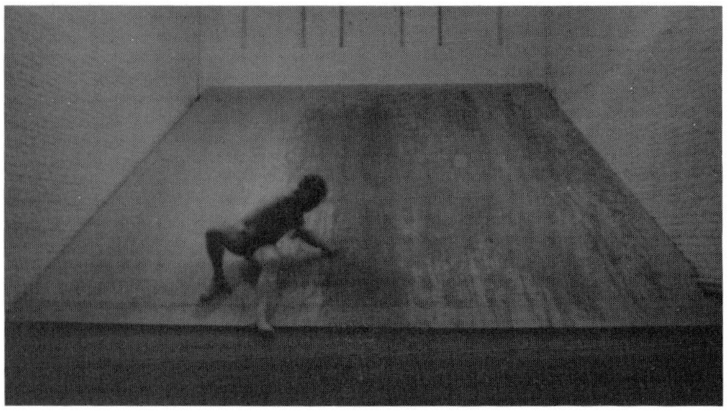

heard on the radio as a child, the tape shifts between Brisley reading out definitions of various cooking techniques — blending, beating, blanching, kneeding, pureeing — and observation of various incidents outside his house: the casually violent lives of the tramps in his neighbourhood. Read in a flat, unemotional voice, bodies and objects, history and the quotidian become interchangeable, creating a space of suffocation and compression. Listening and looking take on the aspect of dulled passivity. If Brisley is the collector in *1 = 66,666* then here, as in the Television South West video *Second Level First Degree* (1983), (which involved him dressing in a balaclava and dark glasses for a day's work looking through his spy-hole) he is the caretaker or functionary. He sweeps the floor, looks out of the window and sits at his desk "shifting and fidgeting covered in dust". He becomes an observer of the dead or dying, of history as that homogeneous time of the ruling classes; he is a caretaker of the dead, a dead culture.

In the tape-slide piece *Minus One* (1984) also a part of the *Georgiana Collection* Brisley uses the same format of first person characterisation and factual juxtaposition. Similarly we are also made immediately aware of the vulnerability of bodies. The tape opens with a man and woman exhausted after sex. The rise and subsequent loss of their bodily temperature however underlies a total loss of temperature they soon anticipate: the total loss of temperature that is expected after a nuclear attack (which some scientists have prophesied as the beginning of a new ice age). Lying, waiting, "marking intervals in time", breathing "into each other" in a room with white washed windows, we in fact begin to realise that the new ice age has begun, the attack has commenced. Interspersed with this narrative are various medical facts read by a woman: over 2000 doses of radiation, death within hours; over 10,000 doses, death almost instantaneously. On the screen during the tape is a single black and white image of a man and a woman in profile facing each other. Towards the end, as the sound of an electronic bleeper intensifies, and the bodies acknowledge the increasing cold, a large red rectangle is superimposed over the image, which gradually gets brighter and larger until it finally obliterates the figures.

If all Brisley's work has been concerned with conditions of constraint then here horizons are reduced to point zero; the political space of *Between*, a space of what might be called limited projection, is reduced to the stasis of a sealed room. The heat of performance finds its opposite in technological control. However it would be cheap rhetoric and bad politics to end on such a note of finality; Brisley's work may present a world of dead time, in which actions become half-frozen or endlessly repetitious, but dead-time is also not-yet time, dormant time, time which waits to explode its forms into view. It would be dishonest not to say that the red rectangle is also an image of transcendence.

John Roberts

1. '1984' catalogue p.14.

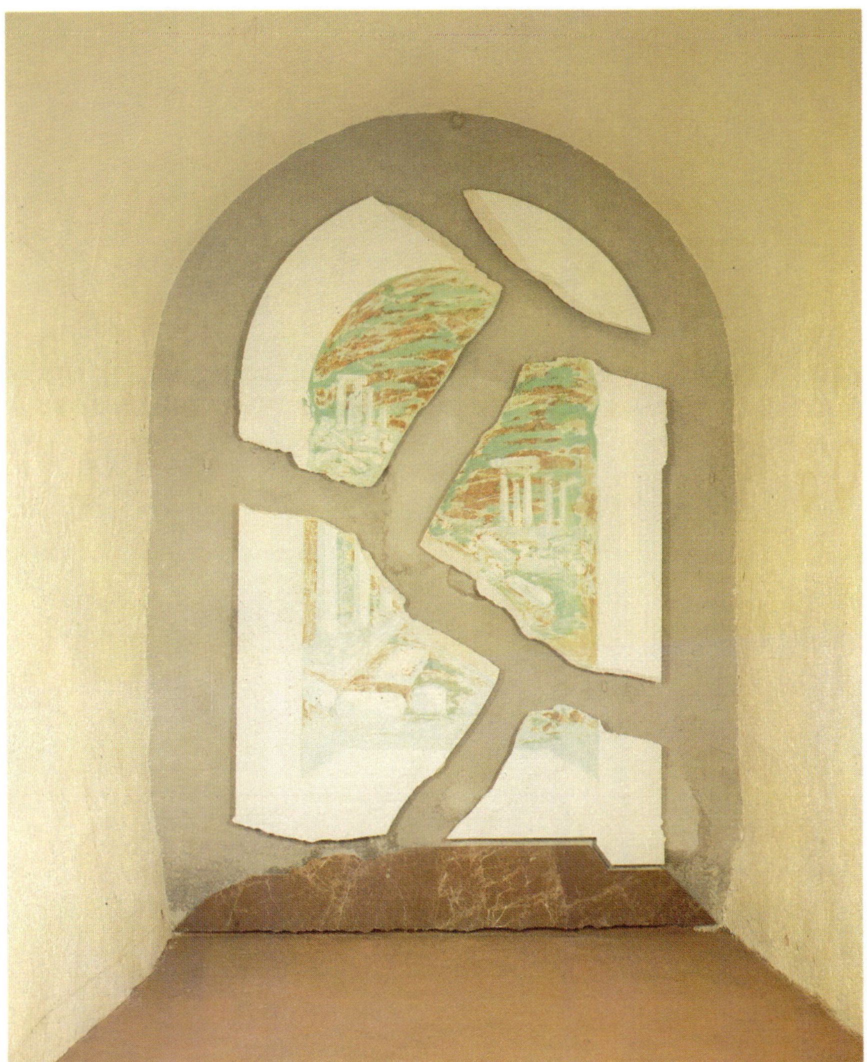

Made with the patronage of I.M.E.G., Massarosa (Lucca) and exhibited at the 25th
Festival dei Due Mondi, Spoleto Italy.

STEPHEN COX

Landscape with Ruins was made for a specific site
(the end-wall of a vault) in the Palazzo de Commune,
Spoleto, Italy, at the Festival of Two Worlds (1982).[1]
The slabs of white marble were cut from the same
boulder, so that some of the contours are repeated.
The three larger pieces represent the same scene
viewed from three different perspectives, and the
whole is enclosed within trompe l'oeil Corinthian
pilasters based on the framing device used by
Masaccio for his *Trinity* in Santa Maria Novella,
Florence. The red marble slab at the base formed a
junction with the red brick floor of the gallery.
Landscape with Ruins was Cox's first large,
'environmental' work using marble, and the first in
which colour is applied as part of the image. The
landscape viewed through an arch, with its
resonances of the work of Turner or Fuseli,
epitomises the spirit of the Grand Tour, looking
through the gateway of the Renaissance onto the
ruins of Antiquity. The arch links present and past,
but intrudes between spectator and spectacle.

   'Yet all experience is an arch wherethrough
   Gleams that untravelled world, whose margin fades
   For ever and for ever when I move.'[2]

Although Cox's interest in the past, and his use of

literary and iconographic references, became
explicit only after his first exhibition in Italy in 1979,
a recognition of the capacity for meaning inherent
in materials and the ways in which they are worked
is, and always has been, basic to his work. After
completing his training at the Central School of Art,
he taught at Coventry at a time when many
members of the staff there were actively re-thinking
the history of art.[3] His notebooks from that time
consciously questioned whether from the analytical
methods of minimalist art (with which he was then
pre-occupied) there might not eventually emerge a
narrative art.[4] This recognition derived not from the
then fashionable axiom that every action is political,
but from a deep love of materials in themselves and
a sensitivity to the way they are handled. He
remembers now that Ad Reinhardt was a
particularly important influence for him, as an
example of purity and honesty of approach. By
1977, a year in which he exhibited both in New York
(at the Fine Arts Building) and in Paris (at the
Biennale des Jeunes), he was able to articulate a
tension within his work between the radical
simplicity of American Minimalism and the need to
express something of the complexity of his own
roots in European culture.

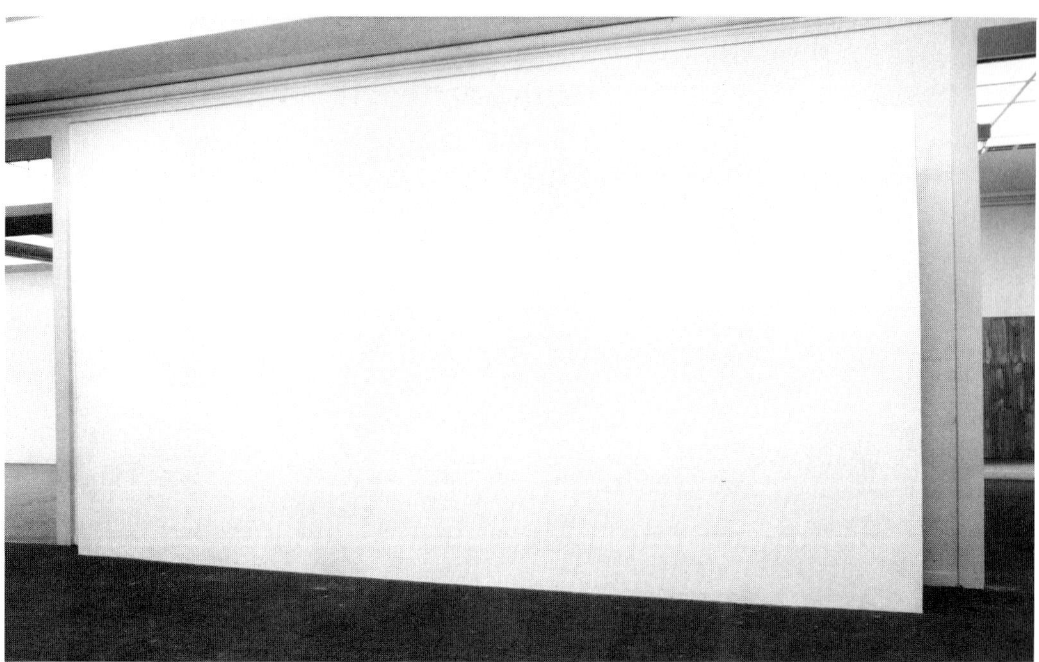

Surface "Spread"
1977

Paris Biennale
252 x 120ins
6.4 x 3.05m
white plaster on plasterboard

He was making at this time a series of freestanding 'walls', faced with different kinds of plaster and collectively entitled 'Surface'. The titles elaborated the resonance of his activity in a lyrical, evocative or narrative way eg *Surface: Spread; Surface: Charm* (named after the sub-atomic particle hypothesised by nuclear physicists); or *Surface: "Shining Forth" to George (Jackson).* He suggests that he saw these 'statements' at the time as artisanal rather than artistic. The *Surfaces* were drawn from two dimensions into three (into sculpture or architecture) in the form of a series of marble reliefs such as *Relief: Alberti I.* These were geometrically regular marble slabs which had been incised with straight lines so that if they were viewed from a particular perspective, the area bounded by the lines would be read as an extension of the slab into which it was carved. In this way, without relinquishing the discipline of self-reference, Cox's work rediscovered pictorial space and representation.

The *Reliefs* were his first carved works (1977). (His earlier work had all been constructed, built up). That he was turning away from America and back to Europe was also reflected in his reading at this time. He studied perspectival theory by Renaissance authors, and learned of the way in which Alberti's discoveries had affected Donatello, Ghiberti and Brunelleschi. He read Adrian Stokes, artist and critic, whose writings (indebted to Kleinian psychoanalytic theory) on carving and modelling in sculpture in particular helped him to rationalise his own attitude to working material. It was Stokes' description of the emerging principles of fifteenth century Italian art which led Cox to see his own elaboration of, and development from, Minimalist discipline as an equivalent to the blossoming of the Quattrocento from the rocky soil of Byzantine convention.

With this theoretical rearmament, when he visited Italy to exhibit in 1979 and 1980 (at the Pittura-Ambiente and Nuova Immagine, both in Milan), he was able to make installations which invested architectural forms with a new sense of emotion. *Relief: Luciano I In Memory of my Mother*, for instance, was a huge curved form expressing his feeling both for his Mother and for Architecture (Mother of the Arts). A deeper relationship with Italy started for Cox when he set out to make a Grand Tour which started in 1981 and continues to the present. He has paid particular attention to the techniques and materials described by Vasari, painter and chronicler of the Renaissance artists. The culture in which he has immersed himself continues to provide artists with a range of images whose meaning has been elaborated through a living tradition over many centuries. From its architecture, Cox has drawn the structural syntax of tondo, tympanum, arch, mandorla, threshold, oeil de boeuf, lunette; he quarries his techniques and structures from Italian literature and museums with the same directness with which he takes his stone from the landscape. Conversely, he arrives at themes and images in an indirect and personal way, often discovering only after the event that they have precedents. The interrelation of material, process and image is highly complex, and from this complexity the richness of his work derives.

The two major developments in his work (although neither is consistent or exclusive) occurring subsequent to the incorporation of pictorial representation, have been the use of fragmentation and, later, of applied colour. There are at least three determinants for his use of a pattern of fragmented pieces of stone as a basic material. It is much easier to handle, transport and install a large work in stone if it comes in several pieces. To slice a piece of stone into thin slabs is, similarly, a practical way to produce a body of raw material which is diverse within overall uniformity. The fragmented pieces are laid out, and then the image and architectural frame are inscribed onto them — it is not a whole image which is then broken. In effect, there is never a whole image other than in

Surface "Shining"
Forth (To George
Jackson)
1977

252 x 120ins
6.4 x 3.05m
Whitechapel Art Gallery

imagination: an image (an abstraction) which we will into being. This is the second determining factor. a spectator will work to resolve and complete a fragmented image, actively participating in the creation of its meaning.

Thirdly, fragmentation has a number of connotations in itself. For instance, Cox is fascinated by archaeological reconstruction and detective work, the 'reading' of old stones to enable deductions about the past or (as with the Rosetta Stone) to discover lost languages. Or, psychologically speaking, fragmentation can connote a state of emotional loss or destruction out of which can emerge an act of creative reparation. It is an important way, therefore, in which the artist's own sense of involvement with the past can be presented with emotional veracity. Lastly, and perhaps most important for Cox, fragmentation of the image ensures that the work is seen as an object in itself quite as much as a representation.

Colour, of course, is intrinsic to stone as a material, but the idea of applying surface colour came to Cox after he had noticed how the Travertine marble of Bernini's fountains has taken colour from its iron and bronze fixings — red iron oxide and blue-green copper sulphate, along with the black and grey of atmospheric dirt. (Surface colour is a misleading term, since Cox stains the stone, using these materials in solution, or rubs in black cement.) Although it is therefore an abuse of his material in traditional terms, serving to work against Neo-Classical preciousness, an historic or intrinsic rationale lies behind even this new attempt to ally his sculptural work to a pictorial tradition (he points out that the Italian language does not have a word

for 'paint', only 'colour'). His use of colour, and this is most important, completes his appropriation of the arts of architecture, sculpture, painting.

Such a broad approach makes it possible to describe Cox's work as mainstream Post-Modernist, if the term is taken to mean a liberal use of symbols and decorative styles as a way of generating 'positive' significations (and where Modernism has by implication come to be seen as a 'negative', purist and alienating orthodoxy). Cox, however, has retained his respect for the intellectual discipline and rigorous honesty of aspiration which Modernism first offered him in the shape of Minimalism. The importance he attaches to traditional craft skills and materials with traditional connotations differentiates his work from that of most Post-Modernists (other than the Italian Neo-Classical painters); and alongside his conscious use of symbolic and archetypal resonances he retains the discipline both of site specificity and internal logic. On the other hand, he does not reject the charges of romanticism and nostalgia which his work attracts, seeing them as endemic to art and its audience at this time. For instance, an accidental stain of red iron oxide revealed when the stone was cut for *Gethsemane* (the first work on which a naturalistic image appeared) has been consistently interpreted as a 'Pietra Ferita' (Wounded Stone) although the artist was unconscious of any such significance. Believing, as he does, that 'self-justification' in art is an abnegation of responsibility, he accepts as an honour the fruitful response between his work and its interpretation in a living tradition.

Lewis Biggs

FOOTNOTES

1. This was the twentieth anniversary of the first Spoleto Festival, for which David Smith was invited to make his Voltri series, all expenses paid. The same terms were offered Cox, and the fine white marble was provided by I.M.E.G.

2. Tennyson, Alfred Lord: *Ulysses.*

3. 1968-72, coinciding with the first efflorescence of the artists producing under the name Art Language.

4. The social and economic context for the production and consumption of a work of art formed part of the 'programme' of Minimalist work by Carl Andre, for instance, using industrial processes and materials. The context of a 'hand-made' tradition could be seen equally as the corollary of Cox's Minimal work.

Luciano I In Memory of my Mother
1980

grey plaster & white marble
installation at Milan Trienale
Nuove Immagine

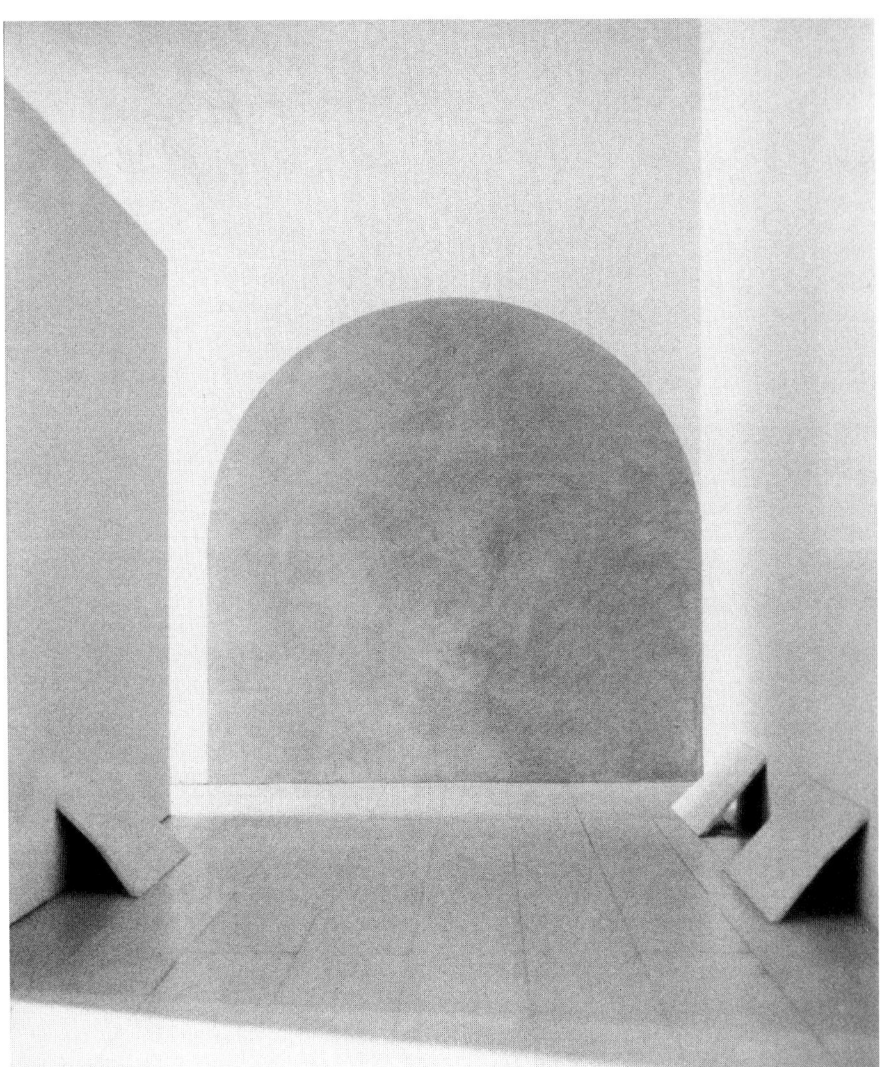

Gethsemane
1982

stone
304.8 x 609.6 x 5.1cms
Tate Gallery London

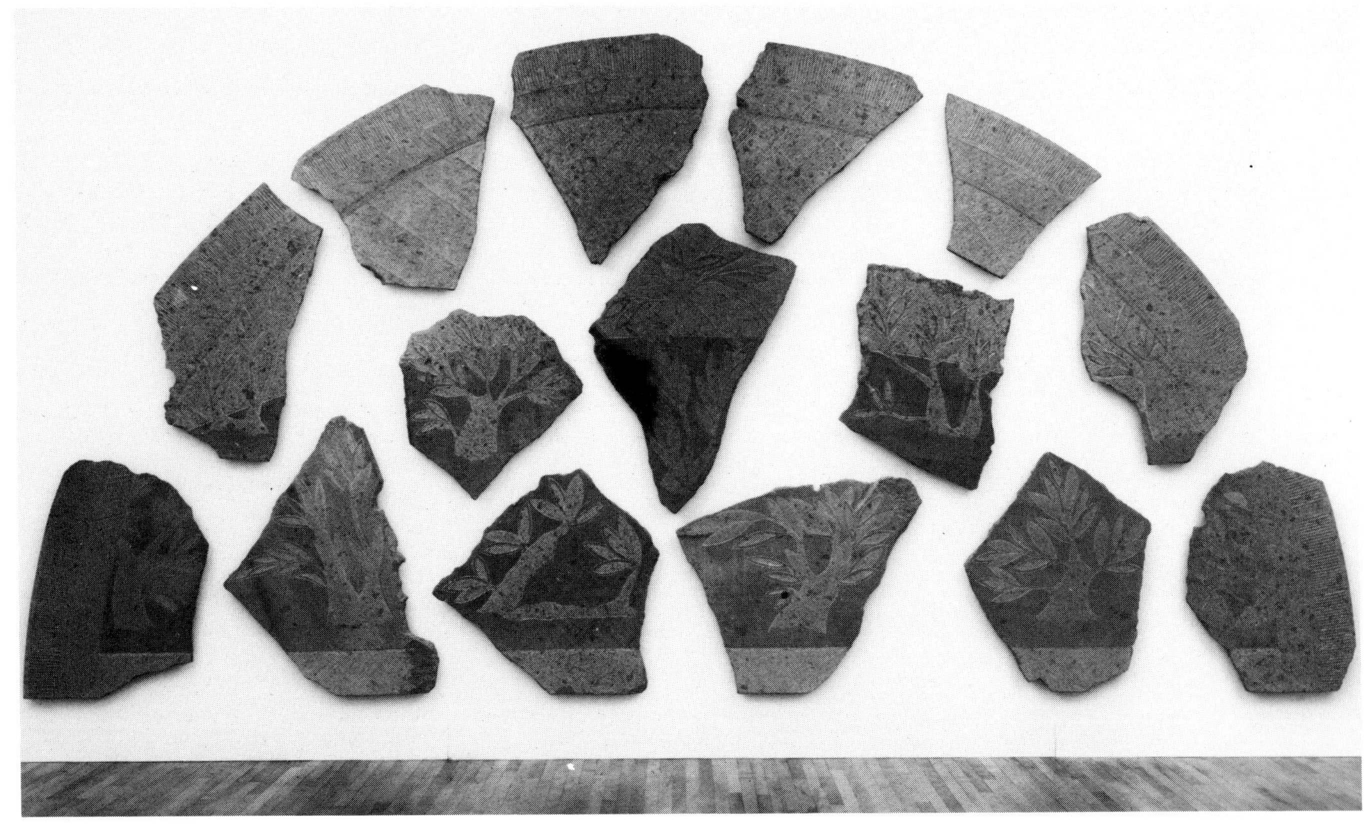

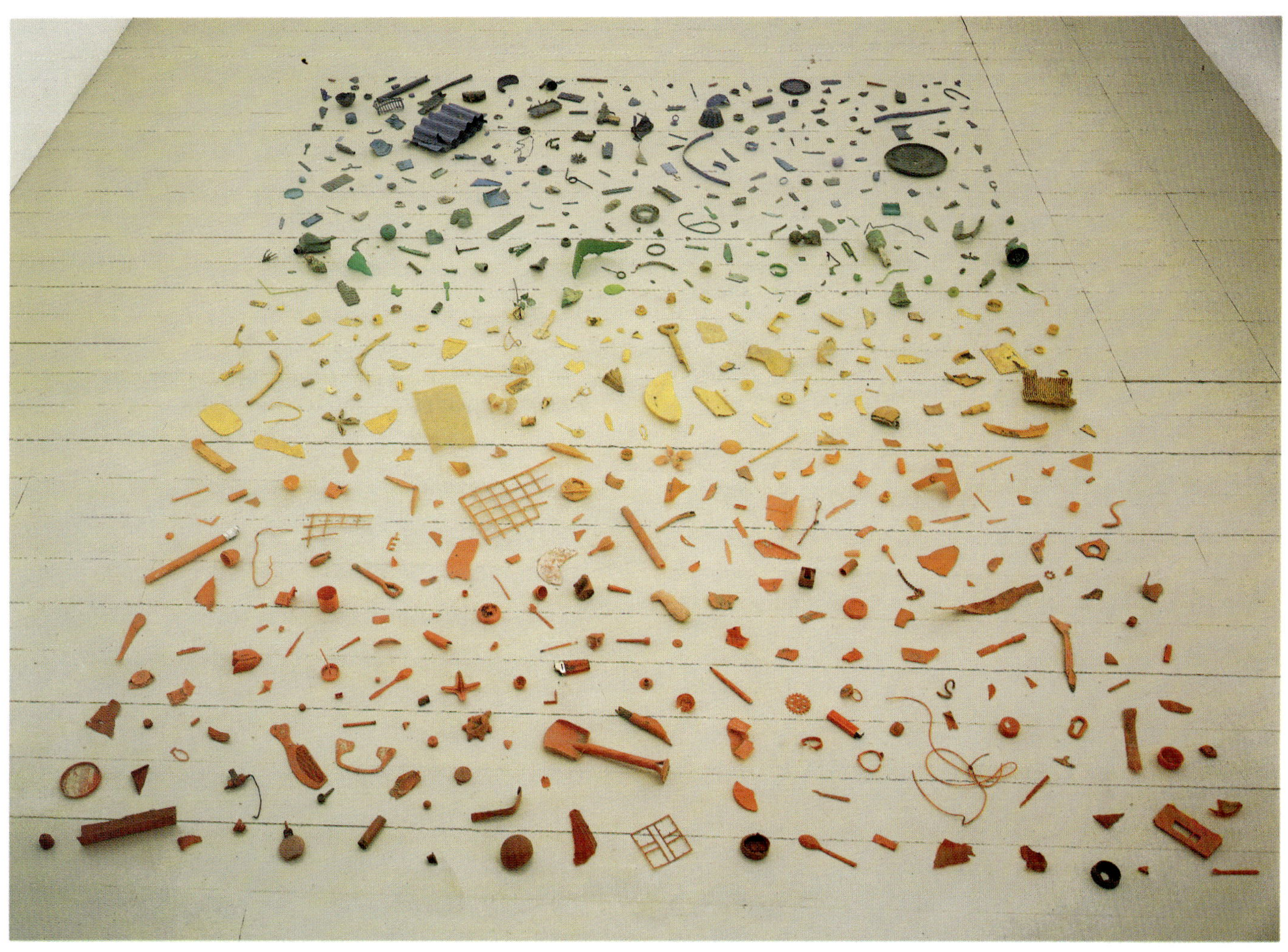

New Stones — Newton's Tones
1978
found plastic objects
366 x 244cms
courtesy: Arts Council of Great Britain

TONY CRAGG

'Here we have a man who has to gather the day's refuse in the capital city. Everything that the big city threw away, everything it lost, everything it despised, everything it crushed underfoot, he catalogues and collects. He collates the annals of intemperance, the *capharnaüm* (stockpile) of waste. He sorts things out and makes a wise choice; he collects, like a miser guarding a treasure, the refuse which will assume the shape of useful of gratifying objects between the jaws of the goddess of Industry'. Thus Baudelaire wrote of the ragpicker who, in amassing his *bricolage* of fragments, could be seen as the antitype of the Enlightenment philosopher Hegel who posited the totalizing momentum of the World Spirit.

These two figures, at the inception of high capitalism, make manifest the double, Janus face of modernity with which we, once again, have to come to terms in the new era of the multinational corporation when the totality is no longer a philiosophical schema but a terrifying reality, and day to day life is lived amid desuetude and fragmentation. In Tony Cragg's work fragmentation

and totality, the additive and the ideal, the prehistoric and the post-industrial, confront one another in a continuing dialogue with modernity and technology. It should not be forgotten that for Baudelaire the ragpicker was also the philosopher of the street.

New Stones-Newton's Tones, 1978, consists of small plastic fragments and objects evenly distributed (not arranged) across the floor to make a rectangle. The form is characteristic of Minimal sculpture but unlike, for example, one of Carl Andre's brick *Equivalents,* 1966, it does not follow by necessity from the structure of the component parts: rather, totality is challenged by fragmentation. The reduction of the minimalist object served to emphasize both its phenomenological environment, the ambient space of the gallery, and the wider context of its production and exchange. Cragg's sculpture also affects the viewer's negotiation of the room, although with a sense of fragility, an unwillingness to disturb the particles, rather than as obstruction. And where the Minimal sculpture adopted the serial repetition and often the finish of the production line, Cragg's recycled entropic fragments are weathered by the vicissitudes of consumption, the unique marks of a history outside the gallery. If they are the shards of an urban archaeology, this is not in pursuit of an archetypal origin or in mourning for a lost meaning. Cragg continues the anti-monumentality of Andre and the ecological discretion of Richard Long in the use of materials as they are found, but he is also decisively marking out a territory of his own, marking it not by a boundary, as property, but by difference. The structure also derives from science: the fragments of plastic are classified according to the colours of Newton's spectrum, thus conveying information about the world which we might not otherwise have noticed, the way in which coloured plastic comes in a limited range of hues. The sculpture could be interpreted according to the two meanings of 'law': the natural law of science and the legalistic norm or contract. To separate the two is to allow a distinction between nature and culture, against the confusion which allows ideology to appear as natural, while at the same time indicating the continuity between a supposedly neutral science and the social effects of technology in the mass produced environment: surplus waste is the counterpart of surplus value in a system of commodity exchange from which art cannot stand apart.

With *Red Skin* (1980) the implications of the tension between schema and fragments are extended to the mediated image. One of the set of red plastic items, a toy model indian weilding a hatchet, is used to determine the configuration of fragments on the floor. The shape connotes prehistoric art, such as the Cerne Abbas giant cut into the turf of a hillside, but insofar as it refers to the red indian through a mass produced toy, it shows the 'savage' as a category produced for consumption within industrial society. In a similar way, the notion of the artist as a primitive outsider satisfies escapist fantasies, whereas real indians and artists are marginalized.

Fixed to the wall, the configuration of fragments becomes an emblem which, according to the O.E.D. is a 'symbol', 'typical representation', 'pictorial parable' or 'heraldic device', all appropriate designations for the imagery in Cragg's 1981 exhibition at the *Whitechapel Gallery, London*: a Union Jack, a white crown, a soldier in riot gear, a submarine and multicolour map of Britain regarded from the north by a life-size figure. Taken together, these could be regarded as a commentary on national pretention and decline, an accurate reflection of the feel of British life at that particular historical moment. The tension between the configuration and the fragment is now translated into the social domain where the configuration represents a dominating mediated image and the fragments the raw immediacy of the street.

That same year Cragg used an alternative method to define an image, blocking it out in white paint on various flat, coloured surfaces. The first of these were emblems of consumption, an overloaded spoon, a form stabbed into a hunk of food, a place setting, an allegorical reference to the consumerism which produced the waste recycled into the art world. Subsequently Cragg used the same technique to define a painter's palette. *Palette* criss-crosses

the boundary between art and non-art not in pursuit of transgression, which only serves to reinstate the border, but as an invitation to consider differences. Colour is not applied but given on heterogeneous surfaces, yet the work invites the sort of scrutiny we normally reserve for painting, an attention provoked by the removal of the surfaces from their function as the disregarded category of rubbish, but which by implication could be extended to the wider environment. That the palette is not painted in but blocked out also indicates the 'other' of art in terms of labour. Like a whitewashed wall, it is the result of what the Germans call *anstreichen*, housepainting, as opposed to *malen*. When we look at a painting we forget the wall on which it hangs, the labour and surplus value upon which art depends.

The group of sculptures from 1983/1984 which involve collections of objects drawn over with black and white marks engage in a similar dialetic of art and non-art. The drawing operates rather like the totalizing schema of the earlier works, and indeed the plastic fragments of the emblematic wallpieces could be regarded as a medium for drawing. In the various furniture sculptures of 1983, bits of found material, fragments and objects are skewered onto rods to provide the medium for three-dimensional drawings of non-functional tables and chairs which seem almost elegiac in their reference to humanity as absent, like tokens excavated from the tomb of a vanished civilization. If *Drawn on Objects* make a reference to art, it is to the Cubist *nature morte* which founded a new convention for the translation of three into two dimensions and opened the question of the difference between life and art through the literal incorporation of collage. Where Cragg had previously eschewed arrangement he now espouses it, not as a given value but as something to be questioned. In a sense the found objects refuse the incorporation into a whole which the drawing attempts to enforce, and continue to assert their obdurate individual identities, their separateness as things. The three-dimensionality of the sculptures conditions both the unfolding of the viewer's experience through time and the resistance of the objects to any assimilation to a single point of view.

Certain of Cragg's work over the past year have been concerned with landscape as both representation and as actuality. Nothing could better illustrate the continually surprising quality of his work and his willingness to break his own rules than the work he made for an outdoor site in Basel, Switzerland. Two blocks of stone cut to resemble houses with the planes cut slightly askew are perched on top of piles of rock like the cairns left on hilltops since prehistoric times as a memorial of human presence. This work is not just monumental, it is a comment on monumentality as a part of human history; it doesn't just use natural materials, it is about the relation between nature and culture, the very moment of transformation of wilderness into human place.

The viewer is confronted with the cumulative, amorphous masses of rock, sloping more on one side to suggest a front and a back, and above them, out of reach the geometrical shapes of the 'houses', the false perspective of which confounds an

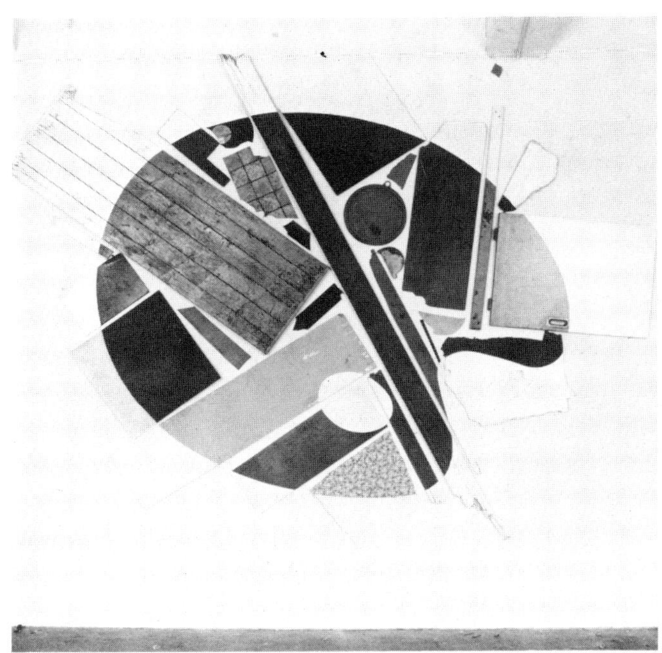

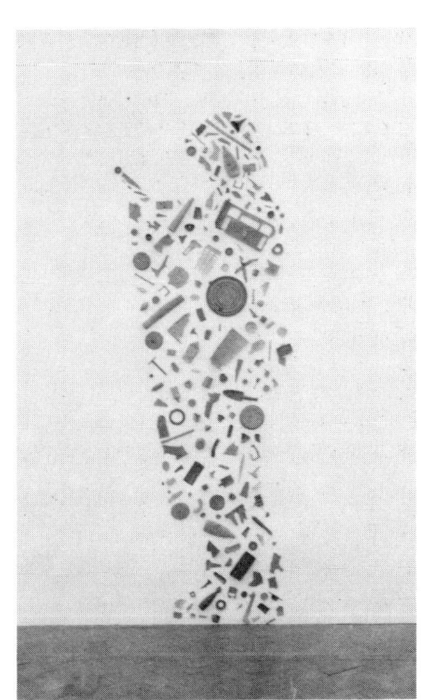

Soldier
1981

found plastic objects
height 2.2m approx.

Palette
1982

mixed material
224 x 252cms
photo credit: Lisson Gallery London

Realms & Neighbours
1984

limestone & red granite
350cms high
collection: Galerie Schelman & Kluser, Munich

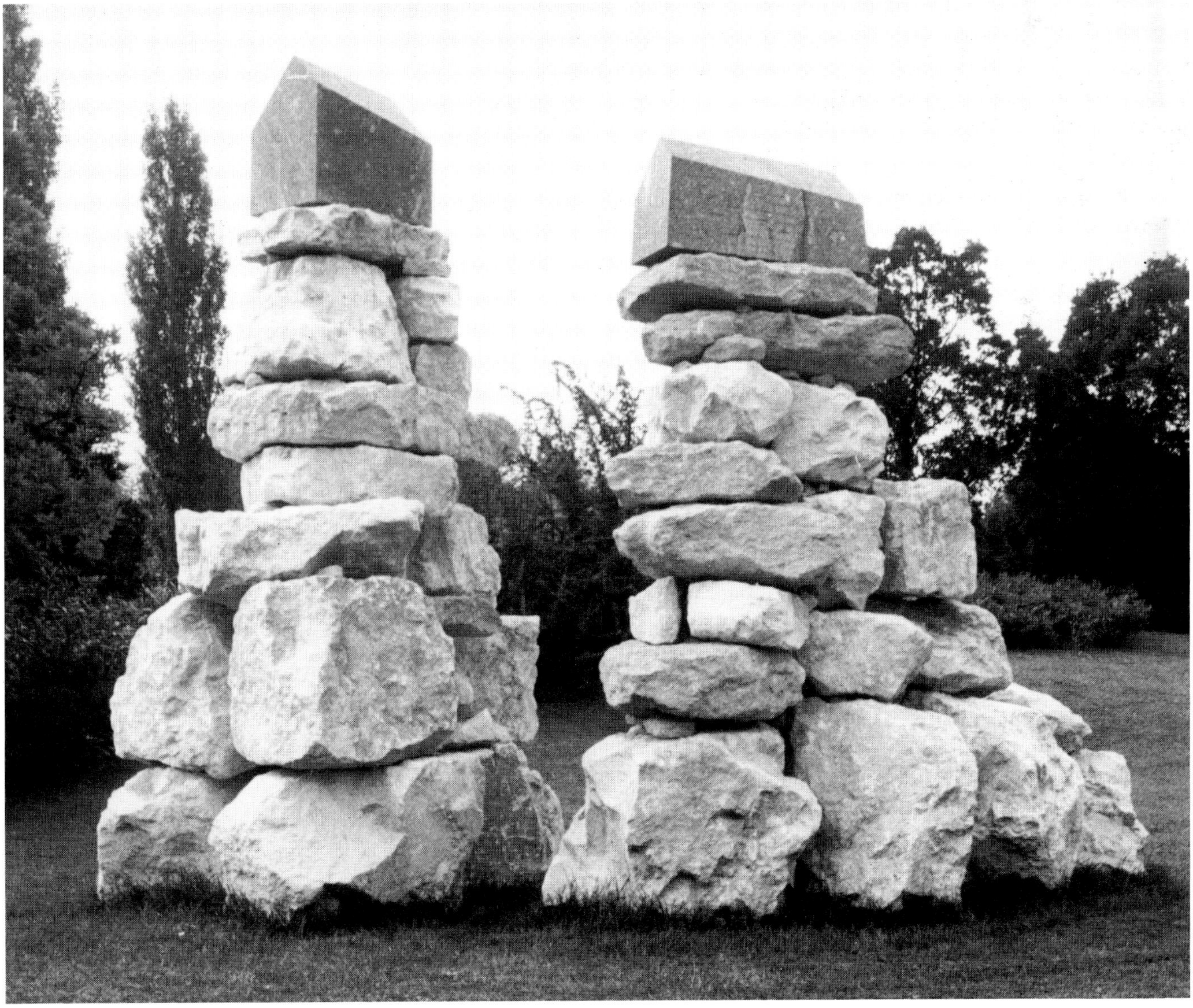

idealized visual projection. The title, *Realms and Neighbours*, brings out the moral implications of the work, the ethical relation of communality and mutual respect as the antithesis of totalization.

The critical interrogation of monumentality through the subversive relation of fragment to totality, which has been present in Cragg's work from the start, is extended in the sculptures that he showed at the Cologne Kunstverein in 1984. These indicated the way in which monumentality as a sculptural mode is associated with a totalizing social structure. Multicoloured plastic fragments, which previously alluded by analogy to the notion of the masses here assumed the life-sized silhouette of a crowd extended along one wall. Breeze blocks and two types of ventilation bricks, the kind of materials from which Carl Andre would have made horizontal, anti-monumental sculpture, are raised into the towering forms of *Three Modern Buildings*,

suggestive of the dominating abstraction of modern skyscrapers. In *Echo* sheets of board are joined to make variously shaped blocks unified by an even covering of hand-drawn marks. These are organized in a curve, giving the structure a definite front and back, and on the inside, leaning against or standing beside the blocks, are a metal container with a funnel top, a concrete ring and a piece of plastic piping. An environment is created around the viewer which evokes both a cityscape and an amphitheatre. In these recent works multiplicity and fragmentation are combined with repetition and construction; and the empirical, pragmatic attentiveness to the specific qualities of materials which has been consistent throughout Cragg's oeuvre is now in tension with an almost baroque theatricality.

Michael Newman

Red Skin
1980

found plastic objects
264 x 194ins
670.6 x 487.7cms
photo credit: Lisson Gallery London

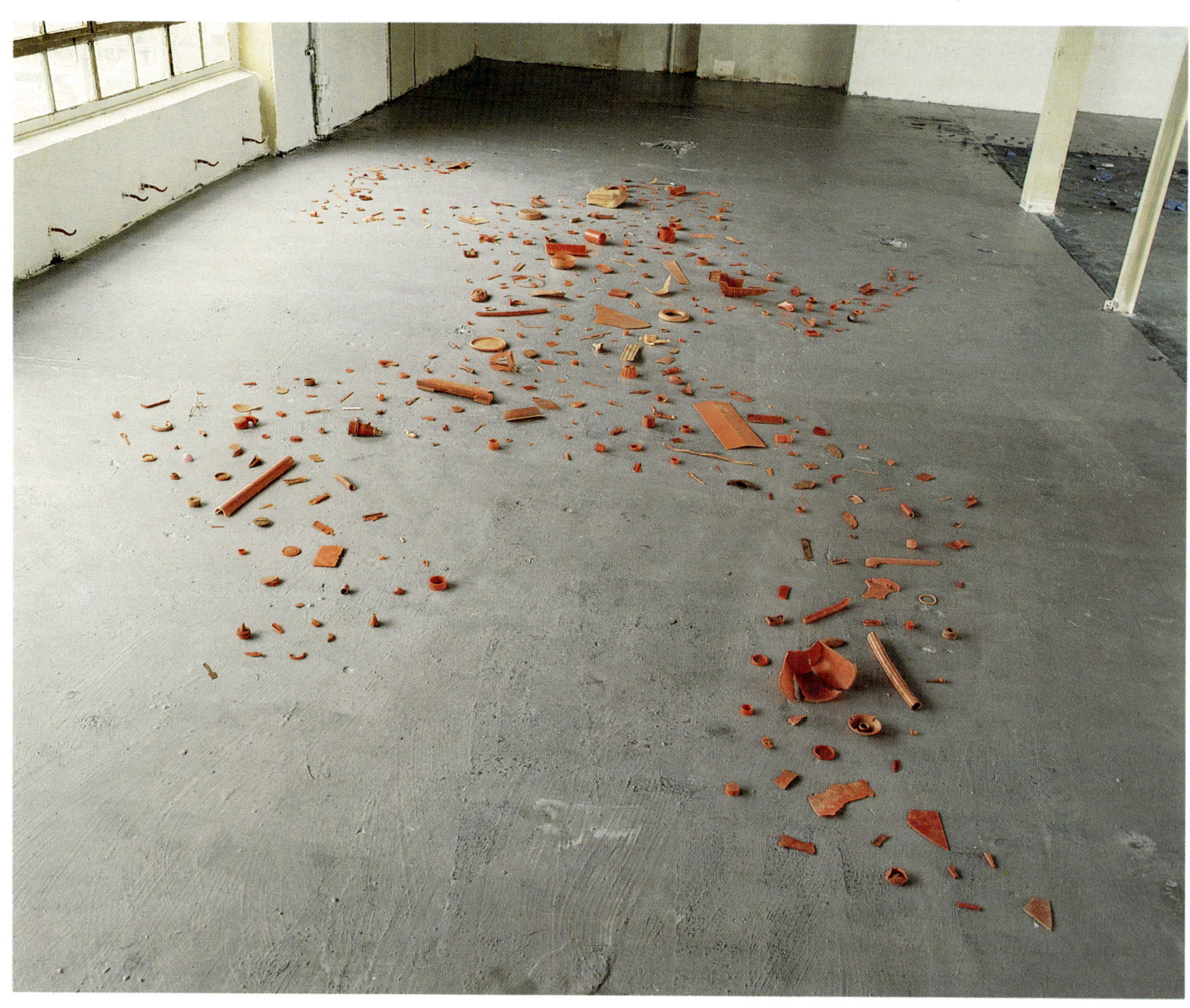

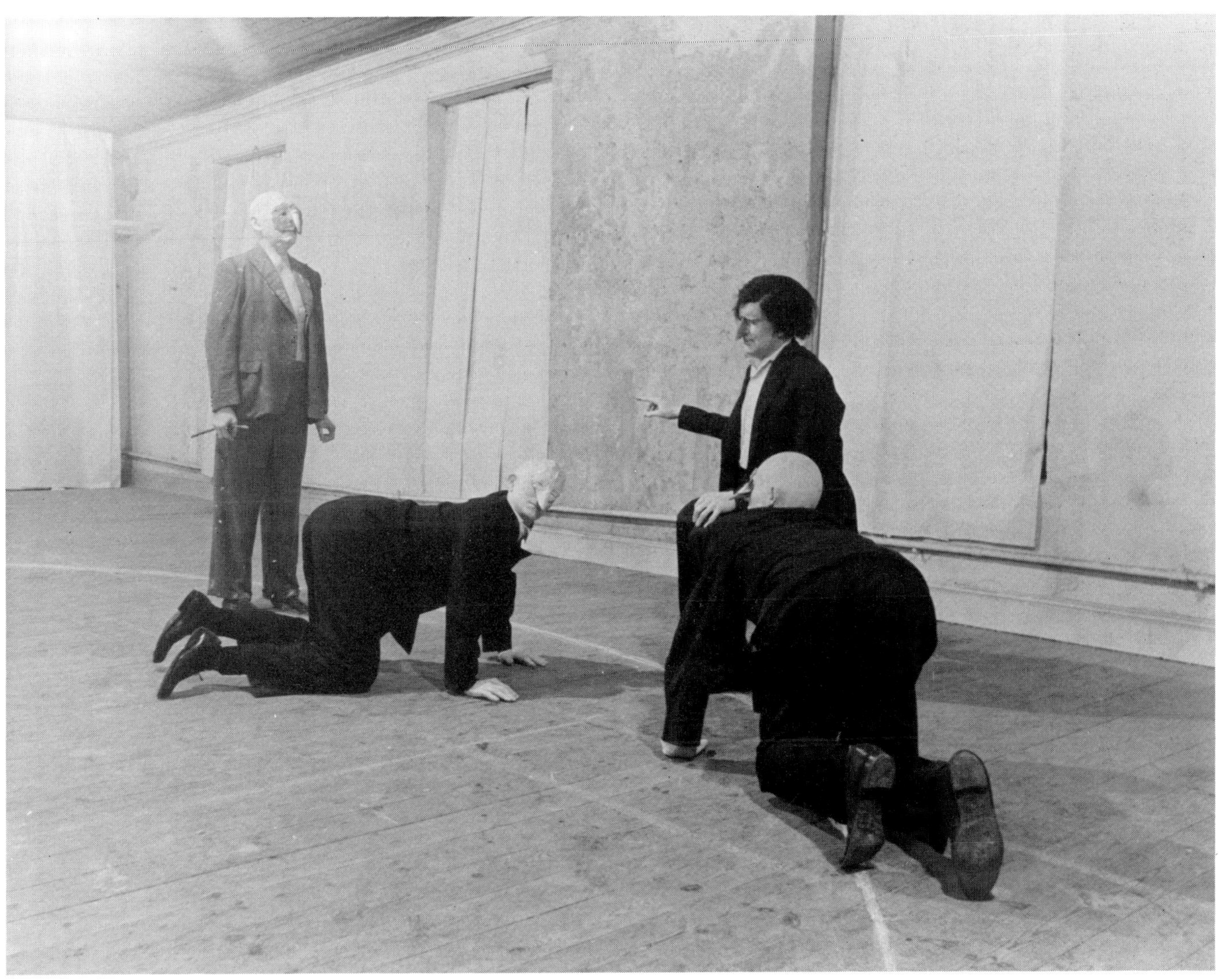

For The Last Time
1972

fibreglass, wax, paint, clothing & shoes
4 life size figures
courtesy: James Kirkman, London

JOHN DAVIES

When John Davies's sculptures were first presented
to the public in 1972 at the Whitechapel Gallery
they caused quite a stir. Figurative, realistic,
permeated with a mysterious symbolism, Davies's
work shared nothing with the abstract models that
predominated in British sculpture of that time. The
difference stemmed directly from his aims which
(while expressing awareness that may sound corny
to some) Davies has summed up as trying "to make
things that are like people, rather than like
sculpture". He felt distinctly isolated as a sculptor
at the time; everywhere he looked he seemed to
see sculpture of welded steel. He was not aware of
the work being done in the United States by such
"photo-realist" sculptors as Duane Hanson and
John de Andrea and though he knew and admired
the work of Edward Keinholz, he didn't actually like
it, finding his aggressively socio-political tableaux
"too crude and gross". Even now, more than a
dozen years later when welded steel has given way
to other more various (and variegated) materials,

Davies's relationship to the rest of British sculptors
remains a distant one.

Parallels for Davies's work, in as much as they are
necessary, have always been easier to find in the
areas of painting, theatre and performance art.
Indeed, anyone looking at photographs of the 1972
sculpture "For The Last Time" without prior
knowledge of Davies's work could be forgiven for
mistaking them for the record of a piece of
Absurdist theatre. The four figures in this piece are
all formally dressed. One, seated, raises his arm,
two of the others are crawling. The fourth figure,
undoubtedly in command, stands aggressively rigid.
The stick he carries is reminiscent of a baton,
attribute of both a conductor of an orchestra and a
sergeant major. Overtones of domination/
subjugation and the associated questions of willing/
unwilling participation that inform so much of
Davies's work are unmistakable.

As with many of Davies's early works all the figures

are masked, a feature that adds to the theatricality of the work and recalls, on the one hand, masked balls of 18th century Venice, with their fascinating degeneracy and, on the other, aspects of criminality. Davies's stated purpose was rather different. At this time he cast many of his figures from the living model but, in the artist's own words "casting will only give you so much". In a paradoxical fashion, Davies introduces alien elements, notably the masks, not to increase the level of absurdity but, as it were, to jolt the figures into life. In doing so, Davies at least side-stepped the ultimate problem of the work of American "photo-realist" sculptors which, though arresting on first sight soon fades. To quote the artist again, "It's like a stuffed dog, after you've seen it for a couple of seconds you want it to move".

Between 1974 and 1980 Davies made a series of figures, some single but usually paired or in groups, that, though clothed in shoes and trousers are naked from the waist up. The single figures often carry or wear a considerable amount of paraphernalia. One, "Bucketman", not only carries the two buckets of the title but supports a semi-circular device from his shoulders and a dense, black, canonball-like sphere on his head. Davies has his own reasons for selecting these bits and pieces, reasons that are often motivated by purely formal concerns. He placed the strange "yoke" that half-

surrounds "Bucketman's" head, to function as a background and locate the head firmly in space in much the same way that a painted portrait is fixed by the surrounding canvas. The devices accrue during the process of making the sculpture and though reminiscent of the Saints' attributes in Christian iconography actually contribute to, rather than unravel the enigma of each figure and its activity. Davies has no objection to others concocting a story around his figures; indeed he enjoys it as an inevitable consequence of peoples' inability to "mind their own business", but it is unlikely that any interpretation will have the remotest connection with the artist's original notions.

Throughout the mid and late '70s, Davies created group sculptures in which the theme of domination and subservience was explicit. He made several works in which one figure sits piggy-back on another, though which figure is stronger than the other remains in question. Is the piggy-back figure being carried because of psychological domination or because of physical weakness? Or is the figure carrying the other one doing so because of superior strength or because of psychological subservience?

In "Figures and Railings 1981", such concerns are notably absent. Young men lean or stand listlessly as if in conversation. The work was inspired by

Figures and Railings
1981

mixed
base: 488 x 366 plus 4 life-size figures
collection: Art Gallery of Western Australia

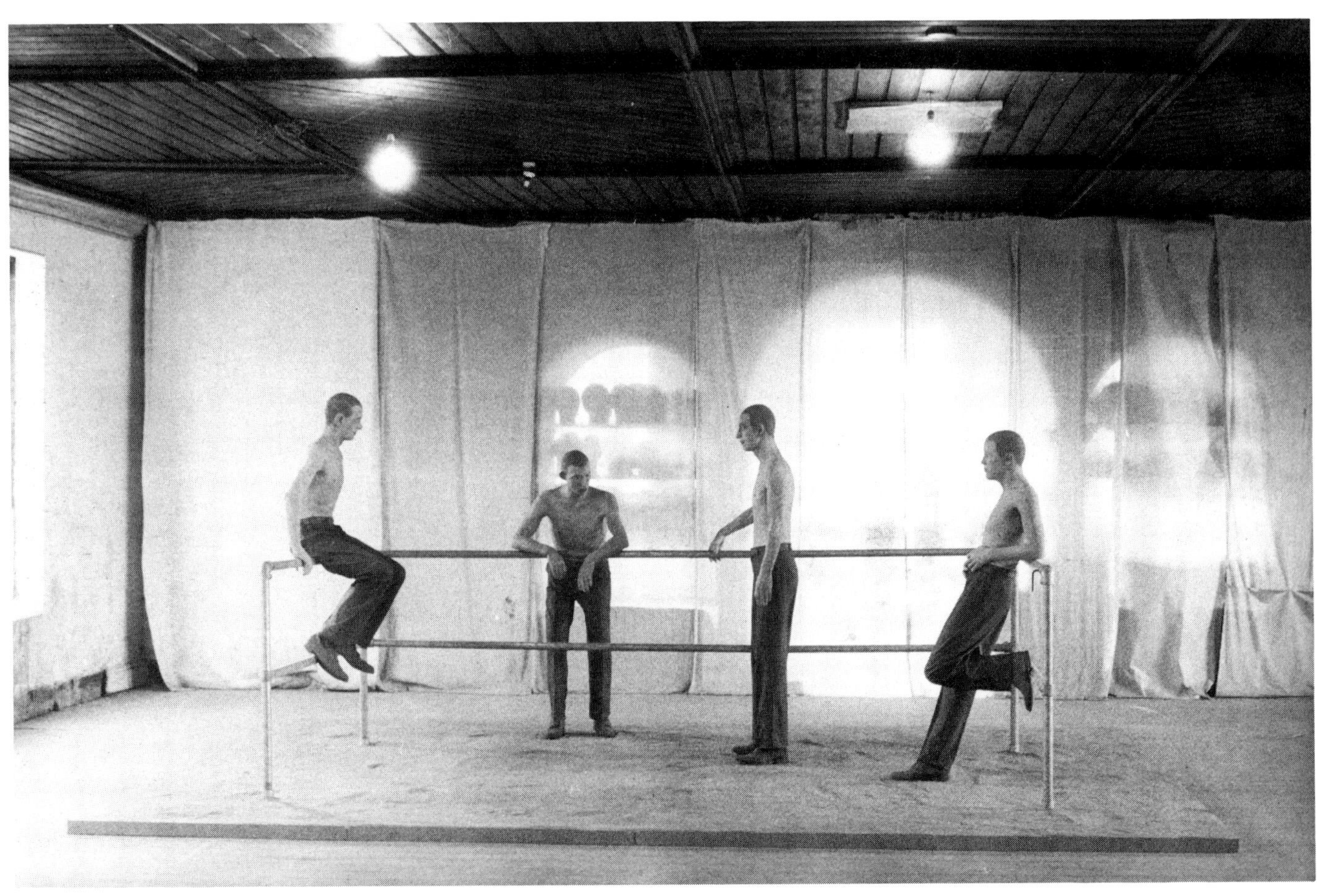

Davies observing people at the seaside. The sense of theatrical action, so apparent in the early work and implicit in the "piggy-back" sculpture, has all but disappeared. Only the improbable "half-dress" of the figures provides Davies's, by now familiar, incongruity and much of the mystery of this group lies in its very banality. But this banality by no means renders the figures harmless or the overall work toothless. It requires no great leap of the imagination to see the figures as conspirators or as bored young men waiting for an excuse for action. In this case, Davies has solved his "stuffed dog" problem by portraying inaction itself and allowing the viewers' inquisitive imagination to do the rest.

"Figures and Railings 1981" was the last work for which Davies employed the direct casting technique and some of the heads in this work are, in fact, modelled. Since 1980, Davies has worked exclusively with modelling and, partly as a consequence of this, has varied the scale of his figures. Between 1980 and 1984 he worked on a series of half life-size and smaller figures, going through the motions of acrobats; climbing vertiginous rope ladders, standing or sitting on trapezes, walking tightropes. These were accompanied by a number of colossal heads, each one over a metre high. Saying they are "the audience for the little figures" Davies compares our experience of viewing the small figures and the large heads together to that of being seated in the audience of a theatre and looking first at the performers and then quickly at our neighbours beside or in front. The large heads also represent an attempt "to get very close to people, to look down their ears and up their noses". By contrast, though, he also likens our relationship to the large heads to that of a baby and an adult. Our hand on a giant head's cheek appears minute and we shrink to a subordinate state. Once again, the question of domination and subjugation occurs and once again it is unclear as to who has the final say: the viewer, by subjecting the head to impertinent scrutiny; or the head, by its extraordinary scale. Either way, the interplay between spectator and performer has become increasingly potent and the viewer has been drawn ever deeper into Davies's exploration of how individuals perceive and relate to one another.

Graham Beal

Bucketman
1974

mixed media
life size
collection: University of East Anglia (Sainsbury Purchasing Fund)

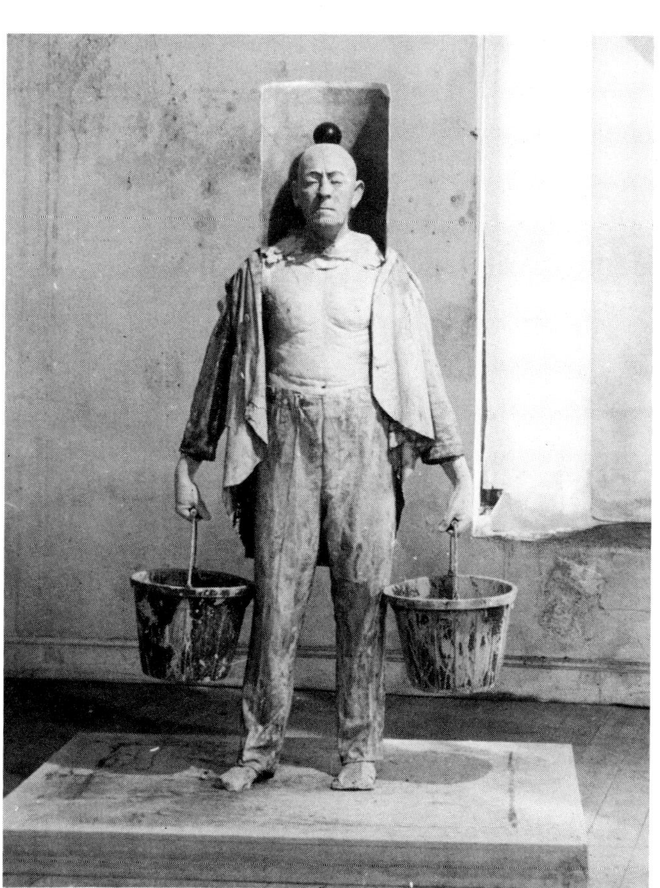

Drawing of D.Y.
1984

mixed media
58 x 43¾ins
147.3 x 111.1cms
Marlborough Fine Art London

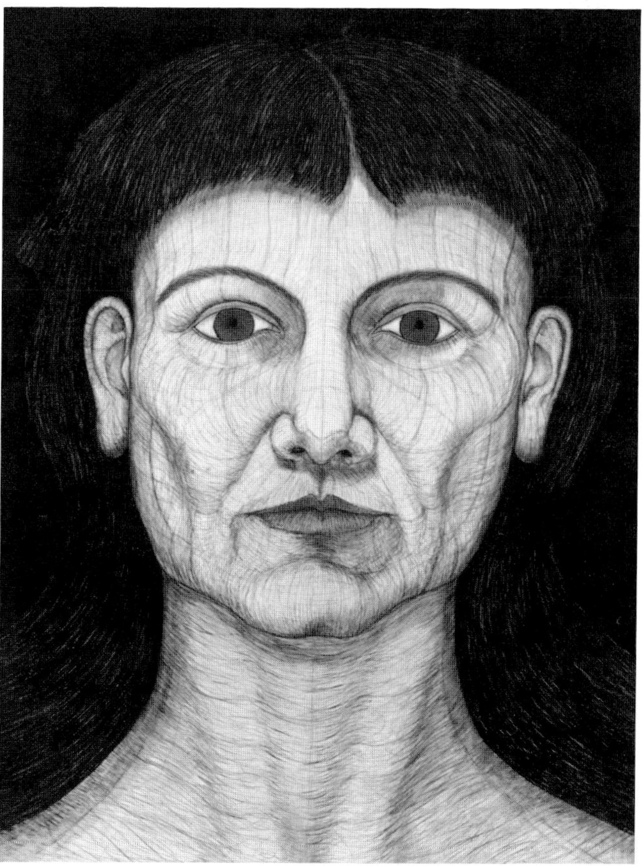

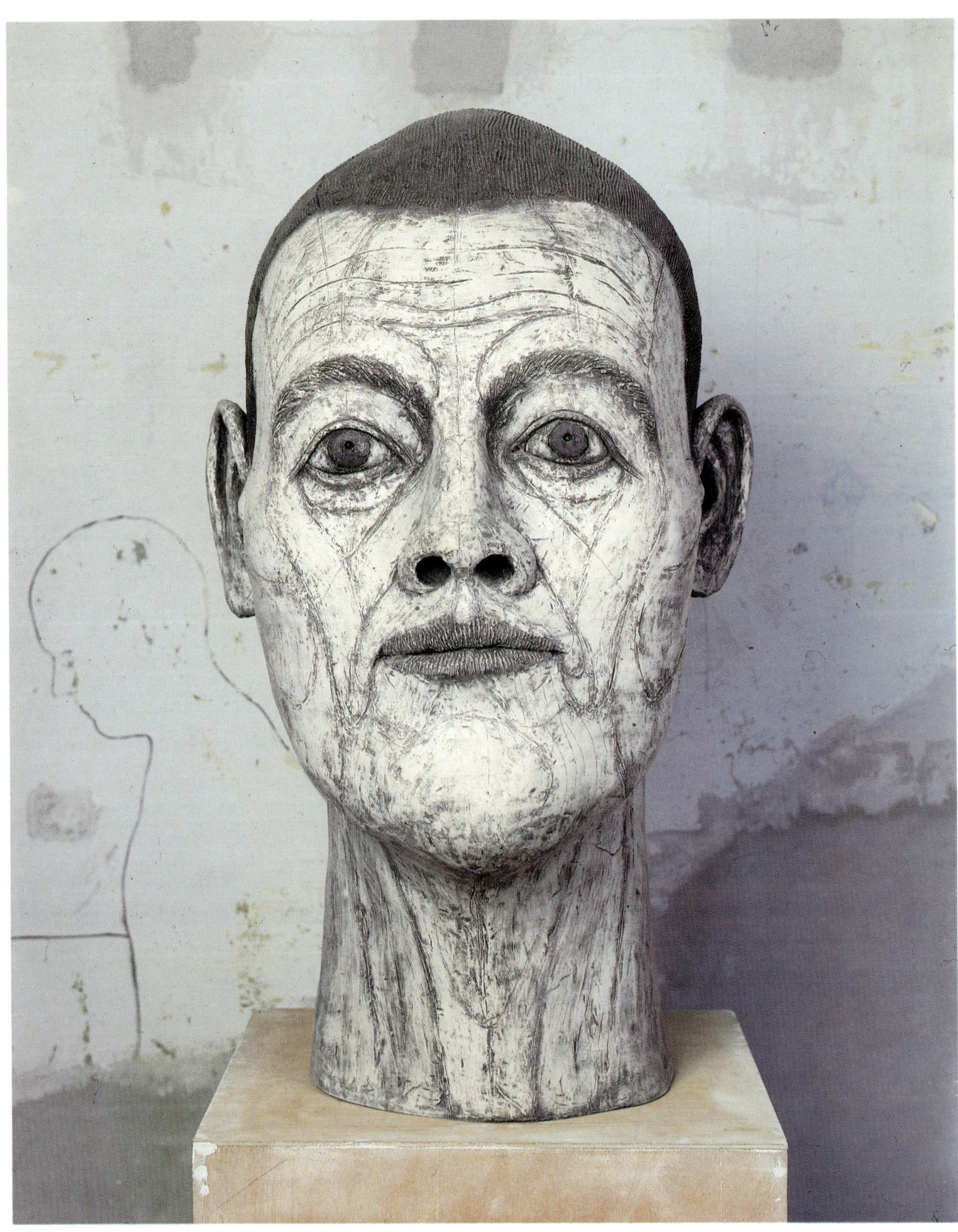

Head (white with lines)
1983-84

paint on fiberglass cast
height 42 5/8ins
height 108.2cms
collection: Queensland Art Gallery

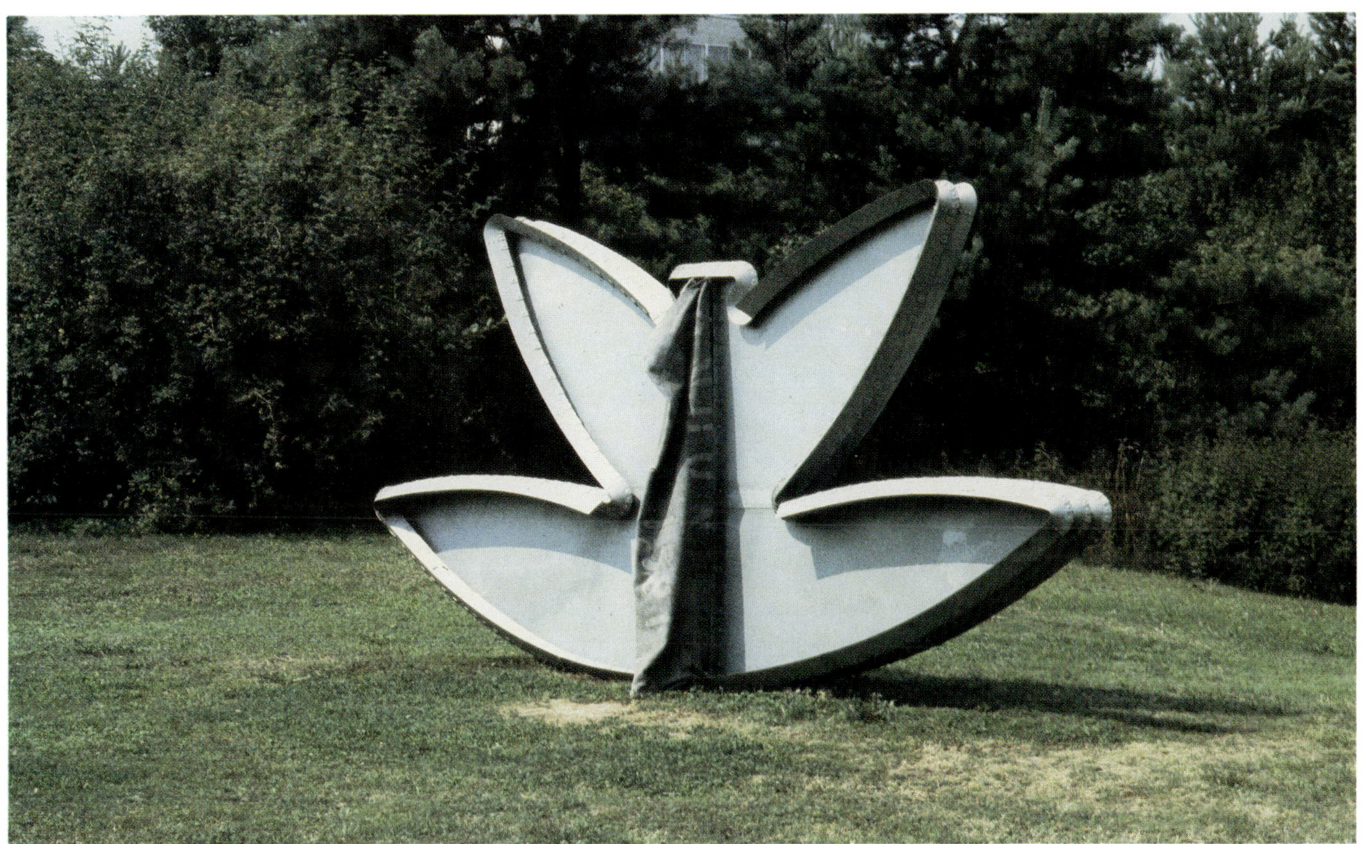

Between the Two of Us
1984

galvanised steel, canvas & rivets
214 x 396 x 31cms
Lisson Gallery London
photo credit: Kurt Wyss, Basle, Switzerland

RICHARD DEACON

For a recent commission by Vogue magazine, Lord Snowdon, photographer to the Royal Family and now to Britain's great artists, was sent to photograph Henry Moore. Snowdon did what all photographers do with sculptors. ''The hands, the hands'', he demanded, and old Henry Moore, now barely able to work, did what he had courteously done for photographers for fifty years and ran his hands lovingly, firmly along his work, round the curves, into the nooks and hollows of a reclining figure.

The hands, the hands — they want to run themselves along Richard Deacon's sculpture but if they tried to the chances are that the screws and rivets would take off a layer of skin. And yet how these objects cry out to be coaxed and rubbed and touched and smoothed and puzzled over.

A wooden skeleton on the floor, is it a lobster or some strange device for sifting? What about this little piece growing like a mushroom, this thing entitled Art For Other People No 6? with its precious green suede bag and its ring of shiny brass it looks like the protruding end of an old nautical instrument, something for measuring the stars perhaps. Deacon's sculptures play with that curious part of the mind which loves to investigate and play around.

And yet though they seem distantly familiar we have never seen such shapes in the world before, the mark, I think of great sculpture. As Frank Auerbach once said of painting: ''What I am not hoping to do is to paint another picture because there are enough pictures in the world. I am hoping to make a new thing for the world that remains in the mind like a new species of living thing.''

The extraordinary thing is that the hands, know Richard Deacon's sculptures well even if the eyes swear that they do not recognise them. The hands are familiar with the touch of the old tarpaulin that sags at the centre of Between the Two of Us, and they long to lift it up and discover the woodlice underneath.

Yet ultimately it is neither the hands nor the eye which derive most pleasure from Richard Deacon's work. It is the spirit. For a very simple reason, it is on work such as this that the spirit finds absolute harmony and through it experiences the delicious, soothing sensation of peace.

When exhibition organisers are asked to decide where Deacon should be placed they usually assume that he belongs among the fashionable new British sculptors, the so-called Object Sculptors or Lisson Boys. Geographically, yes. Emotionally, no.

Emotionally Richard Deacon is no Post-Modernist. Indeed, I think it would not be too far off the mark to call him the last of the true modernists, for he belongs, surely, in the tradition of Cezanne and Brancusi, Moore and Hepworth, Calder and Caro. His sculpture achieves order rather than destroys it. It celebrates harmony, not chaos. At a time when so many artists can work with their tongues rammed firmly in their cheeks, I respect Deacon's deep show of faith enormously.

Inevitably — and this is very British of him, his work reminds you of nature's own handiwork. With Henry Moore it was the rock formation and the female figure which was echoed. With Hepworth it was the bird and the egg. Deacon's nature is more complex than that. It is assimilated, constructed. It is not the nature which produces simple, single forms but a nature which adds and dabs on, which builds one harmonious form out of myriads of tiny relationships. Some of his sculpture reminds you of a giant fruit in which the soft flesh has rotted away leaving a hard wooden skeleton. Or, as in Between the Two of Us, of a large plant budding on the floor, a cactus, a dramatic jungle lily. The smaller pieces, the Art For Other People, have an indoor scale, little things growing around on window sills and coffee tables, things that people bring home from their long country walks, animal skeletons and strange shells. There are echoes of nature everywhere in Deacon's work, *but they are always balanced by the harsher, harder echoes of man's work.*

Deacon's art was conceived in the English school room where, ever since the time of Sutherland and Nash, children have been taught to draw shells, leaf skeletons, twisted roots, feathers. But this is only its *background*, something vague, something generalised that tickles the memory and gives it pleasure. His foregrounds are man-made in an assortment of ways. Deacon assembles his sculpture by cutting, sticking, rivetting, drilling, screwing, sewing, stretching and folding them together. When perceived as a whole his sculptures have no rough edges or incompleted balances. But from close up they are seen to be the result of

Art for Other People No 6
1983

leather & brass
2 x 1 x 1 feet
61 x 30.5 x 30.5cms
Lisson Gallery

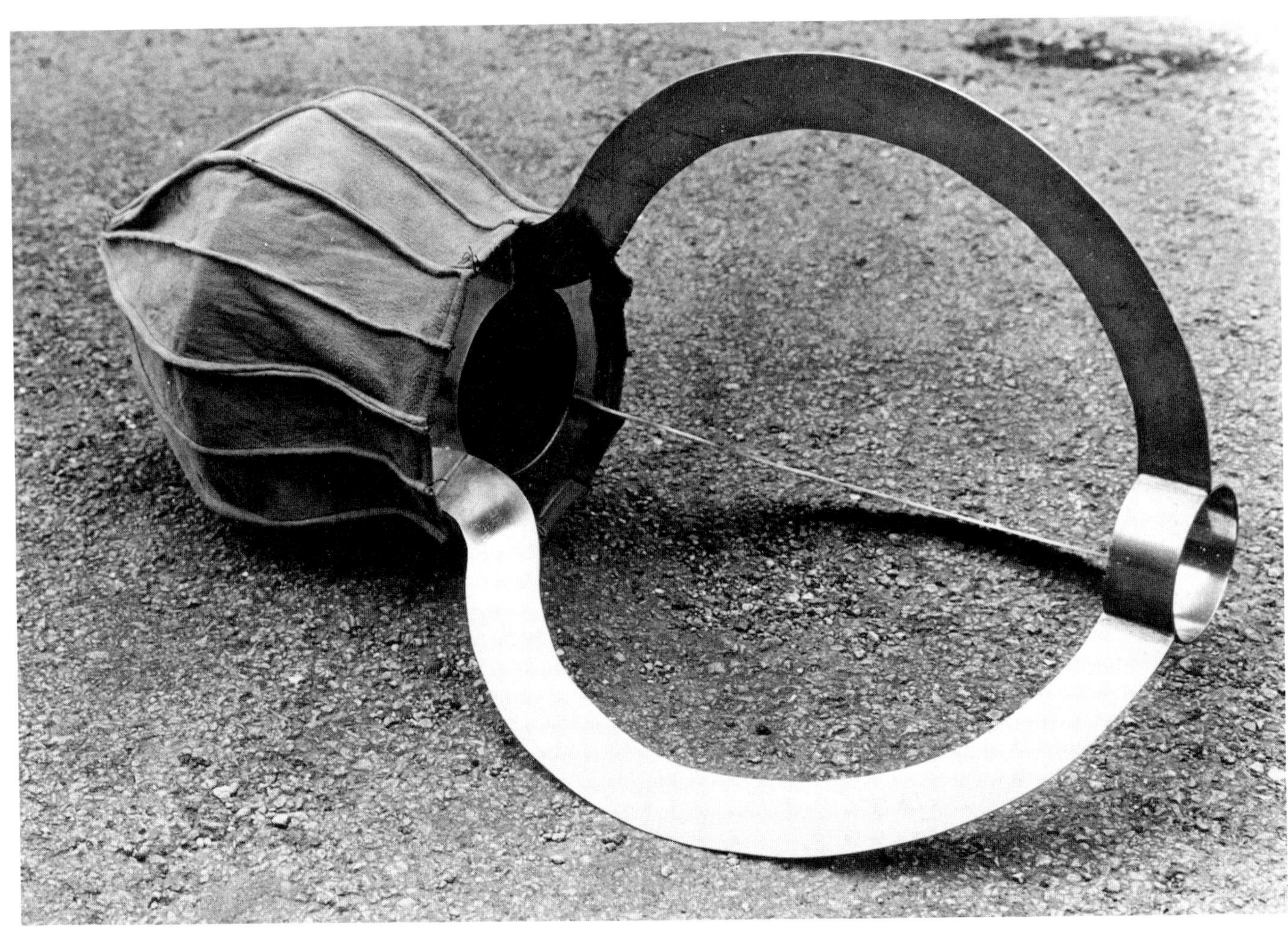

much monotonous labour, of fixing and adding and bending and bolting together. It is this labour which smoothes off the rough edges and allows the final form to emerge in the same way as water smoothes a pebble or wind smoothes a rocky outcrop. For the whole of this century great modern artists have tried to compete with nature, to match their own handiwork against God's. Deacon is the latest of these humanist modernists.

How are his harmonies achieved? It has been said that Richard Deacon loves to experiment with materials and shapes. Why else would he range from bronze to suede, from galvanised steel to old tarpaulins, from great lumps of metal to delicate wicker work? But the word "experiment" implies hesitancy, uncertainty about the experiment's outcome. No such hesitancy exists in Deacon's sculpture. The materials are exactly the right ones needed to achieve a permanent balance. His work exists at the crucial point where — to change any element in it — you would have to take the thing to pieces and start from scratch.

A profound balance lies at the centre of every Deacon sculpture. In Art For Other People No 6 it is the balance between hard, shiny brass and soft, green suede, an open form and a closed one, an inside and an outside. In Art For Other People No 9 it is a balance between one side of the heavy ear-shaped slab of metal, the indented side, and the projecting side, between positive and negative, the side that listens and the side that speaks. For Between the Two of Us, even the title joins in the game. All around the sculpture there are critical balances to achieve, between metal and tarpaulin, flat surfaces and thick edges, outlines and forms, figurative references and abstraction.

Deacon is a poet, a great admirer of Rilke from whom he sometimes borrows his titles. As in Rilke, I think the end result of his search is the ultimate balance between male and female. Only when the yin and the yang combine in a sculpture do you feel that gentle hermaphrodite self-containment which is Richard Deacon's precious gift to modern art.

Waldemar Januszczak

Art for Other People No. 5
1982

laminated wood
3,6 x 3,6 x 6 feet
106.7 x 106.7 x 182.9cms
The Saatchi Collection

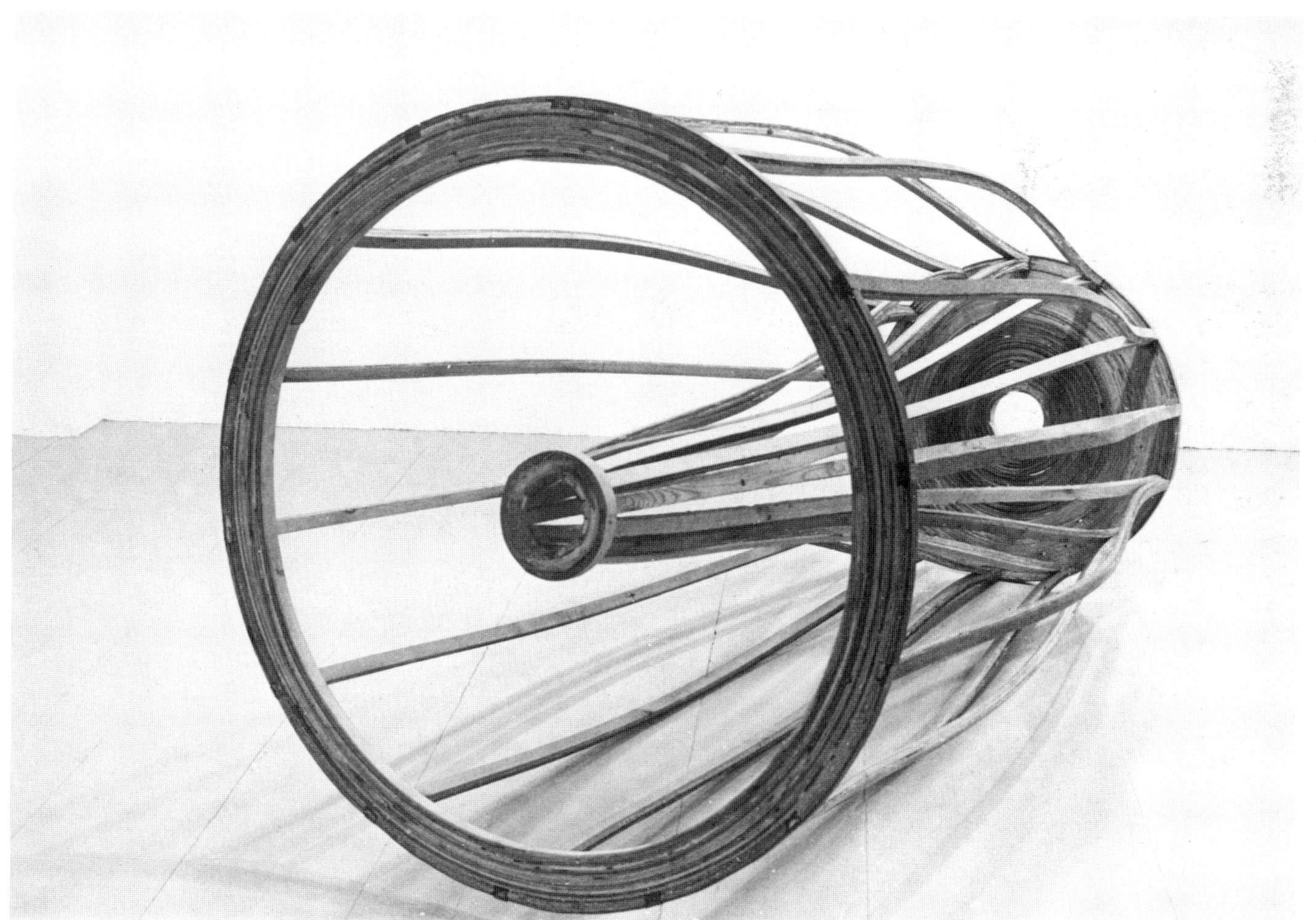

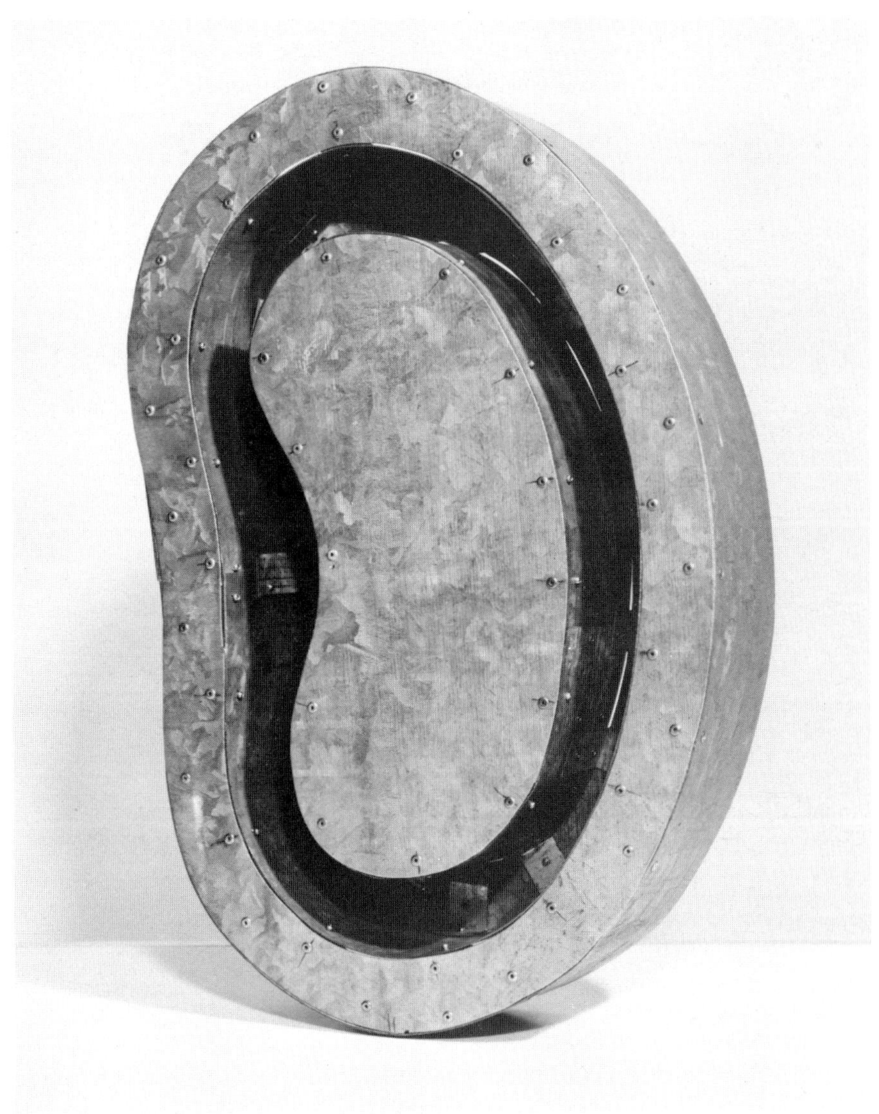

Art for Other People No 9
1983

galvanised steel
53 x 34 x 11cms
Saatchi Collection, London

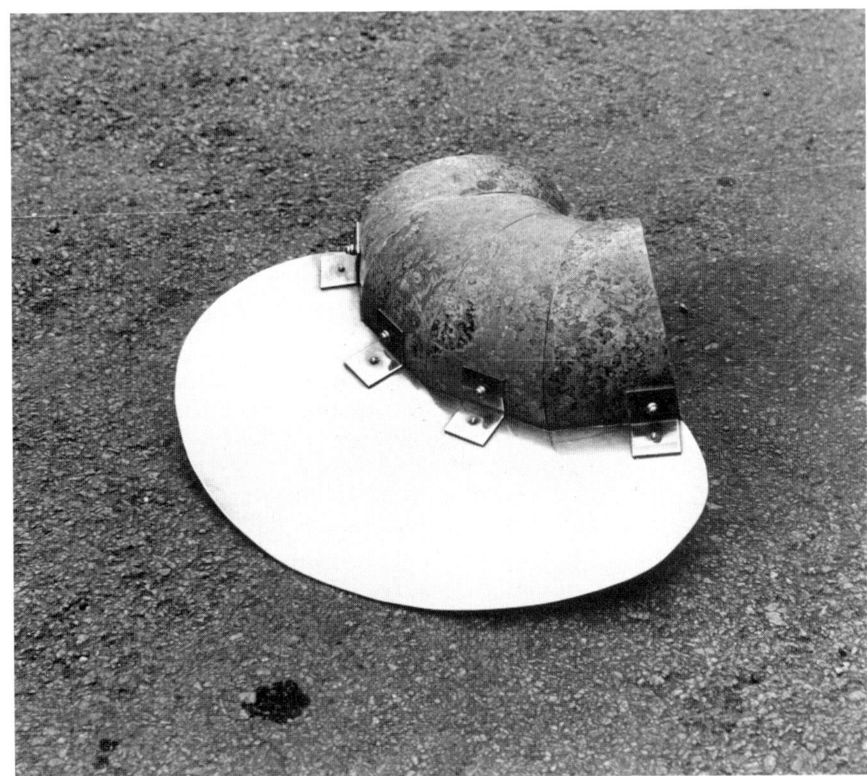

Art for Other People No 8
1983

brass and lino
35 x 35cms
Lisson Gallery London

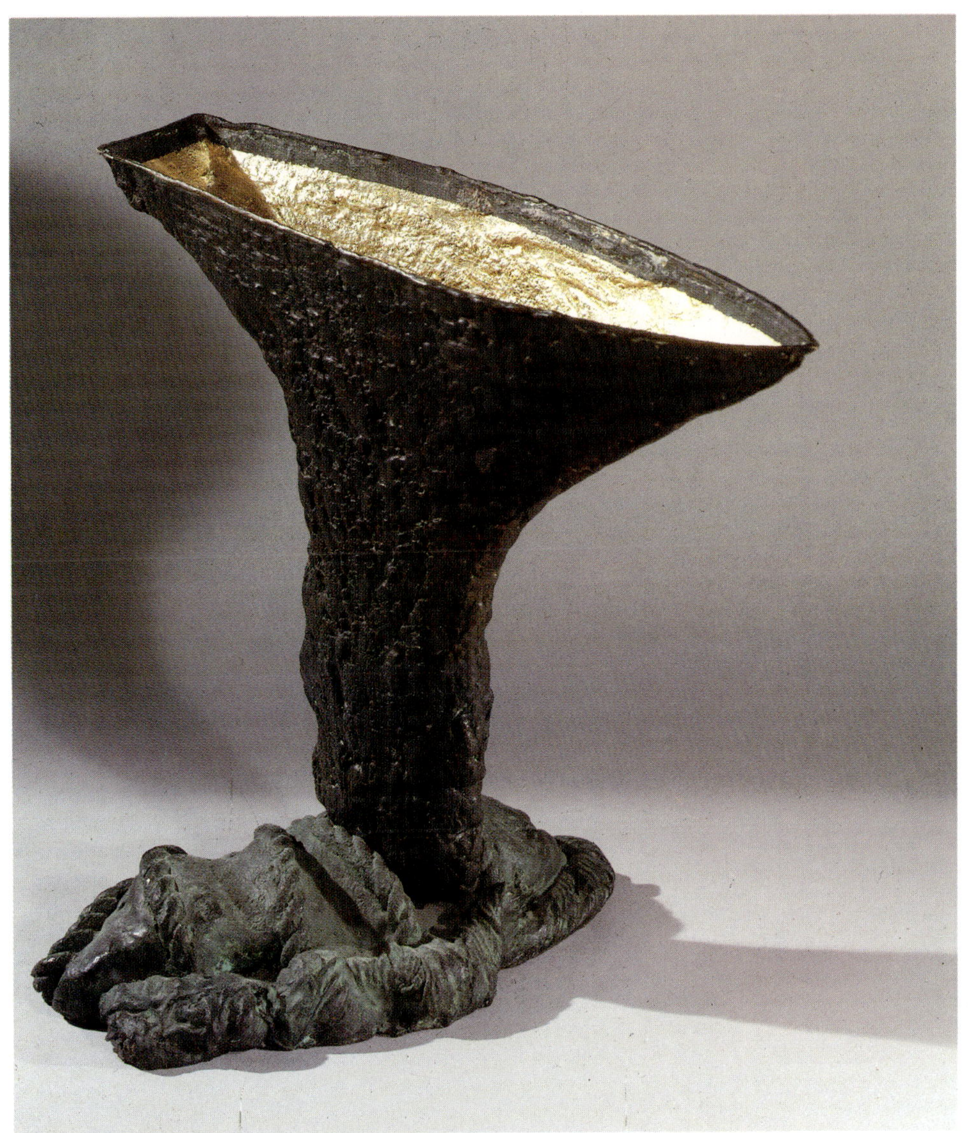

Vessel (In Memoriam)
1981

bronze, gilded inside
23 x 24 x 18ins
58.5 x 61 x 45.7cms
unique
Museum of Modern Art New York

BARRY FLANAGAN

The majority of ideas which inspire Barry Flanagan's action are expressed through encounters with a readily manipulable material. Sometimes the results hardly appear to have been man-handled, yet a beautiful clarity resides in the objects. Not infrequently Flanagan has invented prototypes, for example the cut-out spirals in sheet steel and the frolicking bronze hares: however, these images fit within, rather than highlight, his oeuvre. The progression of hessian, rope, felt, steel, stone, ceramic and bronze works (to name only primary materials) collectively testify to his faith in the human capacity to 'unveil' art. After looking at a number of sculptures (the present selection is a good one) his authorship becomes recognisable. The reticent treatment of surface and silhouette belongs to the expressive dignity and understatement of intention, and thus to the object's stature as triumphant underdog.

In 1969 Flanagan explained that he preferred sculpture to painting because it was 'not in the forefront of our thinking about art and its history', consequently the sculptor is less a slave of 'other people's thinking'. Throughout his career Flanagan has engaged himself in short-term apprenticeships, some in sculptor's trades like carving, gilding and etching, and at other times in ones distantly related, like choreography and accounting. The lengthy chronology prepared in 1982 for the Venice Biennale catalogue gives an impression of the activities and professional company which attract Flanagan. The engagements are usually pursued intensely for several weeks, but, like research, finished when he has mastered the formula of raku-firing or the habits of live cougars. A consistent feature is how uninhibited by contemporary fashion are his enthusiasms. Flanagan was bronze casting in 1968 (a portrait bust) and carving in 1973 (in the traditional stoneyards of Pietrasanta). During the same period he left landmarks in avant-garde areas in the form of temporary installations using projected light, rope and mixed media (as in the surviving assemblage **60s Dish** with cello, sofa, mirror and photograph).

A nonconformist choice of activities and materials are not the only signs of Flanagan's independence. The bias of his thinking in the early seventies was far more visual and less sociological or linguistic

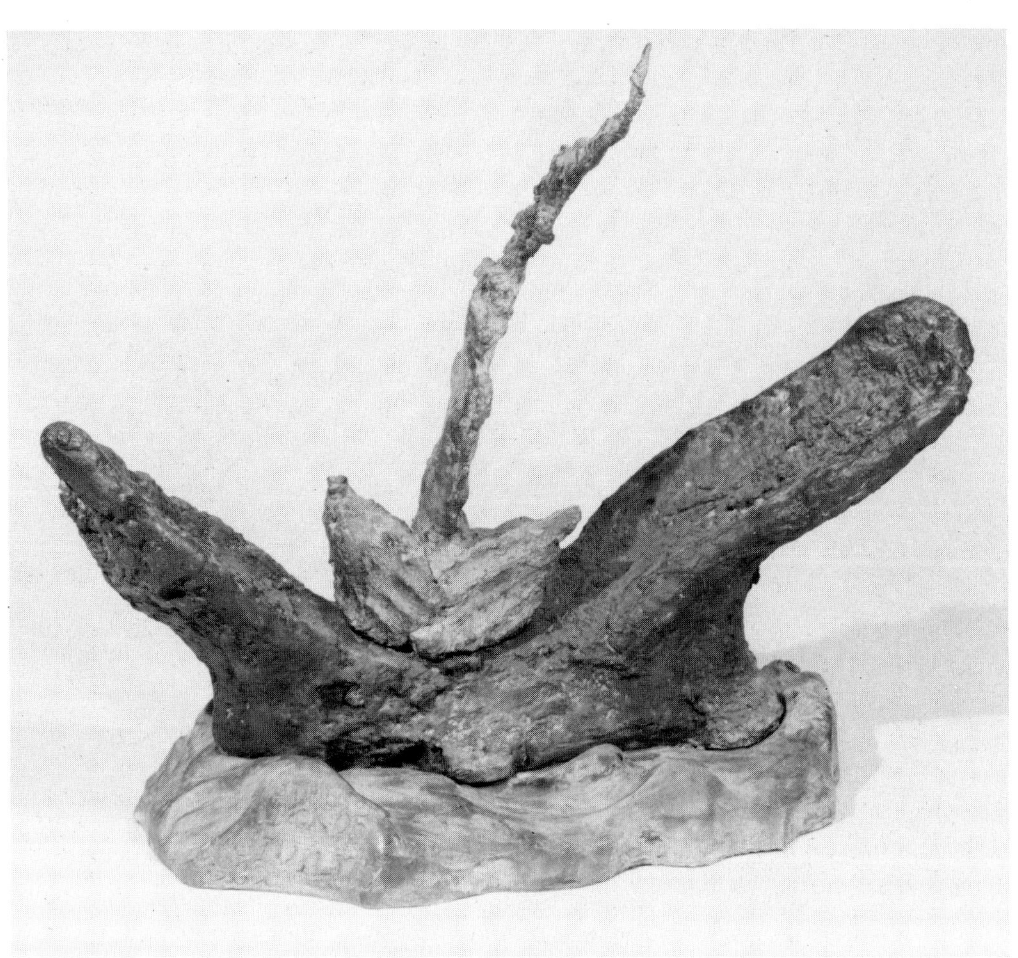

Untitled (2Bx4)
1982

29.2 x 60 x 30.5cms
Romano-chiaro marble

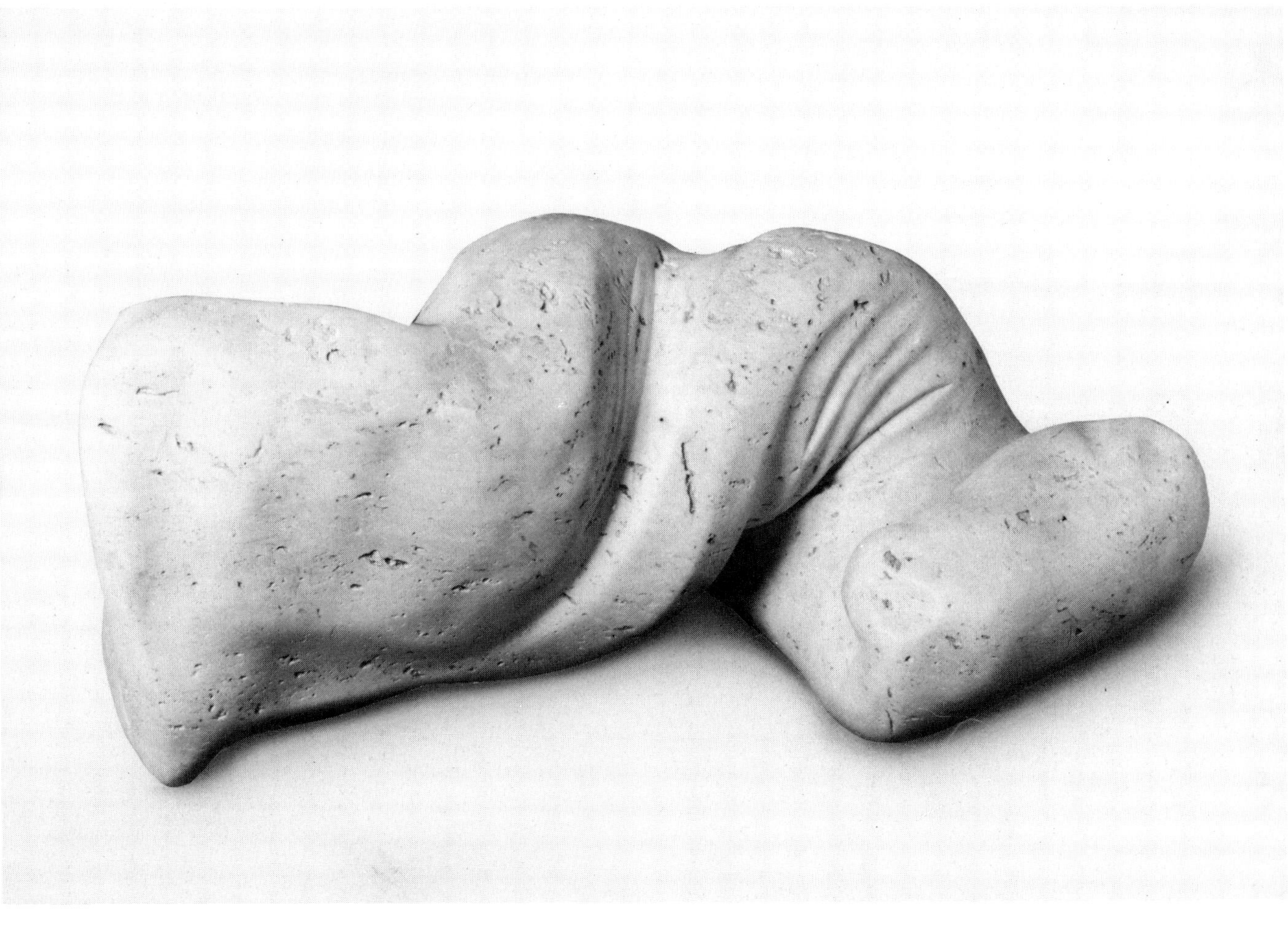

than that of his peers, not least those on the same vocational course at St. Martin's School of Art. Flanagan pinned his communication to tangible things; nevertheless, the criteria he applied to a success deliberately circumvented the formal approach of his elders, particularly David Smith, Anthony Caro and the slightly older 'New Generation' group, several of whom were teaching at St. Martin's. These artists manipulated rigid materials, including plastics and scrapyard steel, using a judgmental eye to design a declarative work, viable in the round. Flanagan countered this control with his faith 'one merely causes things to reveal themselves to the sculptural awareness. It is the awareness that develops not the agents of sculptural phenomena'.

Flanagan proceeded as though his materials were capable of becoming sculpture with only the slightest degree of human assistance. His first celebrated sculptures consisted of stuffed sacks of coloured hessian which varied between anti-heroic tapering columns to piles of floppy tubes. Isolated within a gallery these still-powerful works somehow share a mood of Gallic irony reminiscent of the important work of Flanagan's tutor Phillip King (particularly his winged purple cone, **Genghis Khan** 1963). In a subtle way Flanagan's art dismissed the biomorphic, honed-down seriousness of Henry Moore. Attracted to the anarchic, Flanagan sought the company of concrete poets. The revival of Alfred Jarry's **Ubu Roi** (in a 1965 anthology) and his study of Pataphysics or the 'Science of Imaginary Solutions' plus exposure to the strumpot motif encouraged Flanagan's contrariness, his punning and his mystic spirals. Language in Flanagan's work — at its inception, in the inscriptions and finally in the titles — has always been handled idiosyncratically. This is so because seeing, hearing and reversing clusters of words actually relates to the artist's dismantling of conventions and his own reassembly of an idea on a previously unforeseen plane.

For many years the primary outlets for Flanagan's meditations on the role of artists and on his own autobiographical memories were his relatively representational prints and drawings. Figurative notations entered the sculpture in 1973 when female anatomy was carved on the face of stone, acknowledging the archaic frontality of Etruscan and Tantric art. The first clear road ahead indicating Flanagan's own contribution to the genre of carving came following a temporary move to the Northamptonshire countryside in 1975, when he was first attracted to Hornton Stone. Smooth lumps and irregular fragments of this soft, variously pigmented material were appropriated from the local quarry. Accepting individual characteristics, the stone acquired a stance and usually a linear embellishment, the latter in the form of painted lines along natural crevices and tattoos implanted with the claw chisel in small areas. Thus came a lamb/fish, a marine goddess and 'the memory of the flight owls'. **Bye Bye The Elephant** 1980 is one of the last of these transformations. Its supporting elm blocks are typical of the props which Flanagan invents to set-off his forms in lieu of a plinth. Many props are simple blocks; others are archetypes of the foundry like the anvil, bell and anchor. In most instances the props are partners in a plastic poem, but recently, by means of enlargement they have come into solo roles.

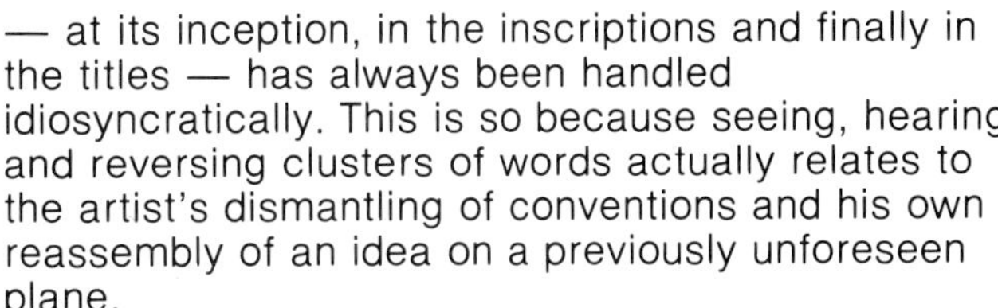

60's dish
1970
multi-medium
62 x 54 x 34ins

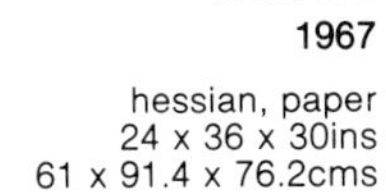

Bundle
1967
hessian, paper
24 x 36 x 30ins
61 x 91.4 x 76.2cms

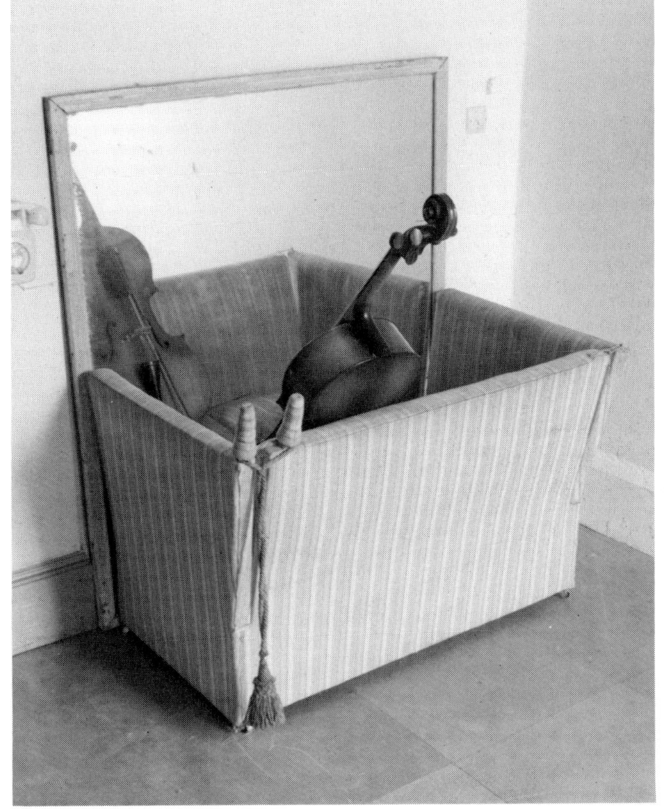

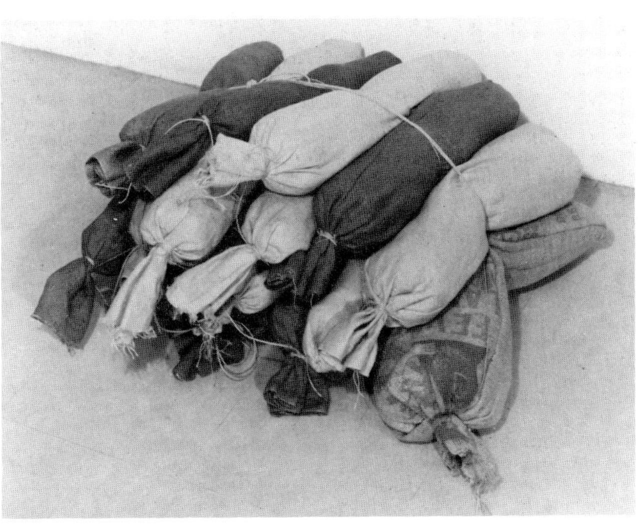

Flanagan's exhibition of these earthy, coarse-grained native stones at Waddington Galleries in early 1980 culminated in another rurally inspired image, the leaping hare. He had always been attracted to observing and anthropomorphically rendering animals including the hybrids of hare/frog and the mysterious axolotl. The hare intentionally communicated the essence of human passion along with its own symbolism. Modelling a linear form with room for expressive details, Flanagan continued to use a lighthanded touch, shaping soft clay (on an armature when required) using his hand and arm as a tool and a measure. What was reminiscent of his conjuring spirit with cloth and stone fragments was the degree of open-mindedness and tolerance of the accidental built into the working process. Furthermore Flanagan especially welcomed the volatile nature of bronze casting and the luxurious acid-based patinas, using their alchemical associations with a natural sympathy.

In 1981 Flanagan returned to Pietrasanta. This time he handed over terracotta and bronze maquettes to the masons to be enlarged and translated to Travertino and other luxurious marbles by means of skilful undercutting and a response to the veined material. In stone as well as bronze Flanagan has insisted on preserving the succulent pliability of clay; hence the spirited waves of green bronze, the mollusc-like vortexes of **Carving No. 5** and the grooved striations on the horse's tail.

The bronzes frequently possess functional attributes, underscoring their classical pedigrees. Vessels are specified as ships, crucibles or money boxes. Many embellishments are unabashedly decorative. When the titles seem most obviously metaphorical they often conceal private significances. We can partially understand **Vessel (In Memoriam)** as an entry for the 'Art and Sea' exhibition and also a reference to his brother's death at sea; **The Lack of Civility**, as a comment on the sinister Exocet missiles blitzing the British warships in the South Atlantic; and **Soprano** his response to Kiri Te Kanawa's part in the royal wedding and a private comment on institutions.

Flanagan's lack of orthodoxy continues in the eighties. The scavenged materials of the 'New British Sculpture', have been tenuously linked to the economic decline of Britain and the salvaging of styles from Cubism to Mannerism. Flanagan's monoliths have a quizzical innocence within an increasingly deliberated and rich material substance. They are intended to be permanent icons, each conceived and published at an unhurried pace.

Catherine Lampert

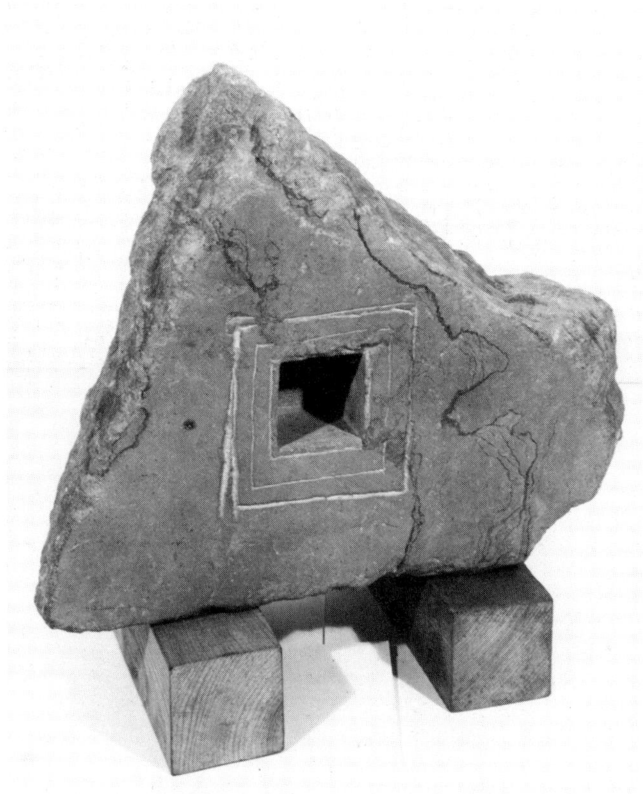

Bye Bye the Elephant
21¾ x 23½ x 12ins
54.2 x 58.7 x 30.5cms
hornton stone
Southampton City Art Gallery

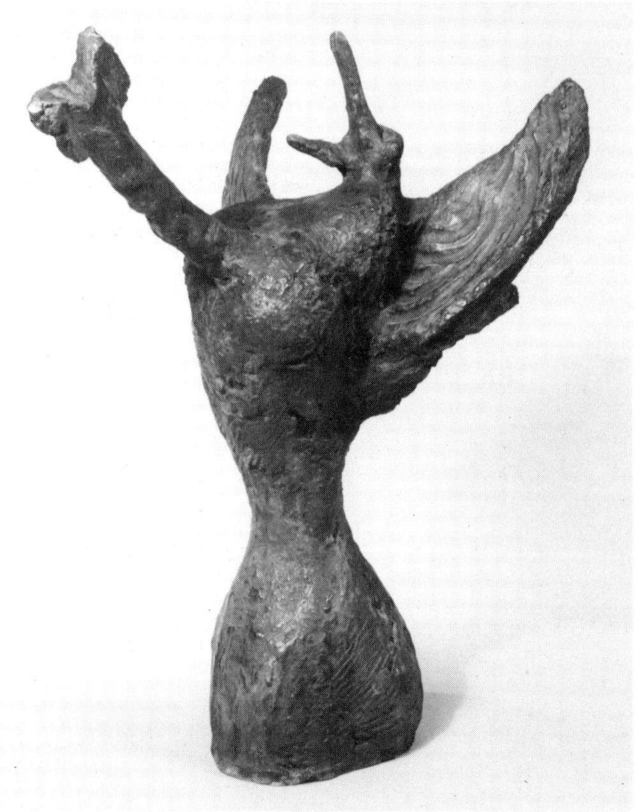

Soprano
1981

bronze
34½ x 19 x 28¼ins
87 x 48.2 x 71.7cms
edition of up to 7
Pace Gallery New York

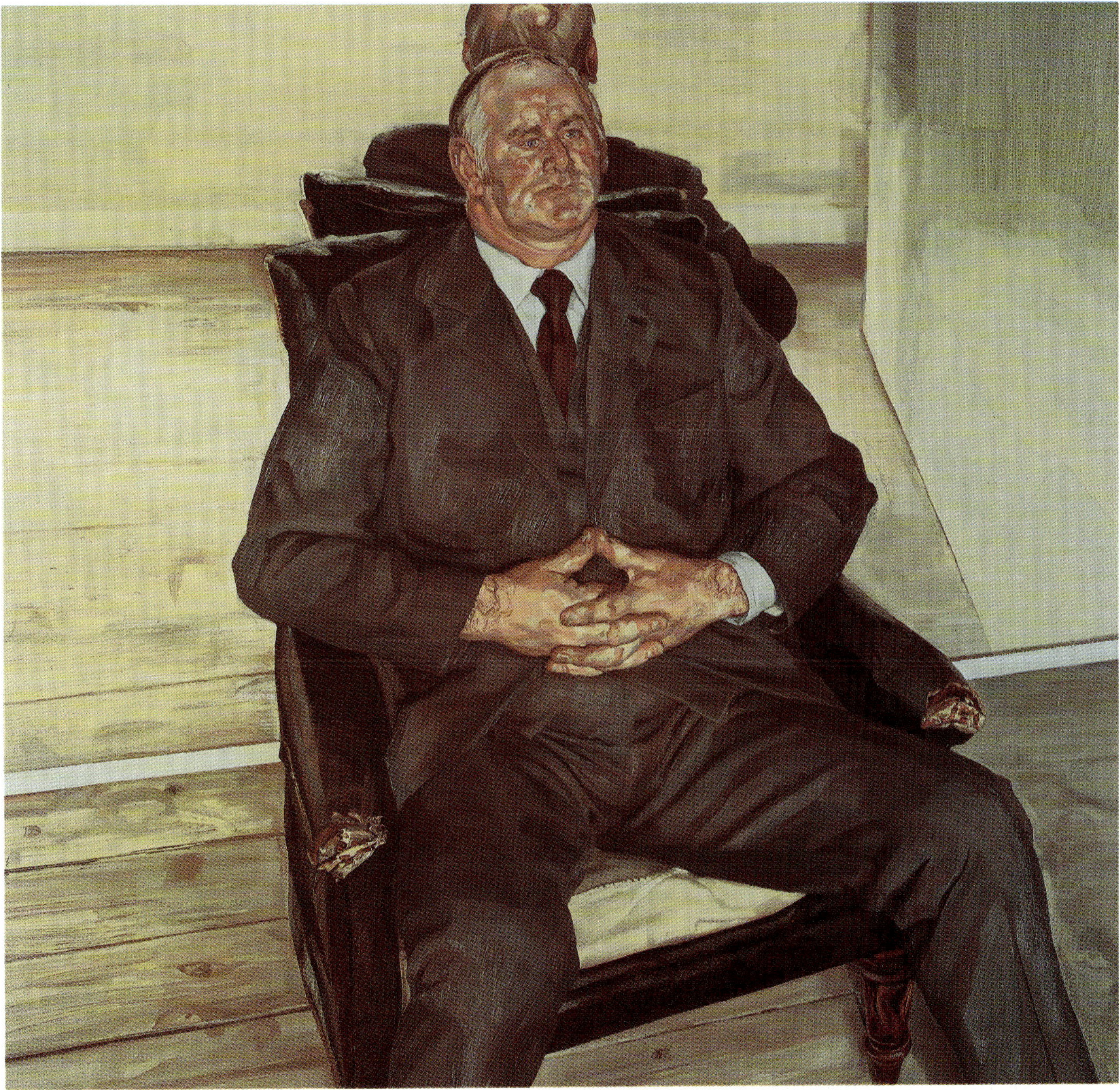

LUCIAN FREUD

The Big Man
1975-76

oil on canvas
91.4 x 91.4cms
S.A. McLean Ireland

In 1981, on the occasion of an exhibition of the paintings of his old art teacher Cedric Morris, Lucian Freud wrote his only public statement. It ran as follows:

'When I was sixteen I went as a student to Cedric Morris's art school at Dedham. Three months after my arrival I accidentally burnt it down. Cedric let me work at his house until the new school was ready. Cedric taught me to paint and more important to keep at it. He did not say much, but let me watch him at work. I have always admired his paintings and everything about him.

The only reference he ever made to the burning of the old school was an indirect one made thirty years after the event. Driving down to Hadleigh one day to take him out to lunch I asked him where he would like to go. 'How about Dedham' he said, 'It might revive old memories'.[1]

Freud, on the whole, would rather not talk about his painting or, much worse, have it talked about. As he says, with characteristic precision, nothing said by the painter can make the pictures any better. But, of course, because he is a grandchild of the legendary Sigmund Freud himself, he is inevitably at a disadvantage when it comes to wanting people not to analyse his work.

Two paintings in the present selection have particularly suffered from misinterpretation, in the sense that no symbolic meaning was intended by the artist: **'Naked man with rat'** and **'Naked girl with egg'**. From the artist's point of view the rat was a pet he had in his studio. The young man in the portrait liked the rat; Freud wanted to paint it, so the man was posed holding the rat. When this painting first went on view the critics directed all their attention towards the rat. Some searched for cheap laughs by suggesting that it posed a threat to the young man's creative powers. Freud, as a realist painter, found fault not with the feebleness of the joke but the slackness of the observation. 'It couldn't possibly have bitten his parts, even if it had wanted to. It is being held very firmly.'[2] It could also be said that its head is pointing in the wrong direction in the first place.

'The egg' critically, faired even worse. An egg on a dish beside a woman on a bed meant ovaries with a capital 'O', but to what end was, of course, unclear. The more art-historically inclined saw the picture as an up-date of Velasquez's masterpiece **'Old Woman Frying Eggs'** (though surely they are being poached), overlooking one obvious difference; that in the Freud, as the title itself makes clear, there is one egg and in the Velasquez there are two, and about to be three. Here again Freud's explanation is much simpler. As with the rat he had long looked for an opportunity to paint a sliced boiled egg — not a sliced hard-boiled egg but one cooked in the Italian way, the white firm but the yoke succulent and soft-centred. The connection between the egg and the woman was one, from his realist standpoint, of physical tenderness, something he tried to express in the softer way he handled the paint in their depiction. The desire to express his physical sensation of the subject through the actual way he brushes on the paint is a realism he always aspires to.

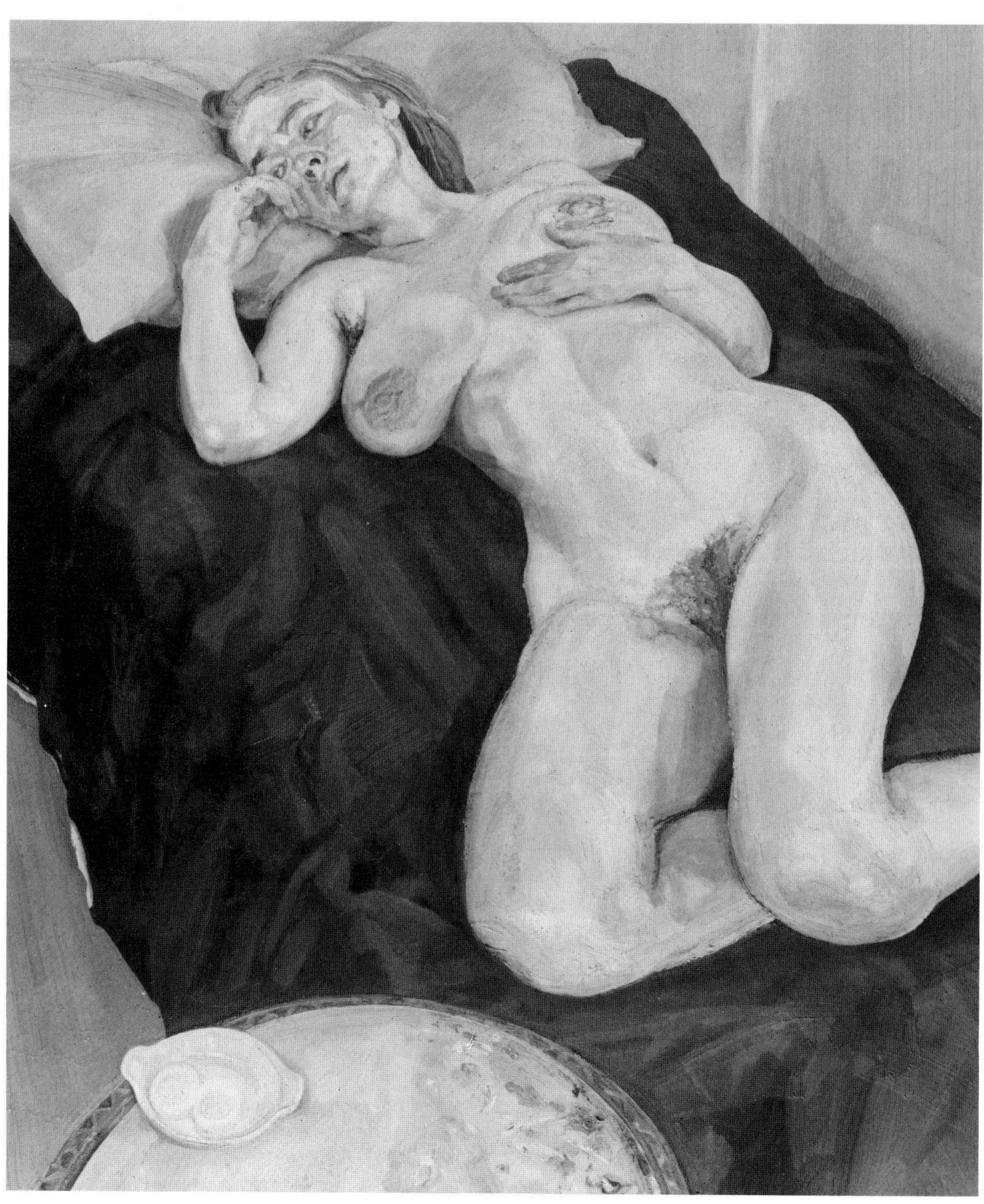

Naked Girl With Egg
1980/81

oil on canvas
75 x 60.5cms
The British Council

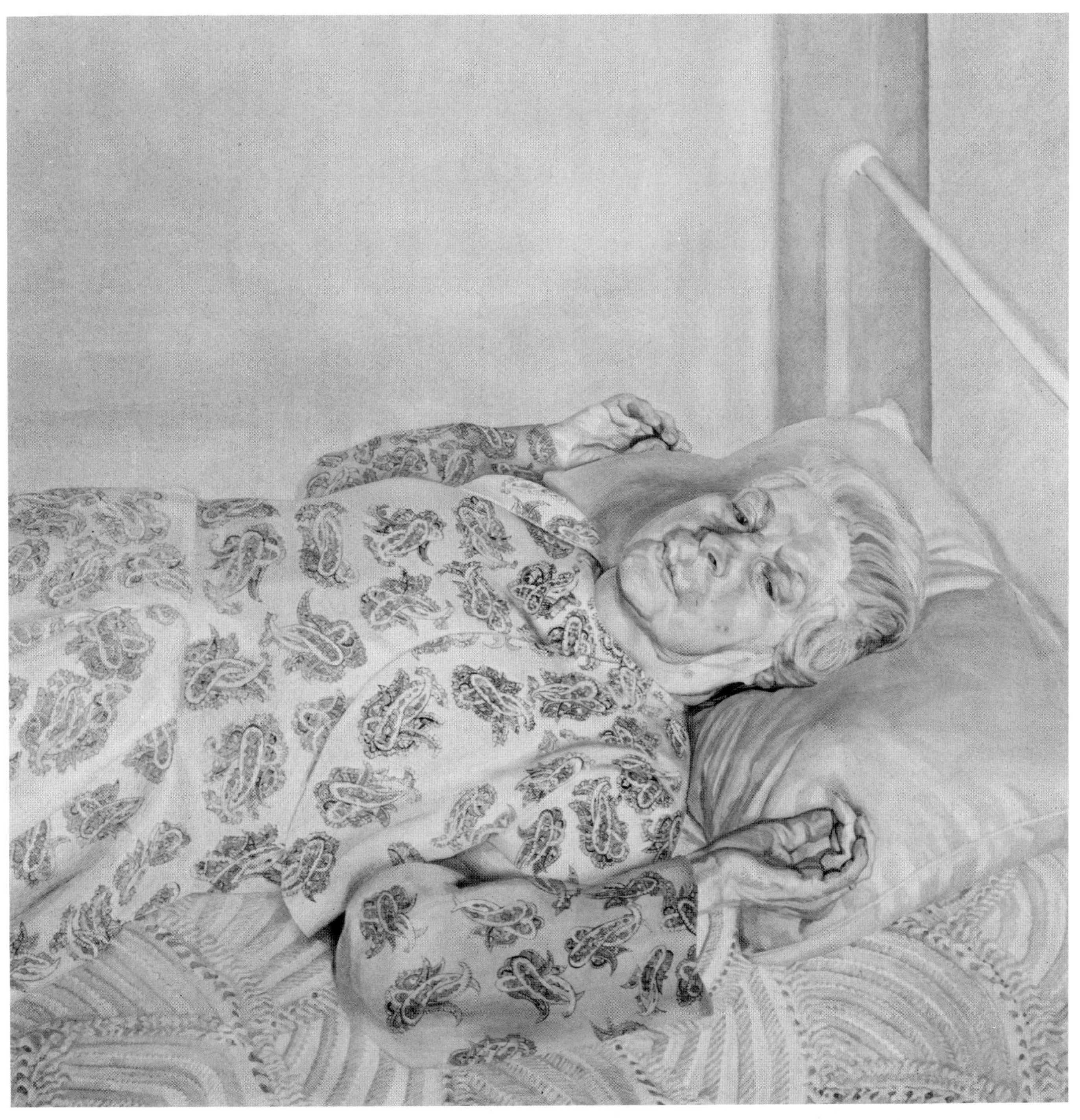

The Painter's Mother Resting 1
1975-1976

oil on canvas
36 x 36ins
91.4 x 19.4cms
S.A. McLean Ireland

This realisation of physical presence has never been more boldly or dramatically stated than in '*The big man*'.

'I want paint to **work as flesh** . . .,' Freud is quoted as saying in Lawrence Gowing's biography of him. 'I have always had a scorn for 'la belle peinture' and 'la delicatesse des touches'. I know my idea of portraiture came from dissatisfaction with portraits that resembled people. I would wish my portraits to be **of** the people, not **like** them. Not having a look of the sitter, **being** them. I didn't want to get just a likeness like a mimic, but to **portray** them, like an actor. As far as I am concerned the paint **is** the person.'[3]

The big man was big in every sense, not just physically but in the expansiveness of his life — an owner of betting shops, a gambler, a great drinker, capable of knocking off a bottle of pernod at a sitting. For all his high colour and swollen neck he is not a dissolute or fat man, he is a big man, seemingly charged — those pressing thumbs, those turbulently haired wrists — with energy and purpose, and wearing an amplitude of cloth that is as hard as it is painted. And yet the back view of the same head in the mirror might be of a different man altogether — older, frailer, losing his hair. Mirrors provide a different view, as Freud has pointed out and frequently exploited, but the truth of the truism has never been more poignantly expressed in his work than here.

What is poignant is that the frailty of that head, as revealed from behind, speaks of death, of the approach of death despite the frontal bigness of the man, still in the glory of his strength, appetite and vitality. Awareness of death is perhaps the most powerful imperative of Freud's vision as a painter. It invests everything he does with a sort of urgency of looking, to see life raw, all fancy stripped away. If there is a sense of puritanism in his work, even of self-chastisement, then it is a by-product of this search for the real, which amounts to a moral obligation; 'a moral teething' perhaps, as Emily Bronte so perfectly expresses it in 'Wuthering Heights', in which the grinding is 'in proportion to the increase of pain'. According to Gowing[4] one of Freud's favourite remarks in literature is that of the painter to the pretentious young man in Henry James's 'The Tragic Muse': 'I wonder what you will do when you are old'. Freud's paintings of young men or women seem to answer the same question — the acuteness of his observation amounting almost to clairvoyance, so that his sitters appear not as they are but as they will become, their faces and bodies molded by age and experience, their flesh more draped to the bone. At the Tate Gallery Freud is hung alongside Stanley Spencer in an attempt to pigeonhole their stark realism, but for Freud the connection is inapposite. He admired the recent Spencer retrospective more than he expected, but he nevertheless deplores Spencer's tendency to paint figures that, in his opinion, are 'boneless'.

Freud's moral flaying in the interests of realism does not, of course, preclude sympathy. The poignant glimpse of the 'big man's' balding crown, the cradled breast and wistful introspection of the girl on the bed, the eagerness of the rat all declare a tender engagement of feeling which, not surprisingly, is particularly notable in the artist's paintings of his mother. Here age is reality itself, the struggle is over and an apparent peace seems to fall on son and mother — artist and sitter — alike. But in 'The painter's mother reading' our expectations are still confounded by the compositional novelty of the solitary thumb holding the page, in the circumstances as likely to catch the spectator off-guard as any rat or sliced egg.

The artist himself has admitted that the pictures that stayed in his head as a child were the ones that disturbed him — Huysman's book on Grunewald remains a favourite — and disturbance is something he consciously seeks to retain. 'Everything I do is a reaction against something' — but always against dull expectation. 'Do you know there is something called picture-making?' He asks Gowing, 'I think it is often simply fatigue. It rules out the hope of making something remarkable'.

Freud has done several self-portraits but none is more revealing than the mirrored glimpse of his legs skipping out of the top right-hand corner of a picture predominantly devoted to a reclining nude, **Naked portrait with reflection** 1980. Skipping is an apt analogy of his tactics as a painter. Tension and clarity in his art have been sustained through an evermore risky avoidance of cliche and classification, both of technique and genre, as he skips clear of repetition or opposition; gaining success by an accumulation of formalist points rather than with the knock-out displays of hair's breadth detail that first won him a reputation in his youth.

These four paintings represent a token sample of those done in his fifties. They are the product of a time which saw him transmogrified from a local hero into an international star and 20th-century master. Art historical attempts to pin him down have naturally burgeoned. Because the first few years of his life were spent in Berlin there has been an understandable inclination to see him as the child of the **Neue Sachlichkeit** or New Objectivity movement in German art of the 1920's. Reading somewhere that he had been influenced by one of these painters, Christian Schad, Freud looked out the work of this artist, previously unknown to him, and found it quite interesting. More recently he and his friend Frank Auerbach, among others, have been used to give much needed substance to the case of the Transavantgarde. Both were included in the Royal Academy's 'New Spirit in Painting' show. Freud, meanwhile, in the best Cedric Morris tradition 'keeps at it' — as remarkably, as reactively, as ever.

John McEwen

FOOTNOTES

1 'Sir Cedric Morris, a retrospective exhibition', Blond Fine Art Ltd, London, 9 April — 9 May 1981. Catalogue, Page 2
2 In conversation with the author, 24 Sept 1984
3 'Lucian Freud' by Lawrence Gowing, Thames & Hudson 1982, p.190/191
4 Gowing, op cit, p.161
5 Gowing, op cit, p.136
6 Gowing, op cit, p.24

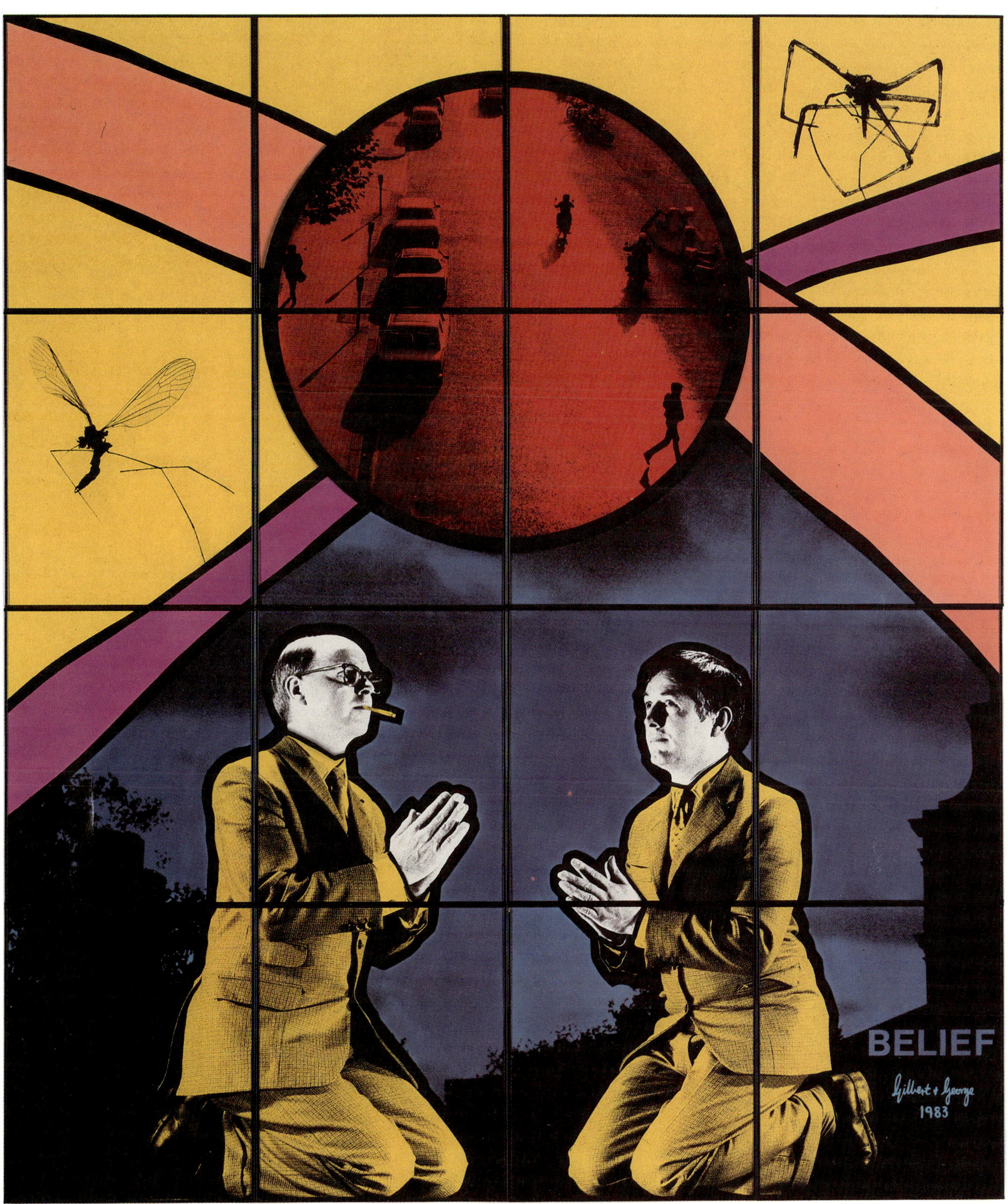

GILBERT AND
GEORGE

Belief
1983

photo-piece
95 ¼ x 79 ½ ins
242 x 202cms
courtesy, Anthony d'Offay Gallery, London

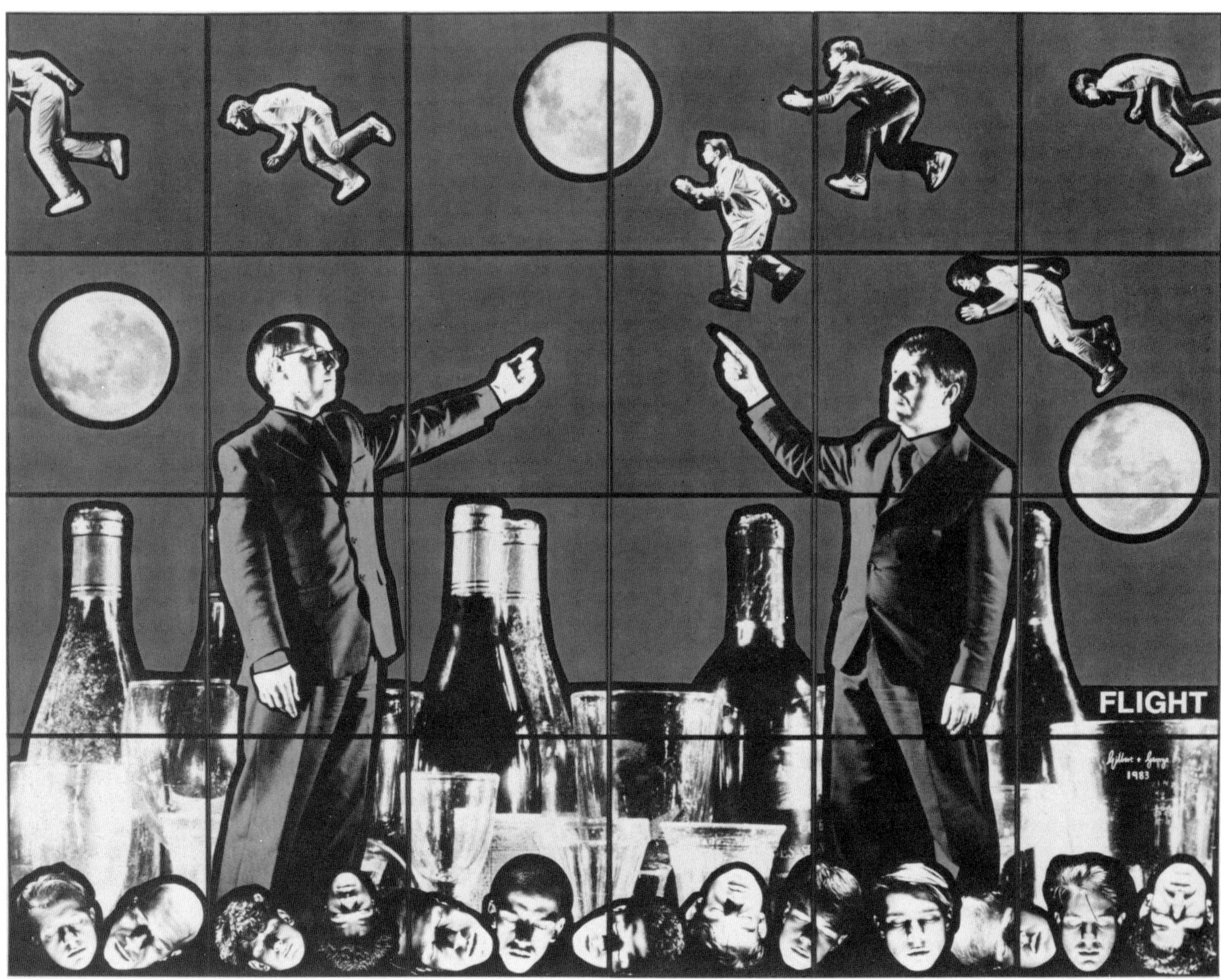

Flight
1983

photo-piece
95¼ x 119¼ ins
242 x 303cms
courtesy: Anthony d'Offay Gallery, London

'Our social realities are so ugly if seen in the light of exiled truth, and beauty is almost no longer possible if it is not a lie.
What is to be done? We who are still half alive, living in the often fibrillating heartland of a senescent capitalism — can we do more than reflect the decay around and within us? Can we do more than sing our sad and bitter songs of disillusion and defeat?' — R.D. Laing, Introduction, **The Politics of Experience** 1967.

'The . . .dislike of Realism is the rage of Caliban seeing his own face in a glass' — Oscar Wilde, The Preface, **The Picture of Dorian Gray** 1890.

A great deal has already been written about Gilbert and George. In particular two substantial essays have appeared in the catalogues of their retrospective exhibitions of 1980 and 1984. The intention of the present, short essay is to present a summary outline of the evolution of Gilbert and George's art, to give some indications of its meaning and to suggest the place it may have in the history of art.

Gilbert and George began to make their reputation in 1969 when they were still students at St. Martin's School of Art in London. At that time art was dominated by two main trends: Pop Art, based on the imagery of the mass media, popular culture and the design, advertising and packaging of consumer goods, and Minimal Art, an extreme form of abstraction. Gilbert and George were among a generation of young artists in the late 1960's who rejected these options, in effect deciding that a new realism should be declared and created. The need to bring art back into contact with life, to revitalise it, is a constantly recurring one in the history of art and indeed it is with such a move that what we know as modern art began, with the Realism of Courbet in the 1850's. Gilbert and George were therefore participants in, and among the progenitors of, one of the recurrent cyclical movements of the history of art. Gilbert and George were not only among the originators of a new phase of modern art, they rapidly came to be seen as being among the leading artists of their generation, gaining an international reputation of a kind relatively rare in the annals of British art. The significance of Gilbert

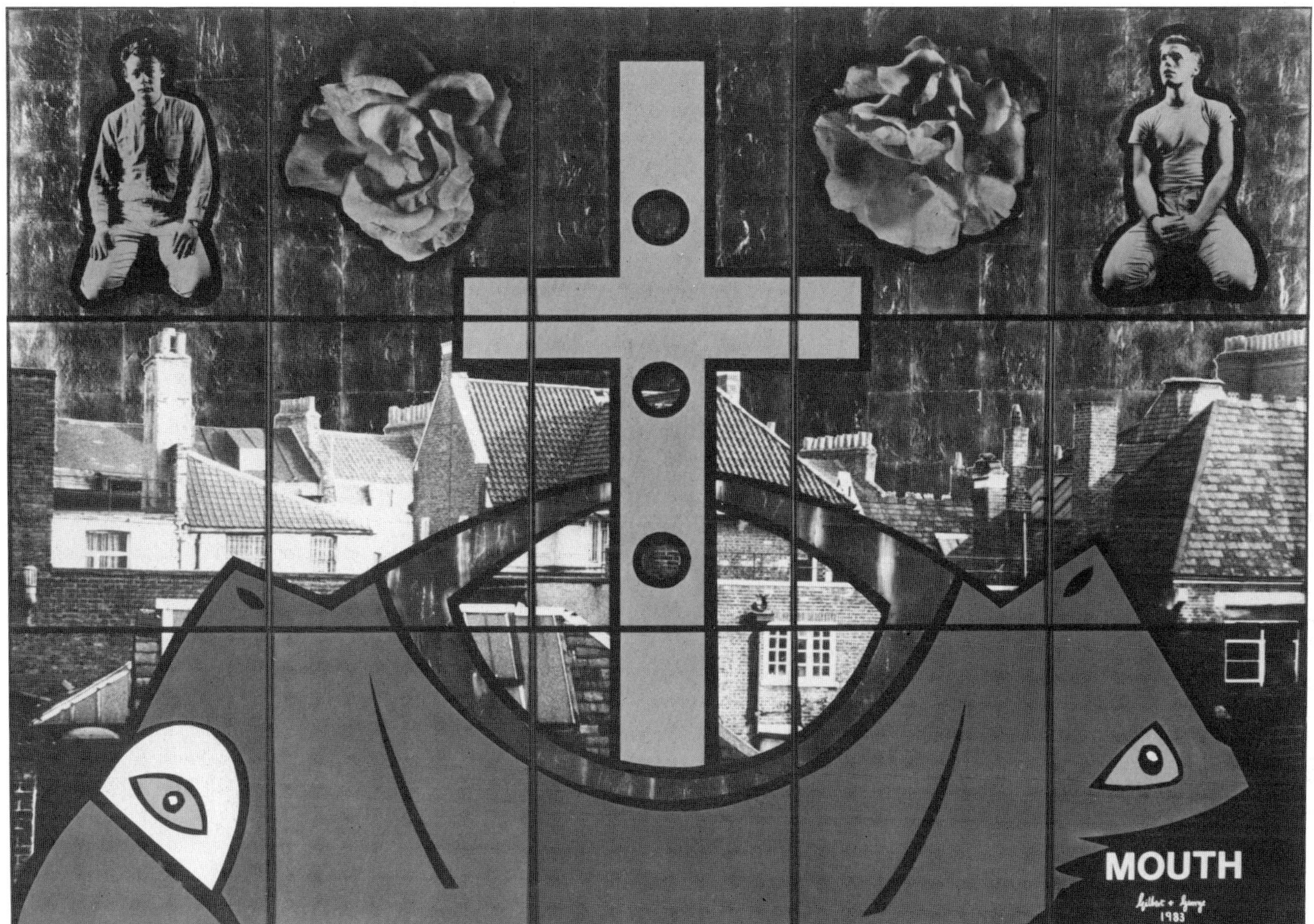

Mouth
1983

photo-piece
71½ x 99½ins
181.5 x 252.5cms
courtesy: Anthony d'Offay Gallery, London

and George's work in those early years lay partly in the extraordinarily fresh and original, almost innocent, methods or strategies that they invented for bringing art into a new and more dynamic relationship with life. An early symptom of their novel attitude was their first exhibition in May 1968. This was held in Frank's Sandwich Bar, a small cafe in Silver Place London W.I. The exhibits were three sculptures, more or less conventional for the time, but given a 'new thought' by their presentation and by their designation by Gilbert and George as 'object sculptures'. In November 1968 they acted as impresarios of a show of thirty two drawings and watercolours of bacon rashers by local youths held in the rest room of a bacon factory in the East end of London. In January 1969 they then took the step which more than anything else lead to their rapid international recognition: in 'Our New Sculpture', later to be called 'Underneath the Arches' and finally 'The Singing Sculpture' they themselves became the sculptural objects, their own living bodies became the expressive medium. Furthermore Gilbert and George extended this procedure beyond specific presentations such as

'The Singing Sculpture', into the whole of their life: in a most remarkable congruence of art and life they became, and with complete consistency have remained, 'living sculptures'. This may be seen as an extension of the 19th century tradition of dandyism by which some of the most radical artistic and literary figures sought by rigorous control of dress and manners to identify with art their whole persona. Gilbert and George's motto, adopted about this time, 'To be with Art is all we ask' also poignantly echoes a central aspiration of (not only) modern artists. At this time too they designated their home in Fournier Street London E.1. 'Art for All' again a poignant formulation of the common desire, most fully elaborated by William Morris, to bring about a world governed by the values of art rather than of materialism and rationalism.

'The Singing Sculpture' and other living sculptures were presented in a variety of non-art, 'real' locations, including the National Jazz Festival at Plumpton, the Lyceum in the Strand and Railway Arch 8 Cable Street London E1: 'all the world an art gallery' as Gilbert & George put it in a statement of

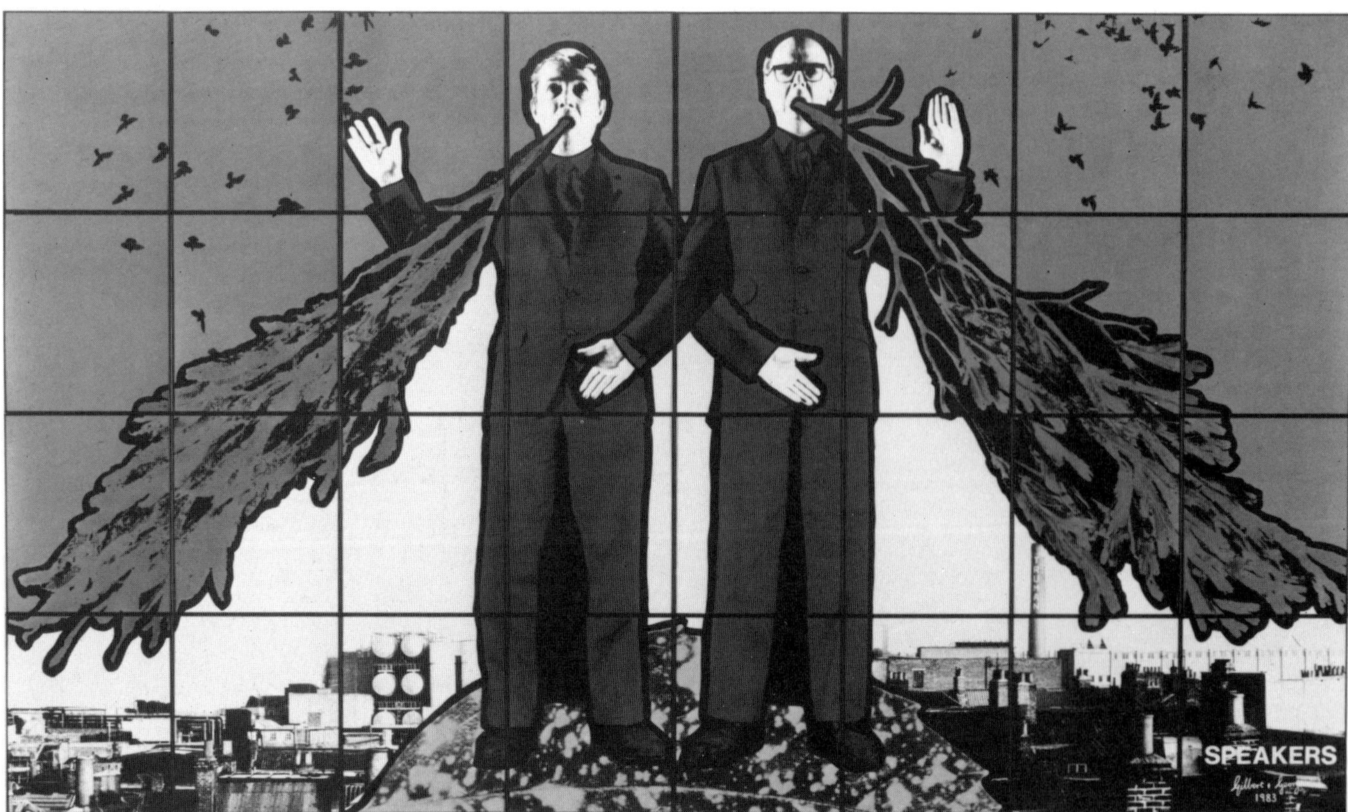

Speakers
1983

photo-piece
95 ¼ x 159ins
242 x 404cms
courtesy: Anthony d'Offay Gallery, London

1969. At the same time Gilbert and George were virtually bombarding people nationally and internationally with 'postal sculptures' — works of art sent direct to the recipients — yet another aspect of the freshness and vitality of their presentation of their art at this time. Their home 'Art for All' also became a venue for their art, a showcase, so to speak, for the living sculptures and they began to publish 'magazine sculptures' and 'book sculptures' both unusual forms of direct expression for artists. The vitality and 'new realism' of form of Gilbert and George's art cannot of course be separated from their vision, a vision, fundamentally, of the moral and spiritual condition of modern urban man. Hints of this vision are already apparent in the sandwich bar and the bacon factory exhibitions and it reached a first phase of maturity with 'The Singing Sculpture' in 1969. In this piece Gilbert and George presented in highly stylised form the pathetic music hall song 'Underneath the Arches' celebrating the life of down and outs in London. Already apparent in 'The Singing Sculpture' is what Gilbert and George referred to as 'the sadness in our art' which, over the years has developed into a full blown tragic vision of Wagnerian sweep and grandeur.

Also a central and integral theme, right from the beginning, of Gilbert & George's art, is a preoccupation with the question of the nature of art itself and especially the role, function and place of the artist in society — an important theme of much modern art. 'We believe in the Art, the Beauty and the Life of the Artist who is an eccentric person with something to say for himself' (from a statement of 1978). Not the least remarkable thing about Gilbert and George's work is the way in which in the early work particularly they appear both, and even simultaneously, as the artist in his special role as detached, priest-like observer of life and mediator of its mysteries, and as everyman, the observed subject.

'Living Sculpture' was, and transformed, remains, Gilbert and George's principal means of expression. Yet anyone who saw their early living sculpture pieces can bear witness to the extreme mental and physical demands made on its practitioners by this form of art, which is by its very nature ephemeral and has a limited audience. Gilbert and George began to seek permanent form for their living sculpture: very interestingly, they began to use the traditional media of painting and drawing, in a novel and witty way, creating numerous 'drawing pieces', 'charcoal on paper sculptures and one huge 'painting sculpture' in all of which the posed image of the artists appears life-size. These works were executed in a competent version of the style of early Impressionism to which Gilbert and George gave a new meaning and freshness by their reworking of it. The drawing and painting pieces remain an important part of Gilbert and George's oeuvre but the artists seem to have needed an even more direct, more realistic or documentary means of giving permanent form to the concept of the

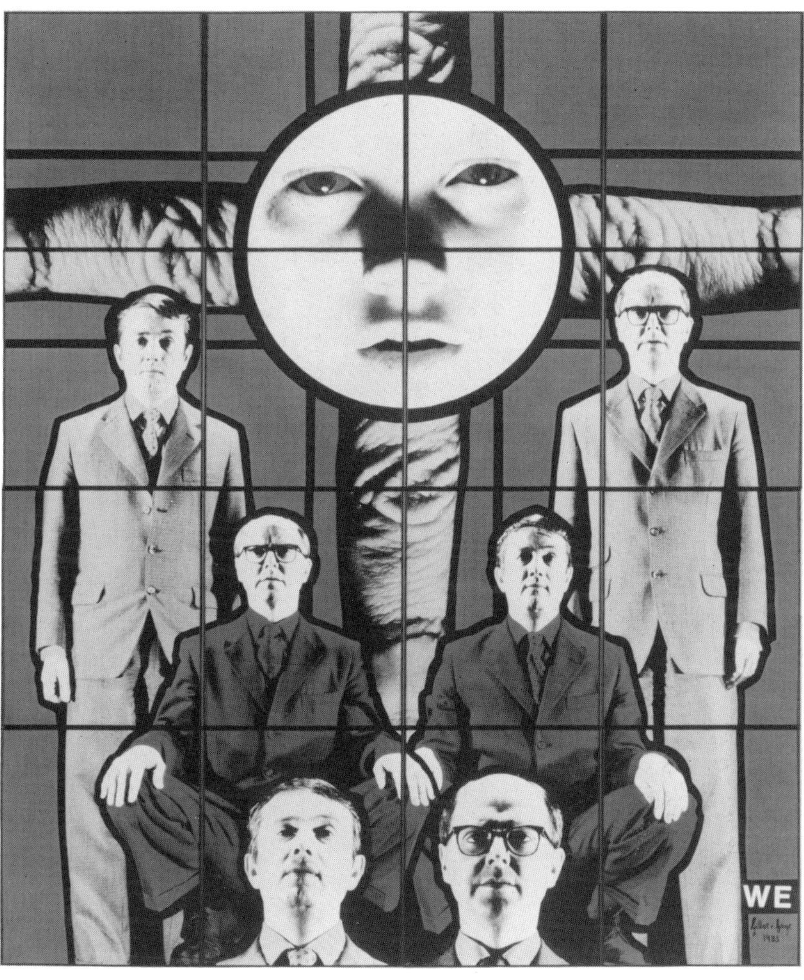

We
1983

photo-piece
95¼ x 79½ins
242 x 202cms
courtesy, Anthony d'Offay Gallery, London

living sculpture. In 1971 they turned to photography, exploiting it with characteristic originality to create the form of the 'photo-piece'. The photo-piece consists basically of an arrangement of a number of separately framed photographic images adding up to a unified expressive whole. The photographs themselves are manipulated in various ways through the printing process to enhance their expressive potential and in the early photo-pieces the framed images were hung in configurations which were emblematic of the theme of the piece. In 1972 Gilbert and George also began to make 'postcard sculptures' in which the ready-made images of postcards are assembled on a flat surface into apposite and expressive relationships. These can be seen as a 'minor' art form analogous to the photo-pieces and bearing the same relationship to them as drawing to painting in traditional art. Postcards are of course a very rich source of fascinating images of the world, going back a century or more. They are brought together by Gilbert and George in their postcard sculptures to create complex and allusive works which repay thoughtful consideration and in which the individual parts are often of considerable intrinsic interest while the whole is nevertheless always greater than the sum of those parts.

Developments of form were accompanied by developments of subject. A prominent pastoral element dominates their work up to about 1973 particularly in the numerous 'charcoal on paper

sculptures' of that period, the 1971 'Painting Sculpture' and the early photo-pieces, in which the artists, in the conventional neat townsman's suits they always wear, appear in various, often lush and idyllic landscape settings. These works evoke the broad theme of man's relationship to the natural world, an important issue in art since the industrial revolution, implicit in Constable, explicit in Turner and the great German romantic painter Caspar David Friedrich.

However, the lyrical pastoral element abruptly disappeared from Gilbert and George's work in 1973 to be replaced by urban settings, mostly pub and bleak house interiors, in a long series of photo-pieces which on the surface appeared to be about drinking and drunkenness. When references to nature reappeared in Gilbert and George's work, after a year or so, it was as a contrasting element in the composition which they have since developed for a variety of symbolic and expressive purposes.

Drink iş often the recourse of those afflicted by otherwise intolerable material or spiritual pressures and artists (often suffering from both) seem particularly to be given to it. During the period roughly from 1973-77 Gilbert and George used drinking both in their life and in their art as a particularly apt metaphor, of some universality, to express what was clearly a state of considerable alienation and existential angst which gripped them at that time. It was by expressing their despair as art that they came to terms with it and eventually

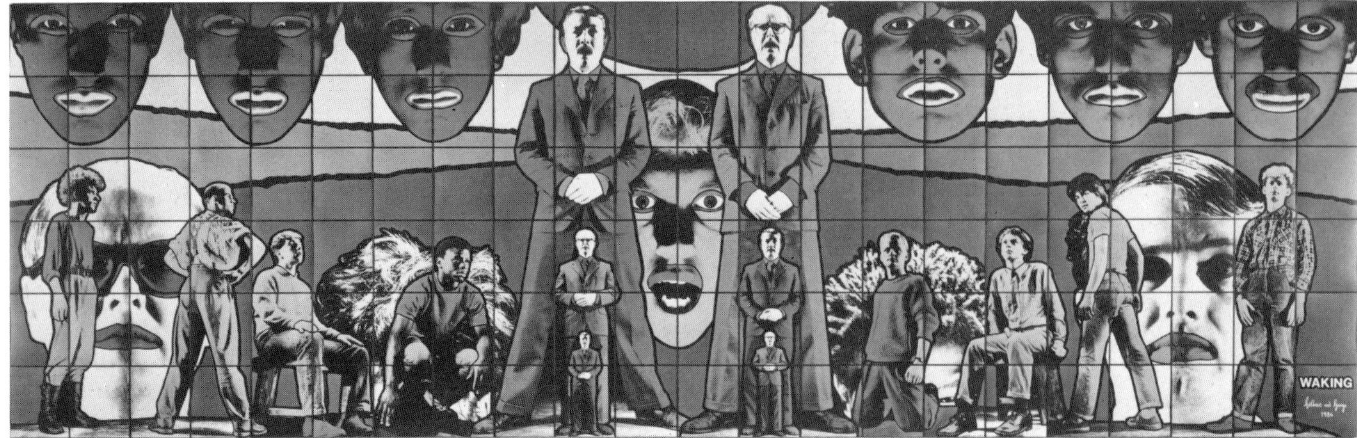

Waking
1984

photo-piece
11ft 11ins x 36ft 6ins
363 x 1111cms
courtesy: Anthony d'Offay Gallery, London

emerged at the end of the 1970's from a period of intense introspection into a new engagement with the world about them. Perhaps in response to the disordered states of mind expressed, their photo-pieces had become increasingly geometrically ordered and disciplined, and by 1974-5 were consisting of standard size rectangular photographs arranged in regular rectangular formats. The scale of the pieces also increased, with the image of the artist moving nearer to life-size. The result of these changes was a new weight and formal grandeur. From 1974 too they began to introduce colour, at first only red, into the formerly exclusively black and white photo-pieces.

The new phase of Gilbert and George's art began, in 1977 with a powerful and harrowing series of essays in urban realism, photo-pieces in which often obscene graffiti words are the principal motif, juxtaposed with varied images of urban decay, both in its physical and human manifestations, and accompanied by images of the artists, pained, silent and sorrowing witnesses.

Since then Gilbert and George have held up a multi-faceted mirror to the world, their chosen world, the world evoked by R.D. Laing's striking phrase 'the often fibrillating heartland of a senescent capitalism', the world which embraces so much of the central issues of our time but which provides material too for works dealing with the great vital constants of human life and experience — sex, death, religion and myth. They have been intensely productive, their works building up and accreting into a tissue of image and metaphor of a density that suggests the sweep and scope of one of the great 19th century novelists rather than the normally narrow focus of the traditional visual artist. The scale of their photo-pieces has increased and their work has been enormously enriched by a dazzlingly original use of colour which is both powerfully expressive and of a theatrical elegance. Above all their structures have developed so that Gilbert and George's works are now symbolic or allegorical compositions which function by suggestion and allusion, by the unreal juxtaposition of real elements, to form a complex poetic

expression of what was in the artist's mind. Art like this can never be given a specific meaning or 'interpretation', the spectator must allow his mind to play over it so that associations, memories, feelings, ideas are evoked and aroused; the titles, of course, provide an important key and it is significant that they are always incorporated as an integral part of the work. One general remark that might, however, be made about Gilbert and George's recent work including the three pieces in this exhibition, is that in them they have taken the image of the youth of their world — working class, unemployed, or facing unemployment — and elevated it to the status of ideal male protagonist, of hero. The young and very young who people Gilbert and George's pictures are late 20th century equivalents, performing the same function in art, of the classicising male figures of Michelangelo and Raphael. Indeed Gilbert and George's photo-pieces in their use of the human figure as the principal expressive element, in their range of human, social and philosophical themes, in their scale and complexity, in their richness of allegory and symbol, now appear as a remarkable extension into the late 20th century of the tradition, the creation of the great Renaissance masters, of what technically are called 'history pictures' more generally known as 'high art'. And whereas Renaissance history painting, strictly speaking, dealt with Greek and Roman history and mythology and with subjects from the Bible, Gilbert and George's histories are absolutely of their own time and they have created their own mythologies. The concept of history, of a high or elevated art using the human body to illustrate significant human themes, dominated European art down to the late 19th century. It then virtually disappeared under the assault of modern art theory and practice.

In recent years, however, it has become apparent that the concept of history has, mutatis mutandis, re-emerged and is now providing us with the most significant art of our time. Gilbert and George are in the forefront of this new movement, as a generation ago they were of an earlier phase in the story of art.

Simon Wilson

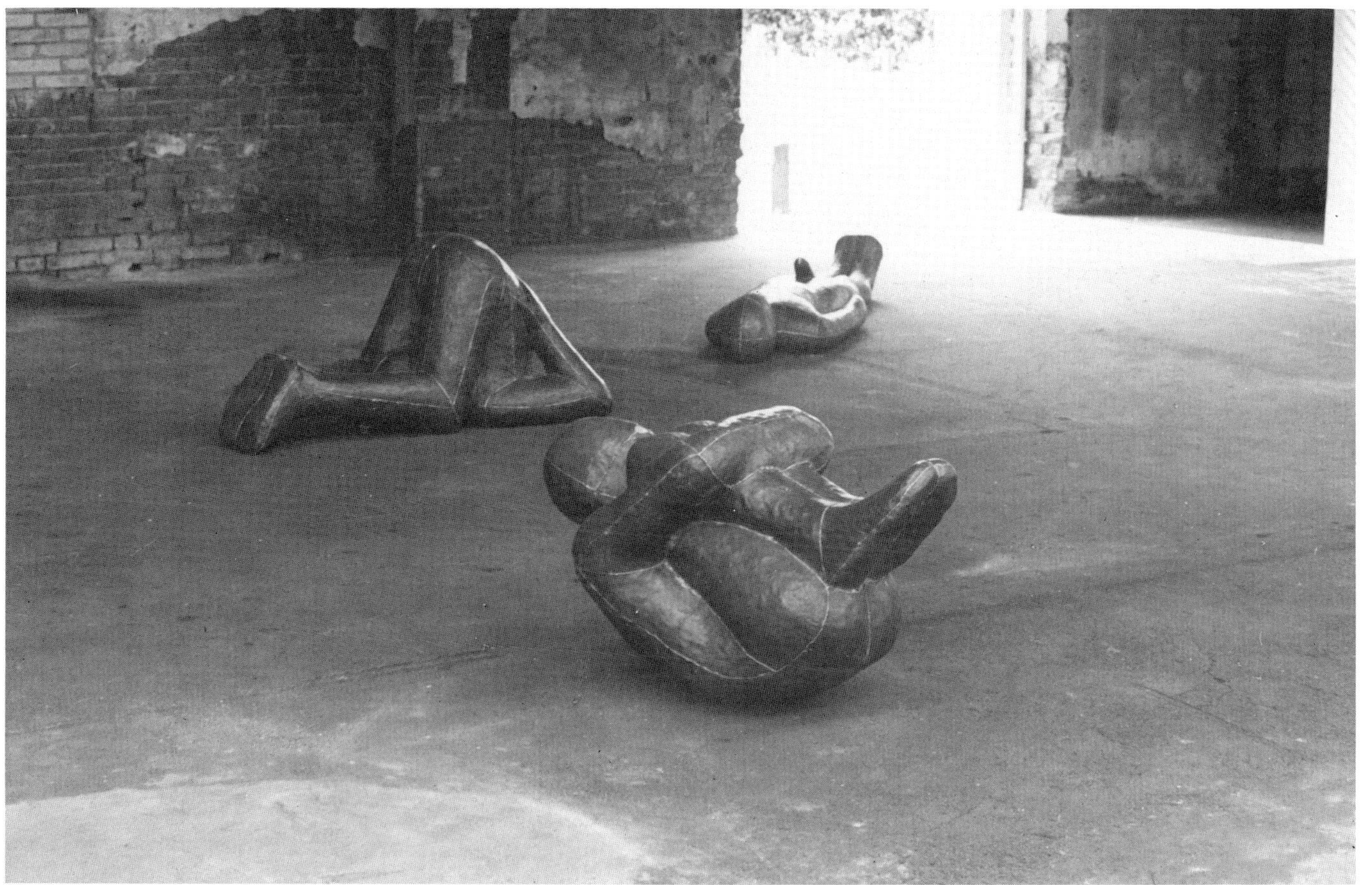

ANTONY GORMLEY

Three Ways
1981-2
lead & plaster
life size

Lead is a strong metal. Not in its physical resistance or tensile strength, but in its ability to insulate, to block all particles, all radiations; to defend and enclose. Infinitely malleable, mouldable and reworkable, it has resilience once it is formed into an enclosing shape. It is also deadly.

Over the past four years Antony Gormley has used it as the principal material of his work. It forms the skin of Gormley's figures — no longer human, frail, or featured, but generalised, undecaying and permanent. The greyness of the lead is the kind of grey that sucks in all other colours, to encapsulate them.

Gormley's figures are moulds of his own body. They are taken first in plaster. Adjusted and refined, they are then coated in glassfibre, and the lead is added in sections. A similar process is carried out over the preserved body of an animal, or a form that has been carved in polystyrene. A series of skills is employed in making the sculpture: the crucial adjustments of the plaster, the structuring of the lead sections and the beating and joining of the sheets. Over the past year the lead sections have been made in collaboration with craftsmen assistants.

The figures are hollow, and the openings that Gormley cuts, the eyes, ears and nose in **Land, Sea and Air II,** 1983, and the mouth, anus and penis in

Three Ways, 1981-2, are the gaps that mark the join between inside and outside. The experience of being, of inhabiting one's own body, the puzzle of locating one's thinking within a physical entity are the first things to be conveyed. The join between in and out, the stress on the skin as the limit of the body, conveys also the psychological division between self and other, between one's own psyche and the world.

"I am now trying to deal with what it feels like to be a human being. To make an image that in some way comes close to my states of mind . . . . all you have to do is close your eyes and you are in a world that is infinite. As infinite as the sky. That is very exciting.".[1]

A generalised, slim, male body, unhuman but not android, is created. Gormley values it not so much as a self-image (though it is) but as a wholeness, complete as an image but not exact as a replica. The pose, the physical position taken prior to casting, tends to be formal. There should be no distracting parts, no misleading or dominating gestures. Each figure has a gestalt, whether kneeling, walking, standing still, lying or squatting. "The body has to stand as an expressive whole. I'm using the whole body almost as if it were a face. Gestures have to involve the whole body. There has to be an integrity to the final form."[2]

'Rise'
1983-84

lifesize
The Artist courtesy Salvatore Ala Galleries Milan and New York

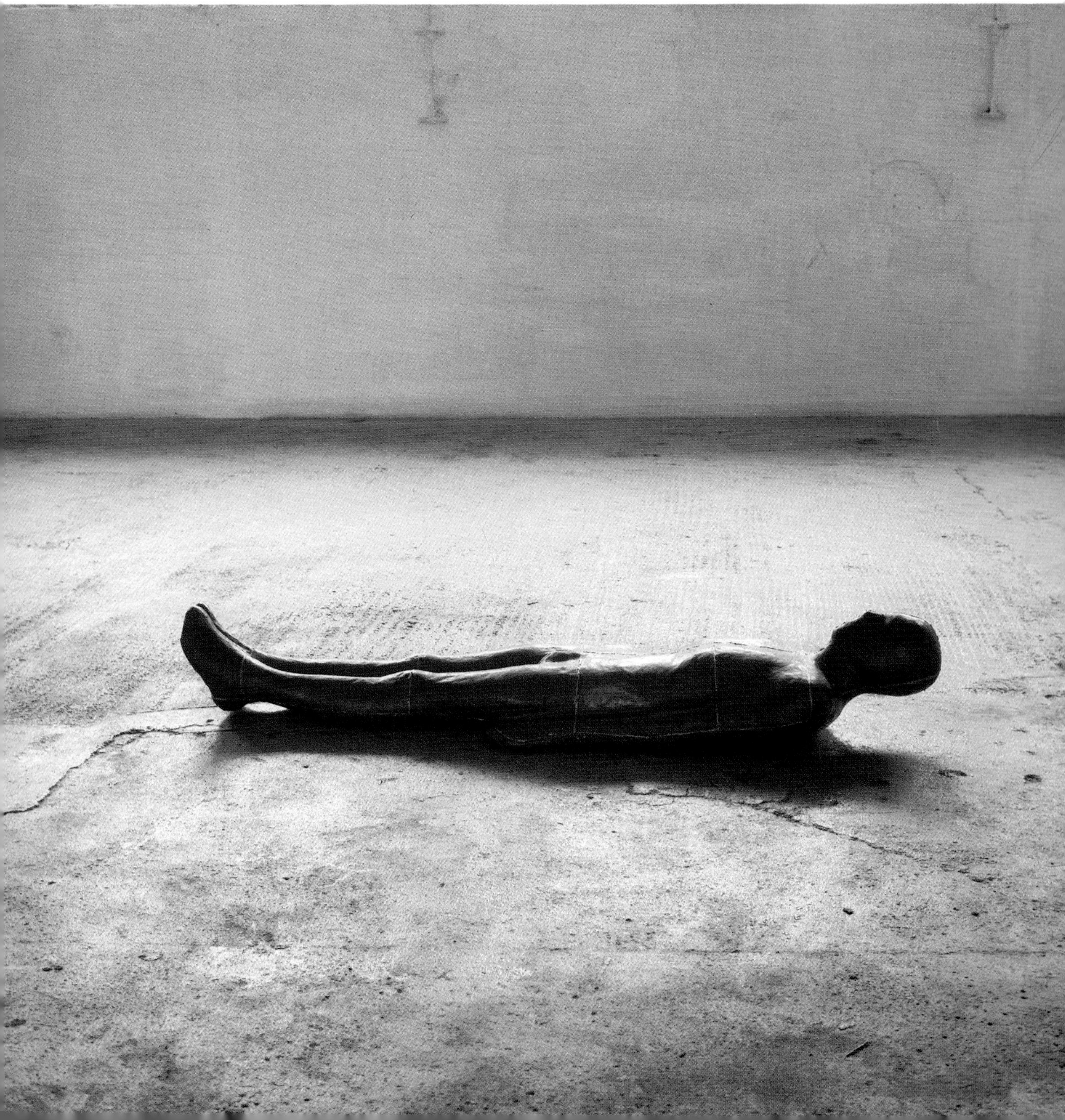

The **integrity** of the relations of all the parts of the figures and the **integrity** of the relations between the figures as a group, indicate Gormley's ambition. First he wishes to make evocative sculptures for a wide audience. (''I am tired of art about art.[3] The spectator completes and becomes the work by the reflective action of relinking the work with the world''.[4]) Secondly, through the increasing use of his own body as a model, he wishes to make an art about his experience as a human being, and to provide the possibility of making an art about human experience in general. Gormley's work is not religious, but its humanism shares many of the aspirations of a religious sensibility.

Gormley's dislike of art as a purely aesthetic activity is equalled by his concern as to how art might function socially. A number of sculptures have been made for public sites, and the locations chosen for

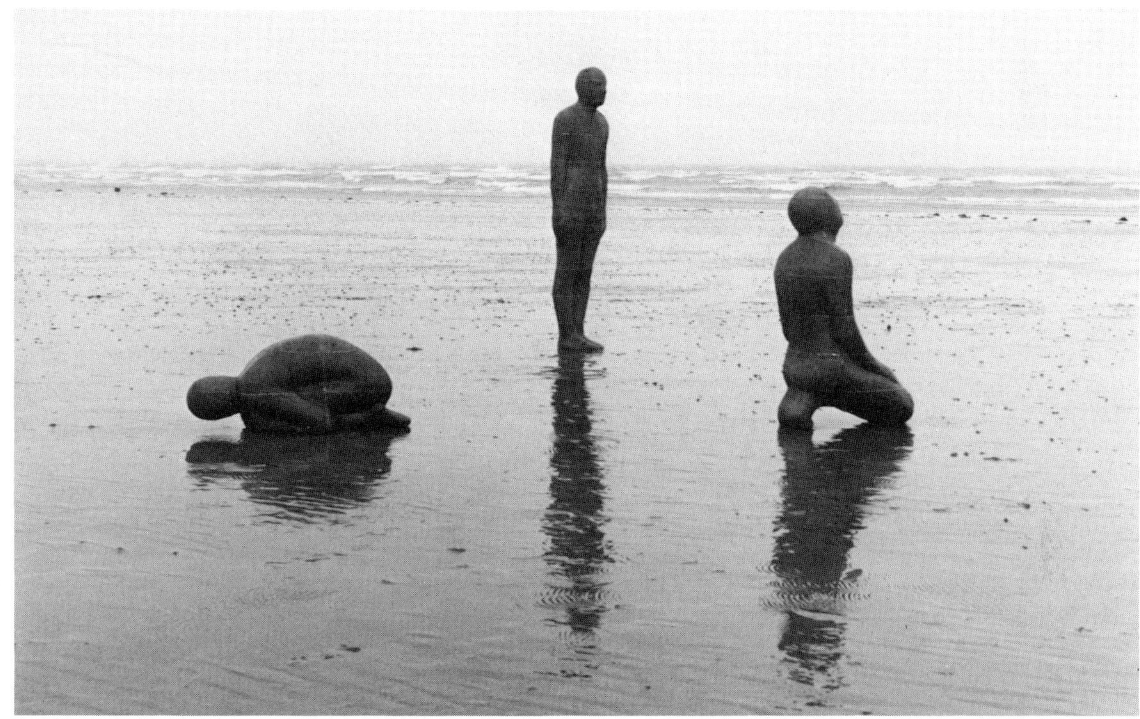

Land, Sea and Air
1982-3

lead & fibreglass
life size
private collection,
New York

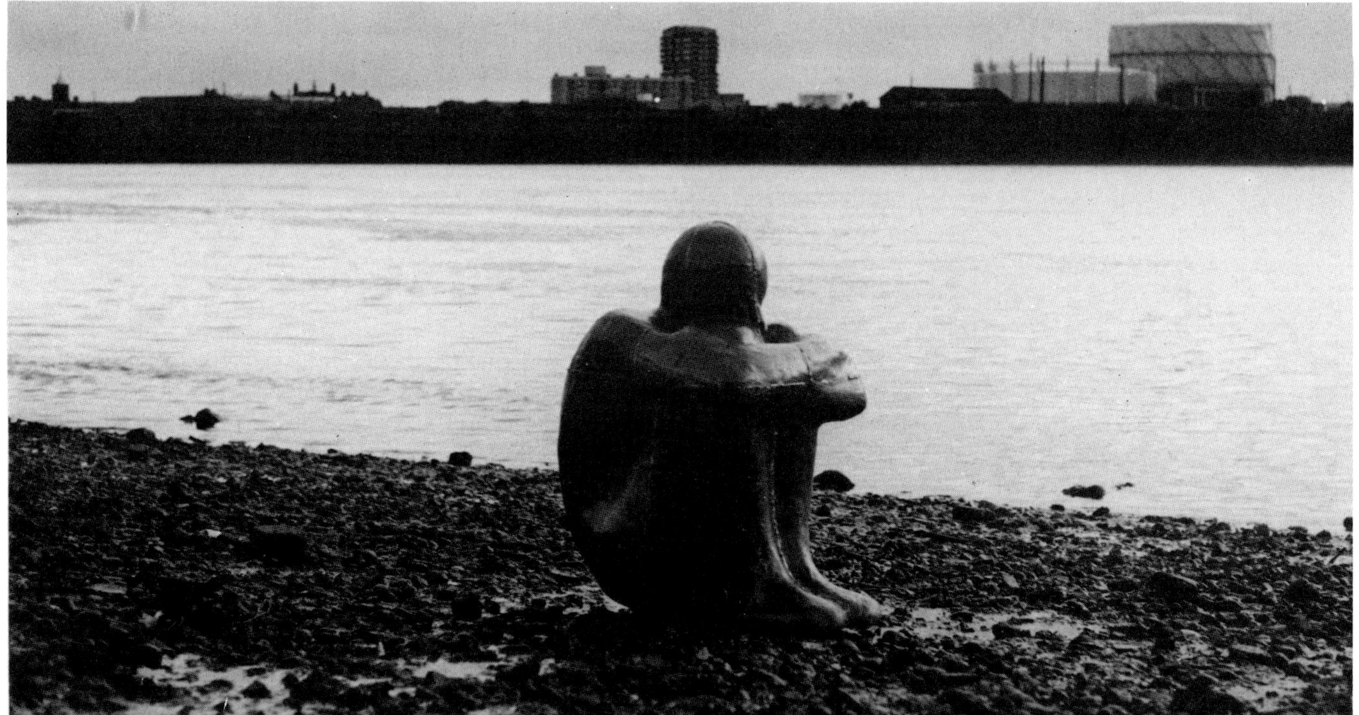

Night
1982-3

lead & fibreglass & air
life size
The Artist courtesy Salvatore Ala Galleries Milan and New York

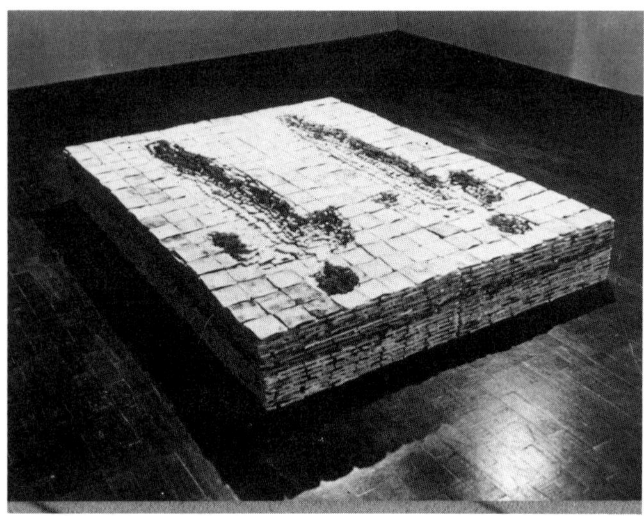

Bed
1981

bread and wax
86 x 66 x 11ins
218.2 x 167.3 x 28cms

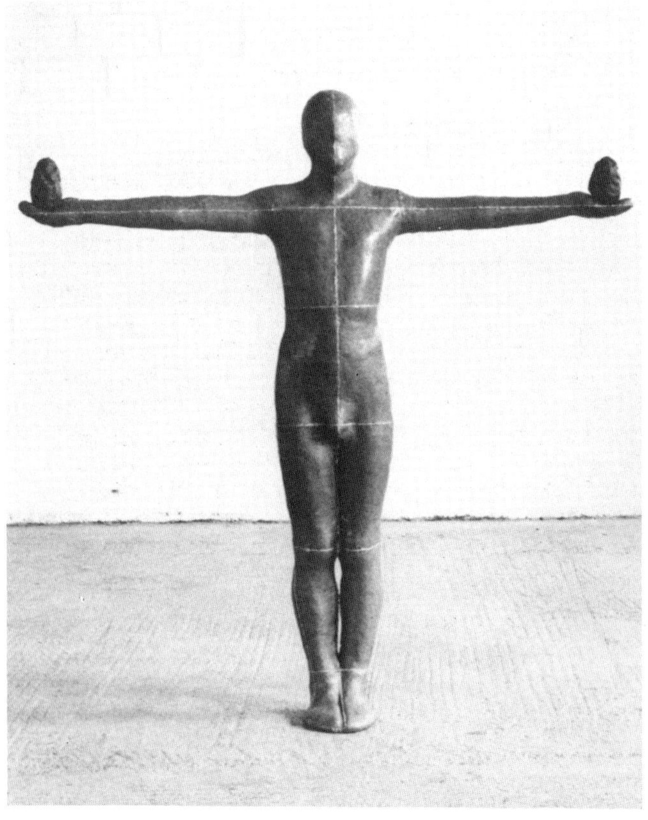

Work
1984

lead, plaster, fibreglass, clay & air
life size
The Artist courtesy Salvatore Ala Galleries Milan and New York

photographing his work indicate a distrust of the white gallery space. He sees limitations in the use of the materials and objects of everyday life (as used in his own earlier works). "Art that deals only with objects is never going to use art to its fullest potential. Objects cannot talk about experiences — they can talk about knowledge, about ideas, about culture...but I don't think that they can carry feeling".[5] This puts his work into counter-distinction, not opposition to that of sculptors like Tony Cragg, Bill Woodrow or Jean-Luc Vilmouth whose work utilises the connotations of scrap materials. Gormley's view of his position and ideas is part of a resistance, felt no less keenly by the other sculptors, to the misinformation of such labels as 'The New British Sculpture' and the kind of cultural packaging they bring with them.

Wood and stone were among the materials used in earlier works, and a notable series has been made out of sliced bread: the principal ones being human figures in negative. The shapes were literally eaten out of the low stacks of bread: the bread appearing as a symbol both of spirit and mortality. Recently, Gormley has extended his use of the lead construction with a figure that has an enormously elongated neck, and a lead 'cloud', suspended from the ceiling, fourteen feet long and nine feet wide; an ominous presence and absurdist reversal of weightlessness. A small crouching figure in clay has been positioned on top of a standing lead figure; the one the conscience, or perhaps the imagination, of the other. The exploration of materials, and paradoxes, has continued with a headless figure, and another with a hand extended to hold a lighted candle. All the works derive from ideas worked out in sketches, the sketch-book acting as a reservoir of pieces to be pursued. Separately, Gormley makes large drawings which, with economy of line and image, are parallel to the sculptural work.

Gormley's position is singular. As has been pointed out[6] his work is presented without irony, and he is uninterested in the fashionable play of images in mediation, or the unravelling of simulacra. "I think that any work that tries to deal with the condition of man is implicitly political; however, the work is the response of trying to deal with those things and doesn't stem from the reading of any political ideology".[7] Gormley proposes the primacy of physical experience over cultural and social experience. While admitting their relatedness, he would put the complex of feelings of being in the human body as the priority for his work. From those feelings he draws out the threads that convey dreams or the imagination. "If you get a sense of extension, of constriction, of vulnerability, or tentativeness, of generosity, or meanness, or love or fear, or all those things, so much the better, for I think all those things are in the work".[8]

Sandy Nairne

1. **Aspects** 25 Winter 1983/4
2. Interview with the artist 5.7.84
3. **Aspects** op.cit.
4. **Objects and Sculptures**, Arnolfini/ICA p.18.
5. Interview with the artist 5.7.84
6. Lynne Cooke, **Antony Gormley**, Salvatore Ala, New York, 1984.
7. **Objects and Sculptures**, op.cit.
8. Interview with the artist 5.7.84

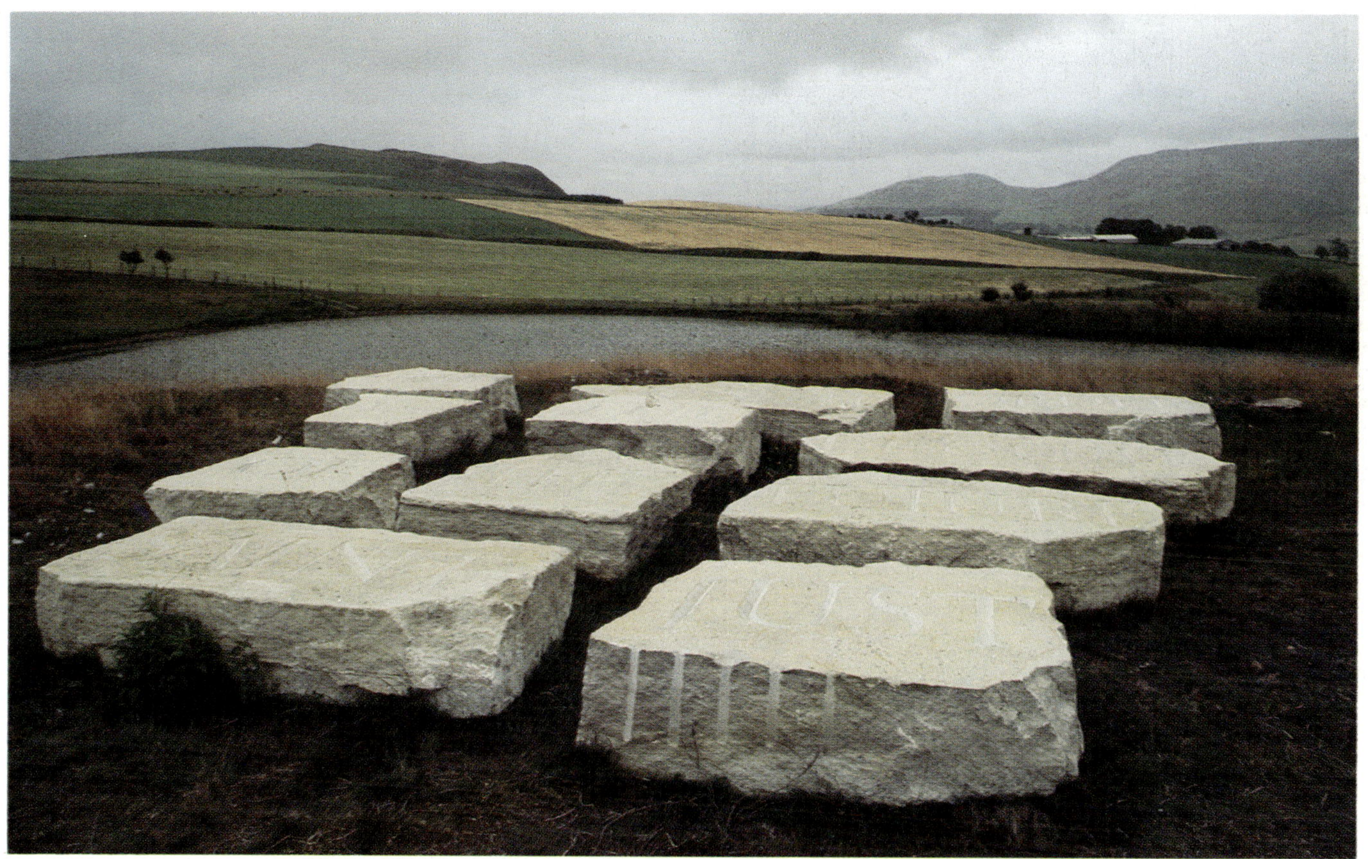

IAN HAMILTON FINLAY

View of Stony Path; Saint-Just
1983

stone piece from stony path
photo credit: Tony Bond

Like every other form of human activity in an industrial society, art is deeply affected by the principle of the division of labour. It is possible for an artist to take refuge in a particular technique, and refuse to acknowledge any responsibility for what lies beyond the detailed and specific treatment of his chosen medium. Yet if this degree of specialisation goes unremarked, the very notion of a unified culture comes under threat. T.S. Eliot pointed out forty years ago, in his **Notes toward a definition of Culture** that even the great artist is not necessarily a man of culture; he may achieve his greatness through a single-minded determination to exclude all that he regards as peripheral to his particular purpose. But if he does so, he makes it all the more necessary for another type of artist to exist — an artist who brings together, instead of forcing apart, the different strands of culture and tradition. In contemporary Britain, there is no more evident example of this second type of artist than Ian Hamilton Finlay.

Highly relevant to this distinctive role is the fact that Finlay has been (and is) essentially a poet. He first made his reputation in 1960 with the collection of poems entitled **The Dancers inherit The Party**, which was enthusiastically received by modernist critics like Hugh Kenner. In the decade that followed, he became widely known as a participant in the international movement of concrete poetry, which had its main focuses in Central Europe and

South America, but elicited a specially valuable contribution from Finlay himself. Whereas his earlier poems had used more or less conventional metric patterns, concrete poetry provoked him to use a new syntax, based on the placing of letters and words on the page. His first collection of concrete poems, **Rapel** (1962), carried the sub-title 'Fauve and Suprematist poems', showing that he was already relating the visual effects of the new poetry to the vivid and memorable styles of 20th century art. The 'Fauve' ideal led him to expressive effects, with coloured inks and connections to figurative genres like the Still Life, while the 'Suprematist' ideal was more severe and geometric. Once he had begun to think of concrete, or visual poetry as providing a kind of equivalent, in graphically displayed language, for the rich and evocative modernist styles, there was no reason why he should stop at the dimensions of the printed page. Finlay began to work on the larger format of what he called the 'poem-print', and around 1965 experimented with carrying his work into three dimensions, with the first 'poem-constructions'.

In moving by gradual stages from conventionally presented poetry to the 'poem-construction', Finlay was in a sense exploring the wider implications of what it was to be a 'poet'. The Greek root for the term which we tend to associate specially with the printed word is, in fact, associated with the one for 'making', and the term 'poetics' can indeed be used

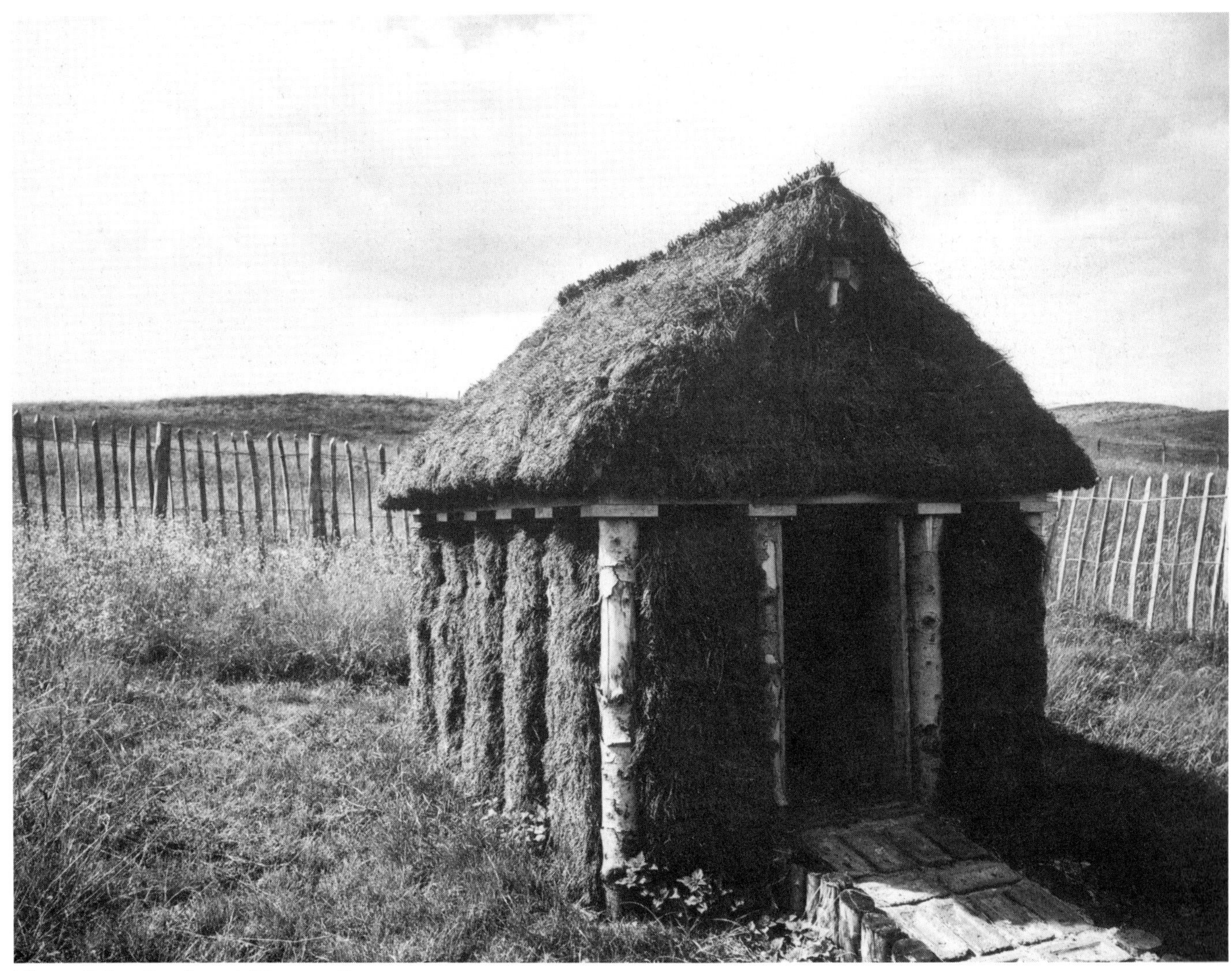

View of the Garden at Stonypath

photo credit: Dave Patterson

to apply to artistic creation in general. For a number of years Finlay had followed the practice of making wooden toys, often small sailing boats, for his own interest, and the 'poem-constructions' were initially just a means of giving an attractive three-dimensional form to a poem whose theme seemed to require it. For example, a lively, optically dazzling poem called 'Acrobats', which mimed the acrobatics of the title through the eye's act of interpreting the distributed letters, cried out for a larger format than the poem-print. What was this to be? Although Ian and Sue Finlay were at this stage living in rented accommodation in the Scottish Highlands, help was obtained for the completion of some experimental works. 'Acrobats' was mounted, with wooden letters, on the side of the farmhouse, while other constructions were designed either for inside the house, or for free-standing placement in the garden.

It was, however, the move of the Finlays to the farm of Stonypath, in Lanarkshire in the Scottish Lowlands, which made possible the conversion of these experiments into a more lasting form. This took place over the winter of 1966/67, and from this time onwards the Finlays have continued to live there. Gradually, over the previous years, Finlay had

begun to envisage a more permanent form for his poetic works than the simple wooden constructions could provide. He was to develop over the next few years a strong interest in the tradition of epigraphy — the inscription on stone — which had been alive in Classical Antiquity and could still be detected in the work of a number of representative craftsmen in contemporary Britain. But, above all, he was to find the solution to the problem of locating his work which had been in a way unresolved since he determined to abandon an exclusive reliance on the printed page. Stonypath was a small farm, on a wind-swept hill-side, with only a small garden which contrived to outlast the long snow-falls of the harsh Lowland winters. But it had what the famous English landscape gardener, 'Capability' Brown, might have called 'capabilities'. A burn running down the hill-side was available to provide water, and to furnish formal or informal ponds if the earth could be moved to accommodate them. From 1967 onwards, this gradual clearing of a larger and larger area of moorland to form a more and more extensive garden has continued almost without interruption. The result is a poet's garden of quite unparalleled richness and beauty, which is retrieved each year from the pall of winter and from the end of May to early autumn displays an extraordinary profusion of flowers, shrubs and trees.

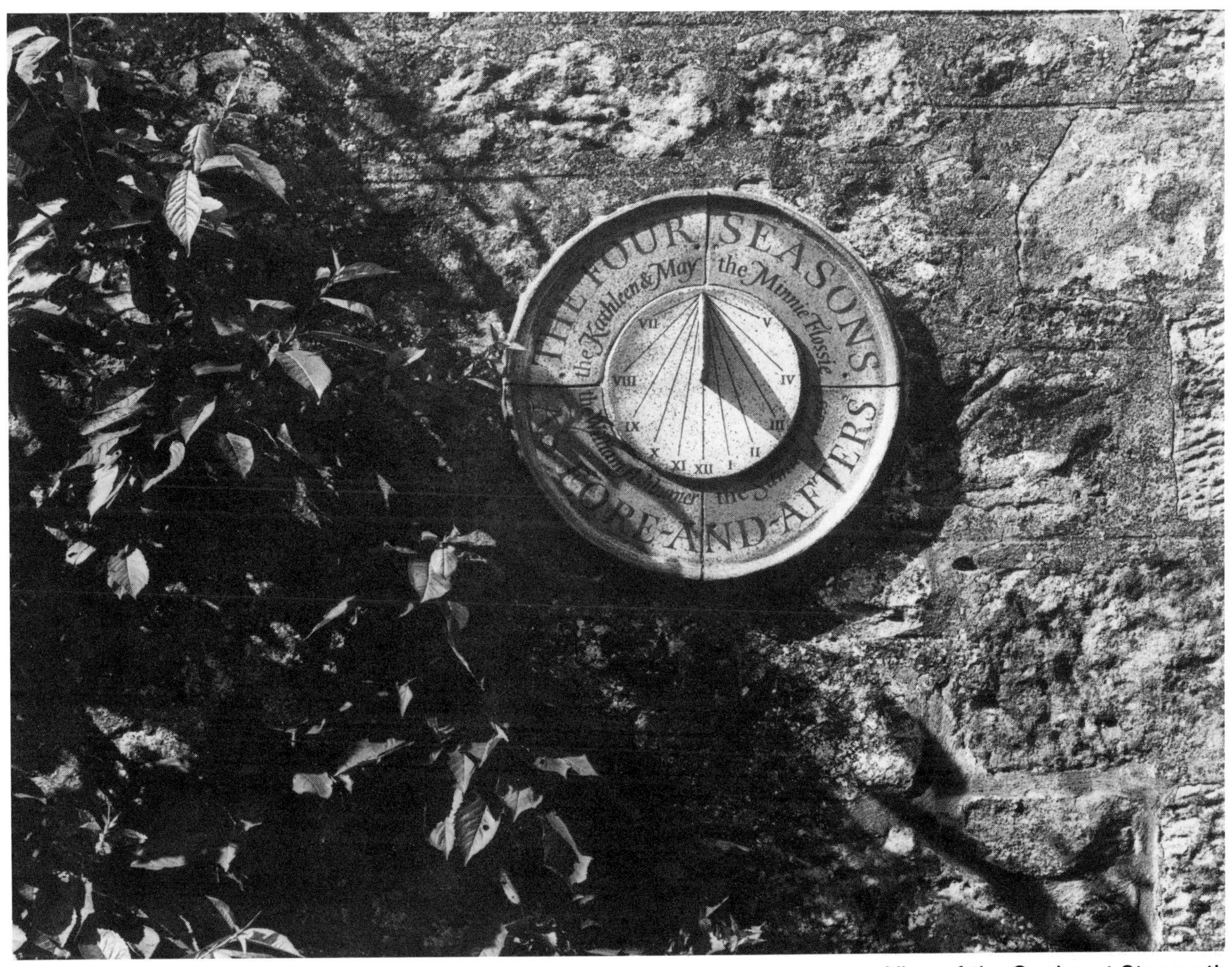

View of the Garden at Stonypath
photo credit: Dave Patterson

If the garden at Stonypath literally gave Finlay a location for his works, it also gave him a cultural background which was of immense value. Certain forms of construction were traditional to the garden, like the sundial which (through Finlay's imaginative exploration) could be used to invoke areas of reference apparently far removed from the inland garden. In the years since 1967, the sundial — with its brief and suggestive motto traditionally alluding to the vagaries of Time — has become an almost inexhaustible genre for Finlay, and it has been the type of work which could most easily be transposed, through commission, to gardens and public places far away from Stonypath (Edinburgh, Canterbury and Liège, to name a few). But in working within the idiom of the garden, Finlay did not merely find how it was possible to adapt his poetics to the kind of furniture — sundials, benches, weathercocks, urns etc. — which was traditionally found within the garden setting. He also established a connection with the tradition of poet-gardeners which was particularly strong in 18th century England, the most noted representatives being Alexander Pope and William Shenstone. For Pope and Shenstone, the creation of a garden was not simply a diversion from the more serious business of writing and publishing verse. It was a way of establishing what Maynard Mack has called "literally and figuratively,

a place to stand". Both these poets were moralists, deeply concerned with contemporary political issues, and they saw in the symbolic recreation of nature which was the achievement of the gardener a way of enshrining their most deeply held values.

The gradual development and extension of the Stonypath garden thus impelled Finlay to develop at the same time his awareness and understanding of cultural tradition. On the one hand, he had himself to rely on the skills and specialist techniques of a wide variety of craftsmen and artists. He had to develop strategies of collaboration with stone-carvers, wood-carvers, ceramicists and a large number of other practitioners who could realise his intentions in the appropriate material form. But at the same time, he had to delve back, beyond the present range of skills, and examine the ways in which the creation of gardens had been implicitly bound within the value-systems of former times. As his knowledge of these precedents deepened, so the polemical force of his position became more and more apparent. It is impossible to understand the significance of Finlay's work without taking into account the principle which he has declared in one of his 'Unconnected Sentences of Gardening' in the manner of Shenstone: "Certain gardens are described as retreats when they are really attacks".

Far from being merely a pastoral refuge from the urban world in which most of us live, Finlay's Stonypath forms an implicit challenge to the dominant values of contemporary culture. It is not simply a question of writing off the greater part of present-day artistic production, but of questioning at its base the ideology which helps to validate and sustain it. For Finlay, the very growth of what could be called cultural bureaucracies, and their increasingly vital role in propagating the art of the avant-garde, threaten to bring the artist irretrievably within the province of the secular. What the artist produces becomes a kind of social service, hardly different in essence from all the other forms of provision which the Welfare State guarantees to its citizens. The sacred or religious aspect of his work is nullified by this regime of unselective, bureaucratic benevolence.

That Finlay is attempting to challenge this situation as far as lies within his power is apparent through what he has called the "neo-classical rearmament" of the garden, which began in the 1970s and has continued unabated up to the present day. What was originally, in many respects, a traditional cottage garden became by stages a garden filled with evocations of Greek and Roman Antiquity. Stone columns are now no less prominent than sundials, and Finlay has devised new neo-classical garden forms, like the inscribed column-bases encircling growing trees which have achieved their most spectacular expression in a 'Sacred Wood' installed in Holland, at the Rijksmuseum Kröller-Müller. Intervening between the Ancient World and the present day, in Finlay's neo-classical Pantheon, is the epoch of the French Revolution which now supplies him with an ample store of references for his denunciation of contemporary attitudes. The largest single project to date at Stonypath (at least measured by the weight of its materials) is a group of massive carved stone blocks originally exhibited outside the Hayward Gallery in London in Summer 1983, which bear a text attributed to the French revolutionary Saint-Just: "The Present Order is the Disorder of the Future". It is a reminder, quite unusually forceful because of its cyclopean

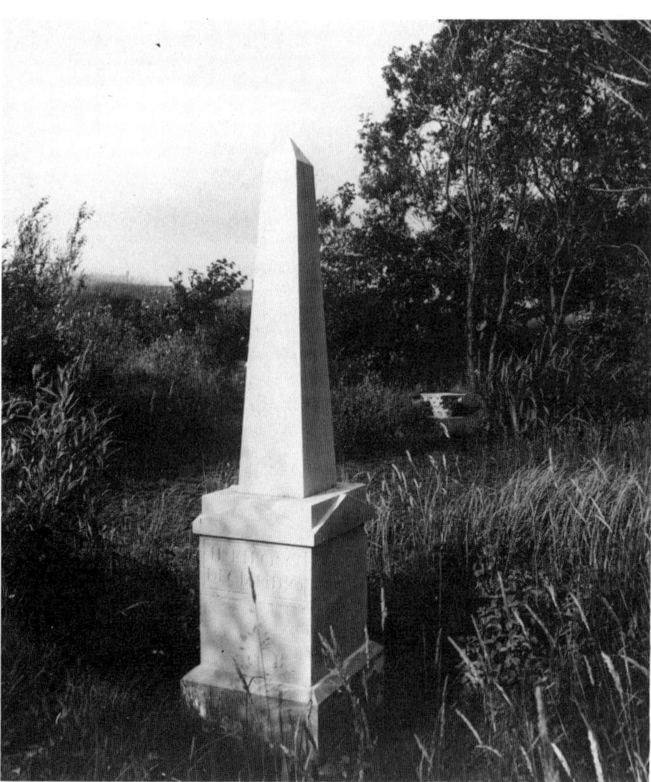

View of the Garden at Stonypath
photo credit: Dave Patterson

proportions, of the intense passion for the transformation of present society which animated Saint-Just and his fellow revolutionaries — a passion which Finlay wishes to contrast with the generally luke-warm engagement of the contemporary artist and his public. His prolonged dispute with the local rating authority over the designation of the 'Garden Temple' in which many of his icons of revolutionary virtue are displayed is therefore not an aberration from his work as artist and poet: it is a necessary attempt to vindicate the deep seriousness of his cultural commitment.

Stephen Bann

Japanese Stacks: Yubari 1 of 6
1979

sycamore wood, carved
10 x 57.5 x 25cms
courtesy the artist and Graeme Murray Gallery, Edinburgh
photo credit: Antonia Reeve, Edinburgh

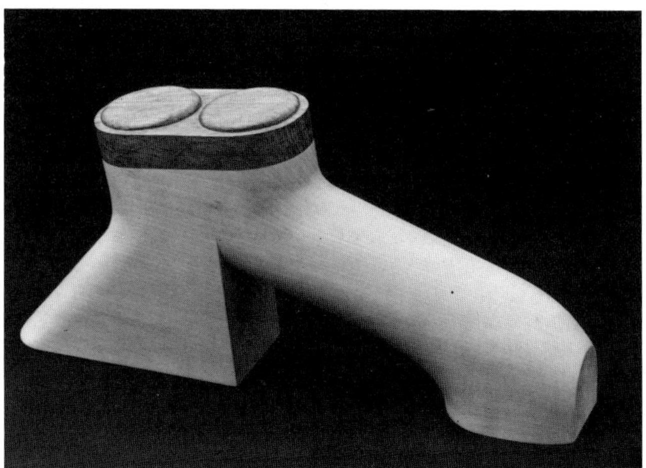

Japanese Stacks: Akitsuki 1 of 6
1979

sycamore wood, carved
27.5 x 10 x 60cms
courtesy the artist and Graeme Murray Gallery, Edinburgh
photo credit: Antonia Reeve, Edinburgh

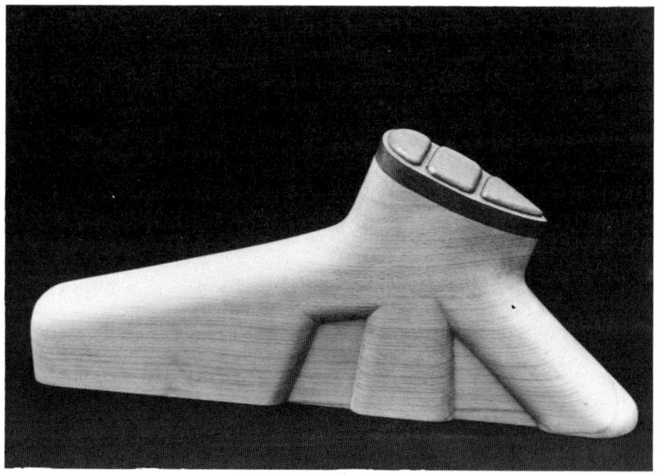

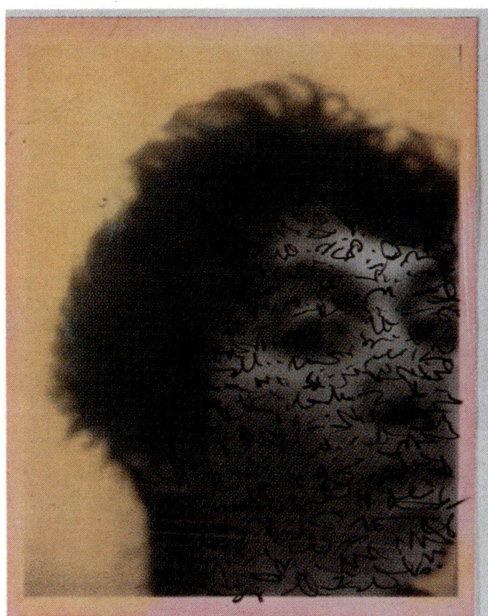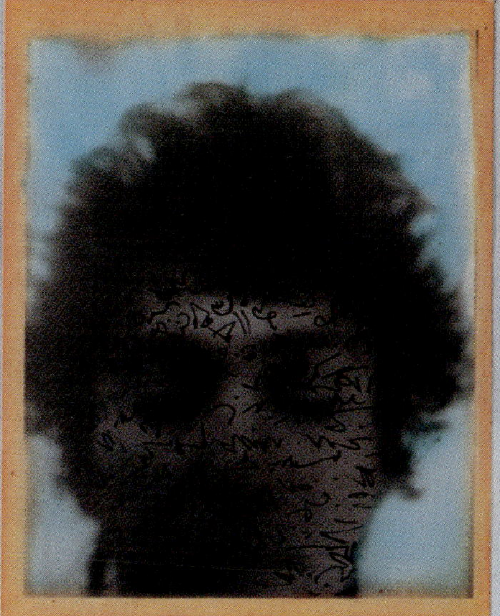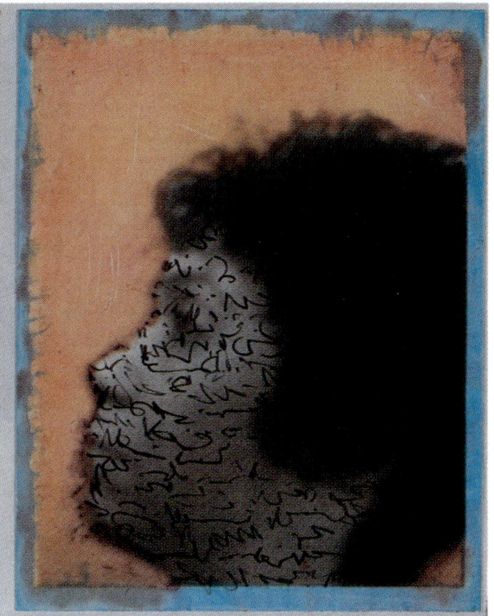

SUSAN HILLER

Midnight, Baker Street
1983

Set of 3 C-type photographs, enlarged from hand-coloured automatic photographs; each 28 x 20ins
71 x 50.7cms

A richly evocative work, *Elan* offers multiple points of entry. Often it is the sound — excerpts from Konstantin Raudive's recordings of "messages from the dead" interspersed with passages in which the artist intones what has been described as a "preconscious song" — that initially captures attention.[1] Barely distinguishable and scarcely audible, Raudive's traces identify themselves as Mayakovsky and Churchill amongst others. Yet in this context they are more preposterous than persuasive, more hilarious than hallucinatory.

With its relatively repetitious simple rhythms Hiller's improvised wordless chanting is very different. At moments an untrammelled muted lament reminiscent of keening, at others, of lullabies and cradlesongs, it seems to partake of both without becoming either. And although it hovers on the brink of speech, it belongs ultimately to some deeper and more primary level of communication. Whilst the splutterings on Raudive's tapes may quite confidently be dismissed as authentic messages from the dead, this no more means that all phenomena which are inexplicable or ineffable are rendered suspect than it implies that communication must be couched in intelligible terms, that it must meet the requirements of logic and reason. For if the stagey melodramatic mutterings of these 'phantoms' in the end rouse little more than curiosity and incredulity Hiller's voice by contrast, even though bereft of words, actually communicates.

With the exception of one word 'elan' (the creative principle) the script on the photographic panels is indecipherable. But since certain fragments resemble words and others ciphers and abbreviated signs, the marks indicate meaning, albeit without revealing it. In various senses this is illuminated writing: literally, in that the photographs are negatives and so the script exists only as light; figuratively, in that the moist velvety background throws forward these letters, burnished and embossed with dabs of colour; metaphorically, in invoking such notions as "the writing on the wall", suggestive of portents and prophecies; and analogously, as a kind of modern counterpart to such precious texts as illuminated manuscripts and sacred scrolls. Just as the chanting manages to communicate without articulating, so it is a recognition of the potential of these runes to convey meaning, and not their literal content, which is crucial. These modes of communication resist rationalist and reductivist methods of analysis. As Hiller wittily if elliptically implies, it is inappropriate to attempt to document, let alone validate them with scientific apparatus, like the tape recorder and the camera, for not only is such equipment a very imperfect witness to the truth, but not all truths are open to mensuration.

In contrast with the mysterious, haunting quality of these vocal and calligraphic improvisations, the white rectangle in the centre of the composition at first seems tersely mute. As Breton conceived it, automatism had as one element in its lineage Leonardo's advice to the painter to find images in the roughened weathered surfaces of walls. This unblemished anonymous expanse remains peculiarly recalcitrant to imaginative fantasy, even though attentive scrutiny rapidly engenders afterimages from the adjacent black panels which sully its pristine appearance. Less a trigger than a screen, the potential recipient rather than the progenitor of visions, it does in-fact provide a perfect arena for eidetic perception, for those instances of waking hallucination in which the normal boundaries between the products of the mind and the evidence of the senses are broken down and the subject sees an image of extraordinary completeness and impact.[2] Eidetic perception has been regarded as evidence of the independence of the mind from enslavement to received sensation and thus of the origins of representation in inner generated perception. By destroying the boundaries between products of the mind and of the senses, between imagination and perception, between inner and outer reality, it also operates at a preverbal level of representation and communication. And, as with automatic speech and writing, it is available to anyone, irrespective of status, and not restricted to the artist alone.

Indeed in *Elan* Hiller in many ways refuses the role conventionally assigned the artist. By not providing the appropriate sort of images from which meaning is normally construed, she deliberately leaves the viewer in the lurch. On the tape she asserts: "outside of its own quotation, the voice is a relic"; whilst on the cassette which forms part of *Monument* there is the related claim: "I'm an audible Raudive voice . . . you can't represent anything in the present; when you represent it, its already in the past". By not proferring predigested visual imagery in a conventional form *Elan* invites, almost insists upon, the viewer's acting in/on the gap. In refusing to supply images which witness her visions Hiller solicits ours. As she says at the end of her tape, language may operate as system, symptom, shock. All three means are utilised here. The script is a relic, a record of activity that took place in the past; if the voice is also a trace it nonetheless provokes an immediate response; the cajolling blankness of the central tablet points to the future. Through this melange of past, present and future, as through the simultaneous appeal to several senses, *Elan* posits the audience between the roles of spectator and participant, author and reader, singular and plural. The somatic, the preverbal, the subconscious, the fragmentary and the irrational possess a latent truthfulness which, however unassimilable by 'normal' channels, render inadequate any straightforward and unitary conception of reality. *Elan* not only makes evident how dangerously truncated and impoverished our capacities to interact and communicate can become but it exposes the patriarchal and mechanistic constructions that construe our world — it is no coincidence that so many of these 'lunatic fringe' modes of perception and communication are designated feminine or aligned with the female.

Yet this is but one level and one pathway into *Elan*: others are equally pertinent.[3] For example, the central space echoes the conventional western format for a painting; a frame closing off what is effectively a window onto a second world. In manipulating the frame and in designating the viewpoint the artist orders his (sic) material, and in so mastering his material he thereby gains control over it. Through its ordering of the world and its possession of meaning, the paradigmatic western painting asserts that the power of art over life is real.[4] In *Elan* Hiller makes a negative frame outside of which she places all her materials. Moreover,

since she employs elements and devices from painting and sculpture, photography and music, the work resists easy classification. By appealing simultaneously to different senses without a rigid priority she relinquishes that commanding position from which the artist typically structures and controls, confines and constrains, and establishes hierarchies and strict boundaries. The result is not disorder and meaninglessness but a suggestive indeterminacy, a congruence of different meanings that all too often in western art remain discrete or deliquescent. As she says: "I believe that art can function as a critique of existing culture and as a focus where futures not otherwise possible can begin to shape themselves."[5] Given the virtually inexhaustible labyrinthine patterns, textures and structures which comprise *Elan*, its mode is contemplative, a means to experiencing presence.

By focussing so exclusively on *Elan* little space is left to situate it within Hiller's oeuvre, let alone to discuss that oeuvre in a wider context. Yet *Elan* is exemplary in several respects. In its focus on issues of identity, gender, representation and language it explores themes dominant in Hiller's art. In its materials and techniques, as in its use of cultural artefacts it invites cross-references with many other works in an oeuvre which is remarkably diverse and fertile in its approach to certain abiding preoccupations. The seminal place it accords to automatism — visual, verbal and vocal — links it for example with *Midnight, Baker Street*.

But here implications inherent in automatic writing are extended in new directions. In its format, a triptych in which the artist is shown in three positions: frontal profile and three-quarter face, *Midnight Baker Street* recalls the portrait of Cardinal Richelieu which Van Dyck painted to enable Bernini to sculpt a bust in the absence of the sitter. Yet unlike the Baroque portrait, which sought to provide all the essential information, Hiller's work (three pictures taken in photo booths, hand painted and enlarged) refuses to render up the sitter. She is distanced psychologically by the fact that her eyes are shut, but more importantly, by the imposition of the script which covers her face, suggesting the way in which verbal discourse structures all experience, and especially the manner in which it intervenes to condition perception. But since it is not legible this wild calligraphy might in fact be a form of graffiti, a cancelling out of the image, a presenting of the self in terms of an act rather than an image[6] (her appearance). Equally, it is reminiscent of tattooing and thus becomes a type of embellishment. What is significant about these differing interpretations is not the question of which is correct, for in some ways they, and perhaps others, all are but their diversity. Contradictions, alternatives and ambiguities cannot be regarded as negative aspects of experience but an inevitable even enriching one. Just as the self is not a simple unitary construct, but a collective collaborative, multiple entity.

Comparison with *Alphabets 1 & 2* confirms that these are not in fact haphazard marks but part of a mysterious (because as yet uncodified) language. As Hiller argues these works should "not just be seen in purely pictorial terms, or as decorated surfaces, but taken seriously as a form of patterned utterance

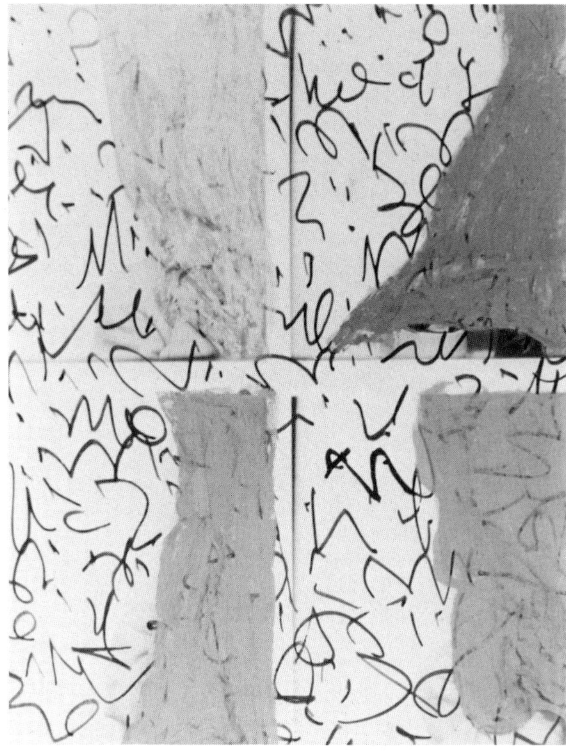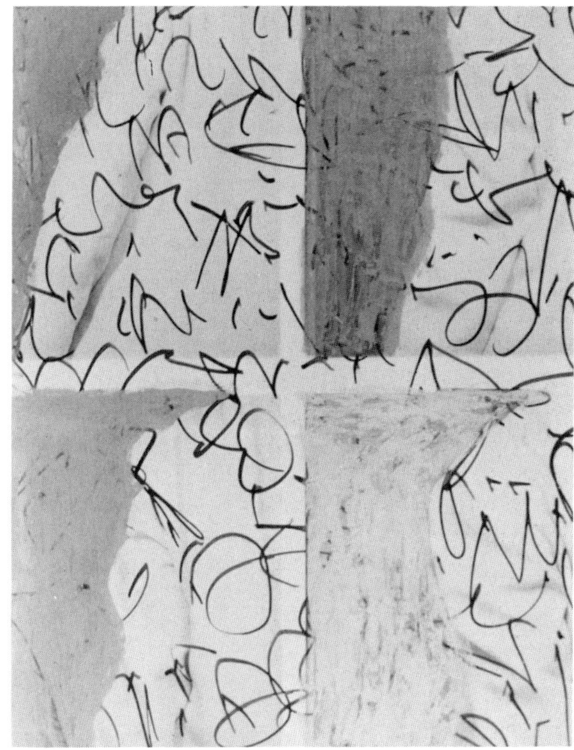
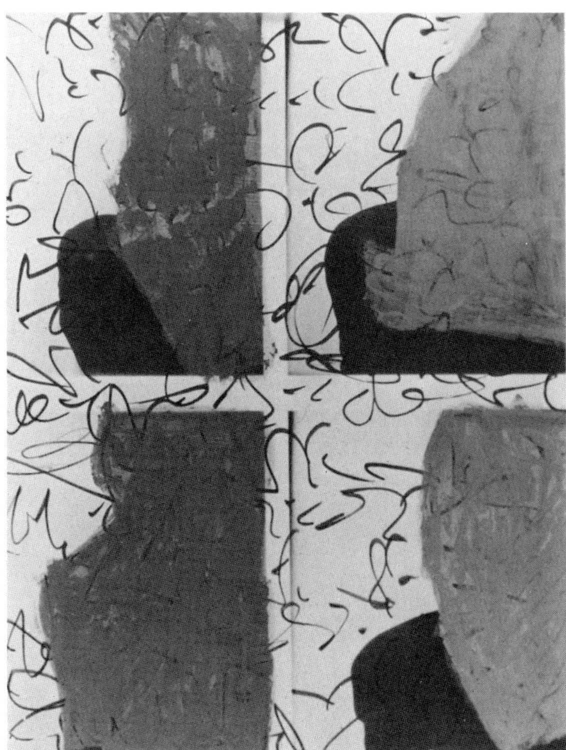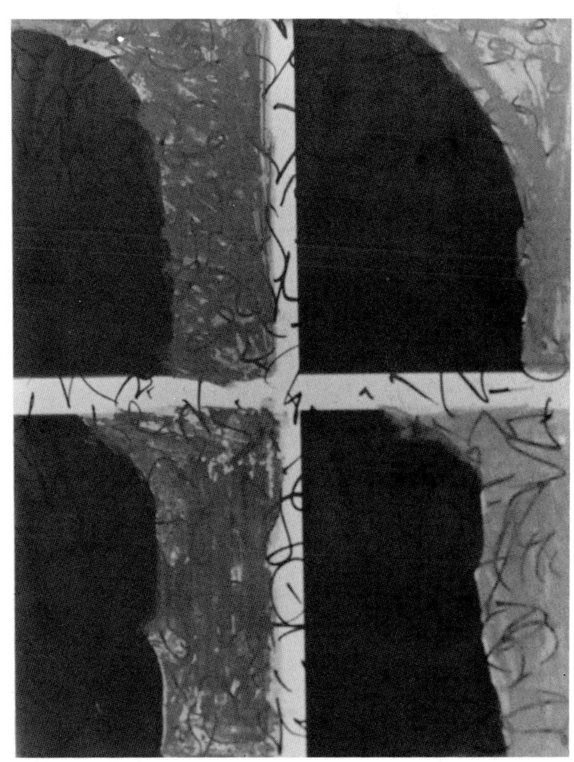

Sometimes I think I'm a Verb instead of a Pronoun
1982

C-type photograph enlarged from hand-coloured automatic photographs;
two panels from a series of twelve; each panel 28½ x 43¾ins
72.5 x 109.9cms

. . .I'd like to see a full phonemic study someday".[7]
Characteristically, the underlying ideas are manifest
in the experience of the work, not simply a
commentary on it. Hiller's work incorporates what
are sometimes referred to as "alternative" forms of
perception and communication, without itself
becoming marginalised. In its focus on such crucial
issues, in its reasonably poetic philosophical
content and in its astute critical consciousness, it
stands at the heart of current activity.

Lynne Cooke

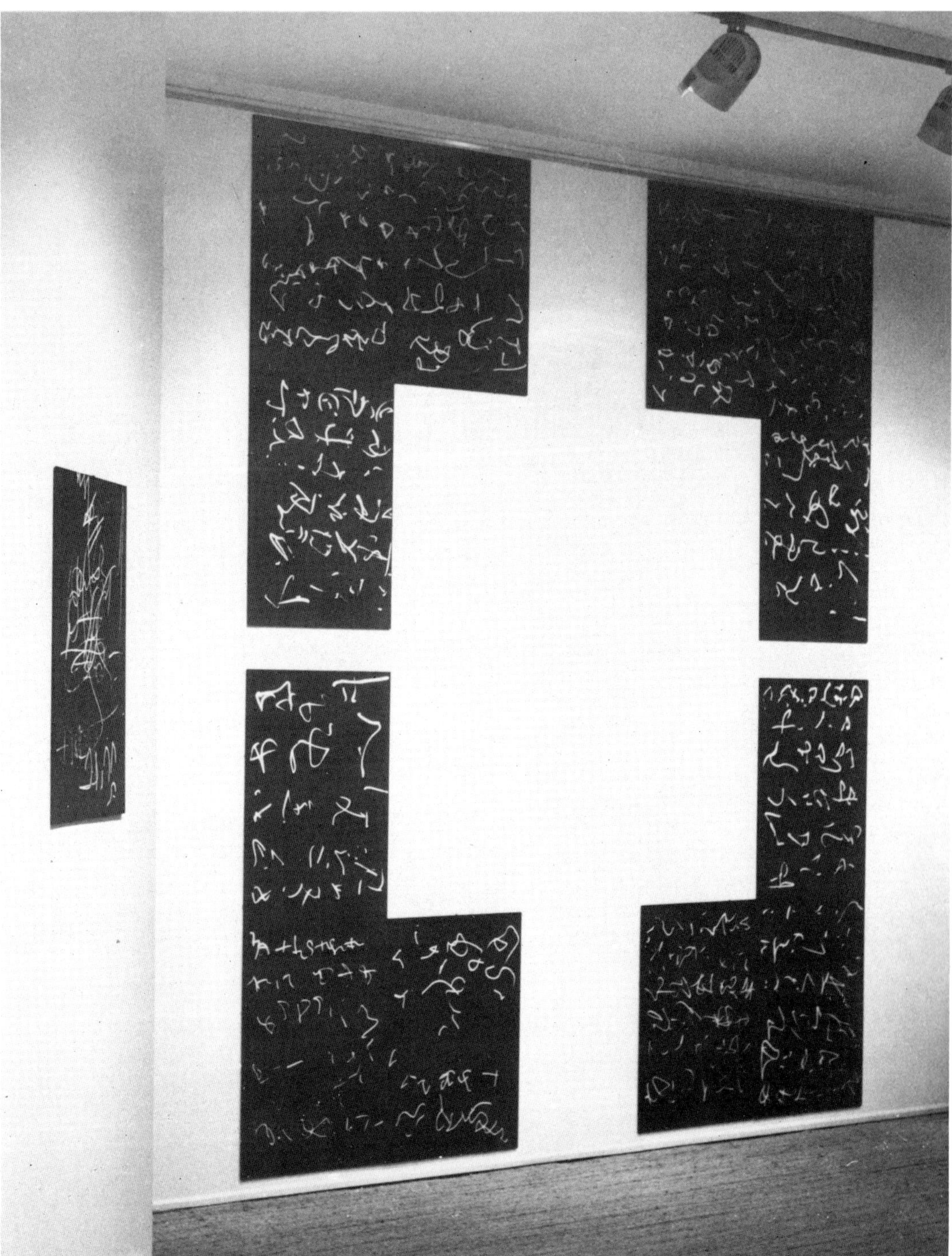

Elan
1982

120 x 92ins
304.8 x 233cms
13 C-type photographs with
coloured ink, each 30 x 20'',
block mounted; and audio-tape;
Installation at Gimpel Fils
Gallery London

FOOTNOTES

1. The Latvian psychologist Konstantin Raudive conducted experiments in the sixties in which he procured what he claimed were recordings from the dead by leaving a solitary cassette recorder running in an empty room, and then amplifying the ''silent'' tapes.

2. In an article on ''Le Message Automatique'' in *Minotaur* of December 1933 Breton referred to the work of E.K. Jaensch and others on eidetic phenomena, arguing that their experiments tended to prove that ''perception and representation — which seem to the ordinary adult to be radically opposed — should only be taken as the dissociated products of a *single, original faculty*, of which the eidetic image makes us aware, and of which we recover the traces in the primitive and the child''. (p.65)

3. Offered here is only one of a number of possible readings of *Elan*. Guy Brett, for example, concluded that *Elan* ''reproduces our cultural conditioning. Our idea of the dead individual is as circumscribed as our idea of the living''. ref. Guy Brett, ''Susan Hiller'', *Art Monthly*, May 1983 p.8

4. Svetlana Alpers (''Art History and It's Exclusions: The Example of Dutch Art'', in *Feminism and Art History, Questioning the Litany*, eds. Norma Broude and Mary D. Garrard, Harper and Row, NY 1982) to which this paragraph is indebted, argues that Northern painting constitutes not merely a different way of viewing the world, but a different mode of art. She provides a suggestive starting point for a fuller discussion of Hiller's art than is possible here.

5. Interview in *Fuse*, Toronto, November/December 1981.

6. This links closely with *Sometimes I Think I'm a Verb Instead of a Pronoun*, 1981-2, and is characteristic of the richly interwoven connections between Hiller's various works.

7. ''Looking at New Work; An Interview with Rozsika Parker'', in *Susan Hiller 1973-83: The Muse My Sister*, Londonderry 1984 p.21

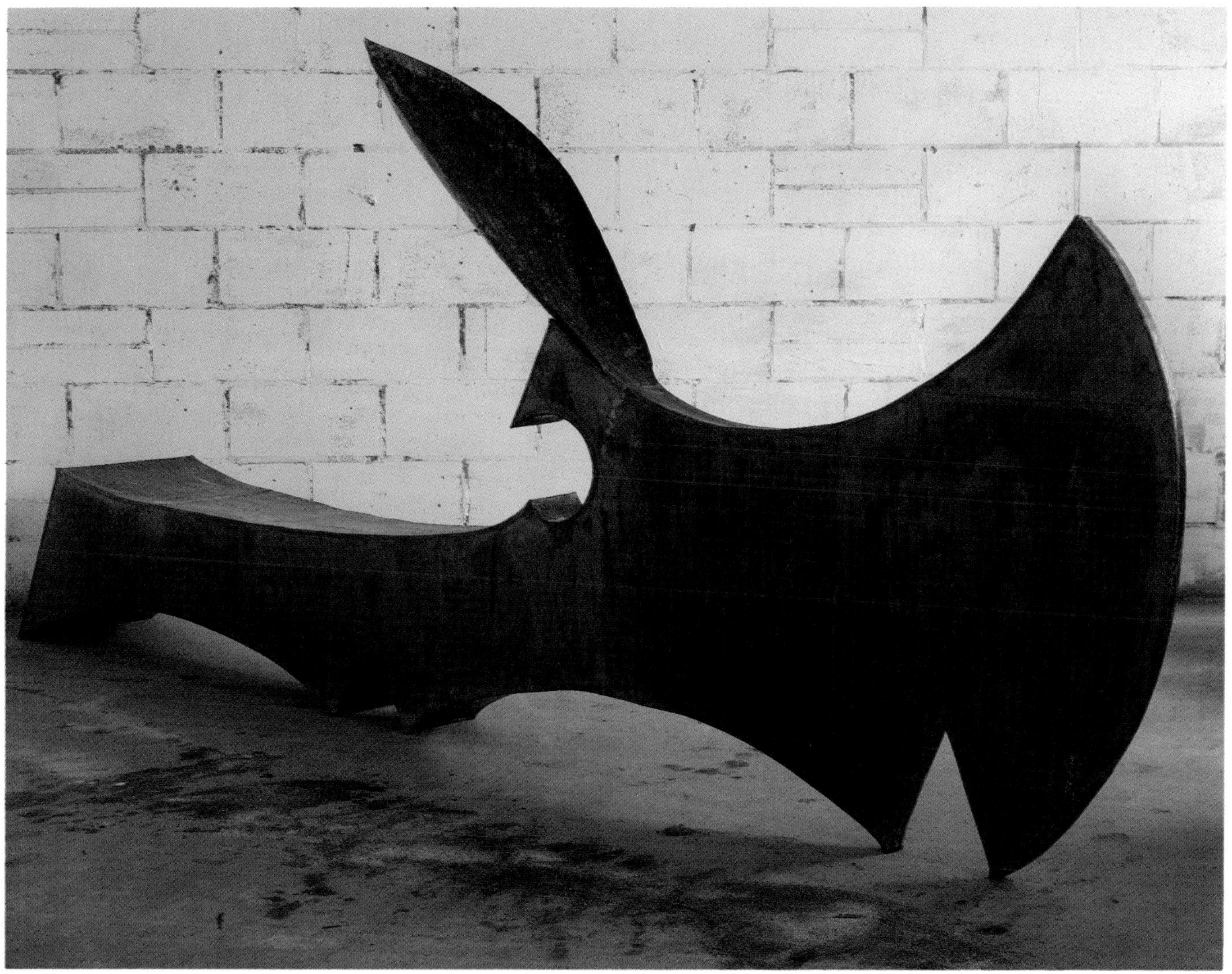

KI
1984

copper
120 x 360 x 75cms
Lisson Gallery, London
photo credit: Lisson Gallery, London

SHIRAZEH HOUSHIARY

The latter part of the 1970s witnessed a return to the object by many sculptors who had formerly been involved with installation, site-specific, performance and multi-media work. Almost simultaneously, a younger generation began making sculpture with recognisable subject-matter, spurred on in part by the revival of figurative painting, and perhaps even by the example of those painters who have turned their hand to sculpture like Baselitz, Penck and Clemente. Concurrent with this figurative revival there has been renewed interest in the poetic-object, and here as in figurative work the tendency has been to fabricate the object by hand, at least in part, in preference to simply assembling it from found and pre-existing objects. In Britain foremost amongst these sculptors have been Deacon, Houshiary, Kapoor and Wilding.[1] Although there is considerable variation in the relationship each established between image and object, each has been deeply stimulated by or engaged with poetry, though once again this has been registered in very diverse ways. In Deacon's case, for example, the poetry of Rilke informs, however obliquely, all his recent sculpture, whereas for Houshiary the interaction between the two arts often entails specific connections. In different works she has invoked Baudelaire and Bataille as well as Persian and Sufi legends. But it would be false to conclude from this that her work has a literary quality just as it is false to suppose that the relationship between the individual sculpture and the specific text will operate in identical ways from one work to the next.

Initially trained in the theatre, Houshiary turned to the visual arts only after her arrival in this country. On graduating from the sculpture department of Chelsea School of Art in 1979 she spent the next year painting before reverting to three-dimensional work.[2] In the first sculpture she exhibited at Kettles'

Yard in 1982, she retained something of the appearance of the calligraphic script or ciphers that had constituted the imagery of her painting, as if however tenuously still maintaining an engagement with the written word. This choice of such imagery, was generated in part by her desire to re-find her roots by drawing on her own cultural heritage and was stimulated and supported by the example of Anish Kapoor, a close friend. Yet the manner in which each drew on their own heritage was distinctive. In Houshiary's case it led quickly beyond somewhat idiosyncratic abstractions towards a biomorphic idiom, as if prompted by an acknowledgement of the limitations of any culture and a consequent wish for a vocabulary that is fundamental and universal, or at least is considered to be.[3] Thus the title of *Listen to the Tale of the Reed*, a work comprising six separate elements made of clay and straw and shown at the Serpentine Gallery later in 1982, evokes a particular Persian legend.[4] This story is unlikely to be familiar or perhaps even accessible to the ordinary Western spectator, yet the piece does not fail to communicate as a consequence; whilst ambiguous and even unidentifiable the imagery is not, however, meaningless. Totemic forms, a sentinel, an altar and a throne with two creatures whose antic gestures seem strangely disquieting, are amongst the inventory of allusions. Moreover, the material, in whose rich textures a light mould was growing, introduces a chthonic primal note as if the forms had been directly spawned from brute inchoate matter. As Houshiary said:

> Made out of earth (they seem as if)
> they had been there forever, that
> they happened by themselves. I don't
> want them to have a maker.[5]

The scale of the work reinforces this effect for it established a context for beings, with somewhat larger than human dimensions. The ensemble is invested with a portentous ceremonial spirit, one that generates emotions which can easily be recognised but less easily named. It is this quality that suggests that the ensemble may be devoted to profane, instinctual mysteries.

In later works like *L'Invitation au Voyage*, 1983, this ritualistic aura has been replaced by something more overtly erotic. All three components have become active beings or creatures whose behaviour can be read as both sinister and playful, alluring and malign. Redolent of fecundity and voluptuous pleasure these tumescent forms seem to have more to do with the body than with the figure, with behaviour than with appearance.

In the past year, fearing that she might become too adept at this language and so sacrifice that sense of unlaboured freshness which has characterised her work so far to questions of refinement, Houshiary began experimenting with other materials. After attempting unsatisfactorily to combine metal, straw and clay in one piece, she began using zinc alone, first beating the sheets then soldering the shapes together. But as seen in *A Pot Can Multiply* the organic basis of her language was, initially, little affected by this change in material. It was only when she experimented with sheet copper that a new morphology evolved. In the zinc sculptures the quasi-bruising of the surface involved in molding each section imbued the forms with a sense of growing from the inner core to the outer skin in a parallel manner to that found in the clay and straw works. Where formerly the skin and skeleton had been separated and the two processes, modelling (moulding) and constructing, distinct, with the copper sculptures, surface and structure are coterminous. The two techniques interact more closely and, partly in consequence the final configuration takes on a more geometric character. Arcs, acute angles and straight edges comprise the profiles of many of these new works, which do not however entirely lose an organic feel and become mechanistic. Because each silhouette has been made by wrapping the edges of the sheet around the inner wooden form and nailing it into place, they thus bear the imprint of the hand, albeit with the intervention of tools. These new sculptures have a hybrid character for they seem to belong neither to the world of fabricated, man-made objects nor to the 'natural' one of things which grow independently, on their own. This sense of an ambiguous genesis is reinforced by the way in which a form may suddenly sprout a leaf-like termination, a protuberance which could equally be read in functional terms as a kind of spoon-funnel. Such ambiguities undermine a naive conviction that these objects originated at the behest of man.

Because the emphasis on fantasy has declined in direct proportion to the growth of interest in objectness these latest sculptures do not beguile in the manner that Houshiary's works have previously. It is not so much the quasi mechanomorphic configurations alone which distinguish them from her former works but the absence of any suggestion of metamorphosis or an imminent transfiguration. Commensurate with this is the substitution of industrially fabricated materials for the former, eloquently 'loaded' ones. (However, the processes which Houshiary is currently using are artisanal in origin and not techniques deployed in industry or manufacturing: her method of handling the copper, for example, was gleaned from workers who employ it in roofing.) This combination of non-anthropomorphic form, man-made materials and a modest scale related these works to certain objects of daily use and, more broadly, to urban vernacular culture.

For Houshiary alludes, however obliquely, to the objects, materials and processes that not only surround us, but in their inexhaustible and often futile proliferation threaten to overwhelm us. In contrast to the casual, often trite relationships which we have with many of these commonplace components of our world, Houshiary's objects indicate the possibility of more meaningful ones. This depends as much on understanding the nature and properties of objects as it does on eliciting any poetic content. In exposing value in this ''raw material'' Houshiary no more provides a critique of her earlier work than she posits an alternative to this environment; it is the deleterious impact that it has in shaping our sensibilities which is addressed.[6]

The starting points of her recent works lie both more explicitly and more deeply in the world that is immediately to hand yet, this need not be at the expense of the poetic. She speaks of the ways in

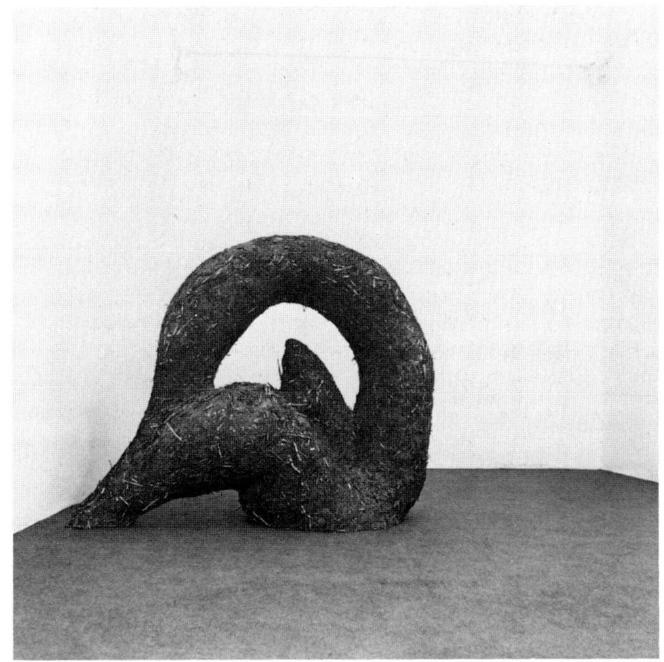

L'Invitation Au Voyage
1983

wood, plaster, clay, straw
140 x 110 x 55cms
photo credit: Gianni Carnera

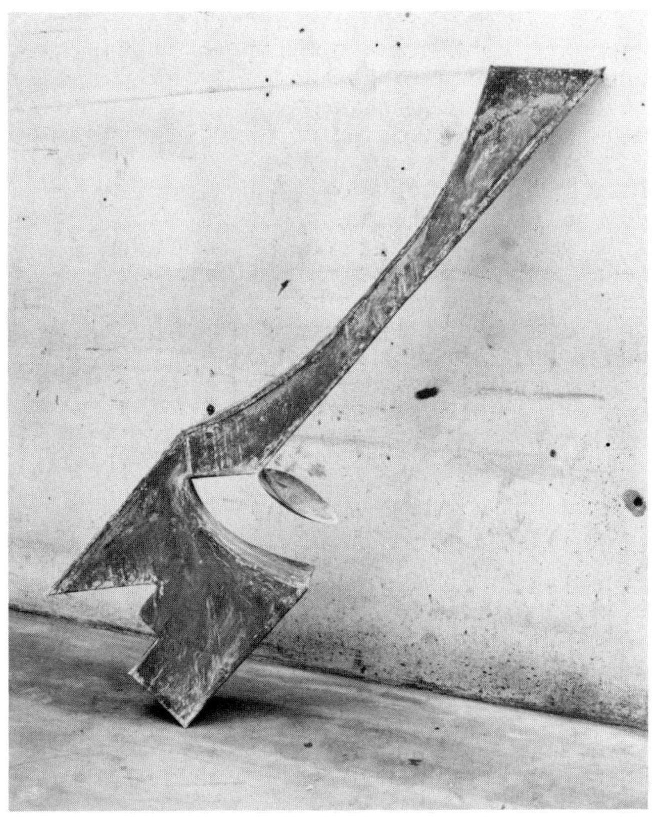

The Pen and the Ant
1984

copper
185 x 120 x 70cms
The British Council Collection, London
photo credit: Lisson Gallery, London

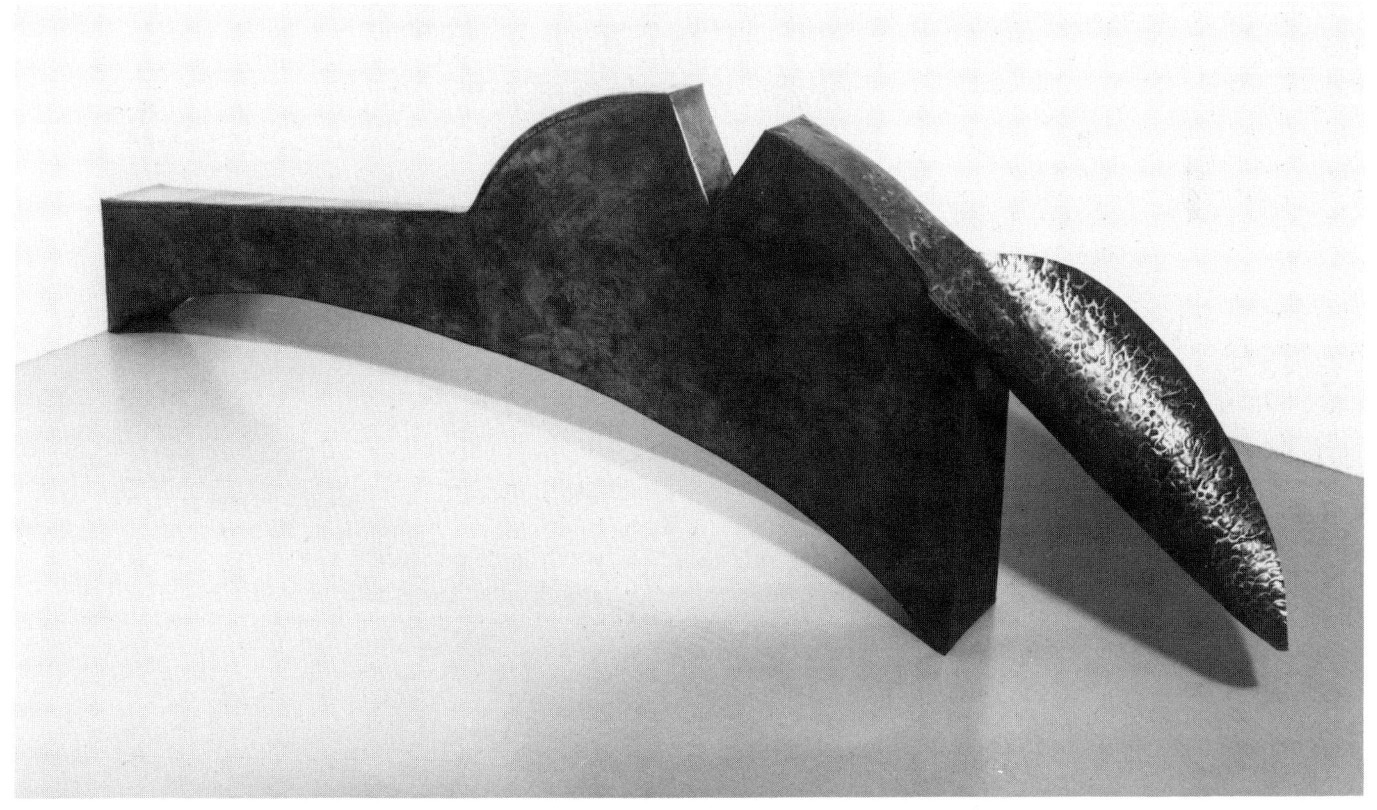

Reed
1984

copper
80 x 250 x 34cms
Lisson Gallery London

which in the spiritual life of any person there is often an initial reliance on an icon or similar sanctified object as a mediator, even membrane, through which the initiate seeks to apprehend the sacred beyond. But a moment is reached when it becomes possible to approach the unknown directly, without intermediaries; or as she says "to go behind the object". The evolution in her own work might be described analogously. In

relinquishing precursors, a more intense, more engaged contemplation of the objects is required than heretofore. Whilst undoubtedly more personal, her current idiom is neither hermetic nor obsessively private: each sculpture is a self-sufficient coherent entity. The best of these, like *Untitled (1984), K1* and *Fire is Three* make a new and significant contribution to the genre of poetic-objects.

Lynne Cooke

FOOTNOTES

1. On account of the strongly conceptual nature, as well as its allusions to the art of the past Ian Hamilton Finlay's work is of a very different order, perhaps closer to a sculptural counterpart of 'pictura poesis'.

2. Houshiary's degree show consisted of an installation in which a carefully defined space was imbued with a ritualistic aura through the agency of light. It tended therefore towards the theatrical rather than being object-based.

3. Affinities could be made with artists like Rothko and Gottlieb who in the mid-forties sought the essence of myth, not an illusion of it, as a pathway to the revelation of eternal truths. They too utilised a biomorphic imagery. And Gottlieb created surface textures which evoked a palimpsest implying not just the passage of time but cycles of death and regeneration. Whilst biomorphism originated in Surrealist circles it was not exclusive to Surrealism practice nor did Surrealism provide its theoretical basis. In addition to Jungian theory, various sciences like microcellular biology, zoology and astronomy contributed to the code, and range of meanings ascribed to it.

4. Titles do not come easily to Houshiary and do not necessarily precede or develop concurrently with the making of a particular work. Often she tries out several before finding one that conveys the range of feeling or references that she seeks. Trying to avoid pinning the work too closely, circumscribing it too literally or naming too particularly means that in not every case it is possible to christen the object.

5. Richard Francis-Shirazeh Houshiary, Tape-Slide, 1983.

6. Of her early works in clay and straw Houshiary stated: "I want to make you dream because that's the only way that I can communicate with this language that I am using". Michael Newman, Interview with Shirazeh Houshiary, unpublished typescript, p.4.

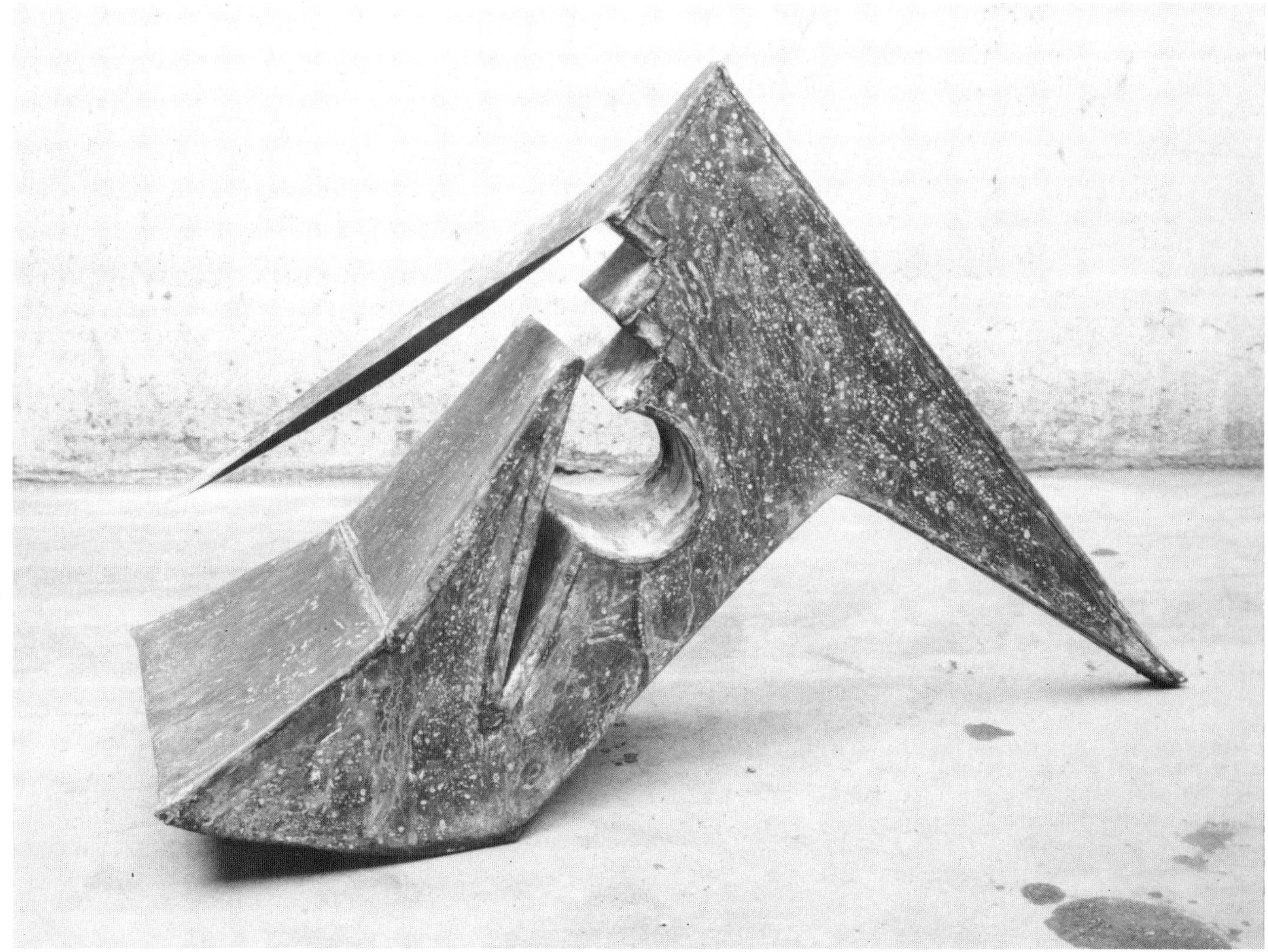

Fire is Three
1984

copper
57.5 x 87.5 x 37.5cms
private collection, courtesy Lisson Gallery London
photo credit: Lisson Gallery, London

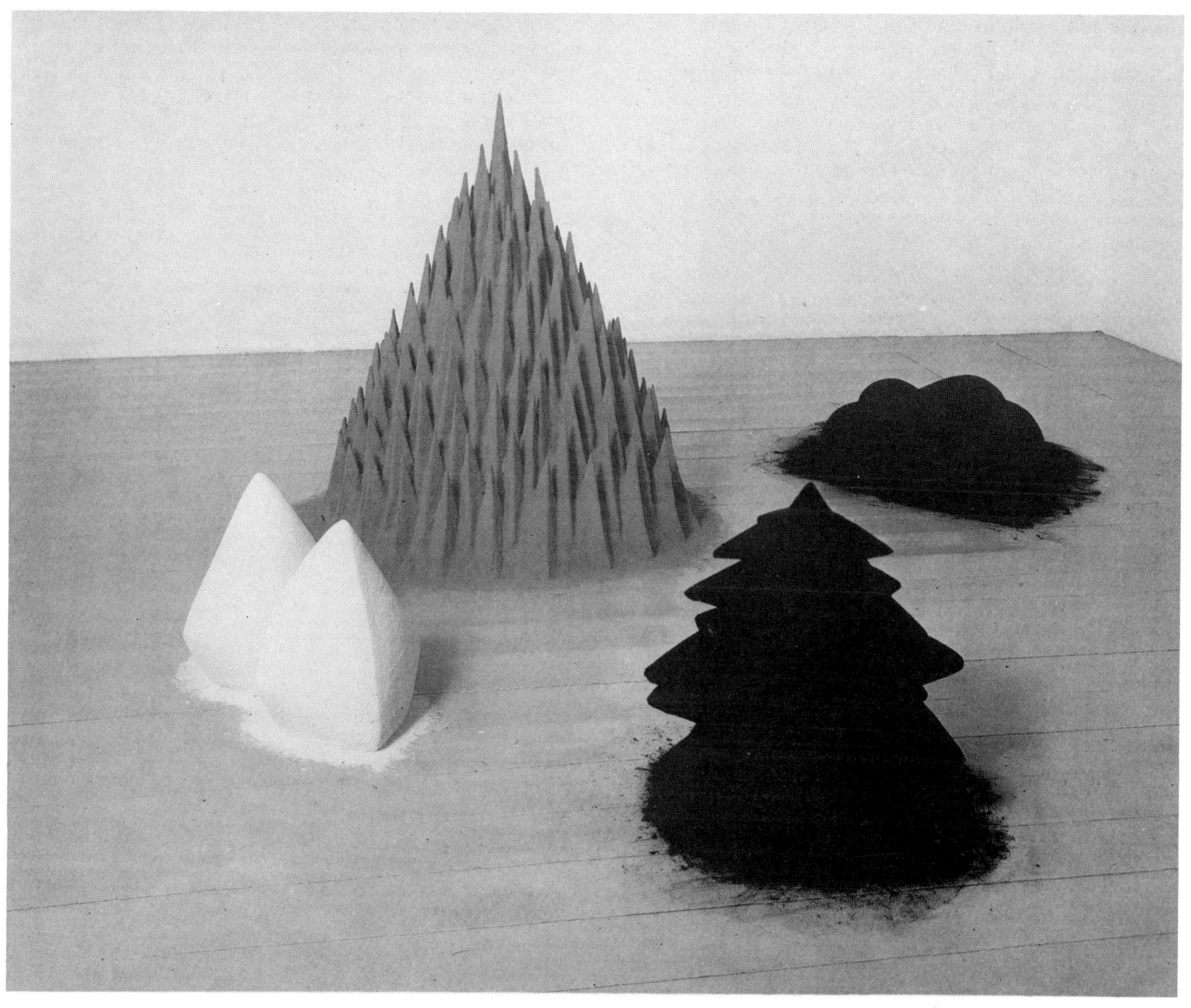

White Sand, Red Millet and many Flowers
1982

mixed media
101 x 241.5 x 217.4cms
Arts Council of Great Britain
photo credit: Prudence Cuming Associates London

ANISH KAPOOR

"[A] noted philosopher who enjoyed provoking rabbis and theologians by using dialectical evidence to demonstrate the non-existence of God . . . arrived in Berditchev to find Rebbe Levi-Yitzhak in deepest meditation. Suddenly, without preamble, the Rebbe looked straight into his eyes and said gently: 'And what if it were true after all? Tell me, and what if it were true?' The philosopher later confessed that this question had moved and troubled him more than all the affirmations and arguments he had ever heard before or since."

The Rebbe never really dismissed the heresy. After meeting the philosopher he reconsidered his faith. Hitherto disregarded strengths and weaknesses occurred to him. After this things would never be the same again. Not better or worse. Just different.

In the second half of the 1960's a new talking-point arose: the possibility that art could exist unencumbered by an art-*object*. For more than a decade the doctrine of "dematerialization" remained a heresy. Anish Kapoor's response was to review the assumptions of formalism in the light of this provocative new contention. His sculpture became a continuing meditation on intuition and knowledge, spirit and substance. In its mature form, from about 1981 onwards, it confirmed Kapoor's status not as a neo-formalist nor a late postminimalist but as a post-conceptual artist. His decision-making has been informed by two assumptions: a Romantic bias and a complex exoticism.

Kapoor's early Romanticism seems to have been based on a mystique of the object. In 1977 he divided a space with a gauze curtain on which

Untitled
1982

bonded earth, polystyrene pigment
10 x 10 x 10 feet
304.8 x 304.8 x 304.8cms
Van Abben, Eindhoven
photo credit: Lisson Gallery, London

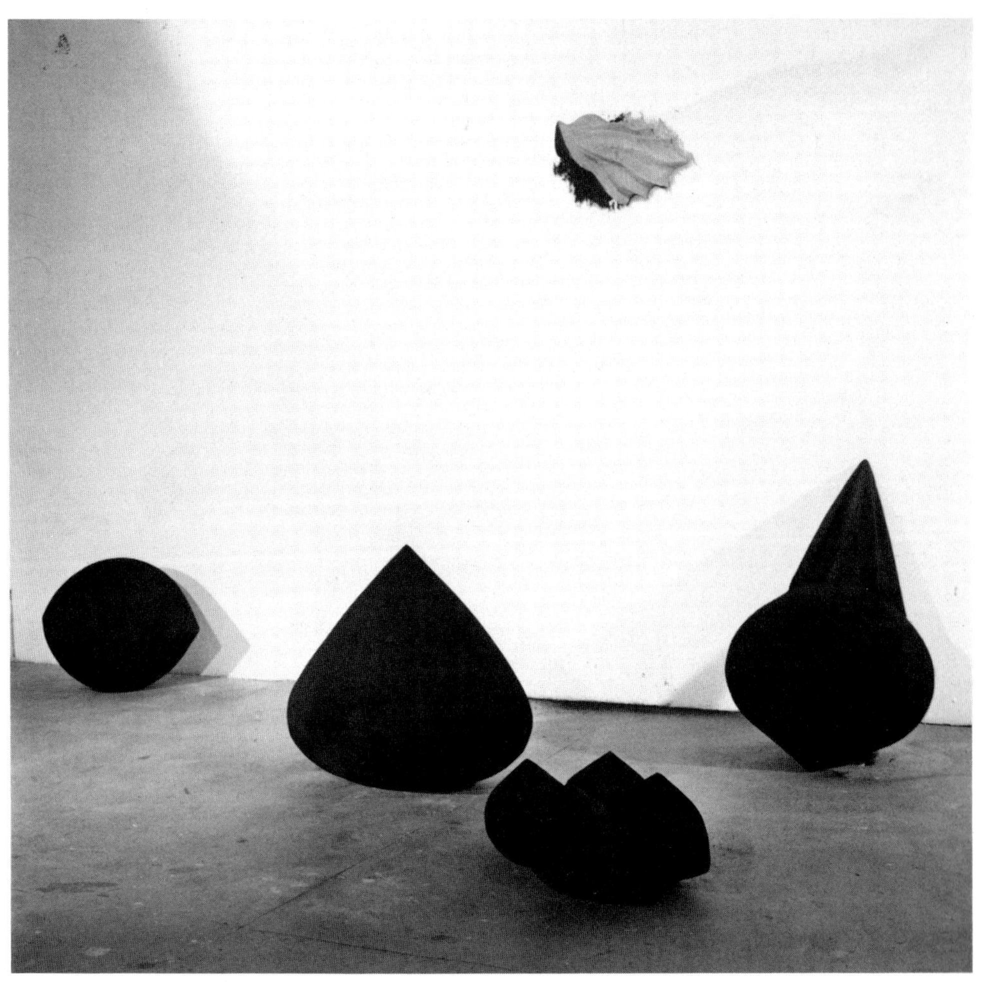

Drawings
1984

charcoal & chalk on paper
9½ x 16 feet
289.6 x 487.7cms

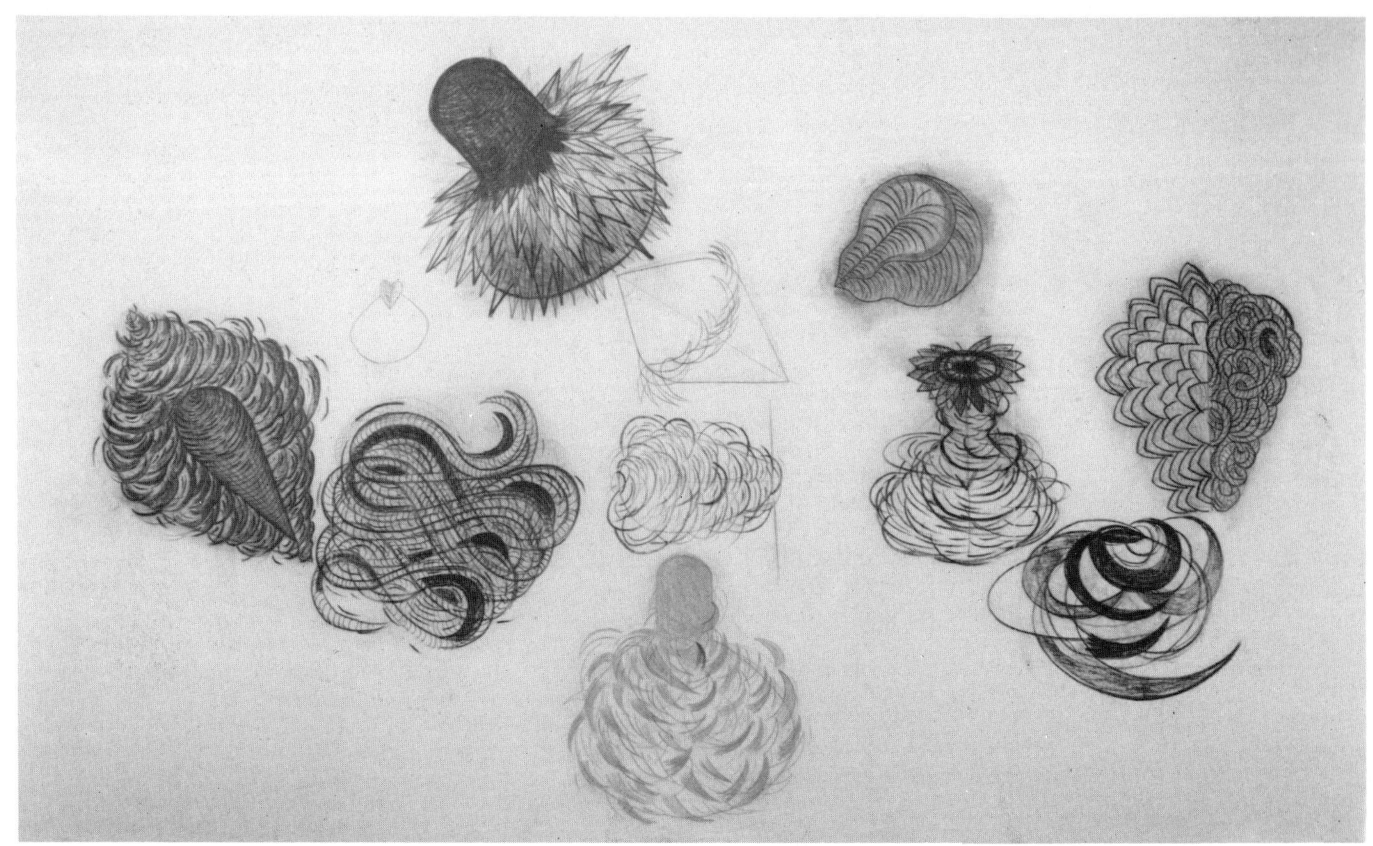

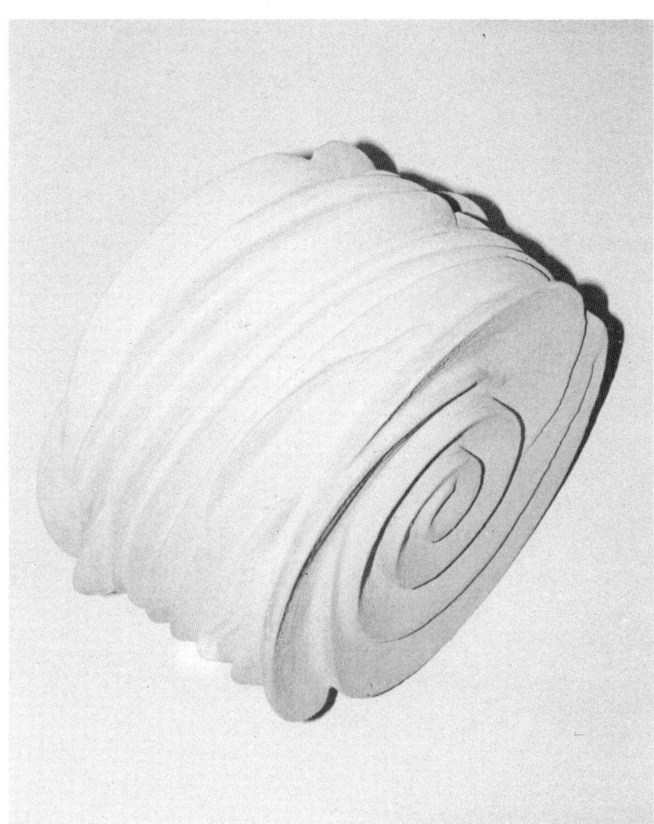

Untitled
1983
63 x 30 x 30cms

expressionist marks were inscribed. In front of it lay
scattered plaster fragments while behind it were
shelves bearing nine bowls. While past and future
states of the objects were displayed the emotions
from which it derived and the debris it would
become, the idea of showing its present existence
as no more than a dim vision, made this a study of
inspiration, invoked in the installation itself by a
repeated mechanical sound half-way between a
production line and an animal call.

Half Indian, Kapoor altered his working methods in
1979 when, after one of his periodic visits there, he
began pressing raw pigment into shapes which
alluded to classical Indian architecture and art. In
time this technique altered; units or groups were
carved out of polystyrene, pigment was attached,
then applied with a brush and scattered like a halo
around each element. Later still, colour was bonded
into the surface itself, holes appeared and forms
became increasingly assymmetrical. Before
concluding that the work is now less obviously
"Indian" it must be asked how Indian it ever was.
Could it be that for Kapoor orientalism is a way of
adopting a split language? Or of insisting on an
opacity which for Westerners is a characteristic
response to the Orient? Certainly a constant
emphasis on surface is essential to his thinking. To
understand why, it is necessary to examine that act
of attention he brings about.

The vivid colour simultaneously affirms and denies.
As forms lose their outlines and shadows are
eradicated, normal spatial co-ordinates are
suspended momentarily and the eye is unable to
judge the position of a solid. Gravity loses its power;
elements stand or hang effortlessly from walls or
ceilings. What they are made of is also in doubt; the
skin seems to exist independently, a thin shield over
empty space. Did they arrive at their shapes by
some act of extrusion? Recently, as holes appear,
there is a suggestion that matter has been flung into
place by rotation. And like all the metaphors Kapoor
offers, we accept it because it offers the prospect
of somehow understanding the work. These are
forms with no past or future. Immaculate, distant,
with surfaces which discourage touch, the pieces
after 1981 show no sign of making. They simply
occur. And although they refer to breasts, tongues,
phalli, pods and other organic shapes, their degree
of abstraction is so high that they finally look
unnatural. Like the tension between attraction and
camouflage, Kapoor's studied artifice characterises
his work. Yet this extraversion is designed to bring
about a seclusion of thought in his viewers. The
eroticism of the shapes, the air of worldly luxury, by
no means challenge this retirement. On the
contrary, they are a reward; in Kapoor theatre is a
stimulus to call into doubt both reason and the
reports of the senses.

After his return from India in 1979, Kapoor said he
no longer wanted to make art; instead he wanted to
make "belief". Frustrating full perception, his art
shifts from spectacle to presence, and that
presence is the sole key to a state in which
ratiocination of any kind is suspended, the
inadequacy of the faculties is accepted and the
viewer advances humbly towards faith. Kapoor's is
a devotional art in which concrete objects become
tokens of a concealed, desired principle. Yet even
strategies of concealment can be discarded; a
recent piece, *Hole and Vessel*, rejects the
polarisation of total revelation versus total secrecy.
One skin, neither completely evident nor completely
hidden, forms an empty pot made up of male —
female oppositions. Homage is also paid to rotation,
an unending dispersal of force. If the pot is a
metaphor for inspiration, the rotating solids a
metaphor for some eternally expended power, it
must be stressed that they are *only* metaphor, just
as materiality is a wretched expedient in Kapoor.
His complete "fragments" are the names of God,
celebrations of His manifold ways of revealing
Himself. And "God" is but one more way of
describing the indescribable: creation itself,
constantly embodied yet inexhaustible.

In the face of heresy, Kapoor opted for a Romantic
elision, regarding a world without objects as a world
without worship. A slender reply? The doubting
patriarch had only a repeated question with which
to arm himself against the ravages of reason. It was
enough.

Stuart Morgan

1. Elie Wiesel *Souls on Fire and Somewhere a Master*
    Harmondsworth: Penguin 1984, 82.

2. Marco Livingstone "Feeling into Form", *Anish Kapoor*
    Liverpool: Walker/Lyon: Nouveau Musee 1983, 12.

Anish Kapoor
Hole & Vessel
1983

mixed media
60 x 150 x 240cms
private collection
courtesy: Lisson Gallery London

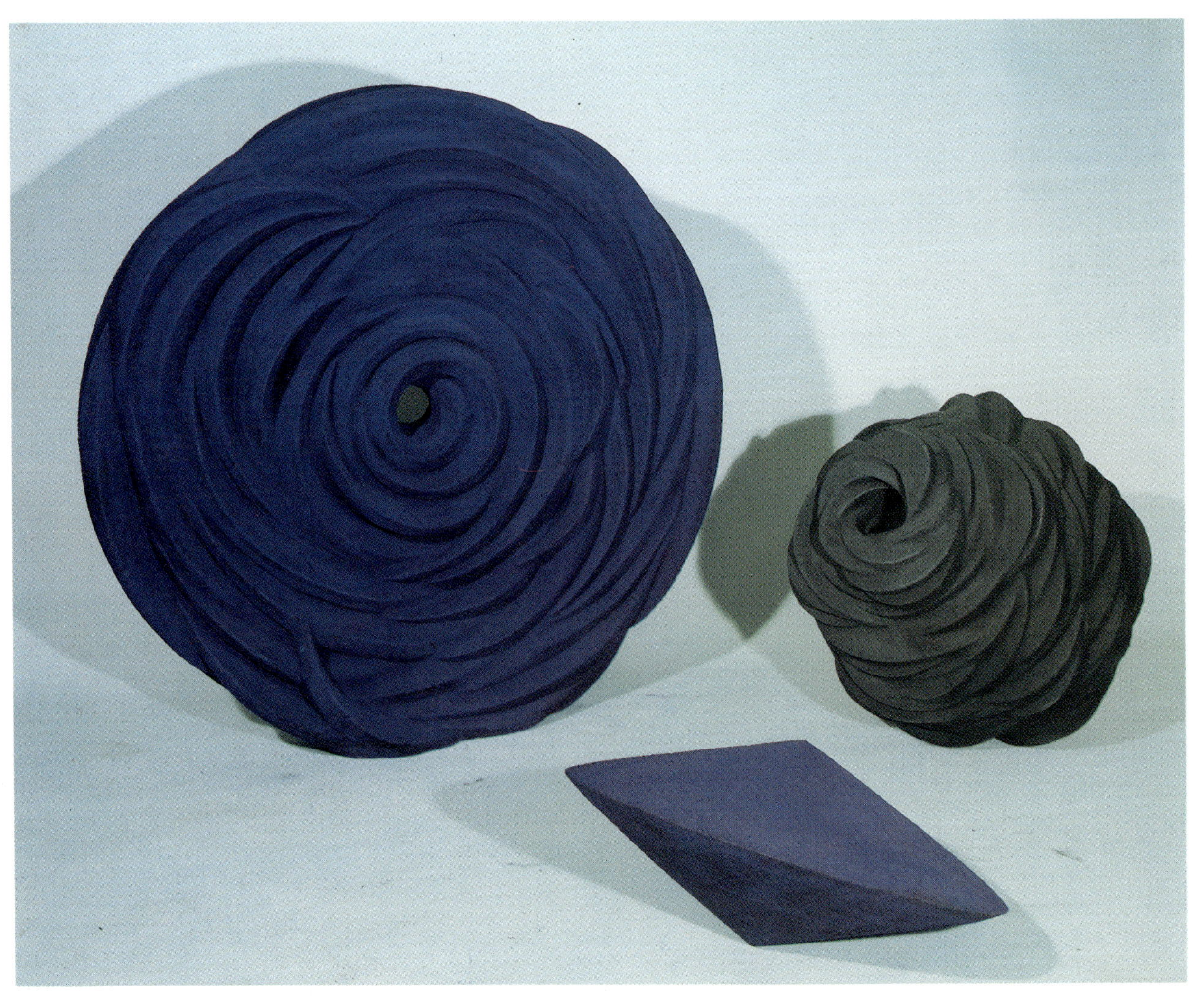

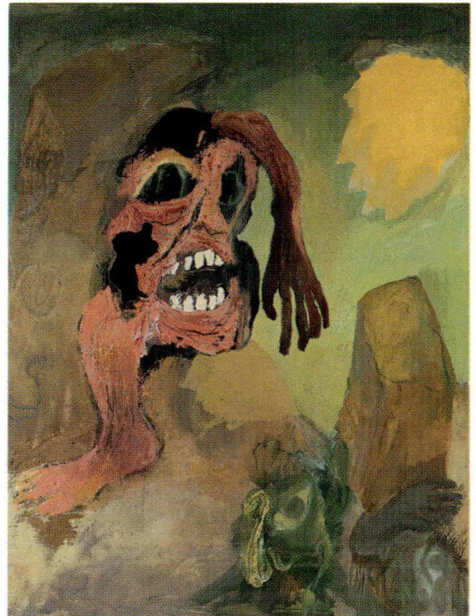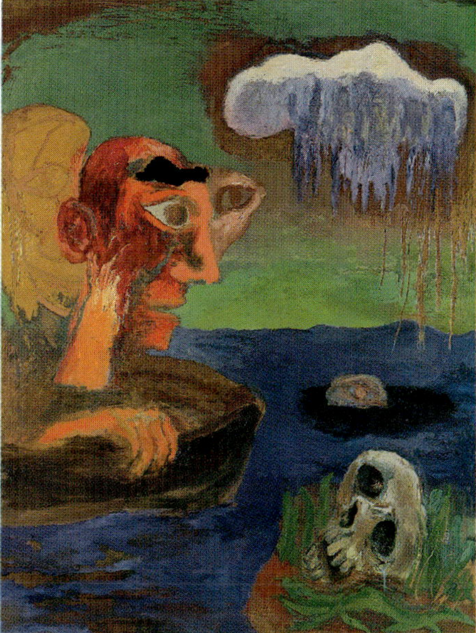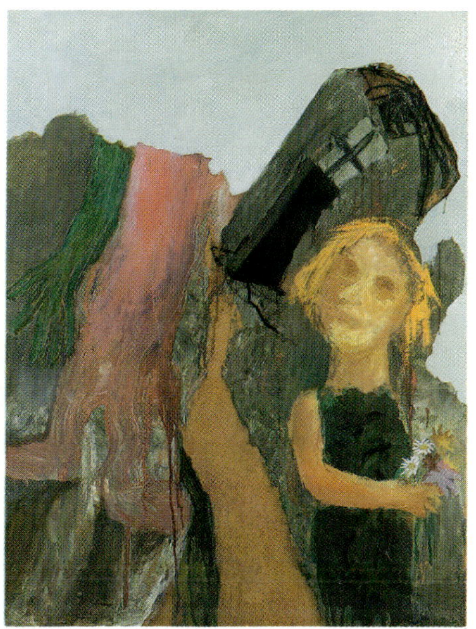

Triptych: The Cry; Rain on the Sea; The Street
1982-3

40 x 105ins
114 x 266.7cms
oil & acrylic on board
private collection New York, courtesy Nicola Jacobs Gallery, London
photo credit: Prudence Cuming Associates London

KEN KIFF

Ken Kiff was both a formal abstract and a figurative painter until around 1966. He first came to the general attention of British art viewers in 1970, when Norbert Lynton included him in his selection for that distinguished annual event, sadly now discontinued, 'Critic's Choice'. His paintings then were much as you see them now, except less specific and detailed in their imagery: a naked little man with a big head, slightly childlike or foetal in effect — an overgrown child like most of us — wandering around an undefined landscape of misty radiance, surveying his strange abode. (Birth in a human body is a shock from which some of us never quite recover). But the unusual element was the optimistic colour.

Kiff's art emerged into an art environment where the figurative alternatives to the dominant abstract art were not to be seriously considered by the British art world in general for nearly another ten years. So it was another three years before Kiff's work got another public airing, at a big exhibition in Liverpool, 'Magic and Strong Medicine' organised by Norbert Lynton, shown in Rochdale just outside Manchester, an area with a strong humane tradition. But it was already apparent that an individual artist had set out on the precarious path of artistic-wise innocence; all the more precarious in our knowing times, when many of an artist's deepest visual memories will inevitably be of images from other artists.

So at first for the critics it was difficult to 'place' Kiff's work; it was not just primitive art, or naive art, or expressionist art, or surrealist art, yet it comprehended all of these. It certainly was not very British (although Kiff, despite that surname, certainly is); expressionism was very foreign to the British art temperament then. It evoked the existential sincerities of early Kokoschka, without the terrible pain; while the radiant, optimistic colours emerging into form evoked the watercolours of Nolde; there was a kinship with the joyful intimacies of Chagall; perhaps a touch of Redon's power with colour too. And — though I'm not trying to stake out a claim for Kiff as an 'honorary Australian' — those who had witnessed the emergence of Sidney Nolan and Arthur Boyd sensed something akin to their painterly, evolving imagery.

In fact, Kiff himself sees his art as grounded in Cubism and its possibilities; and looks to Klee as a model precursor among artists, in the way that he looked for and found new means to approach reality. And he enjoys Chagall as a kindred spirit. However, in discussion about his work, not only does Kiff, like Klee, link the image, in every sentence, entirely to the medium; he will frequently begin by pointing out the particular colour of an area of the painting or of an image that emerges from it, and constantly revert to mention of the colour; it is evidently as deeply an aspect of the 'seed' of the painting as subject or form. Kiff took to using tempera on a white gesso ground in his paintings, so that the radiance of the colour was enhanced because the light passing through it was reflected back again from the gesso; also, because he can 'follow impulse', in rubbing down, reworking and repainting as often as he wishes. However, it should also be noted that he also has in hand a continuous 'Sequence' as he calls it, of painting on paper, now running into hundreds.

Interpretation of paintings is fraught with peril: it is so easy to focus attention on some feature, detail, or form, thus unconsciously demoting, discrediting or disregarding the remainder, which includes the whole emotional ground of neighbouring form and colour, indeed the very whole itself. And this is all the more true of paintings where the colour is neither local and literal, nor subsequent and applied; but rather, part of the whole emotional integrity and being of the painting, of its total transmitted consciousness.

What then, does the viewer new to Kiff's work need to be told, if anything? Or at least, reminded of?

First — if anything — that wholeness, and within this, balance, is an expressed aim and concern of Kiff's paintings. If some detail of imagery in a painting produces the 'shock-horror-concern' reaction that newspaper headlines aim at, then expect that this disturbance will have its compensations somewhere else in the work. It is this concern with wholeness which has evolved the single painting *Cry* into a *Triptych*: in the evolution of that first painting there came a point where there developed a sort of 'overspill' of emotional content, which demanded a further rectangular field of action for its expression, and then another. (There was even a possibility at one point that the work would be a four-frame; but the fourth painting took off as a self-sufficient work.) Had *Cry* remained a single painting on its own, then some areas — for instance, the yellow cloud on the right, forming from its elements in the ether of the mind — would have developed further, emerging into more specific imagery.

The second thing to bear in mind is that Kiff's paintings are not 'calculated' beforehand. They evolve from that seed of medium-subject-colour I have mentioned; and their creative evolution surprises Kiff as much as it surprises other viewers. This can be seen in operation (when it is pointed out

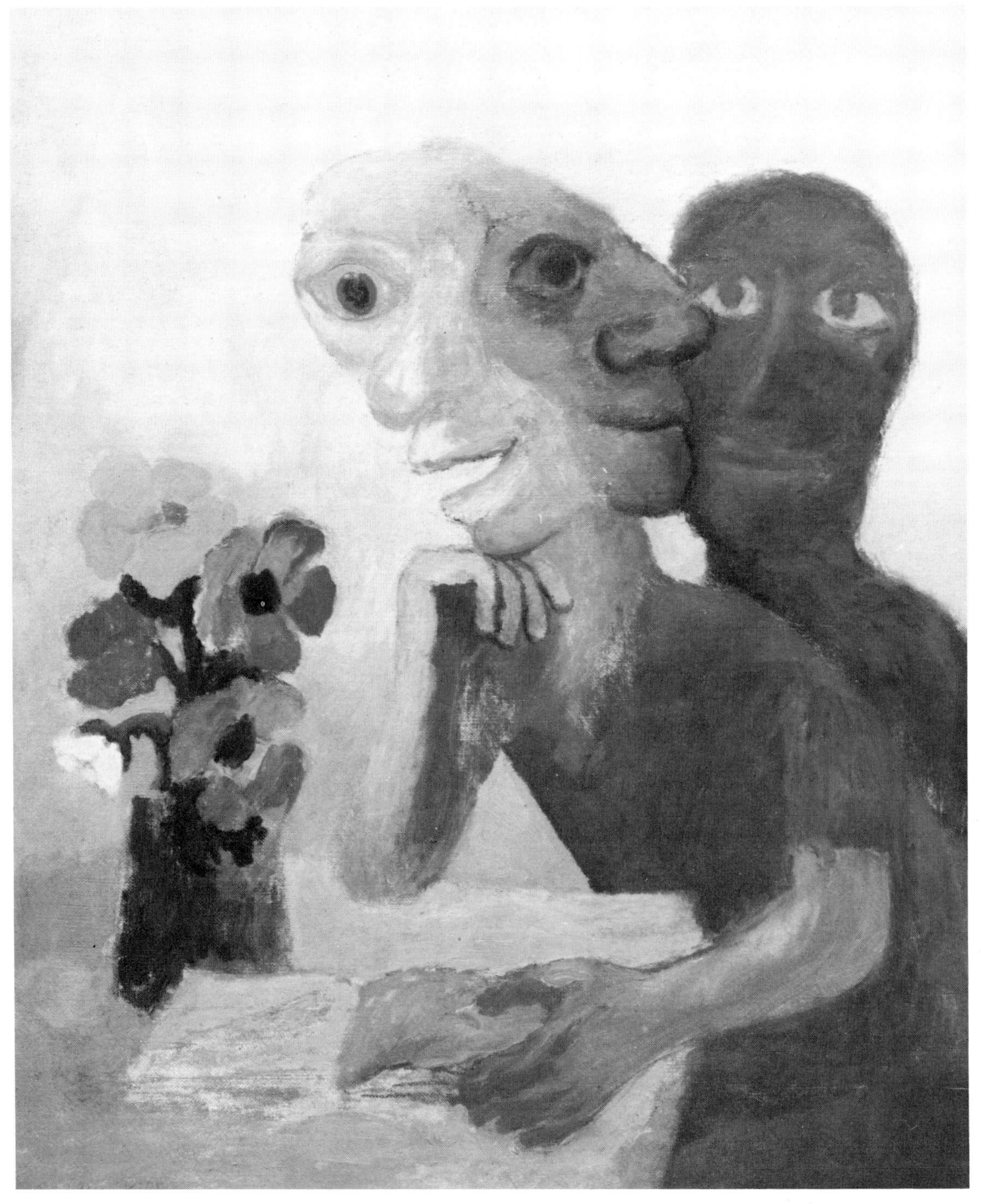

Blue Shadow
1980

40 x 32¼ins
101.5 x 82.3cms
oil on board
Nicola Jacobs Gallery

Green Man
1977

53 x 48ins
134.6 x 121.9cms
oil on board
Nicola Jacobs Gallery

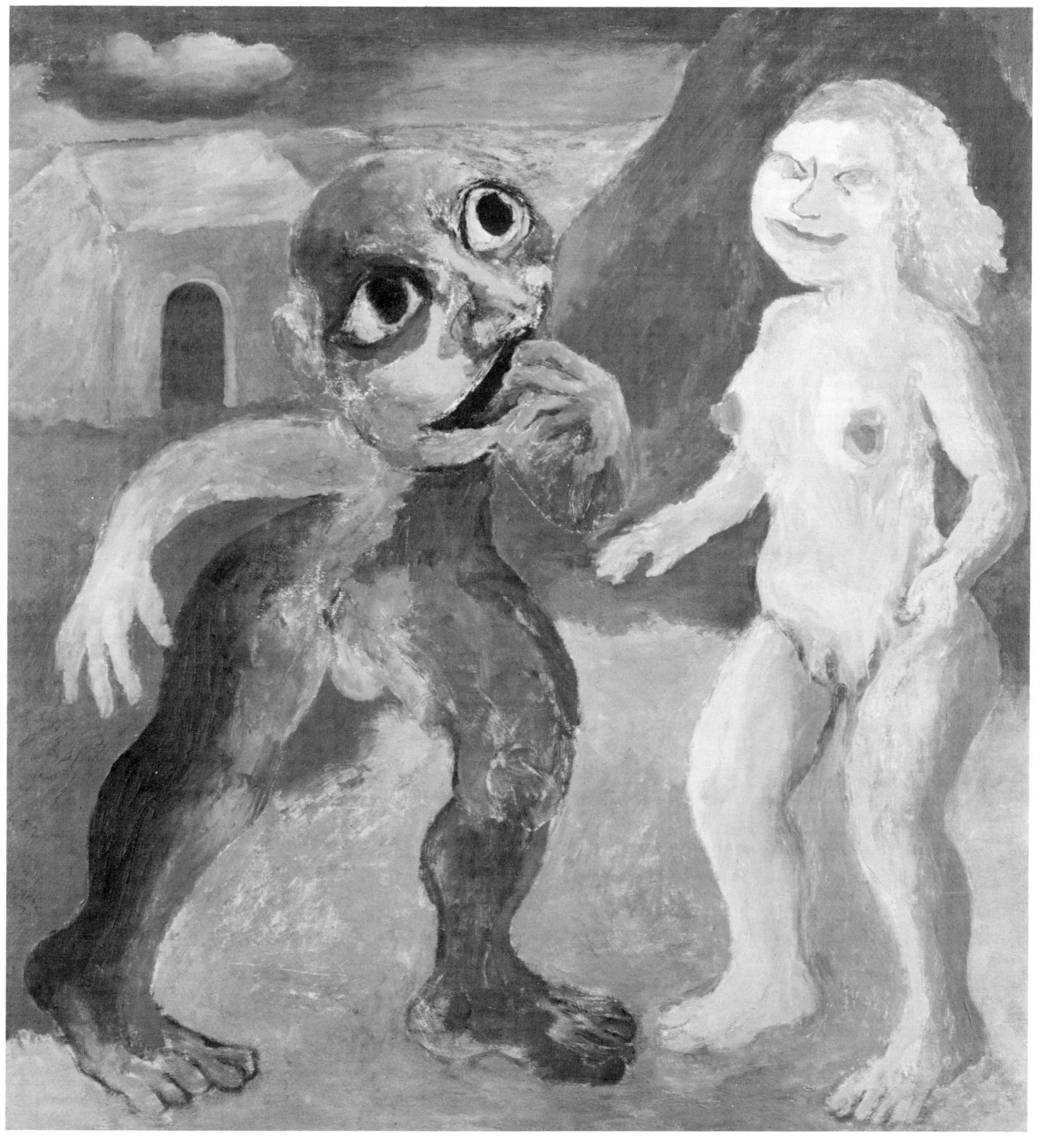

by Kiff) most clearly in *Blue Shadow*: a triangular initial imagery of some emotional seed — self-delight in contemplation? — has found its 'overspill' of emotional content moving towards the right behind the physical figure, developing first a second but opposite face, then a blue shadow, which itself acquires a substantial presence. In other works, evolution may require resolution by disappearance: a painting not in the current exhibition, *Two People*, originally contained three figures, one of which finally resolved into the other two.

The dangers of isolating elements in a Kiff painting are shown by the painting *Green Man*: not unlike Picasso, Kiff has painted a number of pictures where a man of various shape, mood and sophistication of form, looks admiringly at a beautiful woman. In his versions, the whimsical shape of the man should not be isolated from his 'landscape' colouring (evoking memories perhaps of those green men who stalk through folk-tales; Kiff illustrated such a book, by commission, in 1977, with memorable freedom and effect.) And a now almost invisible part of the totality of this painting is that it actually started life as a 'street painting'.

These evolutions can be of long duration: Kiff has several hundred works in hand at any one time. These may turn out to have themes (which for him include such elements as 'yellow hills'), or be in sequence — either way, not by prior intention.

But, wonderfully, he is not plagued in his journey of self-discovery by conscious repetition. He talks of his works with interested surprise, as of living things. *A Talk with the Psychoanalyst* is one of five — and probably the last he will make — in a sporadic sequence on this theme. When he first began his inner exploration, some of the images that emerged frightened him so much that he consulted a psychoanalyst about them. Although some of the most ferocious images (such as *Woman Affecting the Everyday* of 1983, a *Mother Kali* figure dripping menstrual blood) have been recent, Kiff feels that the need for such consultation has probably now disappeared. Refreshingly if tantalisingly, the Jungian psychoanalyst he consulted feels that Kiff's imagery is of no direct concern to him as analyst, and certainly not prime material for analytic dissection. This amicable relationship should be borne in mind when looking at his painting *as a whole*: there are depths of reflection about roles and wholeness to be found in this picture about self-revelation.

Confronted for the first time by the work of one of the many hundreds of thousands of artists who lay claim to our attention nowadays, I suspect we will all have the same initial question: ''Do I trust him/her?'' That's for each of us to say. Kiff's honesty, sincerity, integrity, and the artistic delights of his works, are clearly evident. His exemplary 'journey into the interior' is a contribution to the art, and the self-understanding, of his times. De Kooning has said that ''Every painting brings news.'' The news from Kiff is of the colours of the soul, in the light of the self. To feel that an artist is a valued companion through one's own life is a good feeling.

Michael Shepherd

Talking with the Psychoanalyst: Night Sky no. 113

32 x 54ins
81.3 x 137.2cms
acrylic on paper
Ed Wolf London

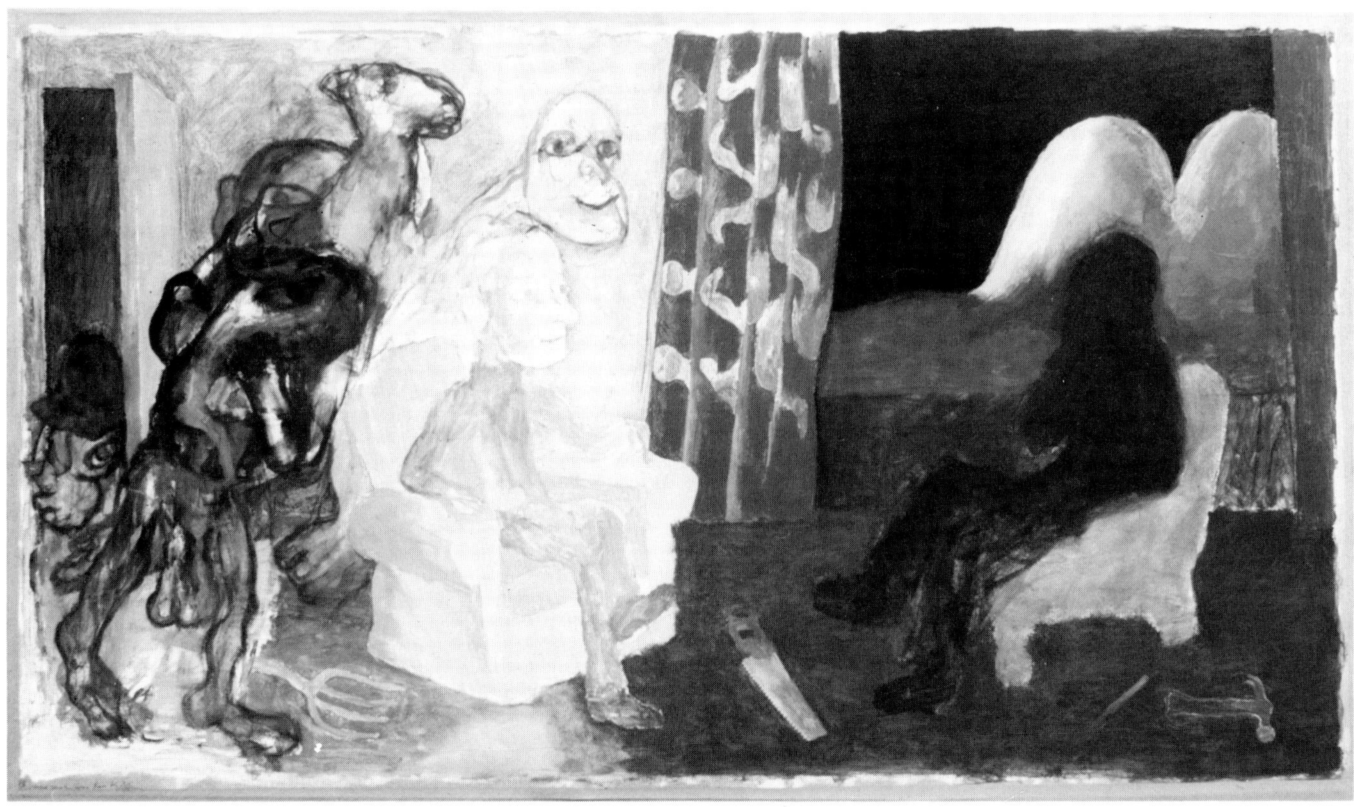

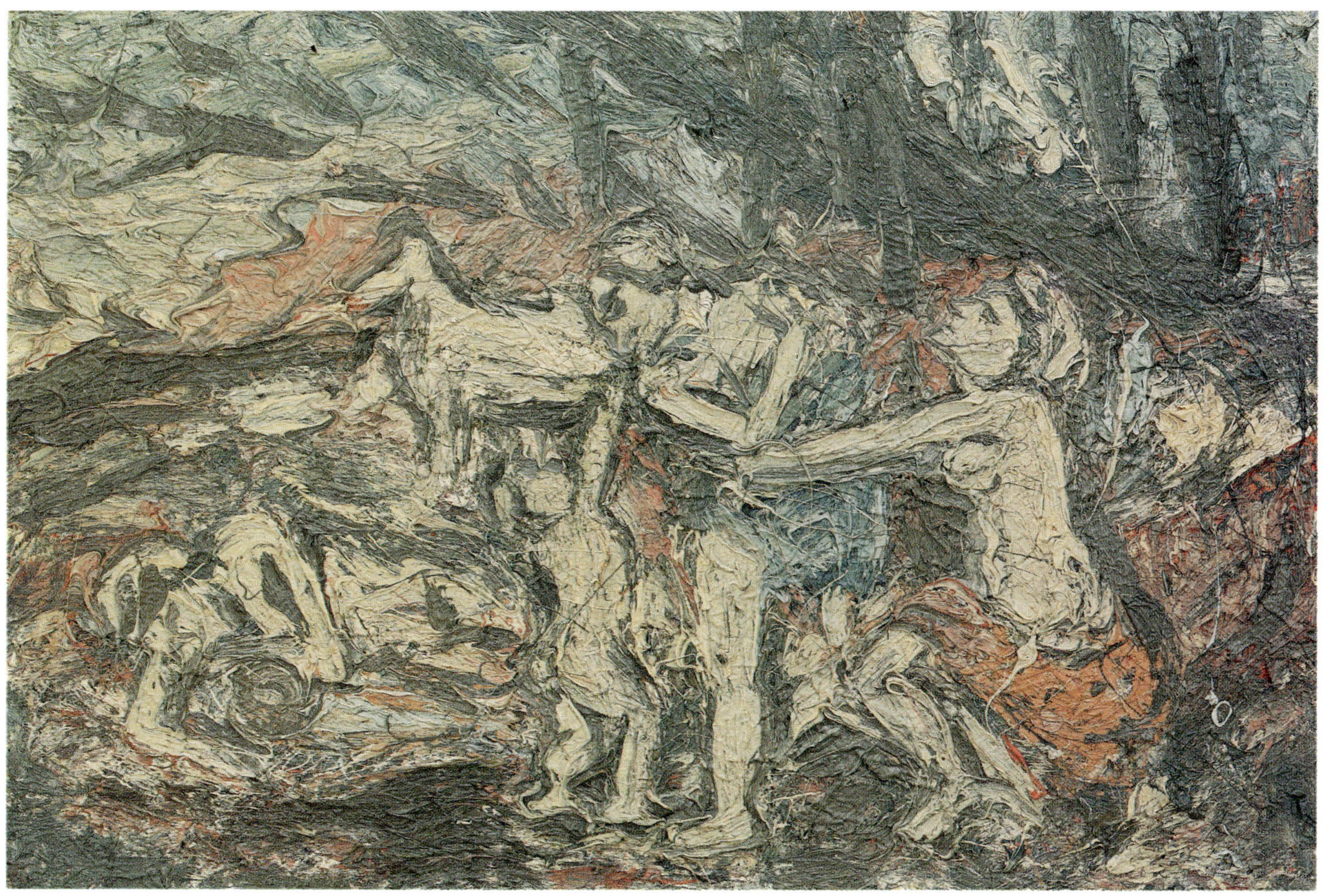

From Cephalus & Aurora by Poussin No. 3.
1983

oil on board
36½ x 51ins
93 x 129.5cms
Art Gallery of New South Wales

LEON KOSSOFF

Although Leon Kossoff began exhibiting at London's Beaux Arts Gallery as long ago as 1957 it is only in the 1980's that his work has begun to receive widespread critical comment or to be included in major touring exhibitions of British art, like this one.

Such acclaim is overdue. Kossoff is among the most consistent and relentlessly dedicated of British painters: more significantly, he has also made some of the finest pictures to have been produced in Britain over the last quarter of a century, pictures like *Children's Swimming Pool, Autumn Afternoon, 1971*, or *Two Seated Figures No. 2*, of 1980 — both of which are now in the permanent collection of London's Tate Gallery.

Leon Kossoff was born in 1926 of Jewish immigrant parents in a long demolished building in City Road, London, not far from St. Paul's Cathedral. Ever since he can remember, Kossoff has drawn his father. Kossoff Senior, who died recently, was a baker: he began by pushing a barrow through London streets, but worked up to a small chain of high quality shops. Memories of his childhood, and the topography of the city in which he has spent so much of his life, were to play an important part in Kossoff's painting.

Between 1945 and 1948, Kossoff served in the army in France, Belgium, Holland and Germany. When he had finished his National Service, he began to study art, first at St. Martin's and later at the Royal College. His early work had something in common with those spontaneous eruptions of expressionist painting which occurred immediately after the Second World War in cities as widely dispersed as New York, Chicago, Paris, London, and Stockholm. At this time a number of isolated individuals and groups of artists struggled, in very different ways, to make pictorial and aesthetic sense out of their personal despair, and their experience of a torn and injured world.

The ways in which they did so were, of course, inflected by the particular cultural traditions which shaped and formed them. Often after a full day at art school, Kossoff would travel to the Borough Polytechnic in south London to study under David Bomberg. Bomberg was to have a formative influence on Kossoff. Having been involved in the pioneering days of Modernism at the beginning of the century, even to the extent of exhibiting with the Vorticists, he underwent a revulsion against the whole Modernist enterprise. At a later stage, he had begun to develop a new way of looking, and of depicting what he saw and felt.

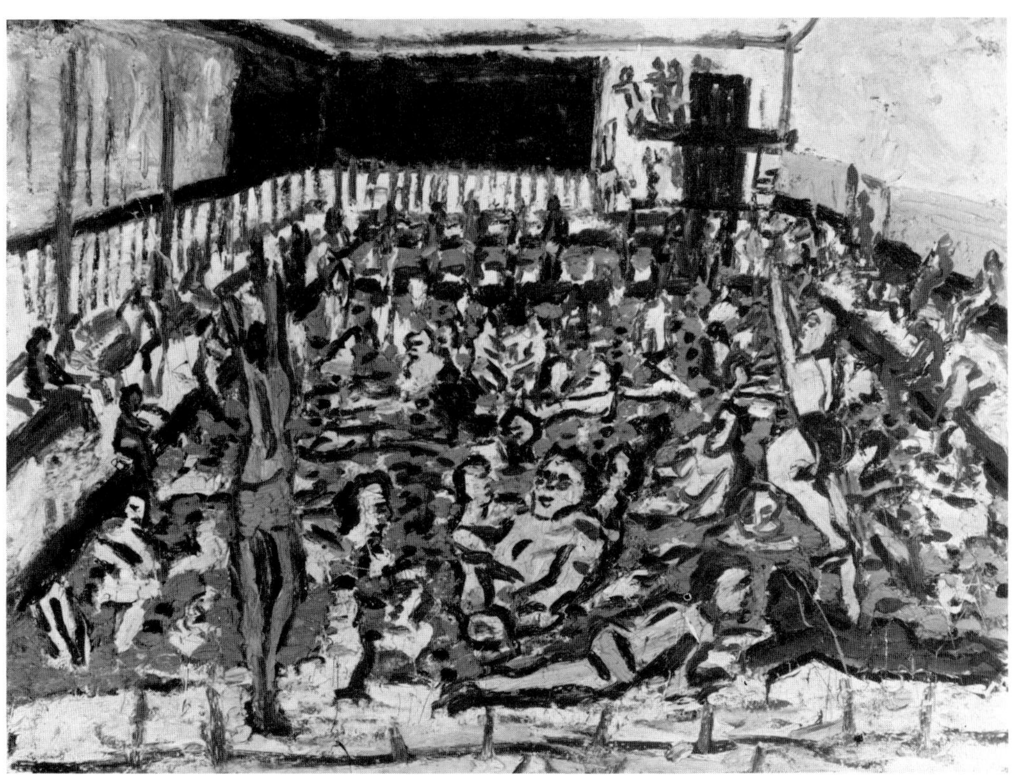

Children's swimming pool:
autumn afternoon
1971

oil on board
66 x 84ins
167.6 x 213.4cms
collection: Tate Gallery, London

Bomberg was an inspiring teacher of drawing. Although neglected and culturally isolated, he advocated an heroic commitment to the pursuit of art. In his later years, he taught his students to search for 'the spirit in the mass'; although he believed in an exacting, empirical study of the object in the world, he held that on its own the eye was 'a stupid organ'. He believed in an imaginative and affective response to human and natural form.

Bomberg gathered around him an exceptional group of dedicated and talented students. "Though I hardly knew him, writes Kossoff, it was Bomberg's presence as a man and a painter and his uncompromising commitment to his personal vision that I learnt from him, rather than his actual teaching. Bomberg was a man who stood alone and took risks, his teaching was not in a way of drawing, but for me an encouragement, in a way of relating to the world as a painter."

In a rare note which he contributed to the catalogue for his 1973 exhibitions at Fischer Fine Art, Kossoff wrote revealingly about his preoccupation with certain bomb and building sites, excavations, demolitions, railways, a children's swimming pool, and, subsequently, a tube station ticket office, in London. 'The strange ever changing light, the endless streets and the shuddering feel of the sprawling city', he explained, 'lingers in my mind like a faintly glimmering memory of a long forgotten, perhaps never experienced childhood, which, if rediscovered and illuminated, would ameliorate the pain of the present'.

In addition to these landscapes, Kossoff has consistently drawn and painted from the human figure. Again here too we can see his unique combination of attention to the living presence of a person in the world, and profound imaginative transformation. Kossoff has always worked from

individuals personally close to him. He once said that he had drawn and painted his father 'ever since I can remember'. For his seated and reclining nudes, he tends to work with the same woman, often in almost daily sessions which continue over a period of years. Recently his drawing has been haunted by images of Pauline and Fidelma. Kossoff once told me that he draws from the model for at least a year before he risks starting making a painting of her.

Kossoff's technique characteristically intermeshes subjective and objective elements. The paint you actually see lying thickly on the surface is usually laid down quickly: often in a matter of hours. Kossoff lays the board on the floor, and the disposition of the paint across the surface owes much to rapidly performed bodily movements. Nonetheless it is also informed by the precise, obsessive discipline of all those drawings from the object which preceded the act of painting. Kossoff combines the rhythmic expressionism of, say, Jackson Pollock with all the tightly controlled, empirical exactitude of a painter like William Coldstream, who developed a system of measured drawing at the Slade. (This is not just a 'nice' observation: Kossoff's teacher, David Bomberg, was, like William Coldstream, a pupil of the great British teacher of empirical drawing, Henry Tonks.)

But Kossoff's painting is always made under the threat of potential loss, and this does not always resolve itself in the artist's favour. 'And always, the moment before finishing', Kossoff himself has written, 'the painting disappears, sometimes into greyness for ever, or sometimes into a huge heap on the floor to be reclaimed, redrawn and committed to an image which makes itself'.

Kossoff affirms the value of commitment to one's

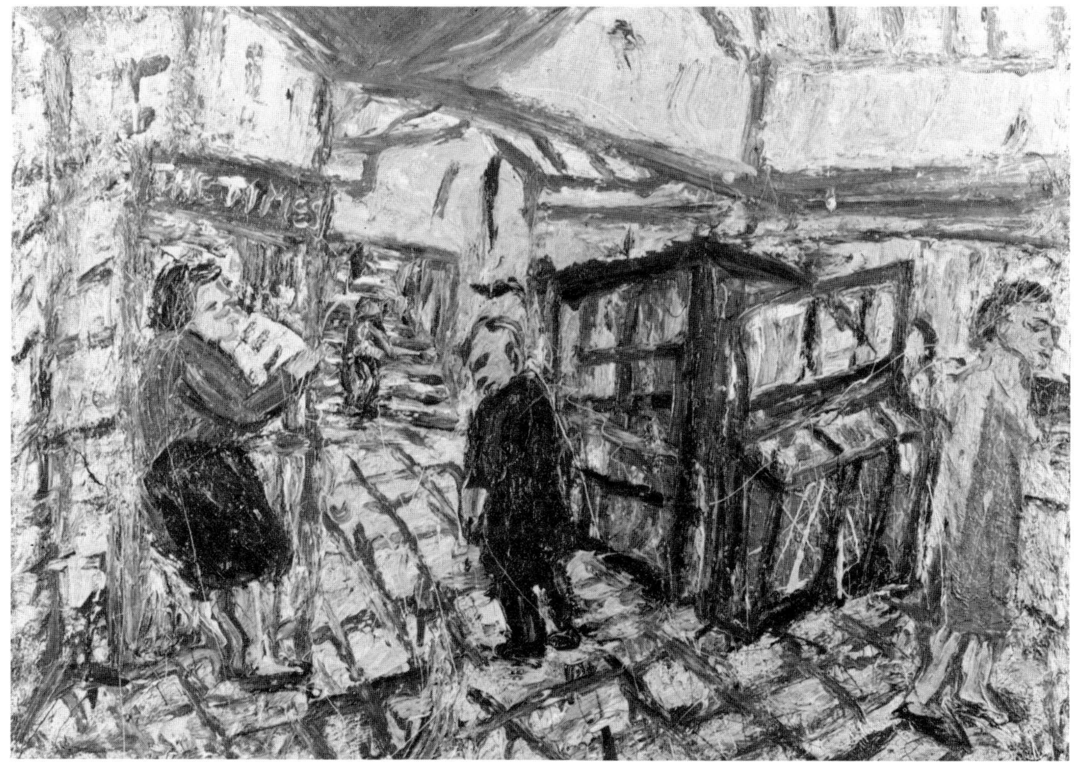

Inside
**Kilburn Underground,
Summer 1983**
1983

oil on board
137,8 x 168,3cms
Saatchi Collection, London

imaginative vision, regardless of current cultural circumstances, or of personal cost. All his works bear witness to his respect for, and mastery of, the skills, disciplines, and traditions of painting, as one of the highest forms of cultural practice. Indeed, he still believes that painting can be the vehicle for the expression of high sentiment.

Many of his pictures — especially those great works based on his ageing parents of which a not entirely satisfactory example is included in this exhibition — are permeated by an undeniable sense of sadness, and awareness of the anguish, frailty and impermanence of life. And yet the energy, intensity, and sensuousness of the way they are painted provides a celebratory transcendence of their subject matter.

For some years now, Kossoff's work has included renderings of certain great masterpieces of the past. For example, he has been drawn to Poussin's great picture, *Cephalus and Aurora*. One of his versions of this work was recently acquired by the Art Gallery of New South Wales, and is included in this exhibition. Kossoff seems preoccupied by paintings like this at least in part because he envies the mythic world upon which these artists could still draw to express and convey their innermost sentiments.

Today, classical myth is effectively opaque to us. The sort of shared symbolic order a religious iconography once provided has also vanished. The artist is compelled to fall back on a private mythology, and to try to externalise from that. He can paint a nude model on a couch, but not Venus; he can depict — as Kossoff recently did — a *Family Party*, but not 'The Holy Family'; he can paint his father, but not God the Father; he can

reveal scenes of a 'long forgotten perhaps never experienced childhood', but not the Holy Land. The danger is, of course, that such images will sink into facticity and particularity: they will end up as just another art school image of a nude woman, or a topographic scene. Kossoff evades this danger entirely. In his work, the element which was once provided by iconography now springs largely out of his expressive handling.

Recently, when I visited his studio, there was a version of Titian's terrifying *The Flaying of Marsyas* leaning against the studio wall. In fact this may turn out to be one of those works which will eventually be consigned into greyness, for ever. Nonetheless, when I saw it, I recognised how there is a real sense in which Kossoff is attempting in our time what Titian did in his. In an uncompromisingly secular way, he is dealing with the psychological and spiritual depth of human experience.

Kossoff's images are dragged from the brink of madness: and yet, in the end, the experience they offer is hopeful — an affirmation. For Kossoff — like Rouault, Soutine, and other true expressionists of the past — offers, through his paintings, an 'other reality', within the existing one. He recaptures a sense of fusion and onement with the world which is usually absent from our adult experience. Thus he creates a kind of 'redemption through form', a hedonistic and *aesthetic* reparation. Perhaps this is the best we can hope for. Certainly, I believe that the way in which Kossoff brings this about in his paintings justifies my belief that he is one of just three, or perhaps four, artists working in Britain today to whom the word 'great' can reasonably be applied.

Peter Fuller

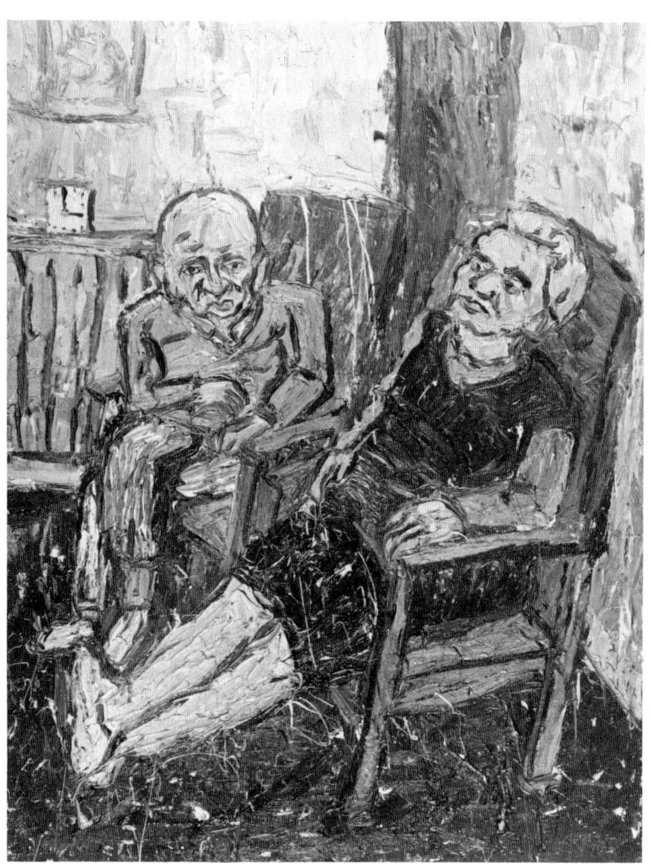

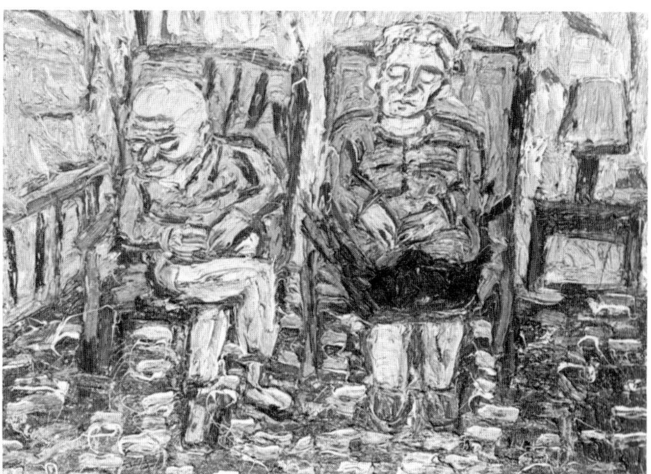

Two Seated Figures No. 2
Spring 1980

oil on board
96 x 72ins
243.8 x 183cms
collection: Tate Gallery, London

Two Seated Figures No. 1
1980

oil on board
48 x 60ins
122 x 152.4cms
Fischer Fine Art London

Family Party,
January 1983

oil on board
66 x 98¼ins
167.6 x 223.6cms

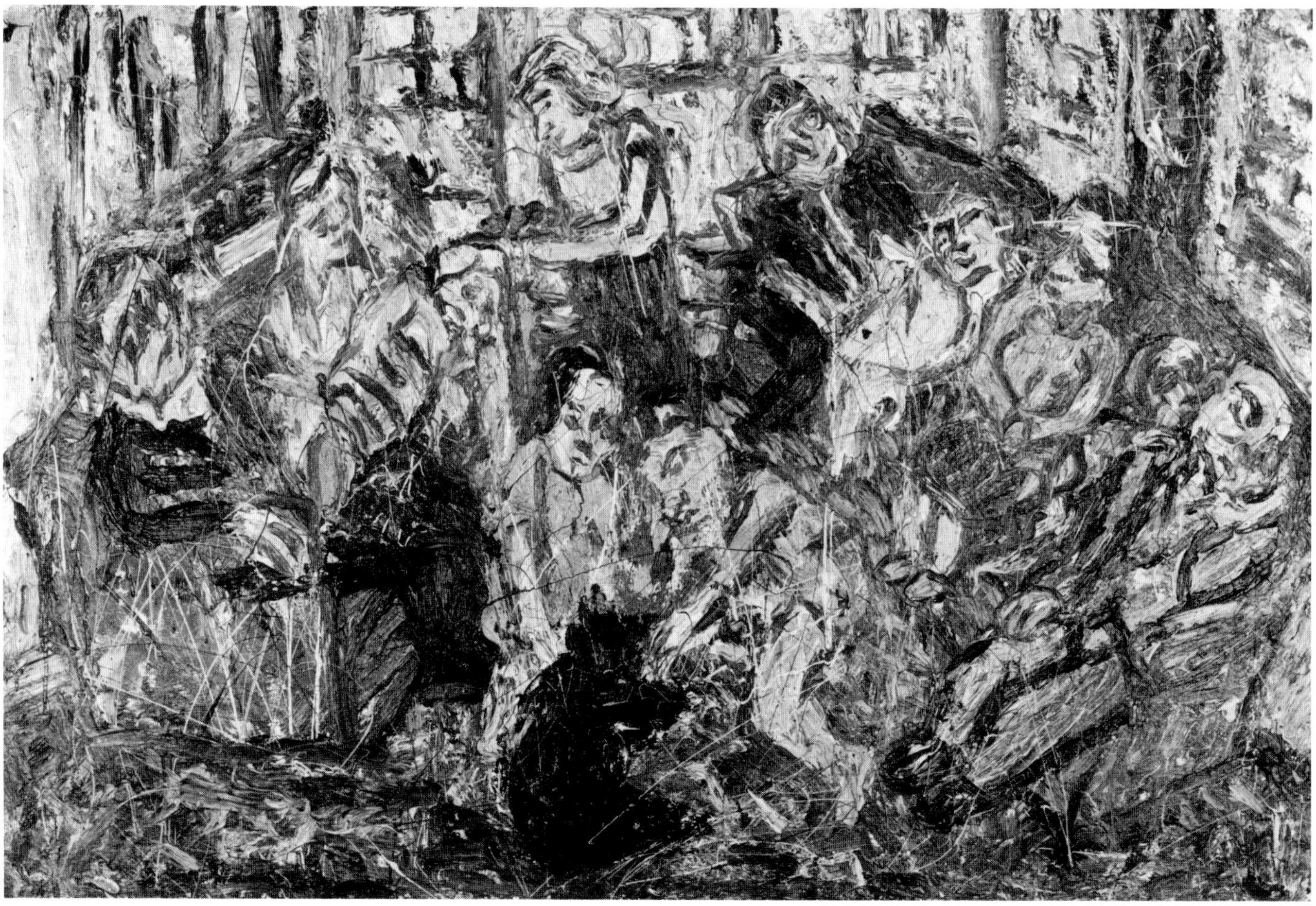

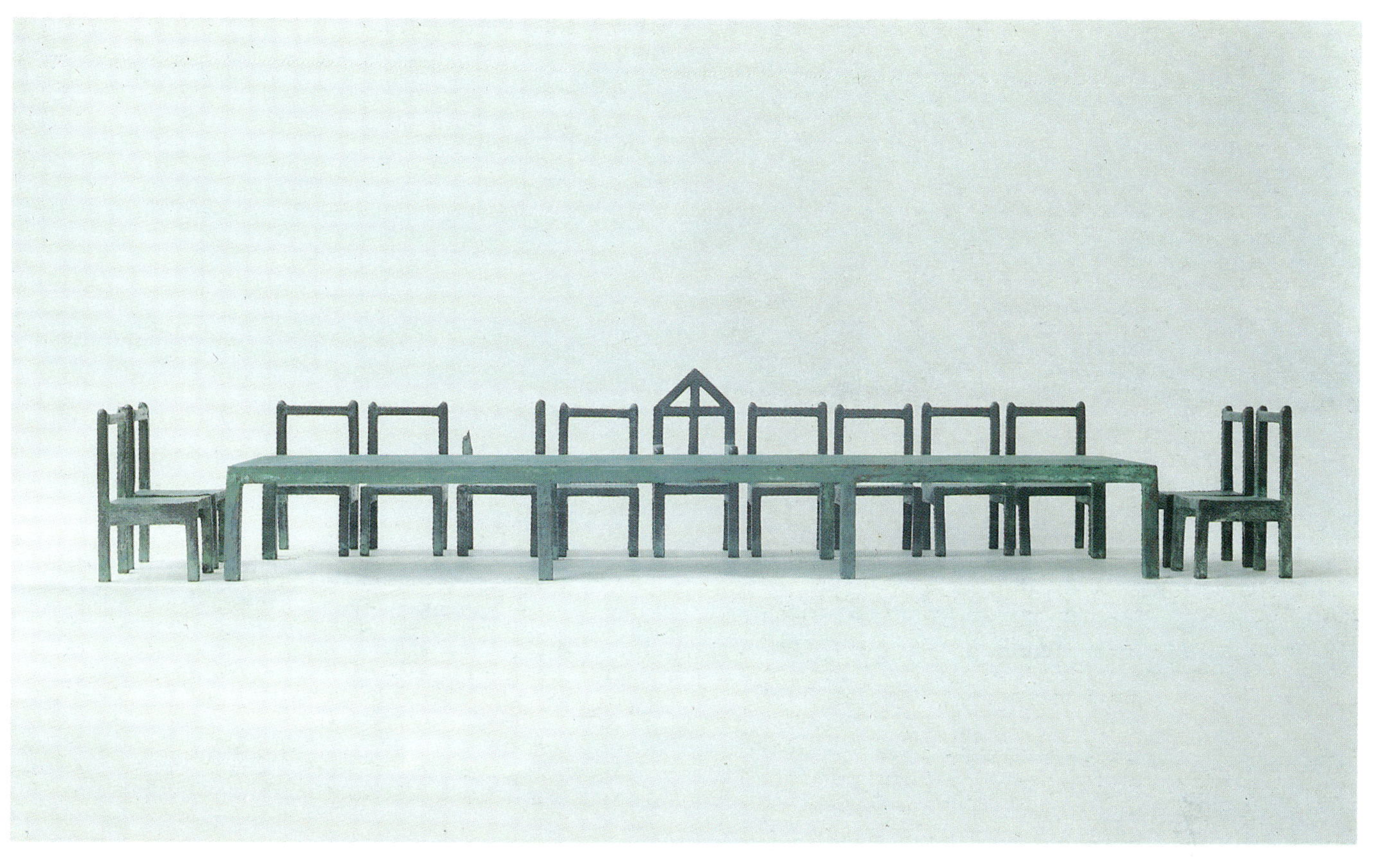

The Last Supper
1984

bronze
81.3 x 20.4 x 10 cms (table)
15.3 x 8.3 x 8.1cms (12 chairs each)
1P.5 x 8.9 x 8.4cms (Christ chair)
Lisson Gallery, London
photo credit: Rodney Todd White & Associates, London

BOB LAW

There is an element of the maverick in Bob Law which makes this work both resistant to categorisation yet intellectually irresistible. From the late fifties to the present his personality expressed through drawing, painting and sculpture has presented a challenging half-mocking conundrum to the viewer.

The drawings of self-location within a cosmos of local events and universal Pythagorean structures made in Cornwall in the late fifties had a somewhat off-centre relationship to the constructivists who advised him there. His work had the appeal of a conceptual Alfred Wallis. The large coloured fields which he painted in the very early sixties were retrospectively interpreted by many of his peers after seeing Barnet Newman. The parallel is in fact specious. Law, like Heron, feels that this interpretation in the face of US imperialism has been unfortunate.

Prior to his black paintings in 1964 Law had already produced a series of minimal paintings. These consisted of 15 foot stretched canvasses with a biro line drawn round the margin about 2½ inches in from the edge and dated at the bottom righthand corner. Law sometimes described these as "Nothing to be afraid of". They can variously be interpreted as referring to psychological alienation or as a whimsical comment on the work of Barnet Newman at the time, echoing de Kooning's comments of Philip Guston after first seeing Newman's large stark convasses "Well we don't have to think about that any more".

These works only have a very superficial resemblance to American minimalism. Law developed his ideas in relative isolation, and far from excluding content, the works are intended to provide a screen on to which the viewer projects his own experience provoked by the artist. The bareness of the image forces the viewer to consider the idea behind the non-event of the canvas. In the "Nothing to be afraid of" works the margin or frame has little aesthetic diversion yet it accents the artist's positive intentions. The viewer inevitably returns to question his own relationship to the work, and his expectations of art. In doing so, he confronts the problem posed by the artist. It is a conceptual attitude to painting with philosophical connections to Zen Buddhism. The void becomes a place of meditation for self-reflection. At the same time it presents a wryly ironical challenge to the tradition of art as an aesthetically worked object, valued for its intrinsic physical properties or its literal message. Unlike American minimalism it is

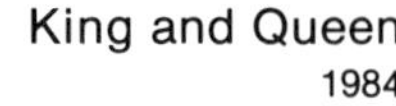

King and Queen
1984

bronze
110.5 x 51.2 x 45   cms (Queen)
104.5 x 53.6 x 43.4cms (King)
Lisson Gallery, London
photo credit: Rodney Todd White & Associates, London

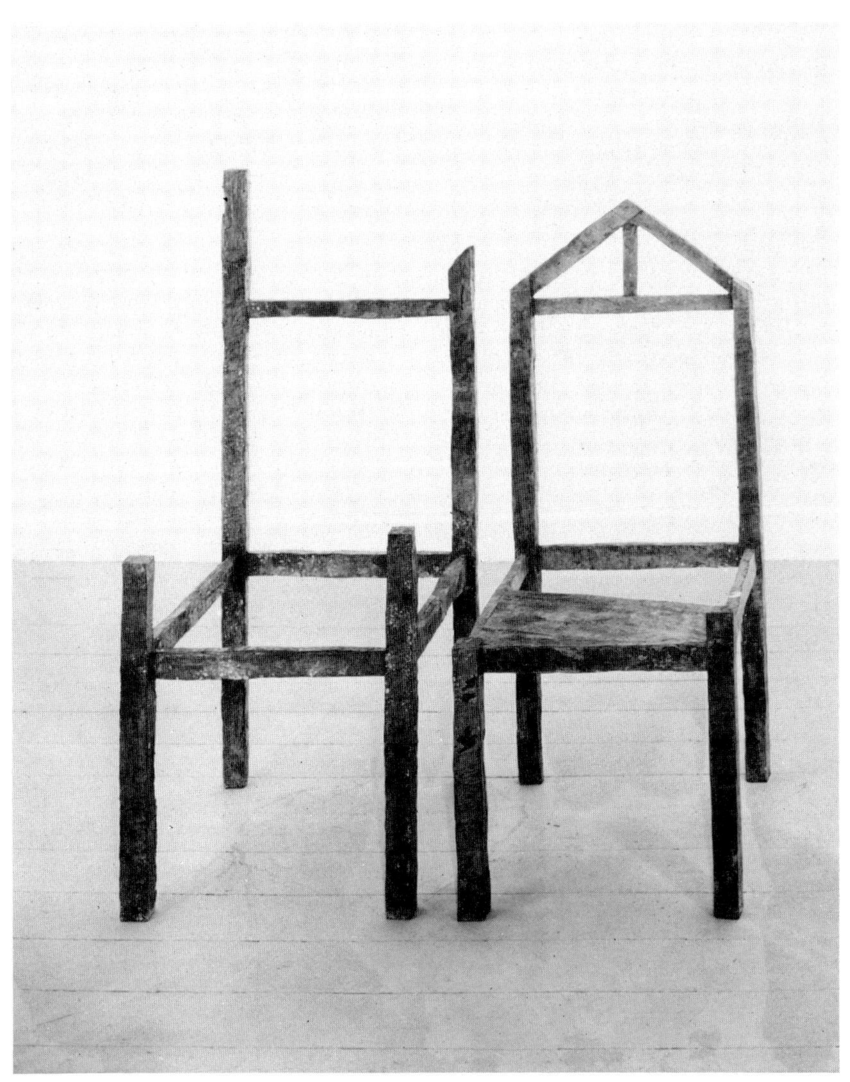

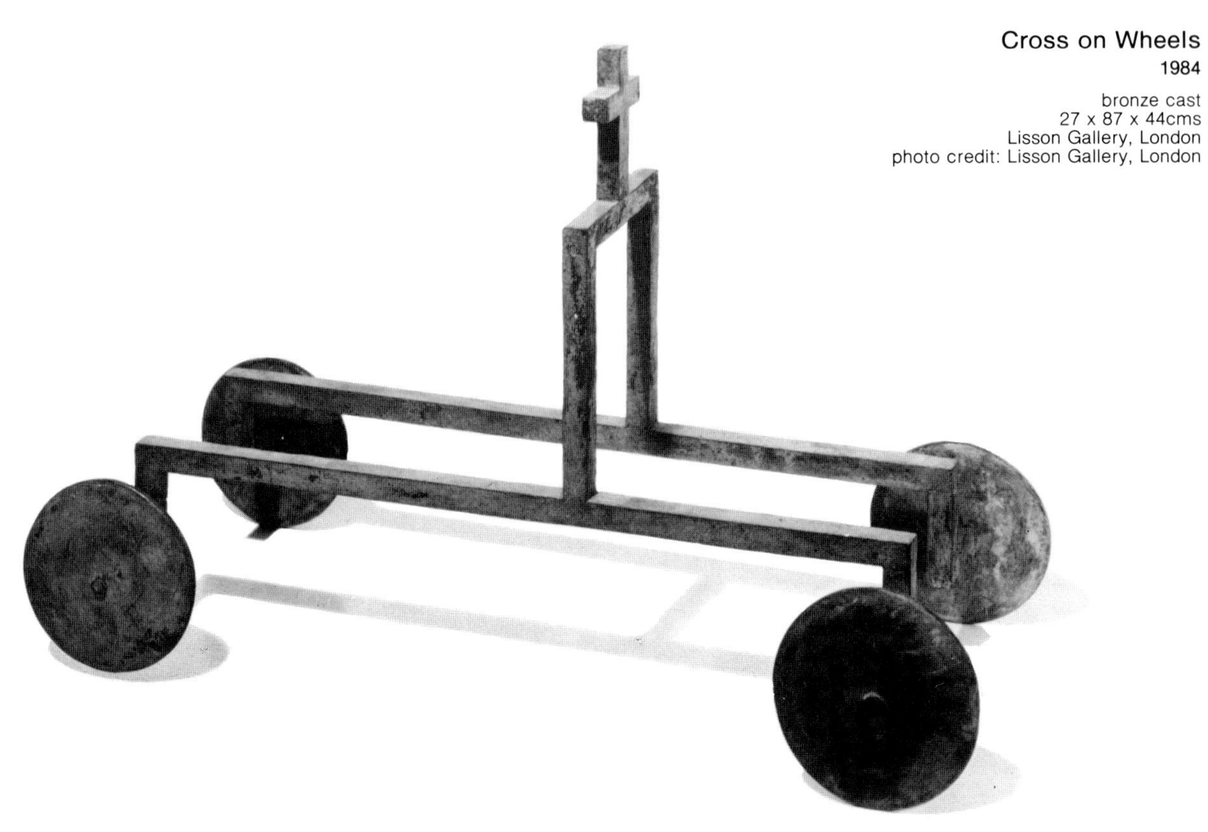

Cross on Wheels
1984

bronze cast
27 x 87 x 44cms
Lisson Gallery, London
photo credit: Lisson Gallery, London

not a product of a process of reduction from a formal proposition but, rather, a direct conceptual leap.

It is a characteristic of most of the artists in this exhibition to employ humour to underline essentially serious conceptual content through rigorous minimal means. The reductive process is not a purely formal one since it is a necessary component of the content itself. The understatement of the best British humour with its sometimes puzzling surreal open-endedness springs from the same roots. In Law's art this attitude appears as its most enigmatic.

From 1962 to 1964 he worked as a shepherd in Hampshire where he made furniture and his first sculptures. His furniture designs were monumental and pragmatic in their conception. They complied with an ethic in which all the functional aspects of manufacture were visible and integral to the look of the piece. In this they pre-figure some of the quality of the sculptures which lead to the work in this exhibition. Like the earlier paintings they are what they are, but the questions they raise refer to an ethical position on the relationship between artist, object and viewer. The object becomes a starting point for a debate which exists chiefly in the head of the viewer but always leads back to the artist who, by a sleight of hand, has become the inquisitor posing existential questions. The disturbing thing is to catch a mocking smile instead of a classical enigma behind the insight.

An element of physical impenetrability is first evident in the black canvasses. In these the pigment is so densely concentrated that the surface becomes too fragile to touch and difficult to perceive in depth. The first sculptures from 1963 and more recent objects came as incredibly dense forms cast in iron. They took the form of wedges,

spheres, cubes, and house shapes. Most of these had a void cut in their centres. These voids inevitably recall "Nothing to be afraid of" paintings. They amplify our experience of the solidity of the objects in the same way that looking into a mine shaft gives us a sense of the claustrophobic mass of the bedrock. The quality of density they exclude is intense.

The hole in the object is sometimes given more pictorial priority, as for instance, in one work where the hole in the top of the stake becomes the form of the work "Hole within a whole". One of the most recent pieces in this exhibition, "Hole within a whole on wheels" continues this obsession of the positive void or black hole. The most impressive works in this exhibition are probably the chairs. The presence represented by the King and Queen chairs challenges Henry Moore's occupied thrones by the very strength of their absence. It is a continuation of the implied presence through absence of the abstract works translated into imagery.

'The Last Supper' is an ambitious essay in classical proportions. It is also an extremely effective piece of minimal theatre. Because the symbolism is virtually universal Law has been able to subject it to a hitherto unparallelled reduction. The intervals of the forms themselves are immaculately worked out. The simple symbol of Christ's chair with its pedimental top and Judas' chair with its broken struts provide a descriptive aspect to the piece, which succeeds by its simple accuracy in avoiding literal narrative. In these works, however, we are offered another feature. The cast bronze taken from wood provides an aesthetic gratification which implies age and weathering. It seems to be an indulgence in the literal which is alien to Law's work, that sardonic smile once more deflecting the obvious interpretation.

Anthony Bond

Christ Chair in Ultramarine
1984

painted wood
120.3 x 57.5 x 52cms
Lisson Gallery, London
photo credit: Rodney Todd White & Associates, London

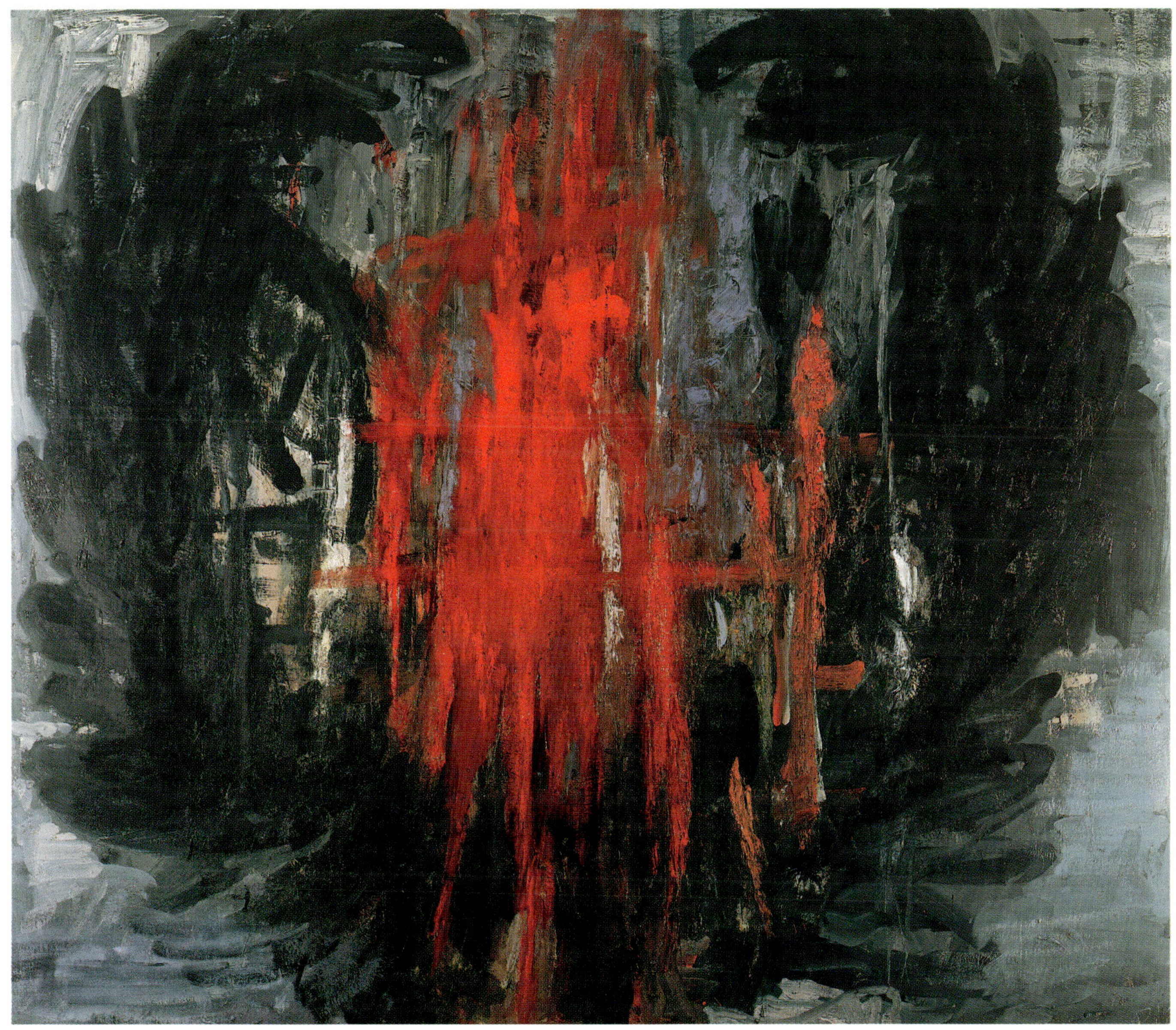

Untitled (Wreath)
1984

oil on canvas
254 x 289.5cms
Nigel Greenwood

CHRISTOPHER LEBRUN

. . . traditional form is so powerful. A Titian painting to me is more wise because what it has is an absolute self-possession, something carved with the brush, the continuity of brushwork . . .[1]

I did a painting of things once considered beautiful — stones, a boat, a wheel, vases — now abandoned by culture . . . images whose meaning is absent. The rhetoric I'm piecing together is broken. Every part of it is broken . . . What happens to poetic utterance when the rhetoric, the basis of understanding, is broken? These objects have a sting of dislocated content. That's why I must work with the picturesque that's been handled and touched by history — stones worn smooth, steps.[2]

Cocteau said that today minds and souls "live without syntax, that is to say, without a moral system. This moral system has nothing to do with morality proper, and should be built up by each one of us an inner style, without which no outer style is possible."[3] Christopher LeBrun's high ambition for painting, his straightforward, unblushing demand that it regain a sovereign role, from whence it can speak authoritatively "of metaphysical and ethical truths", links him more closely to the Abstract Expressionists than to any group of artists since. His idealism, and his admiration for the achievement of these artists, does not however blind him to the distance separating the contemporary artist from those heroic figures, and the consequences attendant on his interval.

There's a bad faith in my generation, a split —

our relationship to the subject has become more complex. By temperament I'm an aspirational or visionary painter after Turner and Blake, but that avenue is closed theoretically and practically. It's a cultural dilemma, not a personal one — sometimes I wonder if post-modernism isn't pathological in its dilemma between the abstract and the figurative.[4]

Of the New York School painters it was Guston who, late in life and almost singlehandedly, tackled these issues once again, but this time in a figurative idiom. And of this group, it is Guston who has proved most inspirational to the younger British painter, through his example as much as through his work.[5] But whereas Guston approached his task by way of a vernacular idiom and a nonchalant, almost self-mocking wit (how else, one might ask, could hoods be painted in a country where *Birth of a Nation* is widely revered, albeit in filmic terms, by all sides of the political spectrum?), LeBrun's approach is graver and less iconoclastic; for example, it seeks to repair the caesura with tradition and is receptive to fitness and decorum.[6] It may be that a wry sardonic humour does not suit him personally but equally pertinent is the degree to which the use of jocose parody and blatant vulgarity, even when employed as masks to conceal a sense of despair, impotence and irrelevance and

even though stemming from the aegis of Guston, have lately become little more than a voguish, mannered ploy. In this, as in his ambition for painting, LeBrun has affinities with Kiefer, whom he also admires, but unlike the German he does not ground his art in the specifics of an historical and cultural situation, nor does he employ imagery which permits a discursive, symbolical or allegorical reading.[7] And because his concerns are metaphysical in character, not social, political or psychological, he is removed too from certain compatriots like Terry Setch, Terry Atkinson and Ian McKeever.

LeBrun's position was not arrived at quickly nor was it the consequence of purely rational deliberation. Following his graduation from Chelsea School of Art in 1975, he continued painting abstract pictures, at the same time using his newly gained privacy to work over the next two years on a canvas which contained a series of images that related almost in a diaristic fashion to his personal life. Against a landscape backdrop the artist, his wife, a dog and numerous other motifs appeared and reappeared at intervals as he struggled to resolve the canvas, worrying all the time about the dichotomy in his practice, the simultaneous involvement with abstract and figurative painting. The dilemma was resolved theoretically but only when his feelings

Serpentine Summer Show III
Headland 1979

oil on canvas
244 x 167cms

Grand Island 1979

oil on canvas
258 x 168cms
installation: Serpentine Gallery, London August 1979

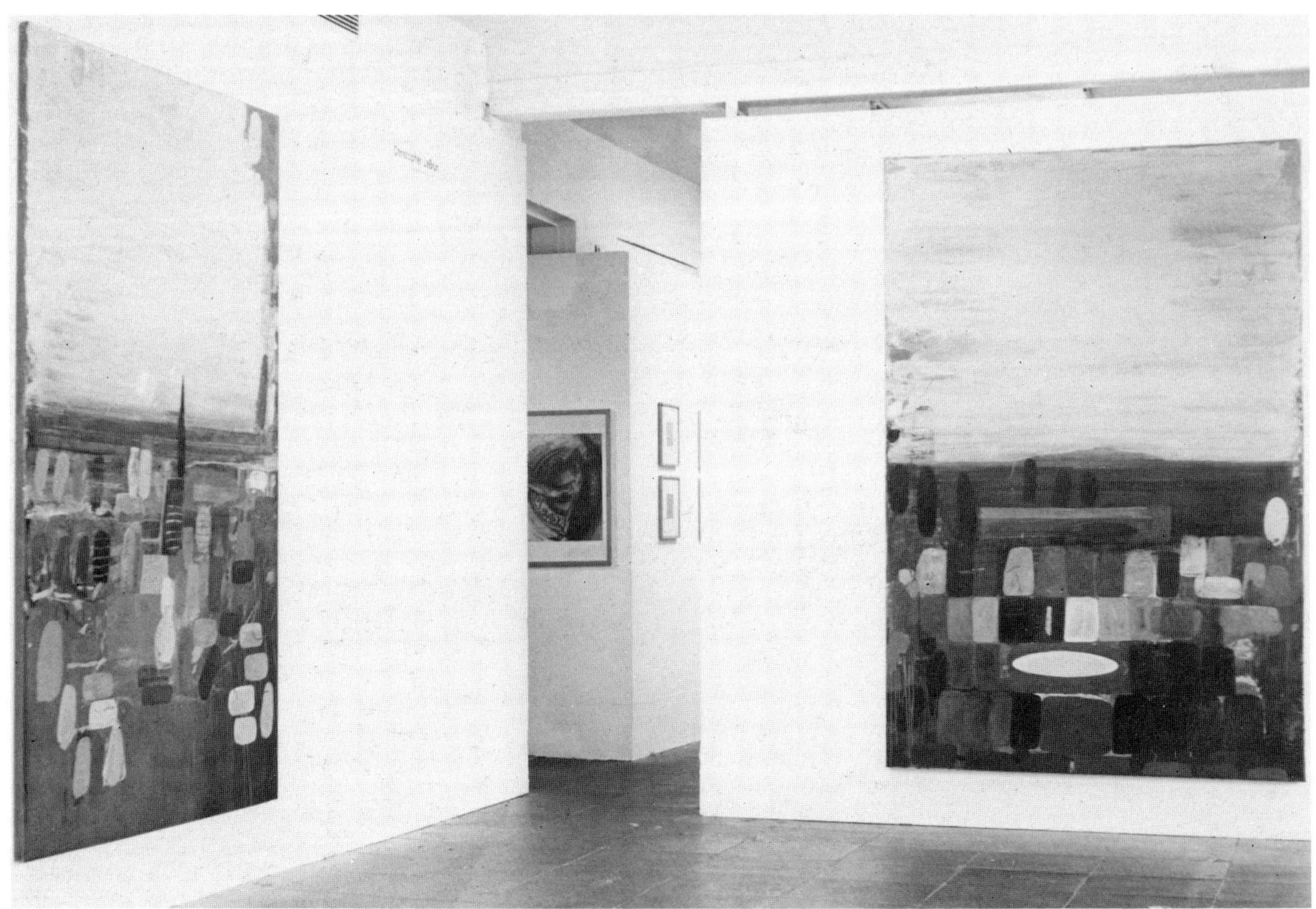

persuaded him of the "rightness" of adopting a representational style. By the end of the decade these two aspects were juxtaposed within a single canvas, in the form of a dialogue.[8] In *Headland*, of 1979-80 an ethereal landscape reminiscent of the distant reaches of a Claudian pastorale occupies the upper registers of the painting whilst in the lower section of the canvas the stained, reddish-brown ground is peopled with brilliantly hued rectangles, like the colour sample of a Dulux paint chart overlying the dribbles and splatters caused during the execution of the scene above. This rural arcadia has obviously been conjured from the raw materials displayed below, yet the illusion is never complete, never seamless. The viewer is not quite transported into this halcyon world: it remains a promise. Although the various constituents of painting are overtly acknowledged, there is none of the cool literalism of, say, Ryman's work where the components have been distilled and then examined, for it is not the basic ingredients per se which fascinate LeBrun. His focus is on the pivot, the point of transformation and the potential for revelation implicit in this metamorphosis.

LeBrun has continued his quest, primarily by means of the image of the horse, for what Cocteau deemed an "inner style" an ethical as much as aesthetic

structure through which poetic utterance might once again be vouchsafed. Because *Pegasus, Xanthus, Mazeppa, Arion* and the others have literary or legendary origins — unlike their modern counterparts, Tonto, Black Bess, National Velvet, Phar Lap and Dobbin, whom LeBrun eschews — he has often been seen as a symbolic painter. Yet the kleptomania of much Postmodernism which, seemingly haplessly, as well as obsessively, plunders or filches from the art of the past in a vain endeavour to convey eternal varieties by nothing more than the very fact of citation, is far from his practice. LeBrun is not in the business of myth-making. The winged horses, elysian fields, knights and even laurel wreaths are public images, images with a notable role within this culture, yet they are real only in the way in which unicorns and centaurs are real. (Even the wreaths which could, arguably, be constructed would not attain the evocative potency in a phenomenal existence that they are permitted within the realm of fantasy.) More importantly, LeBrun does not illustrate his images; generated during the process of painting they are figments of a painted world with no independent existence.

I'm interested in the imagery being innate in the picture . . . Sometimes I feel that the autogenesis of the image will produce stylistic unity.[9]

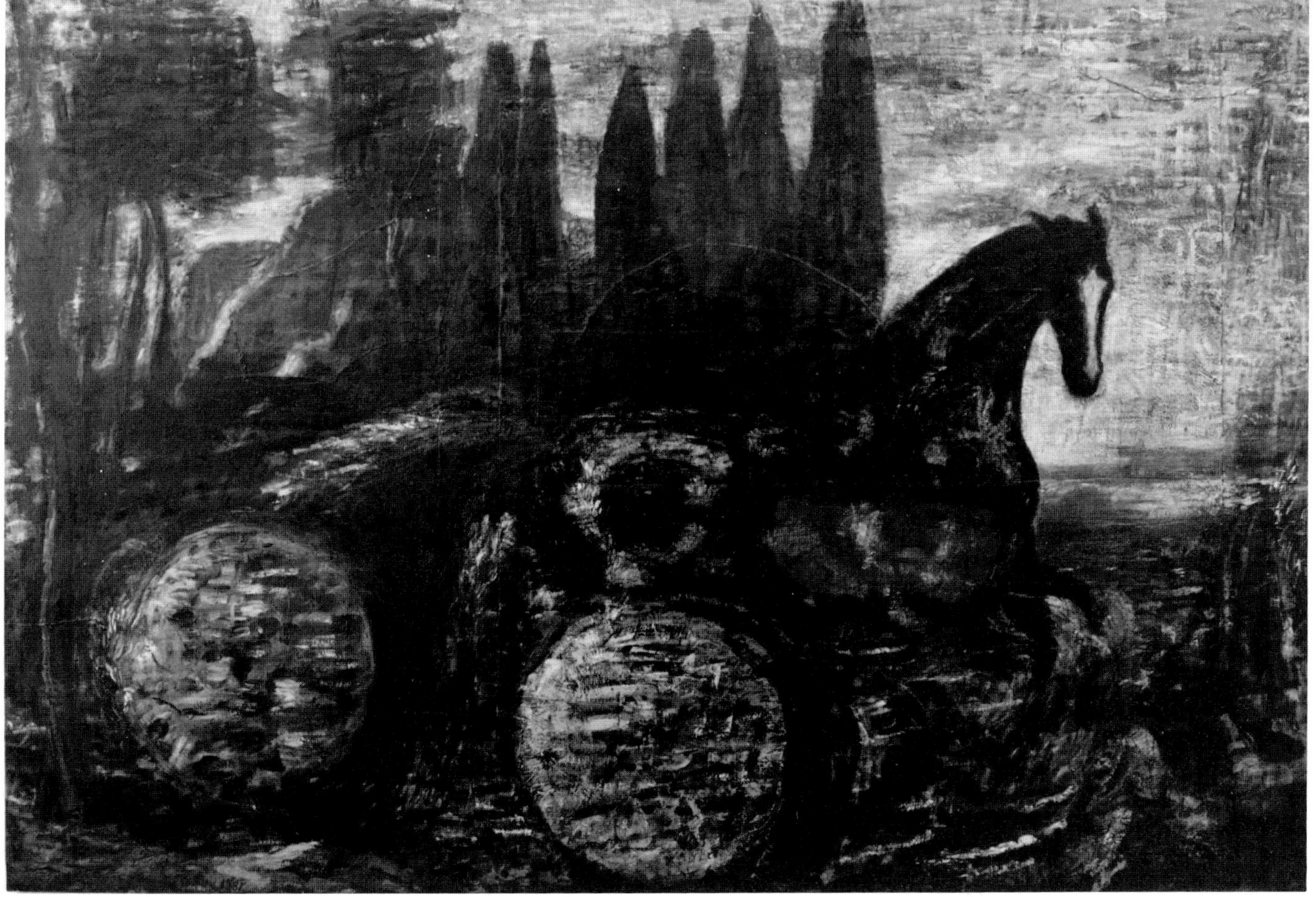

The execution of a painting thus becomes the conjuring forth, the embodying and realising of a vision. It is an attempt to fix, however tenuously, something with an inherently nebulous and fugitive existence. The particular and private significance that these images may carry for LeBrun personally is therefore irrelevant: psychoanalytical inquiry is of no importance. Yet conversely, to view the motif simply as a convenience, a nominal subject around which to make a painting as the horse was used by Susan Rothenberg for a time, is also misplaced. LeBrun's motifs do have a significance, but this significance lies in the fact that they exist in the realm of fiction. That they are fictions is axiomatic for it prevents a reading of the painting in terms of a mimetic relationship with the external world. At the same time the requirement that these fictions are not seamless, not fully illusory precludes them from providing a solace, a Romantic escape from the present. It is what they look like, and not some underlying meaning nor their potential to generate reverie, that is crucial. Indeed LeBrun insists on

affirming the rift between the actual and the fictional. The actual, identified with the materiality of the painting itself, the physical nature of its texture, surface, facture and colour, can never be ignored. The content of the painting thus derives from the act of eliciting a visionary apparition from formless brute manner.

These paintings gain not only their import but their power from this tension between subject and means, material and illusion, the actual and the visionary. In *Sir Tristram*, for example, the diagonally cut ground establishes a locus, though not a plastic space for the knight, and in this area as in that of the protagonist himself, the lighter toned strokes smear and lick the darker base, coming forward into visibility from the depths as nodal points wrested from the viscous inchoate matter. LeBrun attempts to keep the entire surface fluid until the conclusion; since nothing is pre-ordained the whole is continually subject to overpainting. Currently so pervasive, alla prima

Sir Tristram
1984

oil on canvas
254 x 292cms
National Galleries of Scotland, Edinburgh

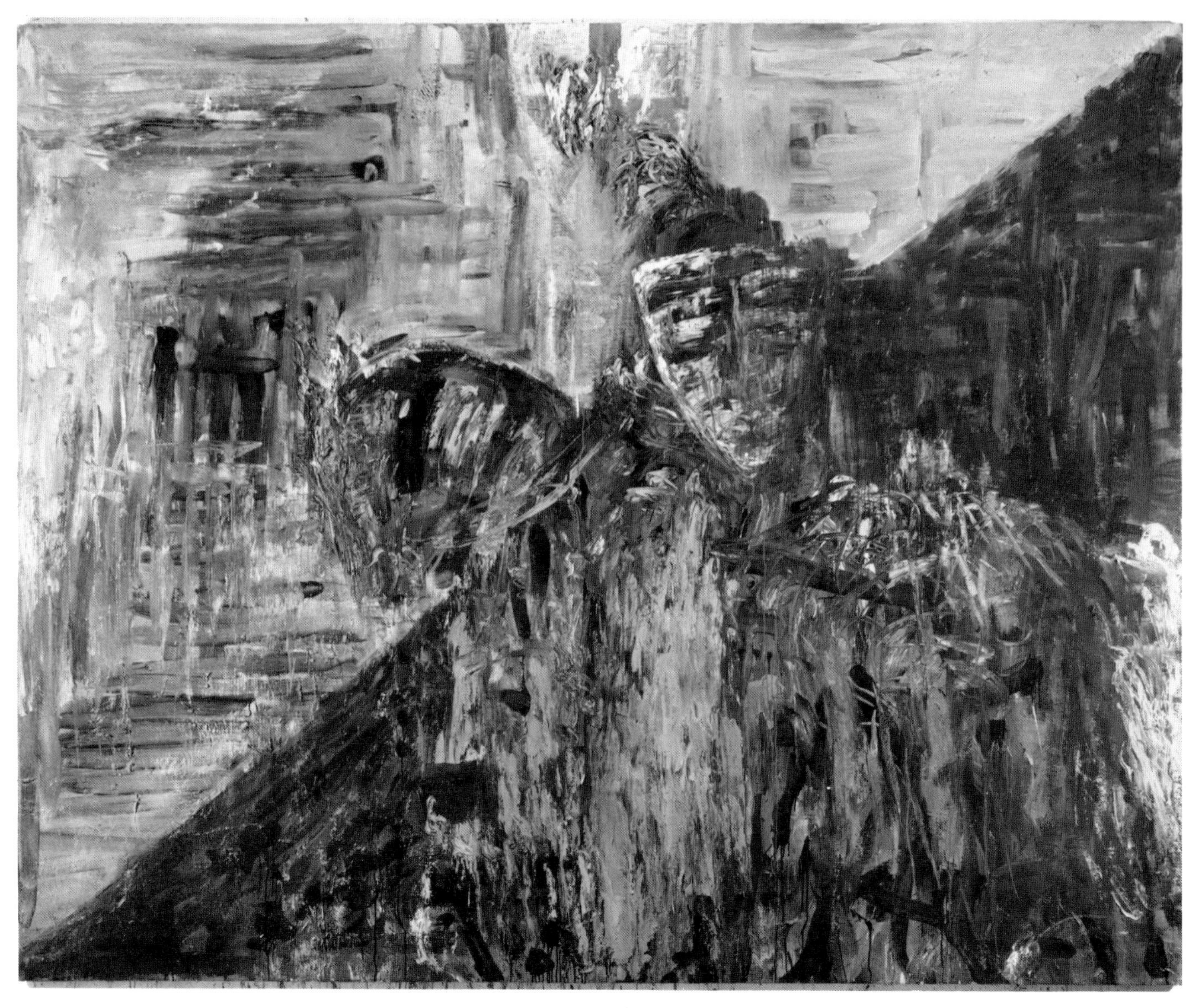

painting is inadequate for his purposes as its impetuosity and speed are inimical to his notion of creation as a holding-in-being by the strength of the vision, the style.[10]

Though colour may be opulent, note the red and red/brown contrasts of *Sir Tristram*, its range is now carefully restricted; Whilst not, in any obvious sense austere, there is a fastidiousness and decorum in LeBrun's manner, a disdain for embellishment, virtuosity and the grand manner for their own sake. Form is designed to discipline emotions at the same time as it arouses them, to engender an attentive involvement with what is there on the canvas rather than inducing reverie. But the image is always not only emotionally but physically out of reach, given the absence of detail, the lack of description. Should the spectator approach in order to attain more precise information, the subject will dissolve. In reconstituting it the observer performs what is akin to a magical act. This is the crux of painting for LeBrun, its emotional as well as metaphysical core: what he terms both a paradox and an act of faith; the establishing of a fiction which stands against and withstands other fictions.[11]

In his recent work a greater complexity is evident, as the fragmentation between image and means becomes less intrusive, through the more supple and fluid handling, the more intricate spatial structure, and the more subtle use of chiaroscuro. Elegiac, almost melancholy, the mood of *Wreath* imbues not only this theme, but a great deal of LeBrun's art. Yet the act of realisation in itself allays resignation. It is therefore entirely appropriate that in one of his most recent paintings, *Shield*, the

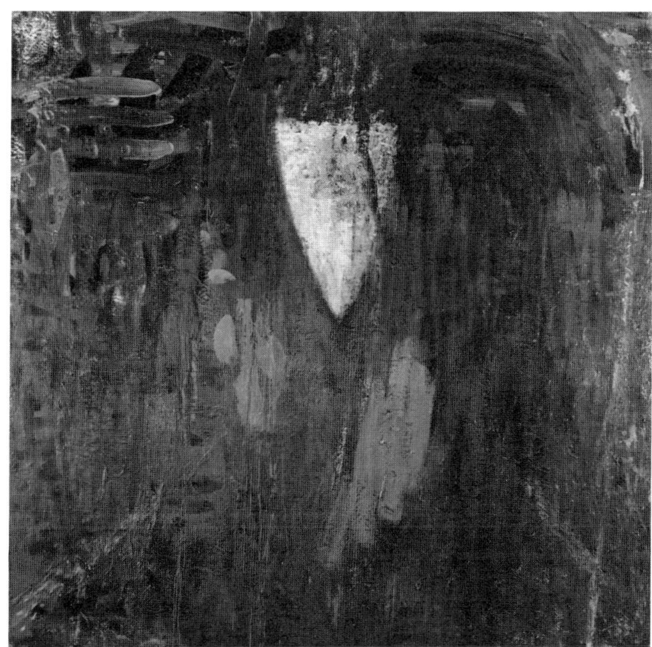

Shield
1982-4

oil on canvas
211 x 213cms
Nigel Greenwood Gallery London

pale weapon looms mysteriously from a lugubrious ground, isolated, almost hypnotic — like a St. Veronica's veil.

Lynne Cooke

FOOTNOTES

1. quoted in Stuart Morgan, "The Field of Rhetoric: An Interview with Christopher LeBrun, *Artforum*, December 1982, p.49.

2. op.cit. p.50.

3. Jean Cocteau, *Cocteau on the Film, A Conversation Recorded by Andre Fraigneau*, 1951.

4. quoted in Sarah Kent, "Art and Artifice: Changing Attitudes". *Artscribe*, February 1984, p.20.

5. Asked about Guston's figurative paintings (Christopher LeBrun Interviewed by Matthew Collings, *Artscribe*, March 1981, (no.28 p.15) LeBrun commented: "I was more interested in his abstract paintings of the late fifties and early sixties. I was interested in the Frenchness of them, the beauty of them". Guston described them as follows: "These paintings were to speak through the inner murmuring of near-forms, of entities nearing completion but never quite distinct".

6. "For me Classicism sets up echoes which can be adjusted to or added to, to make expression. By the term 'Classicism' I mean Raphael, Leonardo: the full condition when the format of the painting is most highly sensitized without the overt expressiveness of Mannerism or the 'becoming' of earlier art, when the painting achieves a non-transitional enduring form". (Collings, op.cit., p.14) and he later quoted Pound: "the Tradition is a beauty which we preserve and not a set of fetters to bind us".

7. In a discussion which took place several years ago with the author at an exhibition of Kiefer's art, LeBrun acknowledged the difficulty of finding a counterpart in British culture for many of the German's themes and the subject of King Arthur came up. He has subsequently painted a number of works titled after the various knights of the Round Table. Significantly, LeBrun reads Tennyson who, in turning to this subject, was writing of a legendary world, and not Malory or other Medieval authors who were giving form to a living chivalric code, one with practical pertinence.

8. Of these works LeBrun later wrote: "It was deliberately dialectical painting in a very obvious sense. I wanted to put an

image, say of cadmium, up against an image of a jar and see which one held, to set them against each other. Those pictures are full of choices. After a while, I found that the aspects of drawing and making figures in space were so powerful that they rendered the demonstration of insights into painting redundant. Before that, I was able to think of all aspects of the painting, from the ground up, as being capable of analysis. It was as if I was working analytically but at the same time I had a 'vision' and the two things started to conflict, and then one gradually came to dominate." (Collings, op.cit., p.14).

9. .ibid.

10. An extended comparison could be made between the works of Robert Bresson and LeBrun. In the Frenchman's films there is a similar sense of decorum, a recognition of the impossibility of penetrating behind the surface to reveal intentions and motivations governing behaviour. With his mythological and historical themes Bresson too makes no attempt at convincing historical recreation or even at a seamless fabrication; rather the film unfolds in a realm in which naturalism and pure artifice coalesce. Meaning is divulged through the filter of style, style manifest not expressionistically but as an ordering vision, and of a composure that holds in check the underlying intensity.

11. The sense in which the terms myth and fiction are being employed here are well defined by Frank Kermode: "Fictions can degenerate into myths whenever they are not consciously held to be fictive . . . Myth operates within the diagrams of ritual, which presupposes total and adequate explanations of things as they are and were; it is a sequence of radically unchangeable gestures. Fictions are for finding things out, and they change as the needs of sense-making change. Myths are the agents of stability, fictions the agents of change. Myths call for absolute, fictions for conditional assent. Myths make sense in terms of a lost order of time, *illus tempus* as Eliade calls it; fictions, if successful, make sense of the here and now, *hoc tempus*." (The Sense of an Ending, O.U.P. (1966), 1970, p.39).

RICHARD LONG

"In his every movement a man of great virtue
Follows the way and the way only.
As a thing the way is
Shadowy, indistinct.
Indistinct and shadowy,
Yet within it is an image . . ."
   Lao Tzu: *Tao Te Ching*, XXI

The subject of Richard Long's work is Nature: the experience of Nature, its rhythms and processes. It is a Nature that includes humankind and our works, but in a texture of natural rather than historical time. A principal means by which Long experiences Nature is to make journeys by foot or bicycle: "it is difficult", says the Bhudda in the *Majjhima Nikaya*, "to live a spiritual life completely perfect and pure in all its parts while cabinned inside." The expressive object arising from and which testifies to the spiritual activity of journeying may be a sculpture or mark made during a walk; a photograph relating to the location of a journey, perhaps showing a work produced there; a text, a constellation of significant utterance elliptically evoking the experience of travelling a particular route; a map indicating a route taken — Long has realised many possibilities. The journey, physically transient and experientially precise, is itself a formally disciplined work, a ritual.

Walking, running, cycling or canoeing over any distance requires a harmonisation of the environment and the body — its physical exertion, the rhythms of heart and breath. Travelling is not a test of endurance. From Tibet to the Australian deserts, dedicated presence in a particular landscape induces a fine-tuning of embodied consciousness, a relaxation of self into natural form through a process that has a close affinity with practices of meditation. This man-tortured earth can thus emerge as an element of total being, rather than as a condition of or constraint upon mere existence. Long's works testify to this sense of a whole relationship between Nature and human being (in presence and biography), and relate (to) a man's scale in the world. They witness totality as actuality, not possibility. The aura of magic and mystery, of ritual and sacred power which attaches to Long's sculptures is in part a consequence of this celebration of the whole relationship, for, as Susan Sontag has noted, the only language we have readily available for totalising-experience is the language of religion. However, travelling is, today, also a political act. We cannot go where we wish, there are political boundaries, property rights, official protocols. Thus, inevitably, the locations in which Long travels are items in an inventory of the places where, and the ways (roads, paths, rivers) in which, we are still able to realise a full and fulfilling relationship with the natural world, simply and without pretensions of ownership.

Long's work employs a familiar repertoire of means and modes of expression, so that his art can be thought of as an art with which and in which everyone can engage. In extending and deepening the significance of our common delight in handling, collecting and (re)arranging natural objects, Long employs a vocabulary of elementary, archetypal formal envelopes: straight line, cross, spiral, and circle. These forms are elementary in a sense which is characteristic of our time, for although they appear simple forms in themselves, they are transformed into complex and resonant signifiers by combination with themselves or with other materials. (Note, for example, the way in which a sculpture such as BUSHWOOD CIRCLE (1977) relates to the space in which it is placed, and in other cases the relation to the horizon-limited ground itself.) They are archetypal forms both in being culturally and historically universal, and in functioning as a deep reservoir of metaphor whose interpretation is dependant only upon being a member of humanity. The journey is itself a metaphor for (a way of) life, and we cannot avoid the senses of meeting and parting, catching and releasing which reverberate within the horizontal cross, a sign which also evokes for me notions of "marking the spot" and "crossing place". Again, the circle conjures the unhindered natural growth of ripples, moss or bush; the primitive enclosures of orifice, dwelling, henge and horizon. These figures are composed of various materials, but they are characteristically of the place to which the work relates, found ready-to-hand, and this is so for words as well as wood or stones. Thus, in FULL MOON CIRCLE OF GROUND (1983) the circular patch of text ironically re-presents the ground on which Long pitched his tent for the night. The words are available at the same time as the objects to which they refer, but they are conspicuously not those objects, nor do they represent the physiognomy of the ground in the way in which a conventional map would. This insistence upon the non-identity of concept and thing is a persistent theme in Long's work, giving rise to characteristic ambiguities and ambivalences in his use of languague, and is another aspect of his commitment to the primacy of authentic experience.

Maps themselves are exemplary vessels of inauthenticity, their method of abstracting Nature subverting the reality of being in the landscape. Our familiar maps, which Long often uses as the basis of his mapworks, substitute a cognitive condition of "being unknown" — an ignorance which can be remedied, at least in principle — for an inescapable phenomenological tension which Merleau-Ponty referred to as *l'être des lointains*, the ever-present and forever unattainable far-offness and allure of horizons. The unreachable horizon locates me where I am, and provides an essential ground of my being and my journeying. This aspect of the experience of landscape is missing from the conventional map, indeed is negated by its rejection of there being any essential incompleteness, a rejection entirely consonant with the dominant industrial-scientific worldview. In this way the map, seeking to comfort and reassure our well-being and self-possession, falsifies our experience of landscape.

The map's inadequacy as a representation of the experience of Nature is brought out in Long's mapworks largely by his seeming to aim at

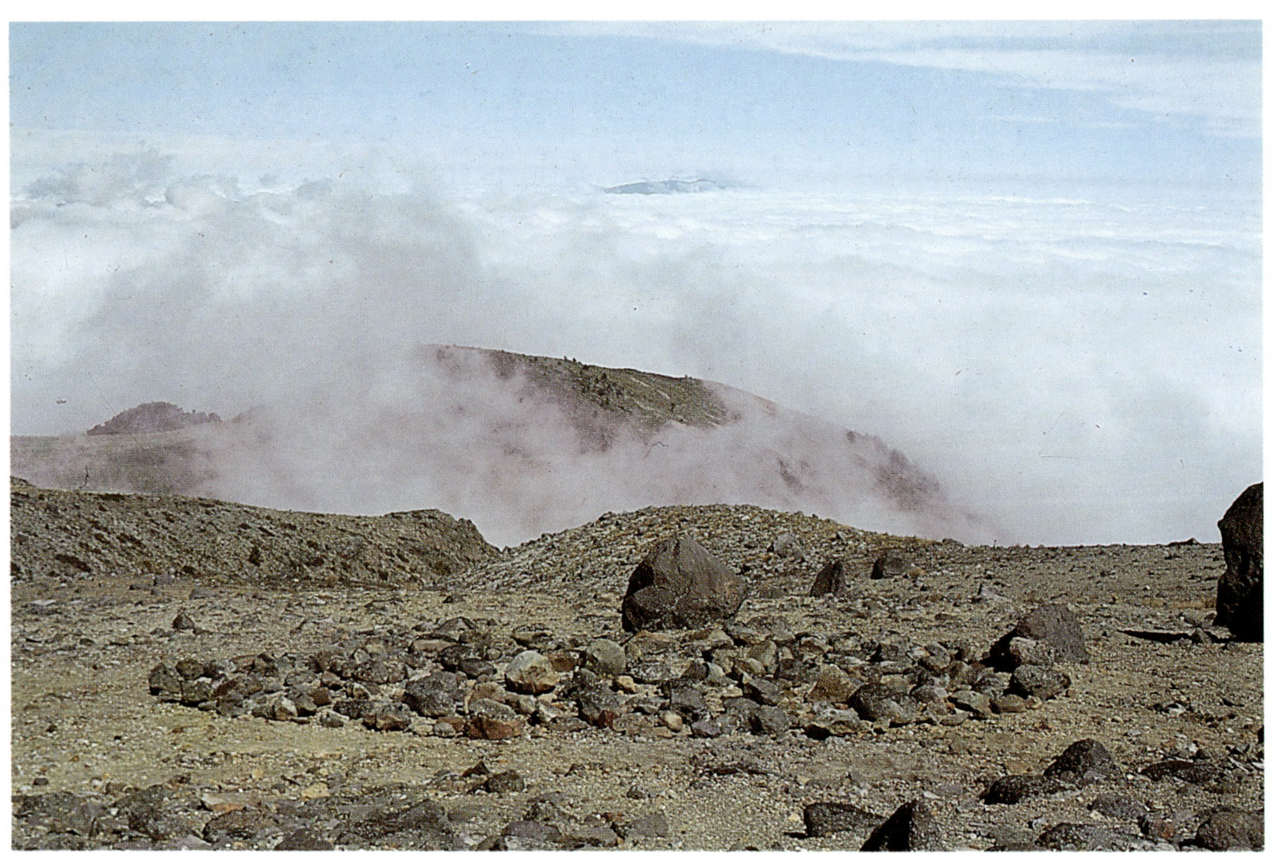

CIRCLE IN MEXICO   1978

completing their work of abstraction. Long's walks activate the self-destruct mechanism of cartographic convention. His geometrical simplicity successfully subverts the map's claim to generic usefulness: all that Ordnance Survey detail, so handy for planning a resourceful and efficient route, over which he goes roughshod, refusing to come to our historical senses! And yet the simple figure is perturbed, by the way the land lies, how the travelling goes. Precipice, deep water, steep climb: these leave their mark not as obstacles to freedom but as occasions for its exercise, maybe making a change of direction, or pace. The mapworks powerfully invoke the experience of being in direct relation with Nature by playing off the pseudo-generality of the map against the work of being there.

Western values have traditionally esteemed an art which aims to transcend Time, creating monuments which demand care and conservation if they are to be preserved against the ravages of entropy. By contrast, Long's sculptures weather, shift, and play host to a variety of flora and fauna: he "let's go", and allows them to participate in natural history. Only when slave to desire do we yearn for stasis, and attempt to transfix the world according to the impositions of goal, of will. These circles, crosses and lines, having been made, are left for Nature to work on, to exhibit itself. In being thus open to process, Long's sculptures remind us of the relics of prehistory, the monuments of past civilisation, and in being naturalised they testify to a community of man and nature, and celebrate the new dispersions and varieties that arise from "letting the world flow through one's fingers."

I am moved by the delicate sureness of touch which has gone towards the making of these works: stones picked and thrown or placed, grass and snow marked by footfalls, the earth brushed clear of leaves, twigs, pebbles. These means of marking an involvement with Nature are neither violent nor massive — even when their scale stretches from here to the horizon — but entirely respect the materials used. Here there is an economy of displacement which produces a distinctive aura to the work, an evocation of care. (This sense is sometimes reinforced, by, for example, a simple correspondence which ensures that each stone in the sculpture stands for each mile of a journey, allowing a spatial condensation of distance into the iconic sculpture, a rosary heap.)

Long's sculptures arise in a compelling abandonment to particular Nature, and in this are not only more than formally classical, but also relate (us) to a radically human way of being in the world. Throughout the world human beings marginally, respectfully and magically mark out their ways with beaten tracks, stone paved paths, cairns and shrines, and Long's works chime with these. In a world mundanely sacred, commonplace materials can remind us where we are and what there is. The concept of the megalithic calendar is itself a commonplace these days, and a circle of standing stones marks a site with reverential precision. But Long's discriminating restraint, his momentary insertion of formality into Nature, also draws into the mind's resonance overtones of the Zen garden's sculptural transfiguration of Nature into an accessible object of contemplation. (Yantras are not far away.)

In the arc of an eye, in a winking, the artist cleaves slates of vision, planes of perception, from air and

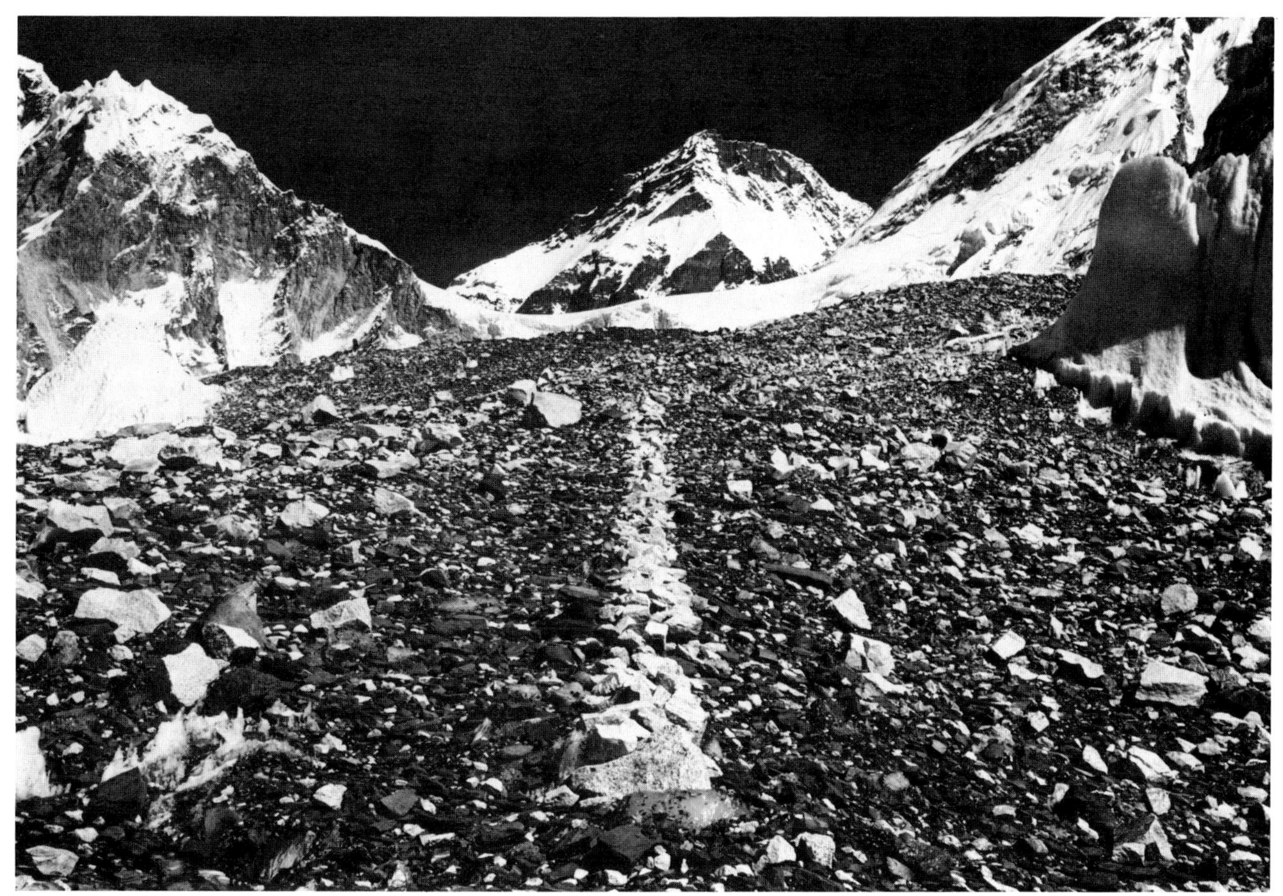

A LINE IN THE HIMALAYAS   1975

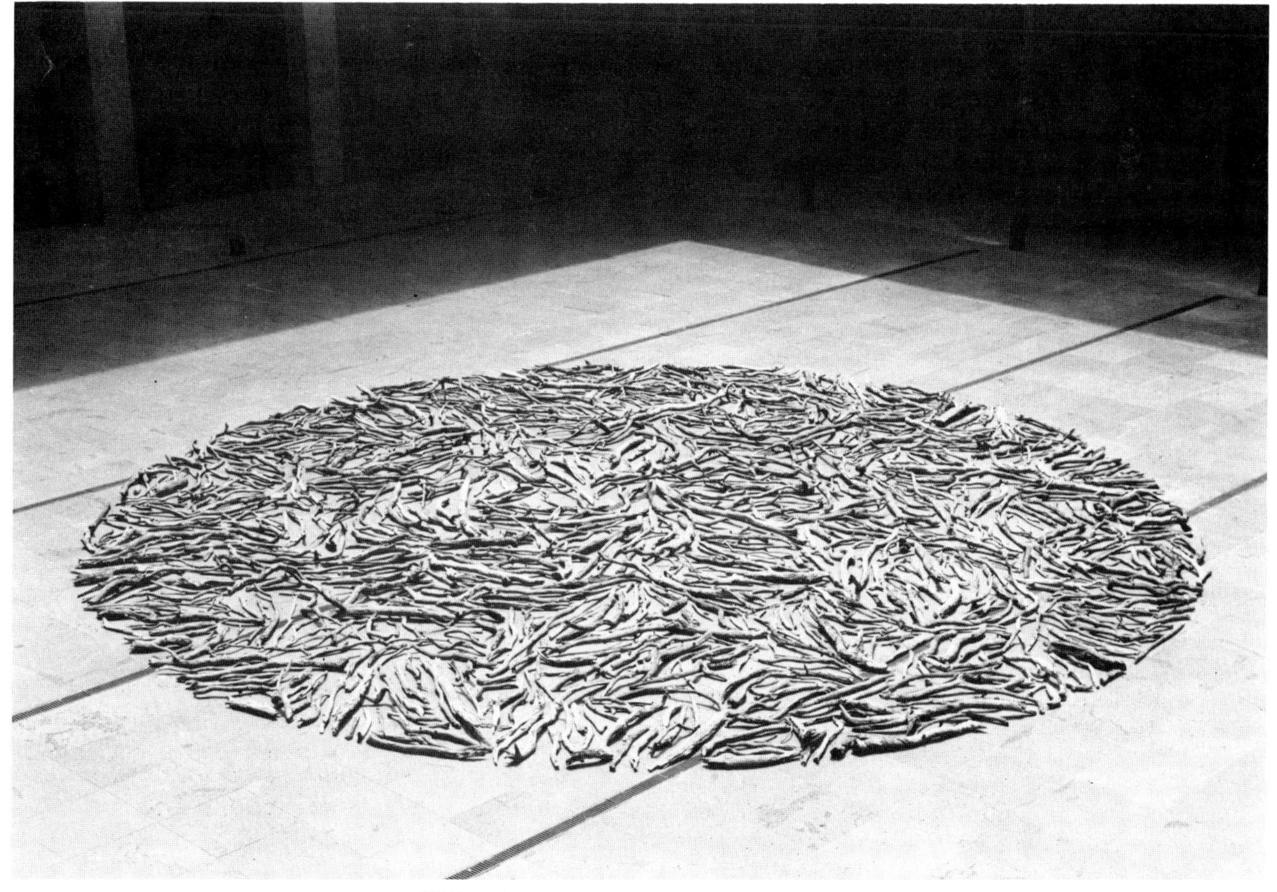

BUSHWOOD CIRCLE   MELBOURNE   1977

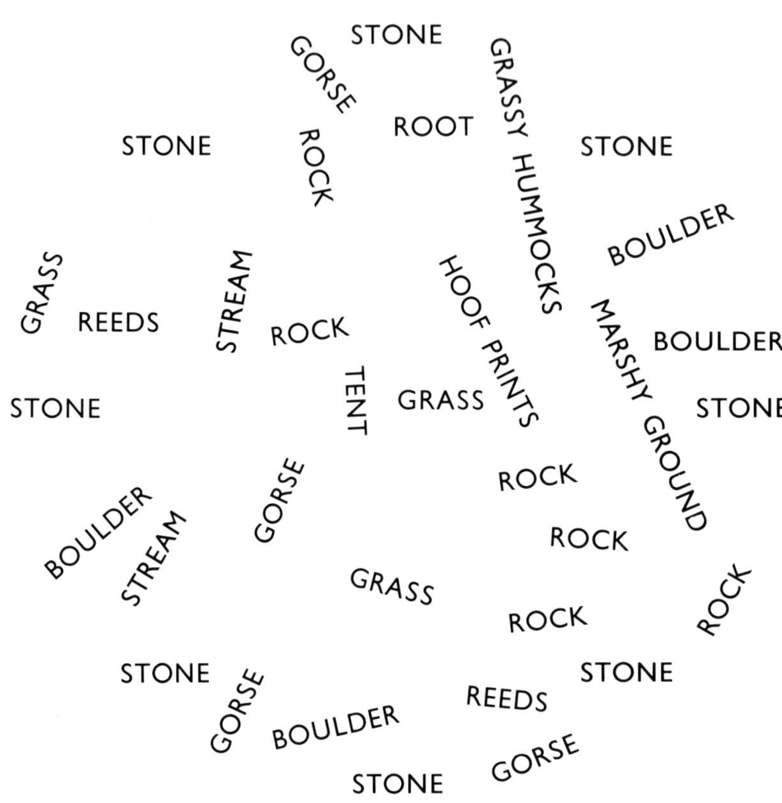

FULL MOON CIRCLE OF GROUND

earth. In PLANE OF VISION (1982) a dusting of words mark the path of sight, settling slowly in the mind. Words have their own powers, names are *tapu*: in my anguish the name of my beloved is pressed from me; I exclaim or recite the names of places in recognition of where I am and who has been before me, of things in assurance of what they are. People are careful with what they name and with the name itself, and this care carries over into Long's work. A text work precisely evidences experience by fastidiously avoiding any suggestion that it captures or represents the totality of experience. That would be a necessarily fraudulent aim and claim. Long's texts witness experience, they do not report or document it, and their enigmatic ellipses provide the essential space for the imagination to illuminate our lives.

Words are meaning's sediment: they have their histories in them, as does mud. Mud is both a material of a place, immediately to hand there, and it is also a landscape summary of a river's course. The river has drawn its way across country, and in its sediment presents us its up-river history. Long carries the mud as the river transports the mountain, and (say) makes a circle: his work of weaving smears of mud by hand onto the wall provides a simple envelope of form, so that the mud may hold our attention. Or the muddy water is (say) splashed on the wall in a gestural calligraphy that emphasises the river's play of gravity, sediment and surface, coursing down the wall in a unity of matter and form that would delight the intoxicated enthusiasm of the Zen artist. The mud on the wall punctuates our orderly world, in which familiarity with the syntax of authority leads us to assimilate the mudwork to bad dirt in the wrong place, to the shit the insane and the prisoner smear on their cell walls. Yet this custodial response is appropriate, perhaps, to the urbane gallery, revealing the regulation distances we insert into the world to keep it manageable and seemingly within our grasp. Nature itself is neither clean nor dirty, it is as it is. Dirt arises from our desire that things be otherwise than they are.

Just as the psychoanalyst assures us that shit is the child's first gift to its mother, so the anthropologist informs us that mud has a central and significant role to play in human life. It is a fertile ground for crops, building material, the stuff of pots. It is among the first materials used for painting, and the prime object for mudwork is the human body itself. (Where Long's walks are about footprints, his mudworks are about handprints. It is pertinent to recall the close identification which is made between the surface of the earth and the skin of the body by many non-industrial peoples, from mediaeval German peasants to the Walbiri of "contemporary" Australia.) Mud is not pollution, does not defile. Splash it on a surface, let the river take its course: see how it goes.

With the simplest of means and the clearest of visions, Richard Long's creativity provides us with touchstones to revitalise our relation to Nature and to ourselves. He challenges the oppressive dogmas of contemporary industrial life by producing a body of work which refuses to succumb to the chimera of inert meaning. The works speak calmly in virtue of a different stance, an authentic attitude. "He who tiptoes cannot stand; he who strides cannot walk", Lao Tzu says. By steadily following his own path Long shows us the way.

David Reason

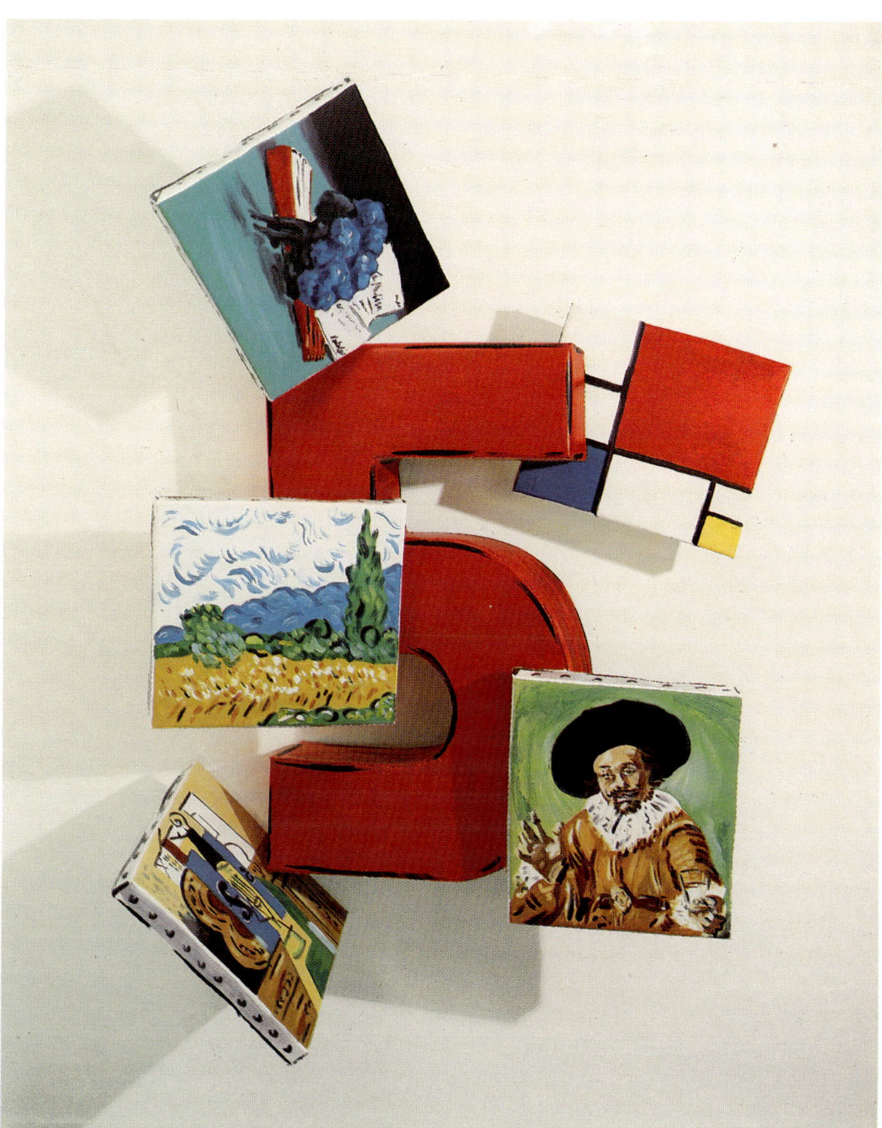

JULIAN OPIE

The film *Blade Runner** based on a novel by Philip K. Dick, invites us to imagine a world where it is no longer possible to distinguish between the 'replicants' produced by a huge multinational corporation and real human beings. The irony is that the film is itself an artificial contrivance, a simulated reality constructed out of a patchwork of historical periods, ethnic cultures, architectural styles and the codes of earlier sci-fi and detective movies. This conceit encapsulates an aspect of our contemporary experience with which a number of artists have been attempting to come to terms: that much of our world — films, TV, advertising, packaging — is already artificial before they even start to work upon it. The paradigm of art from the Renaissance discovery of perspective to Cubism is that of representation, based on the notion of the difference between the original and the copy. What happens when the 'original' is already a copy? Reality, pre-empting the artist, becomes artificial, and the technique of reproduction is displaced by what Jean Baudrillard has called the regeme of simulation. To deny this altogether is to fail to acknowledge that simulation, whether watching *Blade Runner*, listening to rock music or actually enjoying ads, is the source of much of our pleasure. Yet to accept it in a deterministic way can lead to a cynical nihilism. Baudrillard's 'precession of simulacra' poses a moral problem.

Aspects of culture, in the wider sense, which were previously distinguished in an hierarchical manner are rendered equivalent as simulation. When Julian Opie uses masterpieces of past art in his sculpture, he paints them as reproductions. The canvasses in *A Heap of Old Masters* and *Cultural Baggage* are all the same size, and in *Eat Dirt-Art History* they are on pages spiralling out of a book. The components of a still life are painted in the same fast, graphic style as commercial packaging. Boxes from the kitchen cupboard and bathroom cabinet pose as a David Smith *Cubi* while the elements of an abstract composition look like empty cartons. Recently Opie has been making increasing use of abstract shapes in his work, motivated in part by an awareness of the need for the work to cohere in expansive public spaces. There is a limit to the extent to which the representation of a commonplace item or package can be enlarged without seeming monumental and making the viewer feel like some pigmy from a

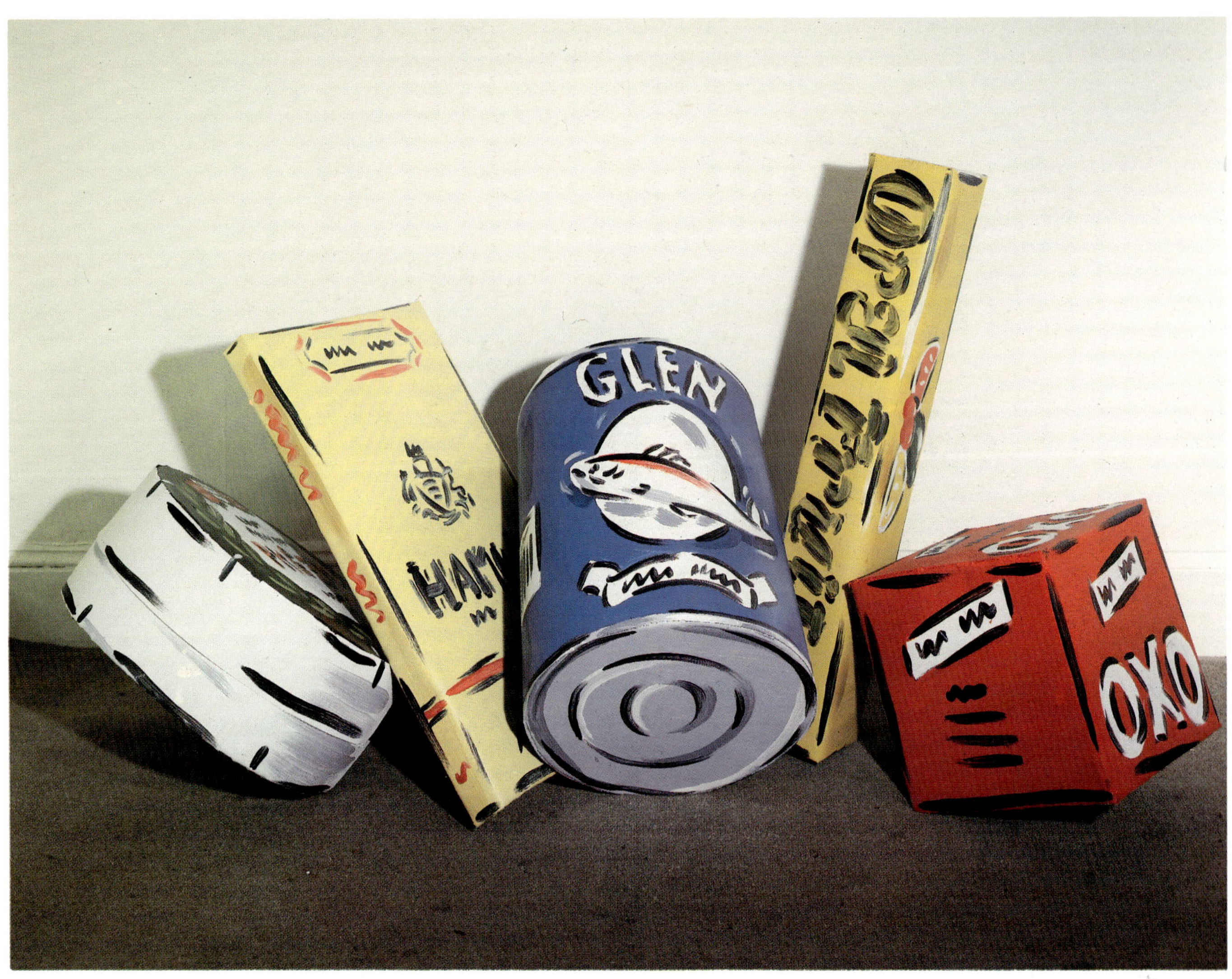

Abstract Composition with Pilchards
1984

oil paint on steel
100 x 175 x 75cms
Lisson Gallery London

latter day of *Gulliver's Travels*. The abstract works are a solution to the problem of how to hold a space but they are quite consistent with his earlier approach in that abstraction is used as representation. A rectangle is not only literally rectangular but also painted as a rectangle, with the edges outlined and the shadows indicated. And the three dimensional shapes allude to the two dimensional representation of solid abstract forms in painting, in certain cases to Leger in particular.

Abstract art, like packaging, functions as a system of signs. There are precedents for the use of demotic imagery: Leger, Stuart Davis, Richard Hamilton, Lichtenstein, Warhol and Oldenburg to name but a few. But in their case mass imagery becomes subject matter to be raised to the level of high art. Opie scrambles his various sources to form the lexicon of a common visual language. The point is not the overcoming of a distinction between art and non-art, but the way in which in contemporary society so much of the visual field has become a confection. He told me in an interview, ''What I find about cliches is the funny way in which they are very flat, like a concept or idea of something. If you

mix that up with things that I call round, like feelings or things to do with personal life, you've got an immediate challenge. That links up with messing around in the sculpture with what is illusory or flat and what is real, the actual shape. Those two things are happening at the same time in the work''. As we stand before it, the painted steel sculpture invites us to take pleasure in the exuberant and energetic rendition of stereotypes, but as we move to the side the illusion crumbles into its component parts. It would be wrong to overstress this device since the conventionalized style of depiction and comic-book primary colours already presume disbelief. Together they are used for various ends: innocent enjoyment is thrown off-balance by tackiness, the minor irritants of life like parking tickets and tax returns are turned into the objects of visual pleasure.

The sham, vulgar quality of Opie's work manifests a resentment of the way in which cliches and stereotypes manipulate and control our lives, evoking desires only to frustrate them, but it is equally a revenge on the way in which the values of 'high' culture are imposed from above: both are part of the same set up. Yet cliches also provide a way

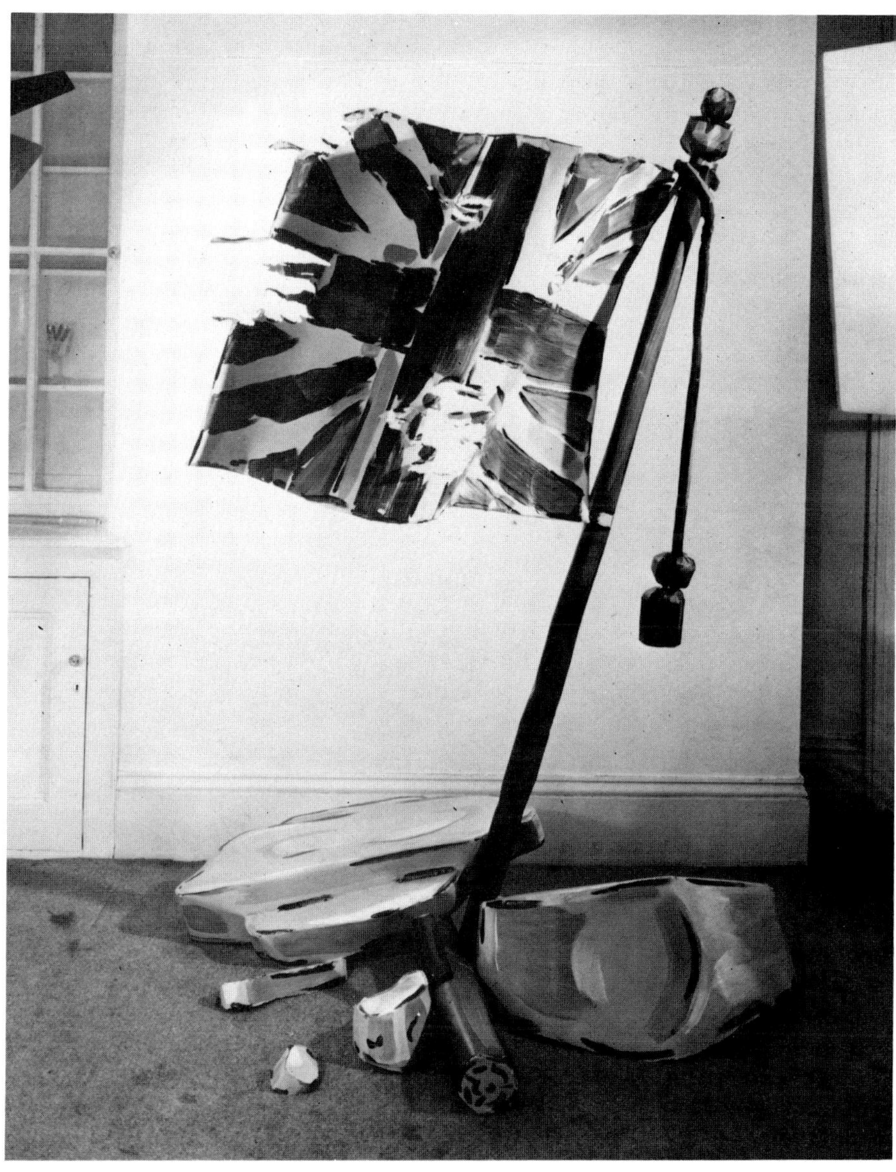

Last Stand
1984

oil paint on steel
75 x 62 x 34ins
191 x 158 x 86.5cms
Lisson Gallery London

of coming to terms with the problems of life in an urban mass society, alienation, loneliness, depression, rejection: enabling an identification with others and an objectification of feelings which can be treated with humour and a sense of the absurd. In one sculpture the letters of the word LONELY tumble down in the solitary pool of light from a red-shaded standard lamp; in another, the words KILL ME are brushed into a dust pan. Another lamp, where the blue-painted letters BLUE support a yellow ceiling shade, is both reminiscent of Jasper John's use of names and colours as two sign-systems which intersect on the surface of the painting, and an evocation of late night melancholy. The word is both a shape in the sculpture and like the lyric in a pop song which you can't get out of your head, both enjoyable and infuriating. In a recent piece the letters RELAX, from the refrain of a hit by the band Frankie Goes To Hollywood, support various items from the domestic environment which the song would have infiltrated, including a bottle, a vase of flowers, a blue dish, a knife and a loaf of French bread.

Dis-illusionment in Opie's sculptures does not take place for the sake of a greater truth, since cliches *are* needed in order to say anything at all, from 'I'm in love' to 'kill me', from the enjoyment of consumer goods to political protest. A tattered Union Jack on a tassled flagpole stuck into some grey rocks expresses the bathos of the imperialist pretentions of the Falklands campaign, the nostalgic *Last Stand* of a nation which cannot come to terms with its own decline. When 'real life' aspires to the condition of cliche, how else to deal with it than by another cliche? To do that is not a symptom of acquiescence but rather the opposite: to assume a measure of control within the limitations of art which is itself a part of the system. When Opie entitles a sculpture *Strong Statement* it consists of an enlarged cheque book, wallet of credit cards, fountain pen and bank statement. Julian Opie matches the banality of contemporary consumer culture with the generosity of his art, taking mediated imagery to make sculpture which is vividly there. In his hands contrivance becomes the means of achieving a certain honesty, what we might once have called 'truth to life'.

Michael Newman

*Editors Note: this film was released in the UK in 1982.

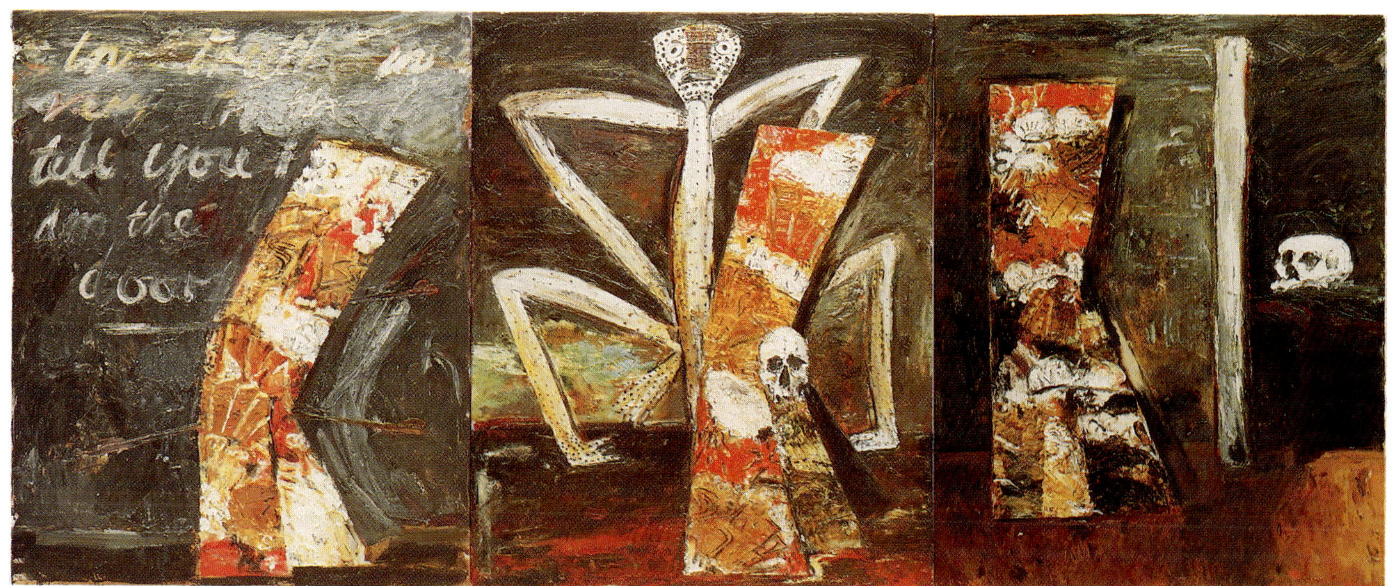

Oceania My Dilemma
1983

oil on canvas
212 x 171cms
triptych
courtesy Art Gallery of NSW

JOHN WALKER

Those that meditate return to contemplate the same few objects, again and again: icons, relics or mandalas. It is not on a variety of things they ponder, but on a few recurrent objects through which can be sensed underlying verities. John Walker's paintings can be seen as a meditation in which we viewers participate. Over the past twenty years the world of his paintings has been inhabited by a relatively restricted number of motifs. These motifs have ranged from geometric shapes such as trapezoids, envelopes or flattened circles to, in the more recent work, more anthropomorphic shapes. The most persistent of these, which appears in each panel of the triptych *Oceania: My Dilemma*, is the monolithshape which first appeared in the Alba paintings. It is on and around these motifs that the painting with its marks and colours, and which can itself be seen as an act of meditation, moves. Although Walker is not overtly religious he has in his paintings always sought what he has termed ''spiritual content''. That such should be the goal of his work has been highlighted by the most recent, and perhaps most curious, motif: the quotation from the gospel of Saint John (10.7) which has often appeared in paintings of the last three years.

''In truth, in very truth, I tell you I am the door.'' So Christ says in the course of telling his disciples the parable of the good shepherd. The good shepherd will enter the sheepfold by the door whereas thieves and robbers will climb over the wall; likewise, the sheep will follow only the shepherd through the door because they recognise his voice alone. Christ is both the good shepherd and the door: ''I am the door: by me if any man enter in, he shall be saved, and shall go in and out, and find pasture,''(10.9).

To know the original context of the quotation tells us surprisingly little of what it means in the new context of the paintings. Despite all its associations the phrase functions primarily as an announcing one, much as ''I will arise and go forth'', or ''I am the vine; you are the branches''. It demands further explication, yet Walker never goes on to write the following verse where the door and salvation are made synonymous: the statement as it stand remains incomplete. It announces the seriousness of the painting's themes, but does not explain them. It is important to remember that here the words are painted, not written. Just as with the American painter Cy Twombly, who also uses writing in his paintings, the act of enunciation is here as important as what is ostensibly being enunciated. The writing becomes a motif like all the other motifs: the Alba-shape, the screen, the skull. At one level it is something to paint, and to which painting carries its own meanings.

In one painting, *The Lesson I* of 1983, the writing appears on what looks like a blackboard at the end of a room, (one recalls that in the early seventies Walker did enormous chalk drawings on blackened walls), while before it one of the Alba shapes stands, doll-like, bowed from the waist up and pierced by three arrows, and with a skull attached to it. Like actors on a stage the motifs meet each other, or pass by each other without speaking as in the large painting *Oceania II* where four Alba shapes pass or follow each other as though in stately procession. Like a Greek chorus four curved shapes watch another bowed and arrow-pierced Alba-shape in another untitled painting of 1984. The frequency with which the Alba-shape occurs makes it seem very much like the main actor (a narrator figure even?). In the triptych here can we read the painting as a narrative in which the same character appears? It is difficult not to try and do so, and yet, it is in fact, difficult to actually do so for, at the last instance, we cannot be sure that the shape even represents a figure.

In an early painting such as *Skyboard* the shapes or motifs moved very much against a large space like a landscape. They moved like the travellers in romantic landscapes do, surveying the prospect; or else like Dante and Virgil in Hell, exploring and commentating. In the recent paintings the space seems more often that of an interior, often darkened. In this shift Walker's paintings echo

paintings by Velazquez and Manet. Consistently the motifs are enriched by reference to paintings of the past. Those paintings called *Alba* echoed Goya's portrait of the Duchess of Alba, while those entitled *Infanta* echoed Velazquez's paintings of the children of the Spanish royal family. Elsewhere when he uses as a motif the skate it recalls Chardin's still life of a skate. It has been vital for Walker not only to belong to a painting tradition with its own history and meanings, but also to affirm his belief in its continuing validity and significance. In particular he calls upon Spanish painting, especially Goya and Velazquez. Even when he derived the motif of the balcony from Manet it was in turn derived from Goya. Walker turns to Spanish painting not so much for its dark meditational, or brooding quality as for

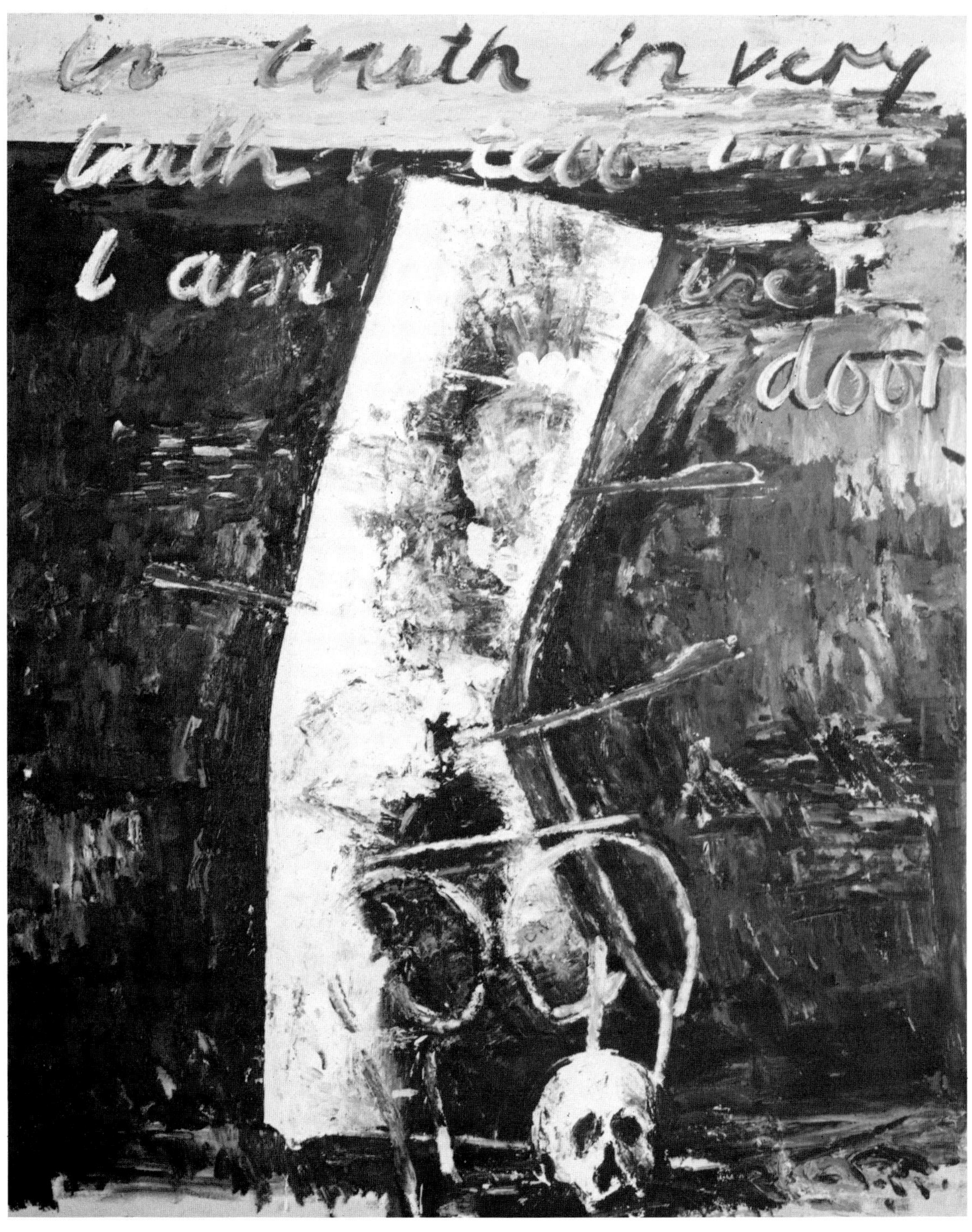

Oceania X
1983

acrylic on canvas
213.4 x 152.4cms

Skyboard
1970

acrylic on canvas
243.8 x 609.6cms

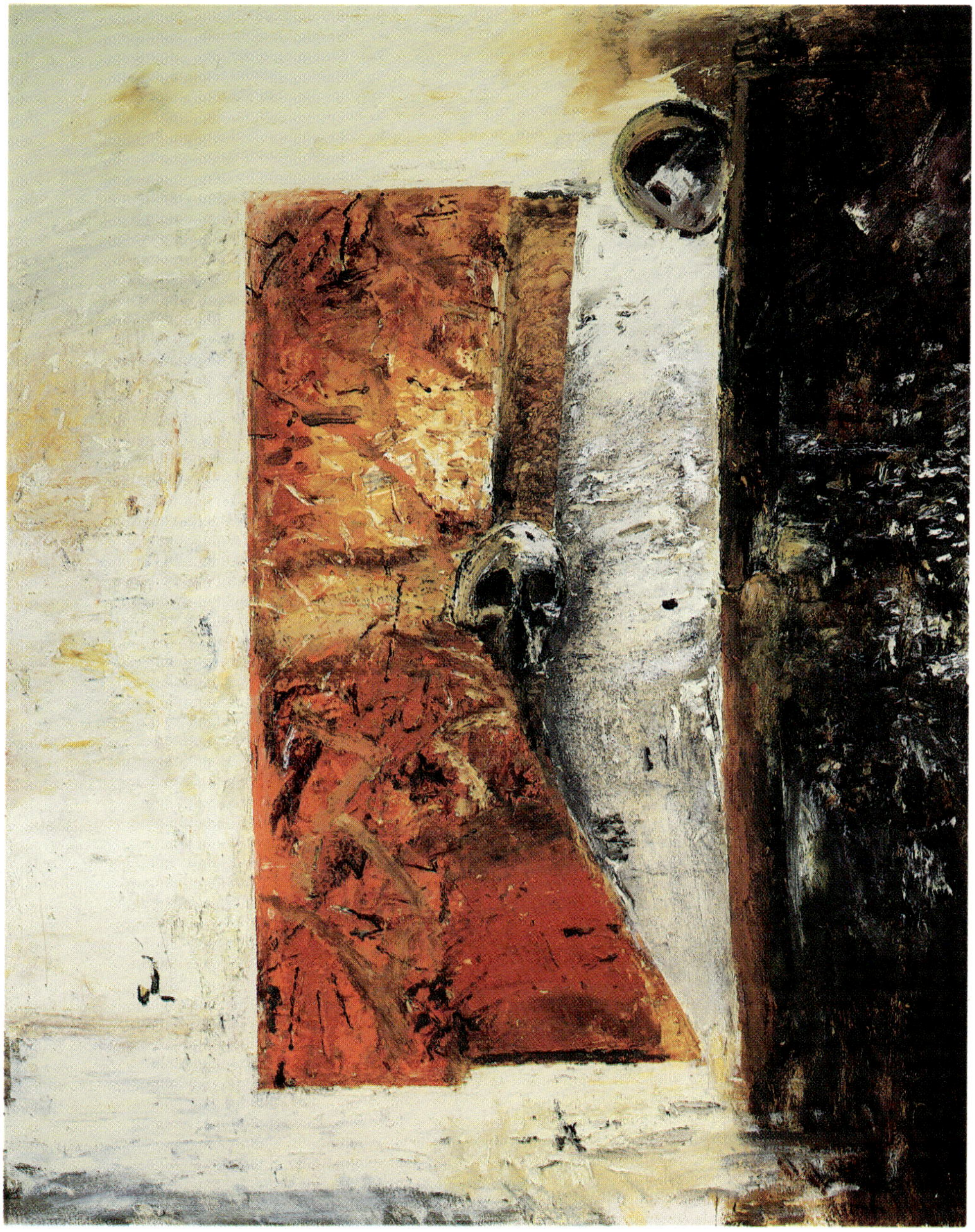

The Red Centre
1984

oil on canvas
213.4 x 167.6cms

its emphasis on stillness and surface. There is a refusal in Velazquez and other Spanish painters to deny the flatness of the paintings surface: our eye is denied the pleasure of voyaging to a clearly defined vanishing point. So it is with Walker: we are continually pulled back to the surface as the illusionism is contested by gestural paint marks.

For all the seeming business of the paint handling these are slow paintings: constructed over a long period and requiring a considerable period of attention from us to divulge their secrets. Just as the motifs in the paintings confront each other so do they confront us as viewers: the skull, like the insectoid head, stares at us, demanding that we make what we will of it. Throughout the history of painting the skull has, eyeless, stared back at us, calling on us to contemplate the lineaments of death that we carry within our own heads. Whittled down to the minimum the skull is what we are left with as the signifying mark of man or woman. It is, and it is essential that we recognise this, also a beautiful and complex form in itself.

In the *Numinous* or balcony paintings shapes peer out from behind the balcony: there is an immanence, a presence to them that can seem both threatening and suggestive of possible spiritual enlightenment. This mixture of foreboding and revelation seems more drastic in the paintings done since he moved to Australia in 1980. There is even an element of cruelty — the St Sebastian-like arrows in the motif, elsewhere severed heads — that in its sardonic humour recalls aboriginal art. Sometimes the world of these paintings seems like that of Samuel Beckett's late plays: nameless characters or motifs move, divorced of context, in a barely furnished, often cruel world. The world of paintings holds, of course, far more hope, or possibility of revelation than Beckett's plays. Most importantly there is in many of the paintings the possibility of a discovery of joy and beauty.

It is in the handling of paint itself that we may discover such joyousness. Walker has always been an abstract painter and these paintings are all ultimately abstract: his marks as a language refer primarily to the tradition of abstract gestural painting, unlike his motifs. It is the brushmarks in all his paintings that are vital: it is they with their variety, ranging from the nervous to the exuberant or joyous, that give a pulsing life to the canvases. The strength and fascination of the motifs may draw our attention away from the background or field against which they stand, but often it is the backgrounds, with their manifold inflections and nuances of paint-handling which carry most of the meaning of the painting.

A useful comparision may be made between Walker and his German contemporary George Baselitz. Both have depended on motifs: in the case of Baselitz normally a figure. But whereas Baselitz has sought to subvert our representational reading of the figure by dislocating or upending it Walker has sought to subvert our formal reading of abstract painting by investing abstract forms with human presence and significance. Both of them have put an unusual emphasis on the importance of drawing, and both curiously use at times surprisingly conventional modelling. Most importantly both use the motif and the field it stands against to confront us: they do not allow their painting to be easy, either for themselves or us.

Walker has always been wary of elegance. Greenbergian flatness and its decorative implications have never attracted him. The physicality of his paintings with their thick paint and elements of collage are partly a reaction against such easy elegance. There are passages of great lyrical beauty in his paintings, but they are never trivial or vicarious. Most importantly he believes that paintings must contain life, that is have content. These paintings are meditations on death and life, on the passage of time, on our doubts.

A comparison with the abstract expressionist painter Clifford Still, whom Walker admires, is indicative of the problems Walker's art gives. Whereas in Still's paintings figure and ground have become synonymous, such is his confidence in his vision; in Walker's their relationship is not certain: our eye and the motif are fought for by the surface and the apparent depth. Whereas Still saw his paintings as embodiments of the sublime, of truth, Walker would see his as a search, or a struggle, for truth. They are difficult paintings, their victories and pleasures hard won. They are also generous paintings, for in them that struggle, those victories, those pleasures are made available to us.

Tony Godfrey

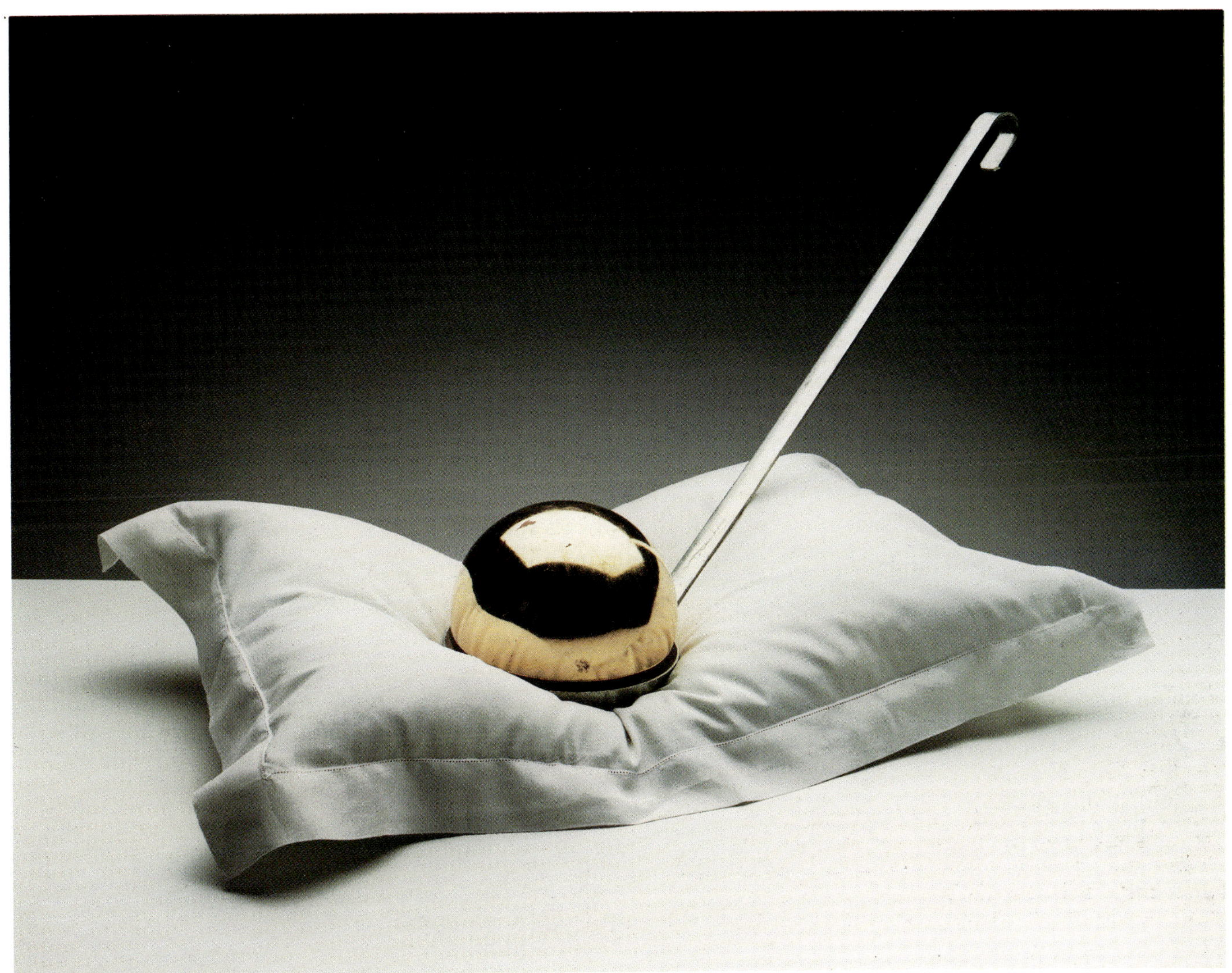

RICHARD WENTWORTH'S ETYMOLOGY

Heist (For S.E.)
1983

linen, duckdown, tinned steel, gilded lead
60 x 90 x 65cms
The Saatchi Collection, London

Etymology n. Account of or facts relating to formation of word and development of its meaning; branch of linguistic science concerned with this.

Richard Wentworth teaches at Goldsmiths College, University of London; he lives in a partly finished house in North London, has an equally unfinished 'country cottage' (a grand title for a converted wooden hut built as a wartime billet on a now disused airfield), and a large cluttered studio which contains as many parts of houses as parts of works of art, both, as he points out, material in a raw state. (He has likened the chaotic landscape of the studio to his own mind.) His two young sons often spend time at the studio with him; his wife works in a major design group. The front passenger seat of his car functions as his office and is cluttered with

papers and catalogues. I mention these domestic details only in order to suggest that Wentworth's ability to construct a unified picture of his world from this ordinary experience is significant in an appraisal of his work. Any one of these elements can, and does, provide sustenance for, and information about, his sculptural work. Perhaps I should mention too his close interest in the oddities of human behaviour and his collection of books about words, their origins and meanings. His own suggestion for the title of this essay was the words on the bag from a French ironmonger: MENAGE — BAZAR — CADEAUX — JOUETS.

Titles are significant to him and unravelling their meanings can suggest multiple, and often interlocking, readings of the works. A semiotic reading, for example, would uncover a *signifier* or "sound image" of the work and might adumbrate the *signified* or conceptual meaning. With Wentworth that lies not only in the formal self-referential language of modern sculpture but in the sculptor's inevitable collaboration and complicity with real events. In some ways Wentworth is a Barthean *avant la lettre*; he can and does offer constructions about subjects of a grand scale through ordinary objects modified or urged together. And, like Barthes and, at another extreme, the tabloids, the subjects that preoccupy him are human frailties, sexuality and mortality.

Wentworth suffered the attentions this summer of the silly season British press trying to raise interest in the story of the sinking of the Argentine battleship Belgrano during the Falklands War. The Arts Council was showing *Toy* (jouet) in a mixed exhibition and had sent a questionnaire asking for information about the work. Wentworth replied that it had been made when his children were very young and at a time when the sinking of the battlecruiser was still a live political issue; carefully, he thought, avoiding the connection between the two, leaving, as he puts it a "gap" for the observer to operate in. A clumsily written wall label that effectively closed the gap and the resulting storm in a teacup, with protagonists drawn in on both sides, sealed the fate of the bathtub and sardine tin as being forever "about" the Belgrano. The title claims no such connection and, in fact, suggested other clues. *Toy* is made from a galvanised washtub (bought near the wooden house) and a sardine tin (purchased in London); they have the same formal significance, being oval containers. Wentworth would admit that formality is his first line of defence (or intended strategy, to put it more positively) when asked to explain a work.

(He, like other British sculptors of his generation, was strongly influenced by the idealist notions of much minimal work.) Setting one oval within another interested him — and he was also affected by the sophistication of the manufacturing processes used to make both tub and can, things normally considered mundane. Then, he is in the habit of taking a bath with his son and he noticed the child's delight when he first floated a tin with water in it and dismay when it later filled and sank. Thinking about the child's discovery suggested to him parallels where a simple childishness is characteristic of the so-called complexities of events in an adult world. It also offered a provisional title — "toy"[1]. He made the work, if you wish, as a correlative of the childish experience. The process of its soldering was reminiscent of the concurrent welding of helicopter decks onto the sundecks of the QE2 in dock in Southampton; the enclosure of the volume in the old tin tub at the moment that the nation was supposedly discovering its identity again through the war took on both sinister and poetic meanings. It was after all the moment when the right-wing *Sun* newspaper, owned by Rupert Murdoch, could print a photograph of the sinking on its front page with a huge headline "GOTCHA". The moment conspired to draw to the surface Wentworth's own scarcely repressed doubts about mortality and morality. He is unable either to keep this out of his work or to safely confine it (and therefore emasculate it) within the polite tradition of postwar formal British sculpture. His reply to the educationalist, borrowed and converted, had thus contained the clues both of his disappointment with the sterility of object sculpture and the request that his sculpture should be allowed to exist within/criticise allusively the discourses of (political)[2] life.

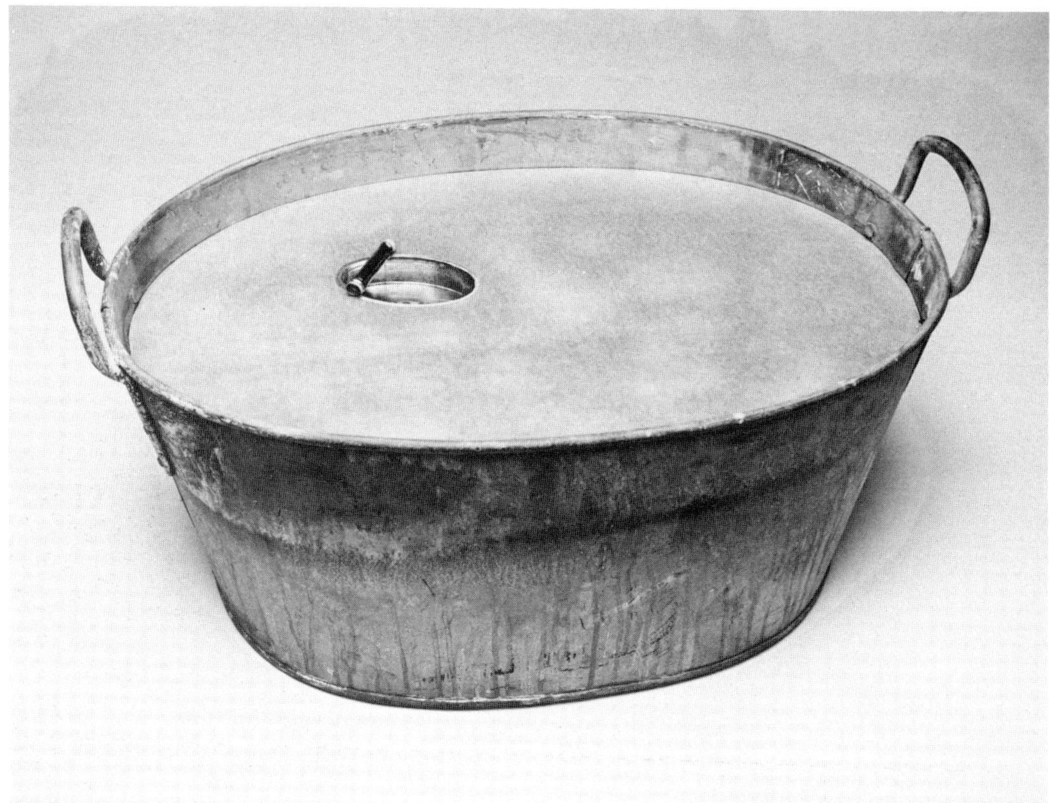

Toy
1983

galvanised and tinned steel
197 x 80 x 80cms
Collection Arts Council of Great Britain

In effect, he would like it to enter the world and to live in the same category of object as the *Citroen DS* when it was characterised by Barthes as *DS*/déesse (goddess). When the titles are working they have that kind of resonance.

Babar and Fido has its origins in the children's bedtime stories and in games where children take and transform objects in their imagination to act out fantasies. Wentworth's paternal grandfather, an upright gentleman, kept spaniels, archetypal faithful (L. noun *fido*) mutts, and the sculptor inherited his dog bowl. It is *made of* a single piece of spun aluminium and is functional since the dog cannot turn it over and it keeps his ears out of the food. It *looks like* a sailor's cap, a view reinforced by the children wearing it, but only the hat worn by lowly ratings in heroic wartime movies. In a modified form, changed that is by the childish procedure of snipping ''V''s out of the upturned bowl, and gilded, it *looks like* the crown with which the wordly Babar celebrates his return from the absurd adult world of the old lady and the city, where he has been both racially and sexually insulted, to be leader among his peers. The irony is that his incorporation and elevation rests on this humiliating experience. Wentworth displays this dual abasement by literally connecting the two ''hats'' by a continuous cord, nailed to the floor and ceiling to form a narrow doorway through which the spectator could tentatively pass, as it were *sub jugum*. Wentworth wishes to make clear the precariousness of the

kingly position, now suspended on high but all too easily dropped.

Being a meticulous craftsman when necessary, and one day having to tidy up his studio, he put the lead ball he had painstakingly made for another work in a ladle resting on a pillow, with its pillowcase on (from another, *Nature, Mort*) for safe keeping. To his surprise the ladle stood up erect — hoisted itself. That same weekend there was a major robbery from a security warehouse (Security Express — SE) near the studio when seven million pounds worth of gold bullion was lifted. The tabloids gloried in the cheeky thieves and dubbed the robbery, in the style of the *New York Post*, a *heist*. Soon afterwards Wentworth found the enormous ladle that finally prompted this work.[3]

He had seen the (French) chairs used in *Lightweight Chair with Heavy Weights* and *Siege* in a cheap furniture shop and speculated both on their debased modern/ist fragility and their feminine, capricious apparent readiness to up and skitter. The first work prevented this flightiness by giving 'balls' to the chair, and by implication the ponderous seriousness of masculinity, but apparently addressed 'proper' sculptural concerns through its title. The second comes clean, for its sexuality is riddled with complaint and its impossible coupling derisory. The pleasure in the chair's feminity is translated to contempt and transferred, by implication, to feminist arguments. An extreme reading suggests two

Siege
1983/4

laminated wood, steel, brass, lead and cable
actual size
collection Janet Green
photo credit: Mike Parsons

Lightweight Chair with Heavy Weights
1983

laminated wood, steel, brass, lead and cable
actual size
photo credit: Mike Parsons

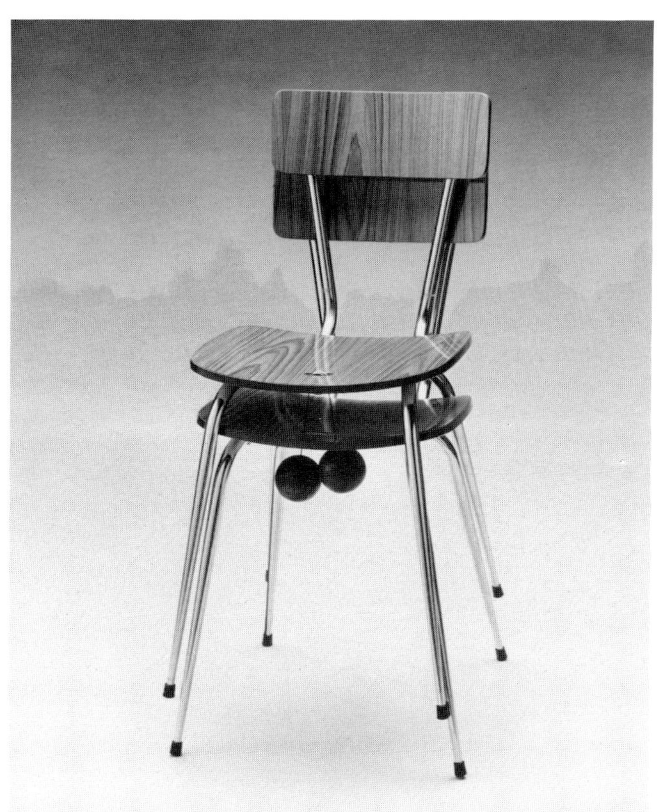

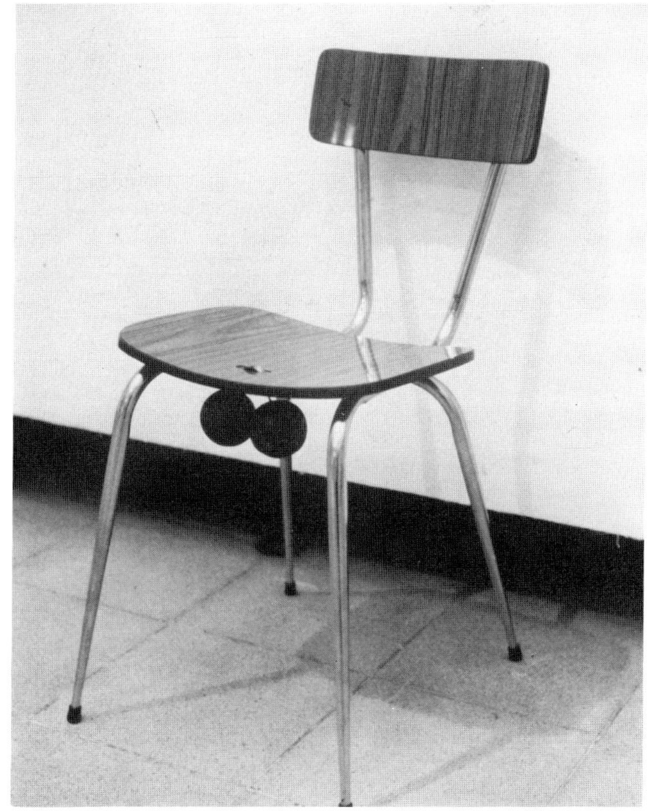

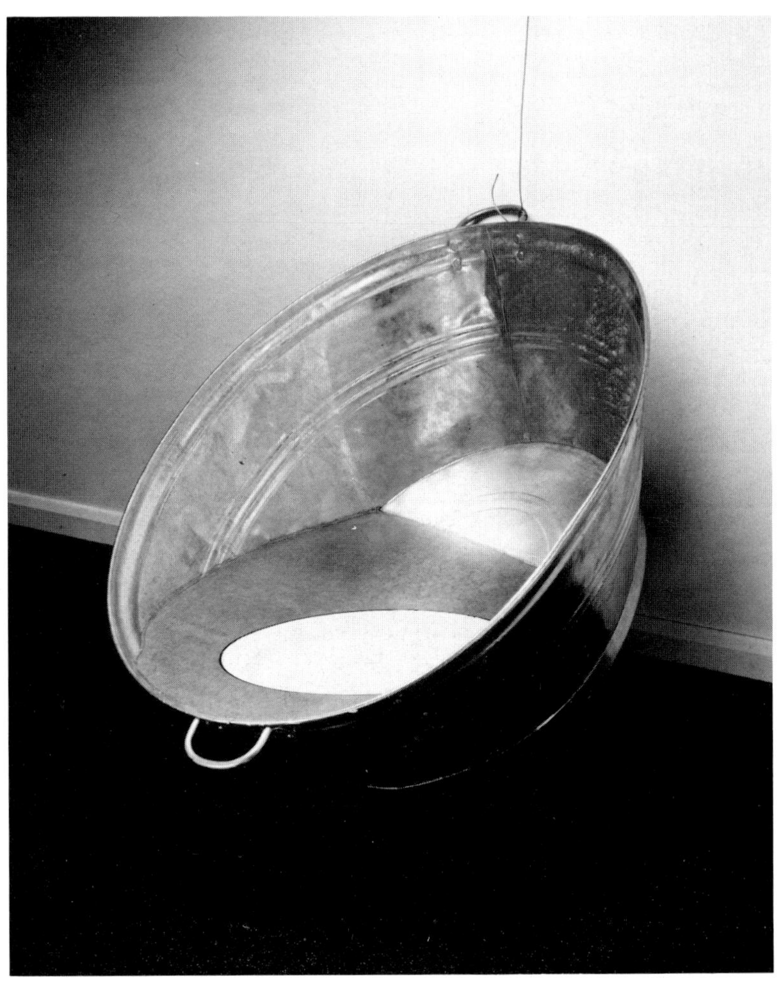

Jetsam
1984

galvanised and enamelled steel, cable
197 x 80 x 80cms
Saatchi Collection, London

women caught in *flagrante delicto* and imprisoned by an assumed masculinity that is not properly theirs. Or, the balls are caught, laid siege to, castrated.[4] In French *Siege* (noun masculine) means not only seat but familiarly as in *lever le siège* to "take oneself off", an act that is prevented here by the balls and their serpentine *vas deferens*.

Flotsam and jetsam normally go together: jetsam is thrown, flotsam floats and is defined as "wreckage found floating". This work was made soon after *Toy*, and is a development of the formal and linguistic vocabulary of that work. The formal conundrum here is the matching of parts of ovals in precarious positions created by the act of tipping (throwing) the large tub. But one of the ovals is an old enamelled dish, similar to those you can buy in army surplus stores, and suggests perhaps that the jetsam or jettisoning (throwing overboard esp. to lighten ship in distress) returns to the subject of war. The artist also mentions the story that Claes Oldenburg tells of

his pleasure at feeling scraps of food in the washing up water where they convey more of human foibles than the grand feast itself.

Roland Barthes wrote in *The Pleasure of the Text*: "If you hammer a nail into a piece of wood, the wood has resistance according to the place that you attack it: we say that wood is not isotropic . . . Just as (today's) physics must accommodate the non-isotropic character of certain environments, certain universes, so structural analysis must recognise the slightest resistances in the text, the irregular pattern of its veins."[5] If we substitute sculpture for text we can recognize perhaps the particular quality of these works, their irregularity and the blood that flows through them and, what is more, the paucity of language's attempts to unveil a project conceived in the gap between image and word, between statement and understanding.

Richard Francis

1. Wentworth noted on the first draft of this essay: "Toying with an idea/political puppet/'forces' used in political games/Games which become serious. Games in which rules are broken/*playing* one's hand/'Theatre' of operations."

2. Wentworth questions the term political; he considers the thought of dying in an enclosed space much more significant than the politics that dictate it.

3. The artist adds: "Inverted corporate identity symbol. Ball is delectable, impossible to steal (lift) except in imagination./

Pillow, sleep. Speculation as to whether SE were asleep/ Cushion — crown jewels, heraldry.

4. The artist is particularly conscious that these are deliberately provocative readings, elicited in conversation. He considers it a *comedy* really, since if you analyse the work's sexual motif, the balls seem to belong to the lower partner, suggesting a woman astride a man, but the upper chair has the mechanism and the lower only a slot. He adds "Don't people say 'Biting your balls off' or something?"

5. Roland Barthes *The Pleasure of the Text*, New York 1975, p.36.

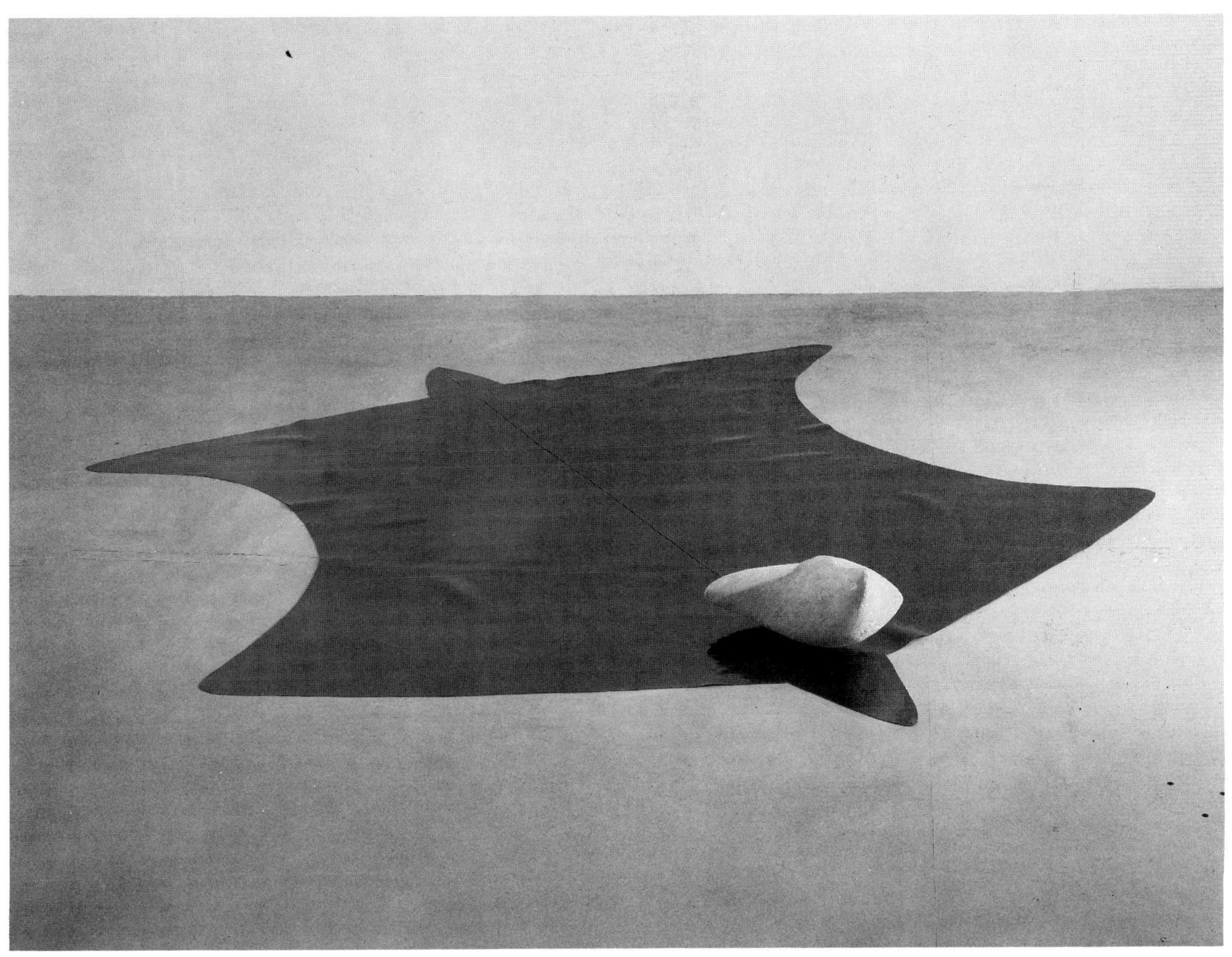

Dark Horse 1
1983

portland stone & rubber
24 x 255 x 312.5cms
The artist courtesy Salvatore Ala Galleries Milan and New York

ALISON WILDING

Alison Wilding's sculpture is essentially bound up with the practicalities of making. Wilding regards her sculptures as 'things', as independent objects in the world and the term 'poetic' which has frequently been applied to her work is received with less than rapture. For Wilding, this description implies 'an inability to see beyond a recognition of the order of things' — a refuge in evasion. The word "poetic" does a disservice to Poetry'. She does, however, acknowledge the metaphorical content of her work, especially of recent sculpture where the expression of ideas has shifted from the surface into its heart.

Between 1981 and 1983, when Wilding's work came to the attention of the British public, she was principally concerned with exploring the nature of surface and balance, employing traditional sculptural materials such as wood, lead, and metal. Often two or more of these were used in the same work providing contrasts of texture, weight, light and hue. Generally the materials were not left in their natural state but altered to achieve a uniformity which would disguise the surface and emphasise its unity. In *Red*, for example, the upper element is coated with a uniform skin of red wax which reduces interest in the surface texture of the wood as wood. In *Pond*, a sculpture where the copper has been coloured by immersion in acid, she explores opacity and reflection and suggests solid and liquid states. The contrast of light and dark is also marked.

Differences in materials are more discreetly handled in *Leaden* an earlier work. Here a wedge of lead is embedded in a solid bowl-shaped piece of wood to which graphite has been applied so avoiding strong contrast. As a result the sculpture, like a number of Wilding's other works, is slow to reveal its full impact and accordingly the concept of time becomes an important element in the work, a concept which she has explored further more recently. Other early sculptures were more confrontational; *Dark Perch* for example is strikingly assertive in its verticality and, as a result of its lead base discreetly merged with the wooden shaft, is

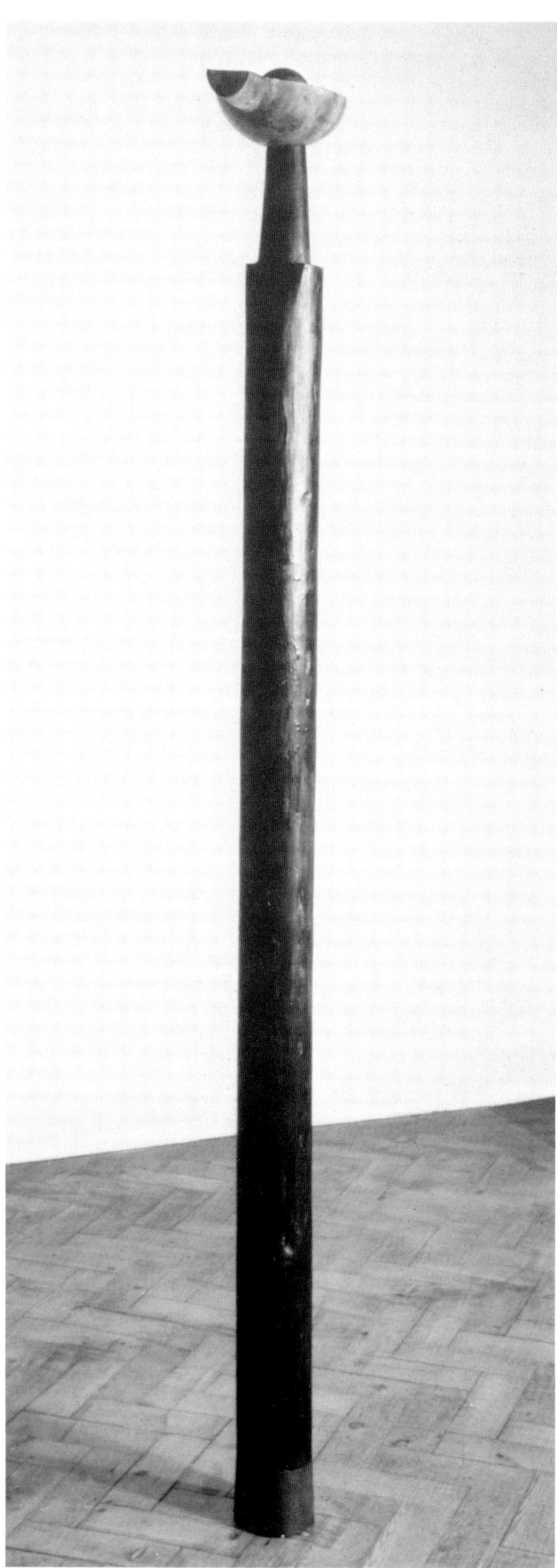

Dark Perch
1982

75ins high
wood, lead and wax

self-sufficient, requiring no extraneous support to maintain this position.

A number of Wilding's floor pieces maintain their equilibrium through the agency of weight. For example in *Red* the lead is embedded in the upper wooden element and causes the supporting mass to alter its relationship to the ground by rocking it gently forward. The same is true of *Leaden*. The concept of balance in Wilding's sculpture, however, is not limited to such a literal exploration, for in a work such as *Pond* the two objects are placed in positions to counterbalance each other. Furthermore, Wilding regards the copper surface as a meniscus, a fluid mass which is itself held in a state of equilibrium by surface tension. Balance has of course been of great importance to many twentieth century sculptors, in particular to Brancusi whom Wilding at one time looked towards. Indeed *Leaden* bears some resemblance to Brancusi's series of cups and to the stools surrounding his *Table of Silence*. The affinity is not simply visual for *Leaden* is also characterised by the mystery pertaining to Brancusi's work; it is not far from embodying the sense of the useless utensil manifested in Brancusi's cups. Other sculptures, for example *Dark Perch*, *Red*, and *Brass Neck*, are variations on the theme of the head which is also of central importance in Brancusi's oeuvre.

Late in 1983 Wilding began to make sculpture which did not consist of balancing components although she continued to juxtapose different materials. In exploring beyond the surface appearance she began to make sculptures which were less literal and more metaphoric. This development coincided with a desire to produce more substantial, volumetric sculpture of greater object quality. Many of her previous works had been small and some were intended to be hung on the wall. *Green Rise*, perhaps the best of these, continues to explore the concept of visually balanced and contrasting materials, weights and densities. Wilding regards such wall pieces as 'a quick way of getting things out' and in some respects they are like maquettes or details of larger pieces; making it 'was like making sense from a shadow rather than making sense of the thing casting a shadow'. She became more interested in the substance of sculpture which was still an unknown quantity to her and which she had always 'kept at arm's length'. She considers *Dark Horse* to be an attempt to resolve this problem but "whether *Dark Horse* marked anything more than a slow turn in this direction is doubtful. Things move so slowly forward and also backwards. This is hindsight to an extent — at the time it was a desire to move away — clarity comes later."

Dark Horse is one of a number of recent sculptures in which Wilding has sought an art which is richer in resonance and meaning. Her increased understanding of materials and her realisation that ideas and materials are interdependent and inextricable have resulted in the fabrications of sculptures of greater depth. Material is no longer simply descriptive of ideas but becomes a metaphor for them. Wilding's sculpture continues to consist of contrasting light and heavy elements employed in the most sparing manner. This reflects her notion of slow and quick sculptural ideas: "Slow ideas are

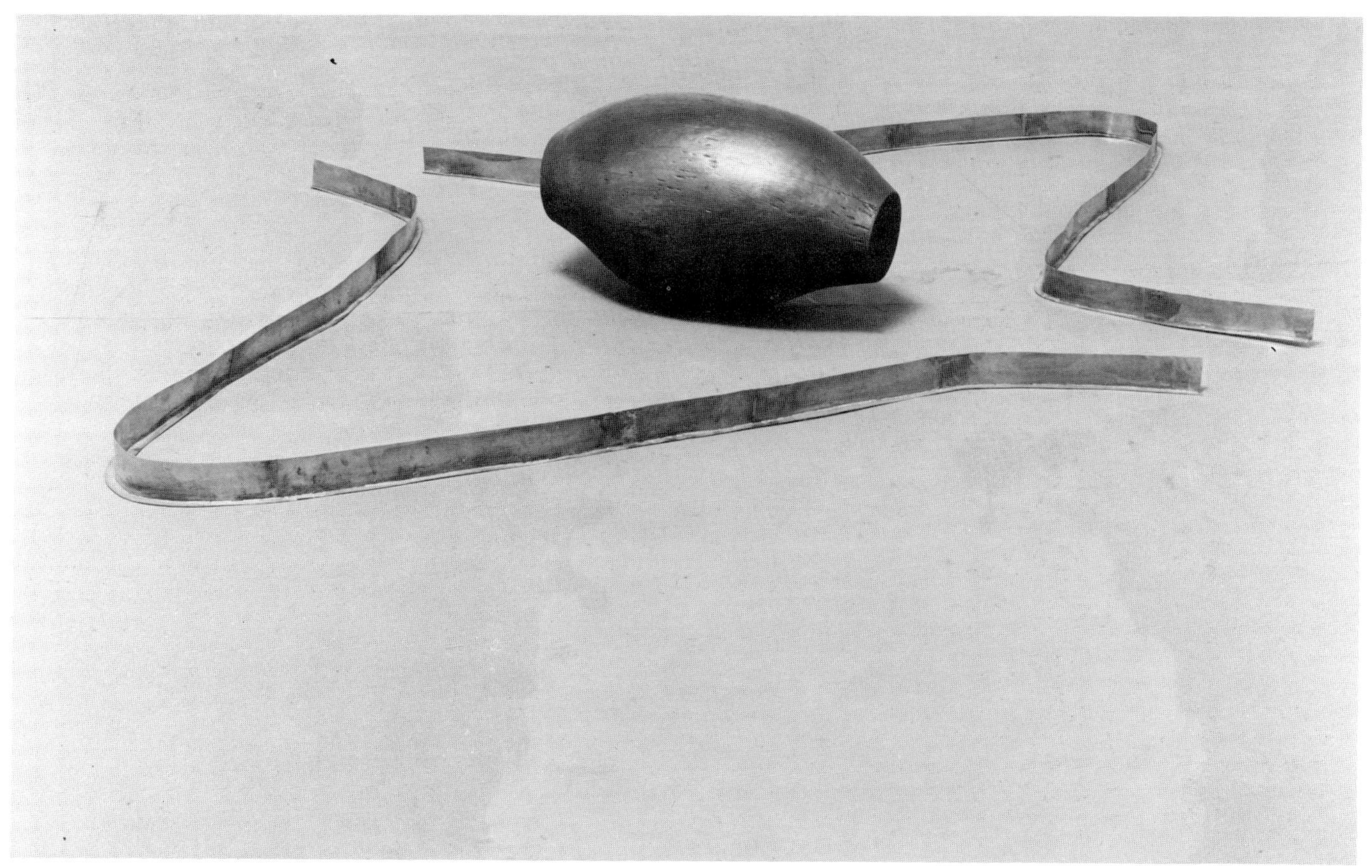

Indelible Field
1984

oil paint, graphite on oak, brass & copper
14 x 85 x 111ins
35.6 x 215.9 x 281.9cms

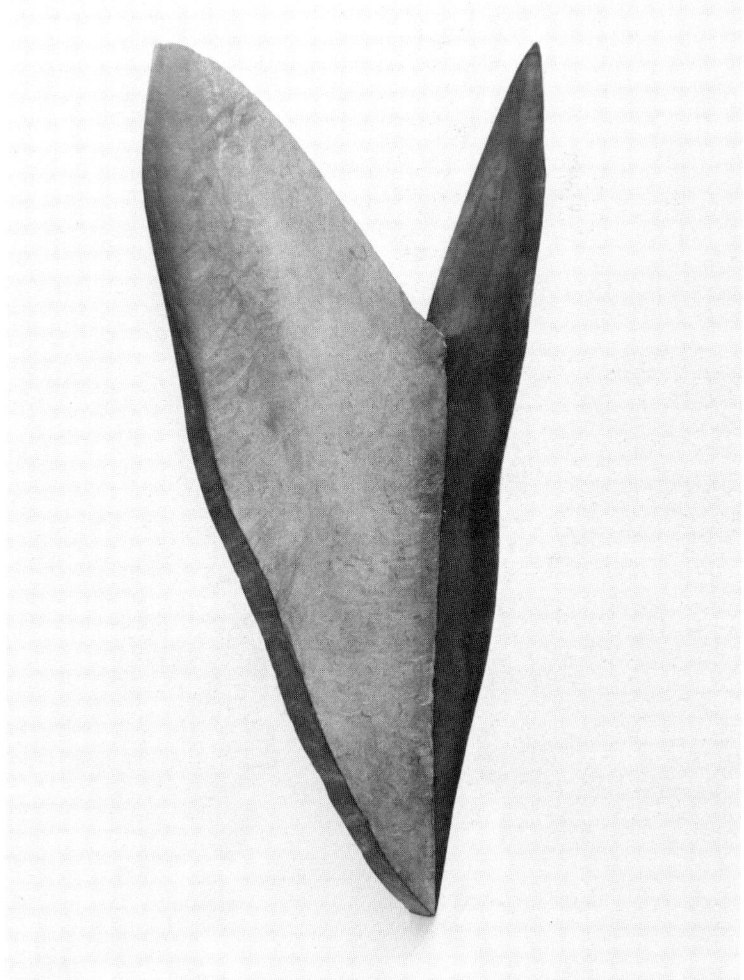

Green Rise
1983

slate & copper
58.5 x 10 x 28cms
collection of the Contemporary Art Society London

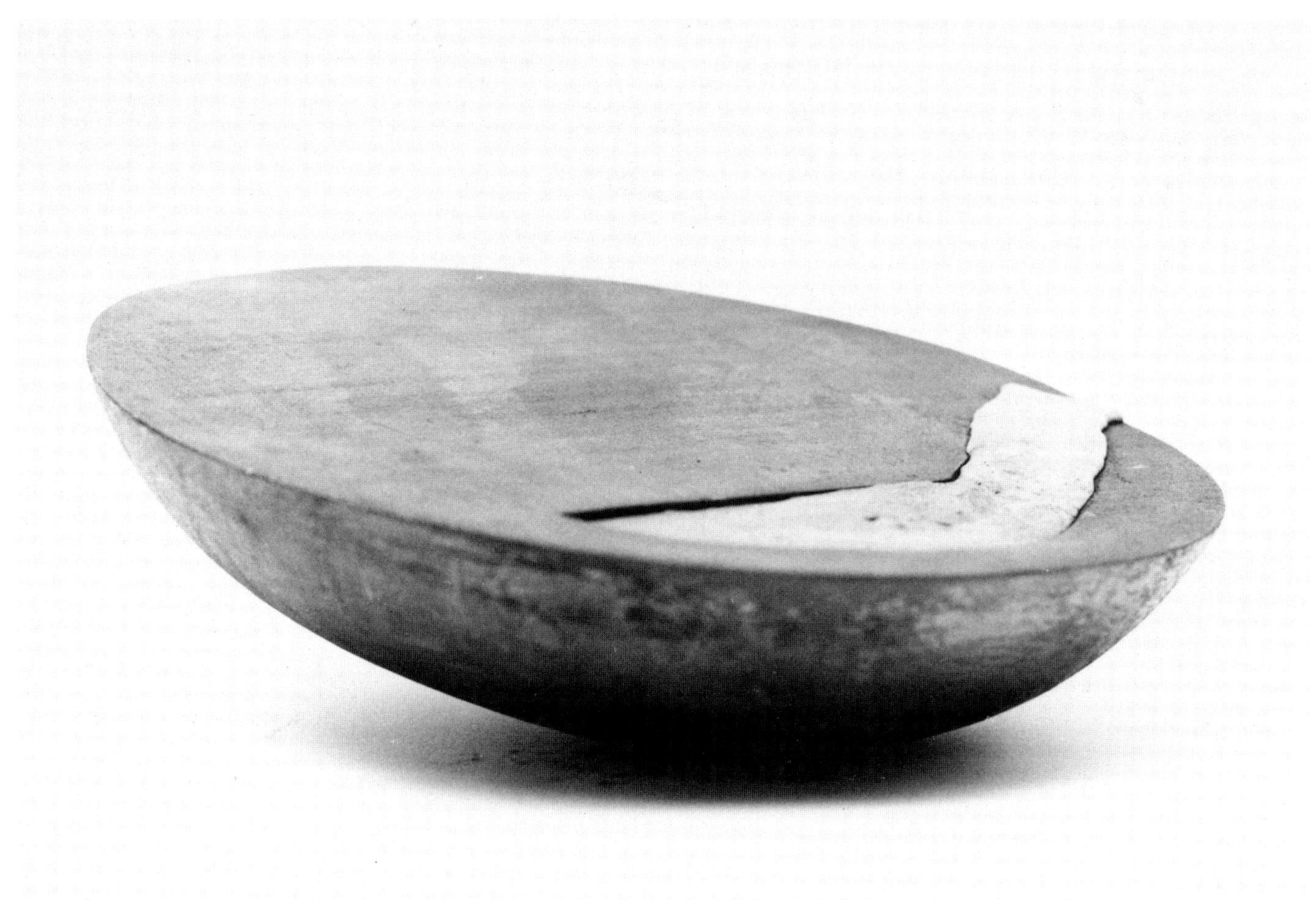

generated through carving stone or wood. That in itself is never enough. It is the quick part — which is a response to the slow — more spontaneous, sometimes like drawing, which tells you how to see it, which changes the nature of the sculpture into more than just a carving.'' The concept of time is not only important in the making of sculpture but also in its perception. The quick part, which often consists of non-ferrous sheet metal either coloured or left in its natural state, is sometimes a linear element which quickens the pace of a work in contrast to the slow, carved element which may be a solid mass. A recent work, *Indelible Field*, exemplifies this aspect as indeed does the earlier *Brass Neck*. Because the quick part is malleable it may be worked swiftly which permits considerable improvisation. It also extends the metaphorical meaning of the sculpture as well as defining its context. In Wilding's words it creates 'a place'. *Dark Horse* was one of the first works in which this was explored. Initially Wilding carved the stone element but she realised that 'the stone had to be on something. I felt the stone's animalism needed to be both enforced and reduced by this other unknown part of the work. I drew a rough chalk circle around the stone on the floor. And then I thought about stuff and not shape. From the materials I knew, I arrived at a rubber sheet — and realised that rubber is a vegetable skin. The drawing

was subsequently made to exclude direction — head and tail both ambiguous — it had to be as non-specific as possible. Cut out, the rubber became both place and body — a kind of tense platform for the stone and an emanation from it. Placed at one end the stone lost some of its ''head'', becoming more like a penis. The piece surprised me, I found it disconcerting, unlike *Green Rise* which had an inevitability about it.'

Many of Wilding's sculptures have human associations and are made to relate to human proportions. The initial idea for the brass and copper line which encloses the carved mass in *Indelible Field* came as a result of laying the wooden torso-like element upon a sweater. Its primal shape may again recall the work of Brancusi but its effect is different. Far from suggesting purity and benignity *Indelible Field* is both mysterious and threatening, a solid which appears impenetrable or perhaps a container whose contents are concealed by a skin. It is both contemplative and confrontational, a subtle combination of two characteristics found separately in Wilding's earlier works. *Indelible Field* is not simply a pure form but a 'thing' which breathes and lives its own existence. In asserting its independence it fulfils Wilding's desire to make sculpture which she is 'able to look in the eye'.

Jeremy Lewison

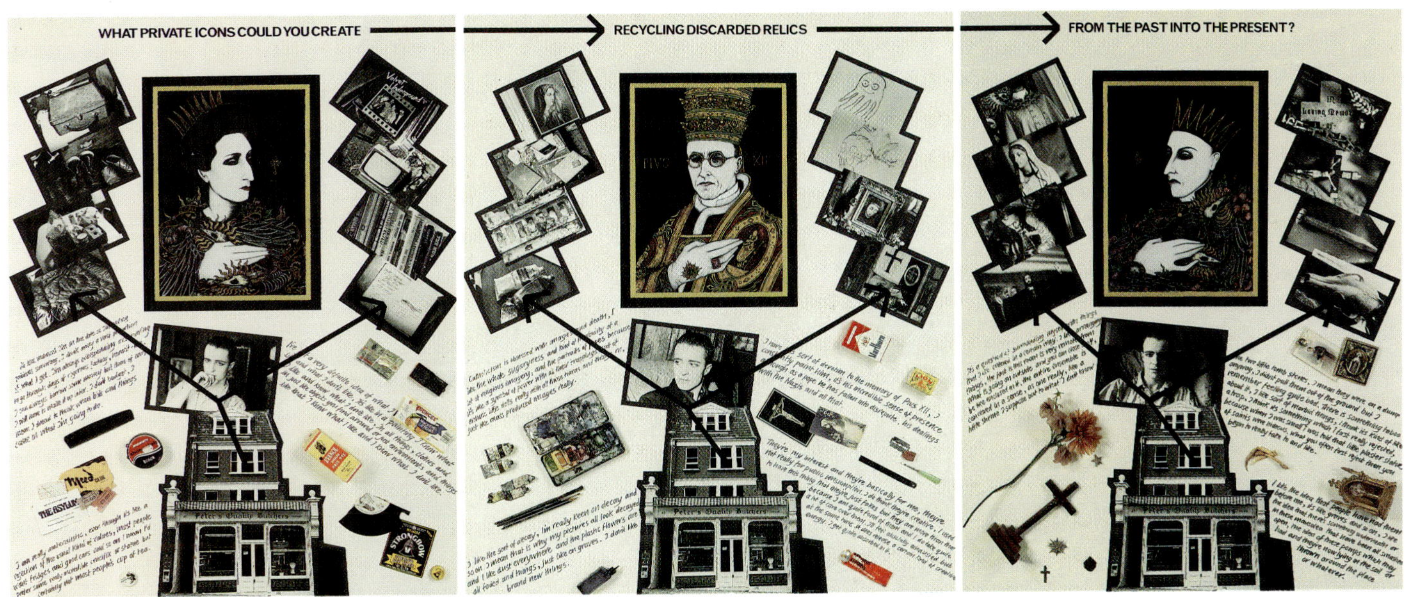

Private Icons
Aug-Dec 1983

photographic prints, photographic dye, ink, acrylic paint, letraset text, felt
tip pen, pencil and found objects on paper and card
three panels 140 x 101cms (each)
Lisson Gallery, London
photo credit: A C Cooper London

STEPHEN WILLATS:
Rites de marge

In establishing his art practice Stephen Willats made strong references to two interconnected disciplines that have become exceptionally significant in the last two decades: cybernetics and social anthropology. After school, Willats worked in a number of jobs including gallery assistant at the Drian Gallery and New Vision Centre where he met leading constructivist artists: he thinks this contact and the principles of self-organisation which it taught him particularly important. Willats then trained at Ealing School of Art from 1961/63 where Roy Ascott's ground course in particular, inspired several generations of students to think in terms of organisation and structure. Cybernetics — the catalyst for the development of computer sciences — offered sets of ideas (feedback, systems of self-organising control, similarities between scientific and social phenomena) which enabled the artist or constructor to make models (mathematical or otherwise) for works which actively involved the audience. Ascott taught that practice should be bonded to a strong theoretical base. Willats' first drawings are therefore more diagrammatic than expressive; they represent conceptual models of systems involving changes of state within those systems. Willats wrote in 1964 of *Organic Exercise No. 2 (series No. 1)*

"In these drawings the observer may view a single part, relate part to part, view the area as a whole, or wander at random over it. The drawings are connected with a way of looking at objects and relating oneself to an object."

These works selected parts from masses of information available from theories of information and communication, the "forms of data . . . for working towards other directions and dimensions".

They generated, for most of the rest of the decade, a series of behavioural machines, (*Visual Automatics, Visual Transmitters*) motorised with flashing or randomly switched light patterns. Willats showed a group of these pieces at Oxford in 1968, and wrote then "In a society whose structure seems to be moving increasingly towards a position of equilibrium in man's relationship with his environment the artist might well perform as a creator of areas of randomness in order to trigger creative behaviour."

But he also revealed in that essay his desire for more direct and complex relationships with the audience and the establishment of a homeostatic model. His text for *Homeostat Drawing No. 1*, (1969) cites the model as self-regulating, and self-assessing, a pluralistic structure that is continuously responsive and by inference a positive force. He wrote "The need for people to find and operate their own parameters can fit in with the concept of a mosaic structured behavioural net . . ." The structure he envisaged is netlike — changes in the internal and external environment are responded to 'intelligently' and the system learns to be self-organising. (We should also remember the developments in structural anthropology at that date and of course, the events of 1968) Willats worked with the homeostatic model in various guises, moving from electro-mechanical machines through primitive computer systems operating a carefully controlled database, to more complex interactions between pairs of spectators as in *Meta Filter* (1973-75). With this work Willats moved openly into the field of interpersonal and social behaviour: the spectators were asked to work with personal and social choices selected by the artist and the process demanded discussion. This had the benefit of deepening the immediate relation with the work but limited its capacity for a more general application.

Willats already used his own personal interaction in a series of projects begun in the mid 1960s where he sought through symbols to define the organisation of particular social groupings. These resulted in two groups of work; "wall-works" that display the result of the collaborative unravelling of the social model and a series of publications about particular models and problems. In these he incorporated photographs of the fetish-objects associated with roles or social behaviour. Willats turned to his childhood "patch" in West London. By 1978, when he made *Living with Practical Realities* in a tower block in Hayes, West London he had discovered a method of working that squared both with his need for structural analysis and his desire for intervention in the social process of making culture. Working class estates where the problems of loneliness, one-parent families, low income, poor housing and vandalism were exacerbated by major economic forces offered models for numerous works. He was not looking for conventional signs of society's disregard for the disadvantaged but for symbolic representations of individuals within a structure. Tower blocks and mass-housing are microcosms of much larger organisations where

pressure is applied to the individual. The "goodness" of the homeostatic model (its ability to adjust to individual needs) remains, but he now posits a necessary further development, that of the "counter-consciousness". The individual at the margins of society creates a second reality. This second world, inhabited in the past by the artist (as *shaman* or *seer*) is the opposite of the New Reality that has been forced with authoritarian and institutional violence on many lives. The quasi-caring agencies of local and central government become the unwitting repressors of individuality and creativity; individuals are forced back inside their homes or outside the "newly real" world to express themselves.

Willats spent a year on a DAAD fellowship in 1979 in West Berlin where these problems were especially severe. While working in Berlin he discovered and developed an understanding of the symbolism of young people's drawings made on the base of tower blocks in which they lived: the world that was represented was an idealised fantasy. He saw Berlin as an isolated land-locked city in which the pressures to conform with an artificially sustained political system imposed psychological pressures on the inhabitants. Berlin, he believed, was an extreme corporate version of the model that he had developed elsewhere.

In a sense Berlin prepared him for the works that he

Organic Exercise No. 2. Series 1.

June 1962

pencil on paper
61 x 76cms
154.9 x 193cms

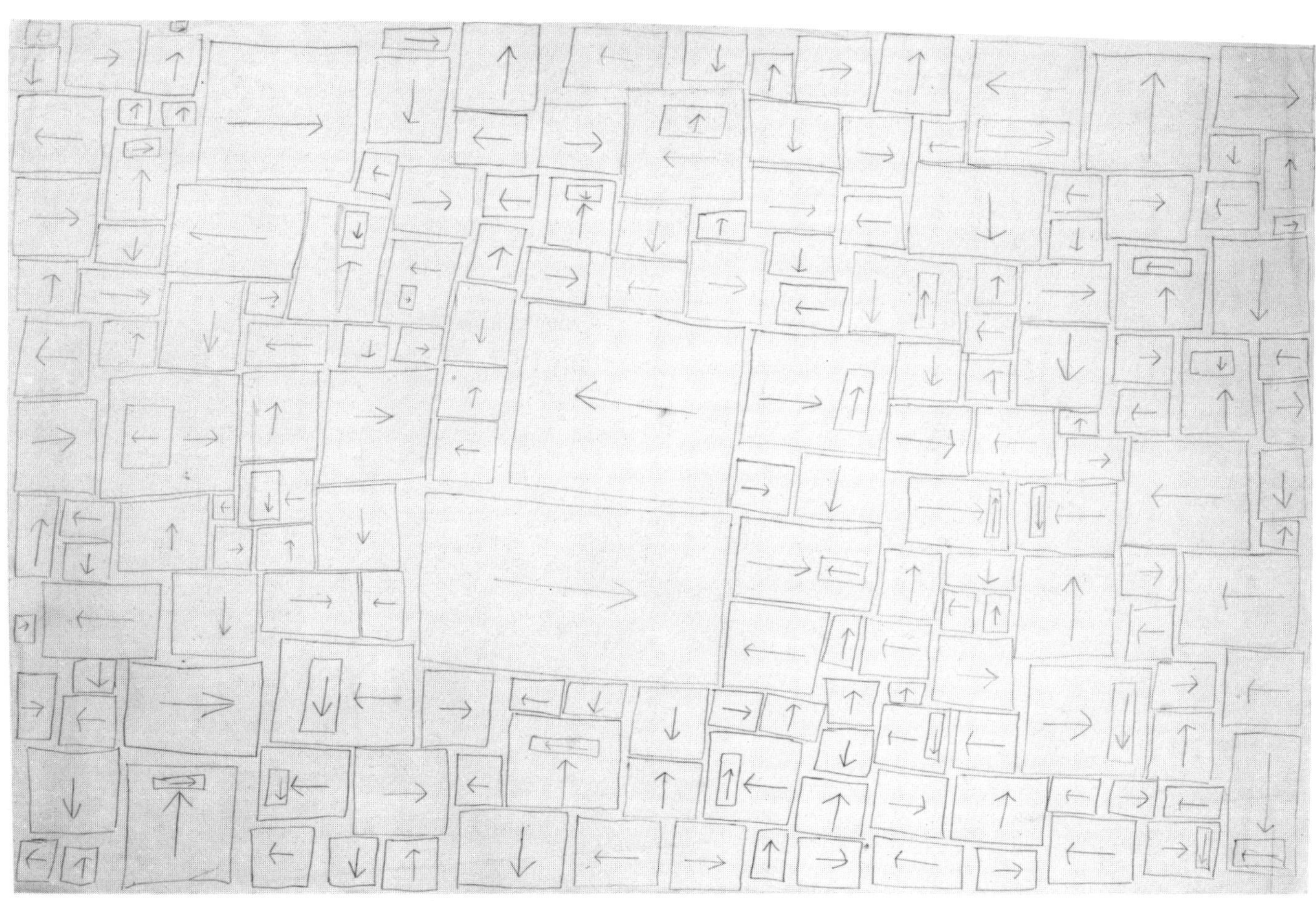

made when he returned to London; he went back to
the Avondale Estate, the site for earlier pieces, to
look for counter-consciousness and found it in the
"lurky place" — a wasteland behind the housing
development. He had collected material here for a
book and a wall-work in 1978. In the 1978 pieces
the place had a sort of innocence in which the
items that were taken to it became part of the
liberated consciousness of the people that used it.
Willats identified camp-making and bike riding on
'the Track' as important social activities but did not
yet uncover the whole meaning of the camps or the
despair that occasioned their use. (It is significant
that the objects in these works are depicted rather
than real.)

Pat Purdy (*Pat Purdy And The Glue Sniffers Camp*)
is the daughter of one of the residents on the
estate, introduced to Willats by the leader of the
residents' association. She, in turn, re-introduced
Willats to the significance of the wasteland and to
the camps where the ritual of glue-sniffing took
place. Here, a small can of Evostik was heated on a
fire and the warmed glue inhaled by the group
sitting around on old car seats. It was outlawed and
because it induced a change of consciousness
chemically, introduced the participants to another
world. For them it was a symbol of anarchy and
freedom. The pressures of estate life are presented

in the left hand panel of each triptych and the
'freedom' of the wasteland in the right, whilst the
central panel present the transition zone in which
objects have meaning in both worlds. Willats
emphasises that this work was fully collaborative,
that Pat Purdy wrote her comments on the boards
themselves. To increase the sense of confrontation
he used real objects recovered from the site. The
work marks a new stage in this working process
and in the interactive effort.

Willat's search for genuine self-expression and his
long interest in popular music lead him to punk
music, records and clubs. Here he found more
extreme versions of disengagement and he
embarked on a series of works which use this world
as a powerful symbol of freedom. He became a
regular visitor to the Cha-Cha Club, for example,
and documented it in a book *Are You Good Enough
For The Cha Cha Cha?* and wallworks. Edmund
Leach describes the rites of marginalisation
identifiable in many societies. He refers to the
initiation process often involving "prescriptions and
proscriptions regarding food, clothing and
movement generally" and the final 'normal' stage
as a return to previous proscriptions.

The general characteristic of such *rites de marges*
(rites of marginality) is that the initiate is kept
physically apart from ordinary people, either by

Homeostate Drawing No. 1
May 1969

22 x 28ins
55.870 x 71cms
pencilon paper

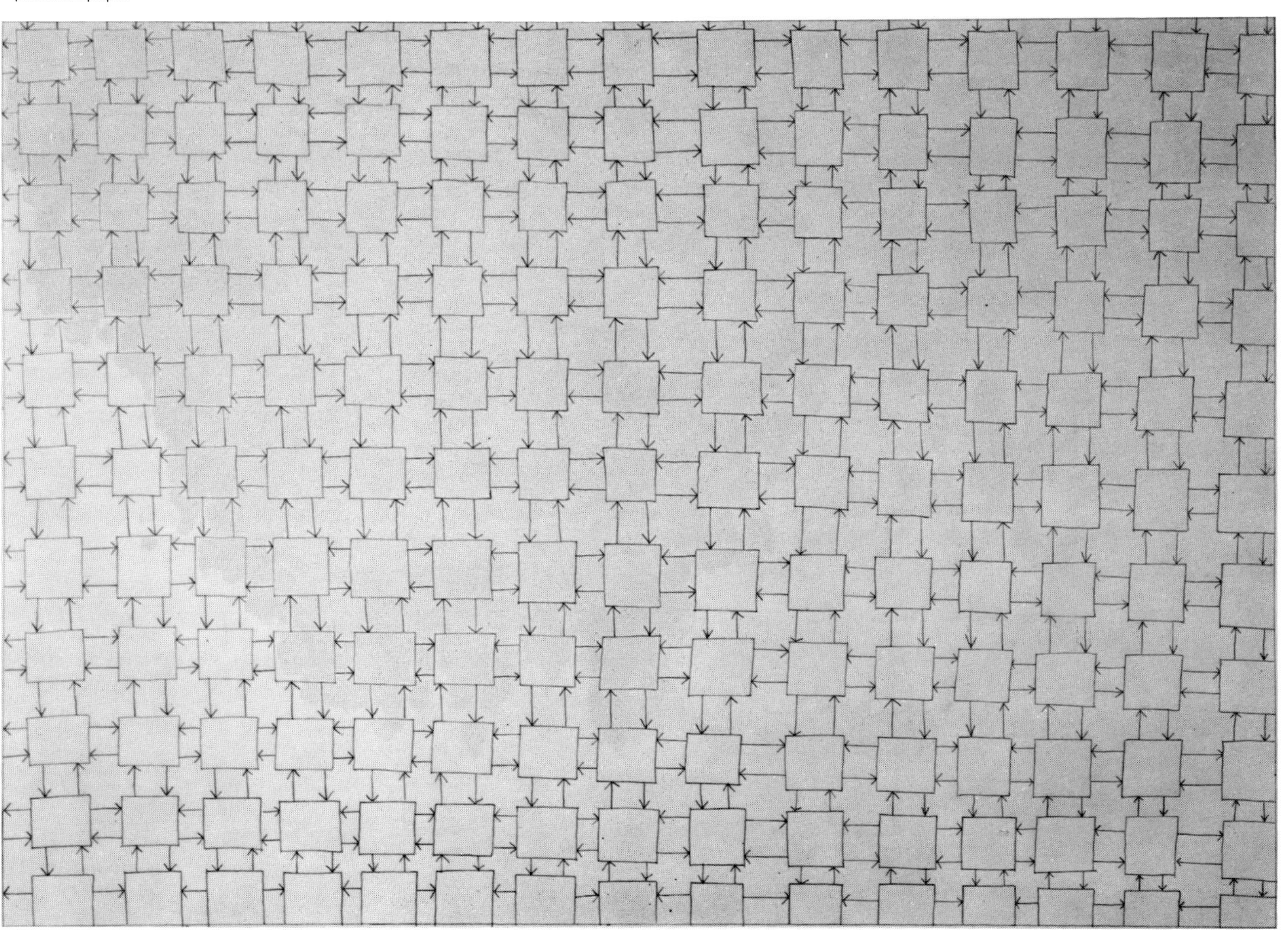

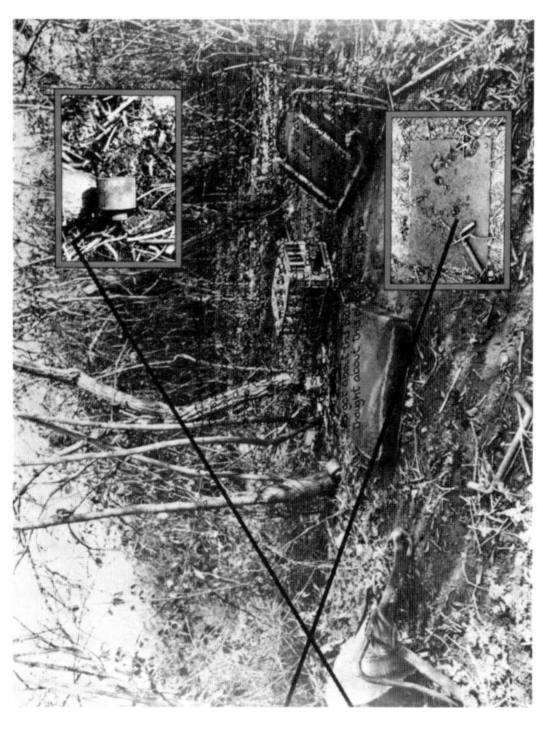

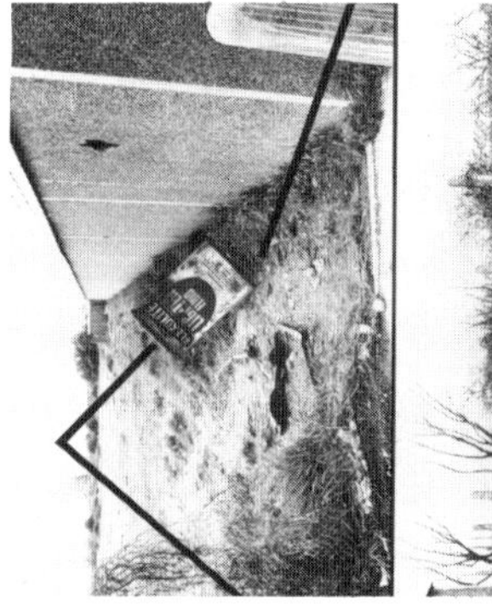

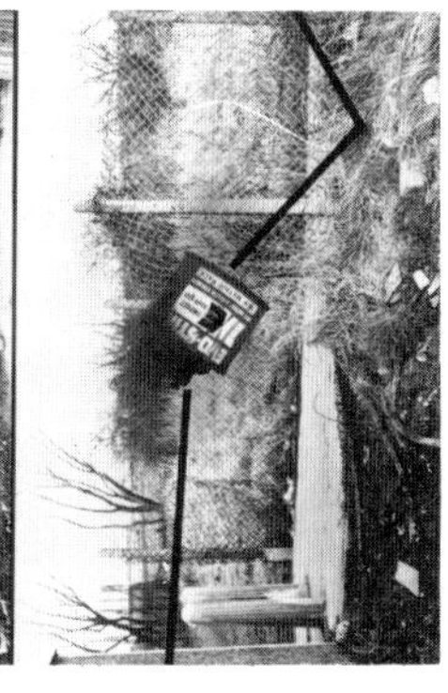

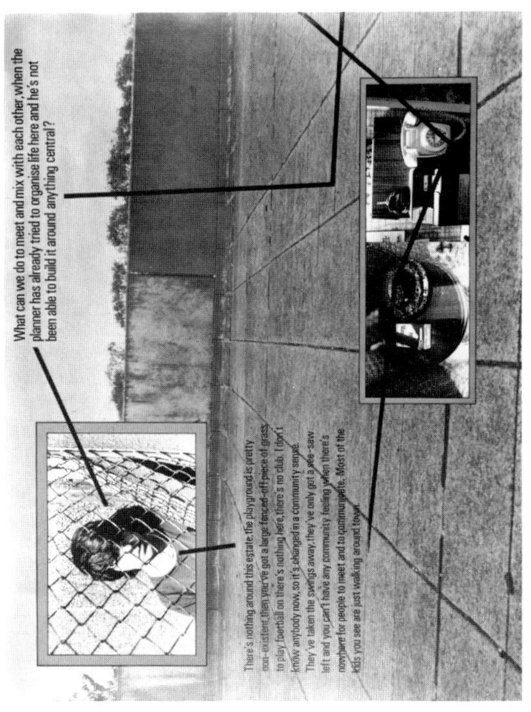

Pat Purdy And The Glue Sniffers Camp

January/September 1981

eight panels 102 x 76.5cms and four panels 66 x 51cms
photographic prints, photographic dye, gouache paint,
letraset text, ink, felt tip pen, and objects found at the
Lurky Place.
Lisson Gallery London
photo credit: Stephen Willats

being sent away from the normal home surroundings altogether or by being temporarily housed in an enclosed space from which ordinary people are excluded. Edmund Leach, *Culture and Communication*, Cambridge 1976.

Willat's youth lives in the marginal state and in his most recently discovered cases seeks to extend this marginal existence permanently. They actively participate in the process of withdrawal.

His encounters drew him further "into the night". Willats enters, however as a collaborator, engaged in a common pursuit and not as an objective investigator. Through the Cha Cha Club Willats met Michael Malapasta who introduced him to the world of the "night opera" held in a basement flat in Earl's Court whenever, in which the participants perform a completely spontaneous opera, to which (it is said) the Directors of the world's opera houses invite themselves. These experiences have led him to groups and individuals who have constructed new realities so complete that their contact with the everyday world has become almost non existent.

Tim, in *Private Icons* brought together, in a structure modelled by Willats, his own paintings and the taboo objects that he collects which symbolise his freedom. The work, like all the others is made from meetings, tape recordings and photographic sessions. Willats emphasises the importance of transformation in these works: objects change status and value as they are moved from one system to another; discarded things are the agents for personal revelation. Presented in this way the work can become an agent for social change.

Willats has always seen his practice as an attempt to make changes in the perception of the social and cultural future through his interaction with his audience. He sets out to create an artwork that will instigate in the audience perceptions, understandings of their own creative potential. "The artwork becomes a social process during its inception, in its development with the participant, and during its internalisation by the audience. All three stages being completely and vitally dependent on the involvement of people other than the artist."

Richard Francis

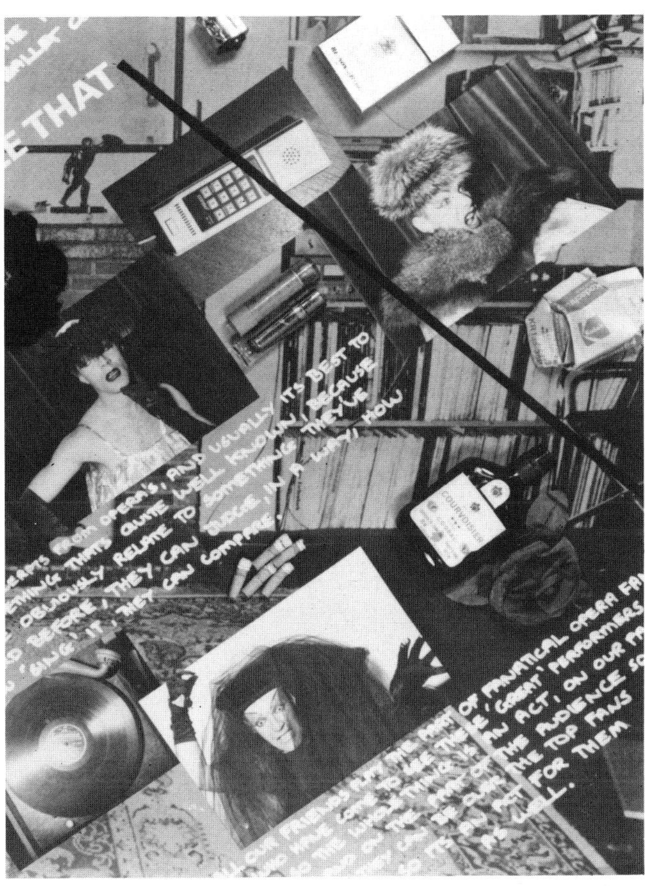

Secret Prima Donna 1983
Detail of 1st Panel
1983

two panels 140cm wide x 100cm high
one panel 102.5cm wide x 100cm high
media: photographic prints, photographic dye, ink, acrylic paint, letraset text, felt tip pen, and objects given by Michael & Keith
Lisson Gallery London

Living with Practical Realities
1978

photographs, letraset, gouache & ink on card
3 panels each 109 x 76cms
Lisson Gallery London

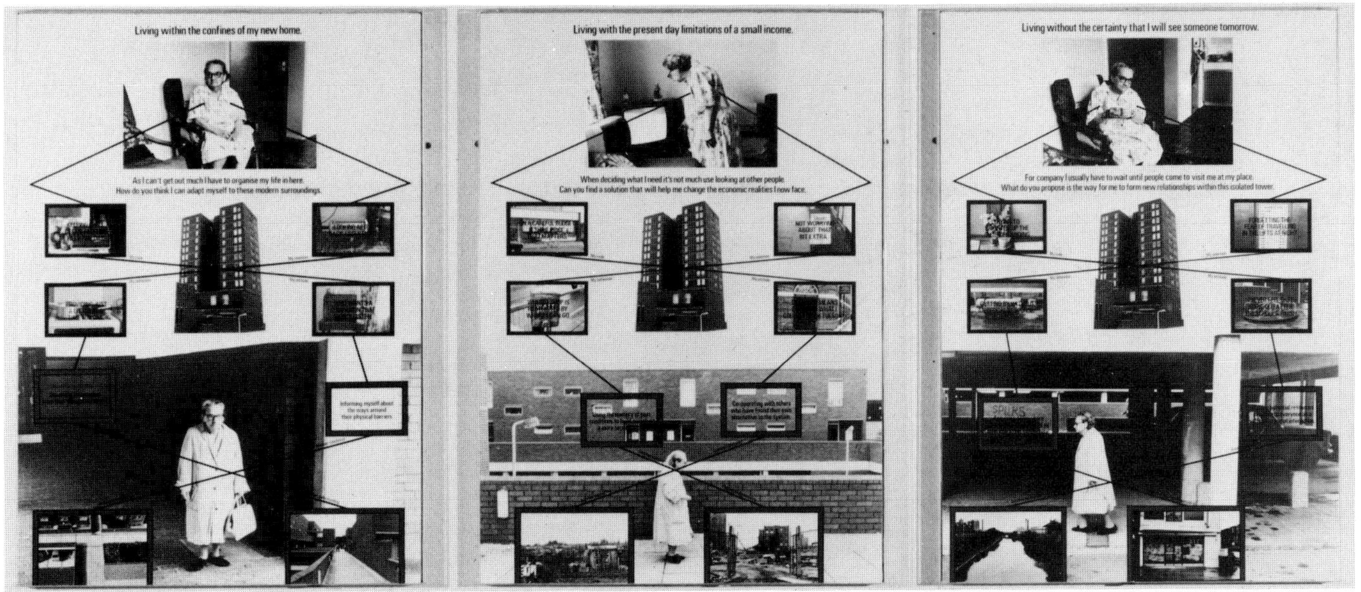

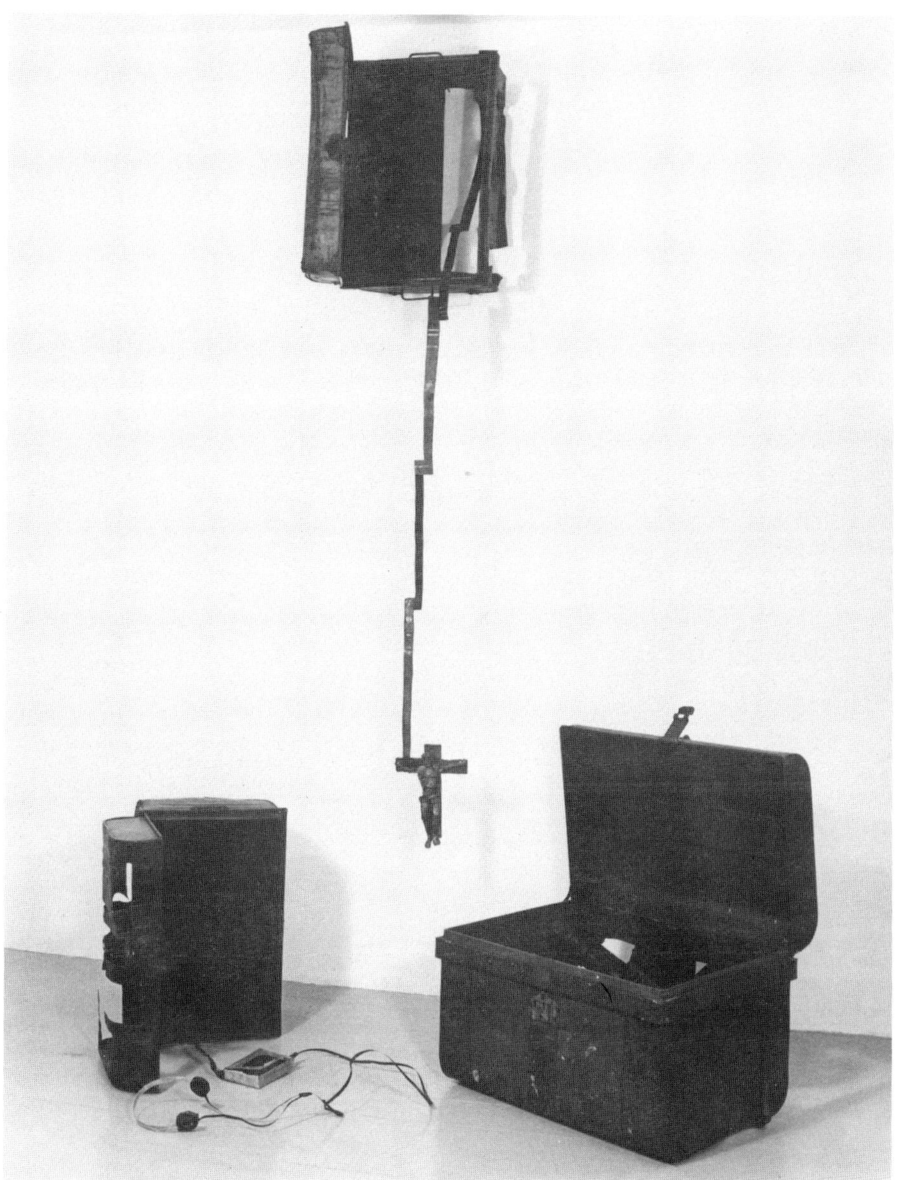

BILL WOODROW

When Dr Gideon Mantell tried piecing together the remains of a prehistoric monster found in Bensted's Quarry, Kent, in 1834 he had no idea what it had looked like. Some sort of lizard, he decided. So he called it an 'Iguanodon' and made it a giant creepy-crawly. Generations later, with superior knowledge of the Lower Cretaceous period, the Natural History Museum in South Kensington revealed that Mantell's dinosaur had in fact two little arms and two long legs. The iguanodon's living descendents are birds.

Bill Woodrow used to visit the Natural History Museum with his family on Sunday afternoons. There they saw the fossilized bones of the creature from Bensted's Quarry, still embedded in a slab of rock, ammonites sliced in half to reveal their structure; the full-size mock-up of a blue whale slung from a ceiling, winking diagrams of human intestines and arrays of stuffed and pickled wild life. When Woodrow encased a clutch of hair-driers in concrete then broke the lump open to disclose them, pathetic foetal objects, he had such exhibits in mind. The broom set in concrete, its sweeping stilled, the vacuum cleaner similarly silenced, these instant fossils were both promoted to museum status and given that traditional gangsters' send-off, the concrete overcoat.

Metaphors come ready-mixed in Woodrow's work. The gruesome incident of the armchair with its brains blown out, splattering the wall; the fish gasping behind the grille of an electric fire; the fish-hook handle of the ladle with a pectoral cross cut from its bowl, resting in an empty saucepan: barbed charity.

At the Natural History Museum you can buy dinosaurs in kit form. Woodrow's compositions are one-offs but many of them have a practised air. The artist, one might suppose, simply follows instructions (as on the back of cornflakes packets), cuts round dotted lines, twists and fastens and there you have it: a Red Indian war bonnet contrived, without fuss, from perfectly ordinary household goods.

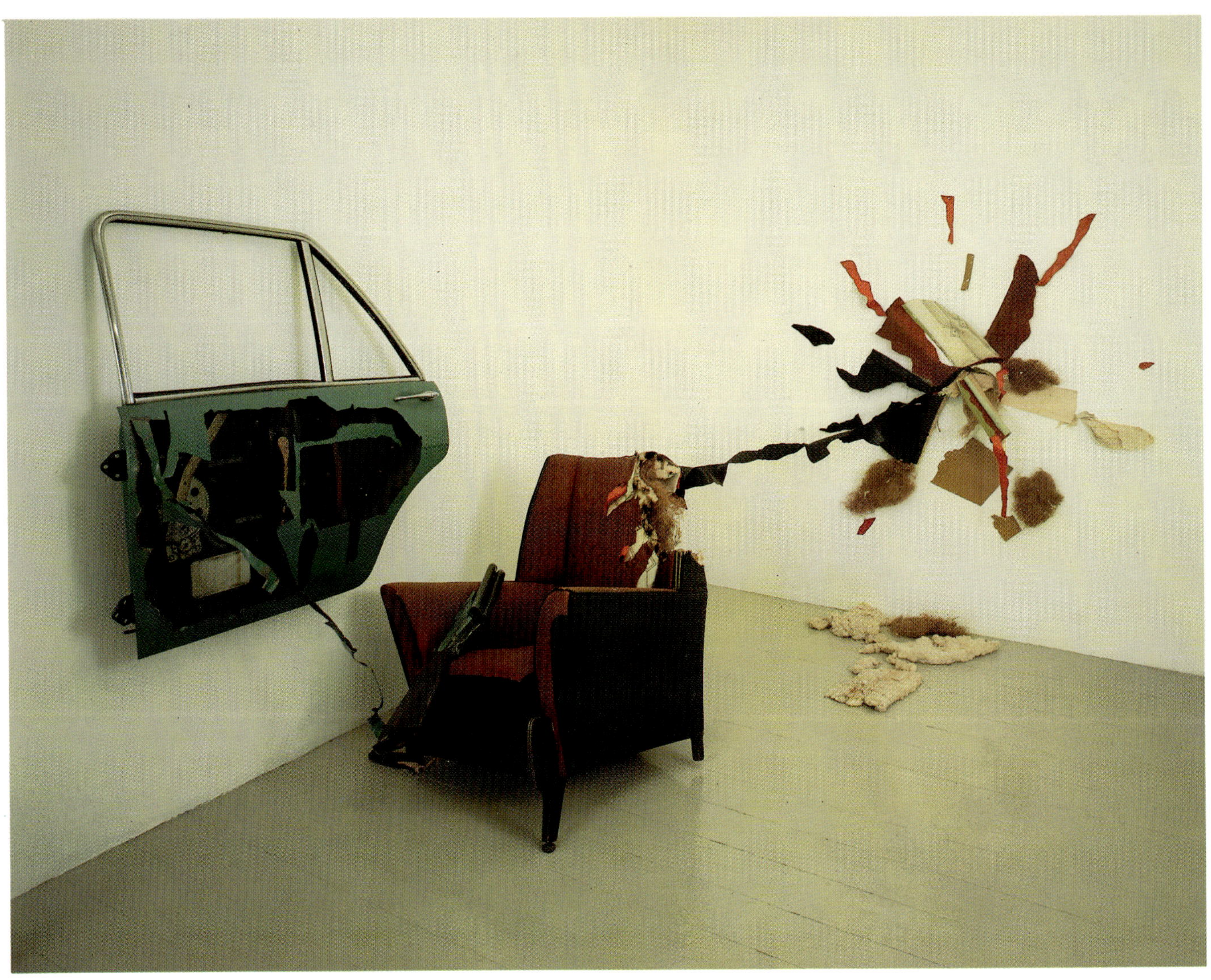

Car door, Armchair and Incident
1981

approx 365 x 365cms installed
photo credit: Lisson Gallery, London

The starfish produced from the side of a bucket, leaving the mop still planted upright, like the mast on a derelict vessel; the lobster similarly emerging from a companion bucket; the crucifix dangling from an old tin trunk with a dummy Sony Walkman and a cine-camera equally immaculately conceived in two other trunks (forming the novel Trinity of *'Sound, Vision and Christ'*), the beaver nibbling at the twin-tub from which it was fabricated are all presented as 'hey presto' miracles. You can examine the folds and joins and work out how the second generation object was contrived from the host body. You can admire the ingenuity and guess at the thinking behind these curious pairings.

Often there's more rhyme than reason. Woodrow repeatedly makes guns out of car doors, ingots out of wash-tubs. The world is a ball of half-perished electric flexes. The message comes over clearly enough: these are cargo-cult goods, fake purchases from the Duty-Free, things to arouse envy, displayed on the conked-out remains of what were once, not long ago, gleaming vehicles and domestic appliances. The products of production line assembly methods give rise to the hand-crafted starfish, the eager-to-please performing seal, the busy beaver.

In 1976 Woodrow made what now looks, in retrospect, a significant model for the processes of cannibalizing everyday things. A photograph of the ruins of ancient *Babylon*, a panorama long enough to qualify as a short scroll, was placed on the floor and held down by a set of 22 adobe bricks. Babylon in image and substance, Babylon the mighty civilisation that became as extinct as the dinosaur, is laid open, guarded by a double column of paperweights.

London, once the Heart of Empire and now a tourist capital, is the White Man's mess, say the Rastafarians. London is 'Babylon'. The Rastas have

Bucket, Mop and Starfish
1983

private collection

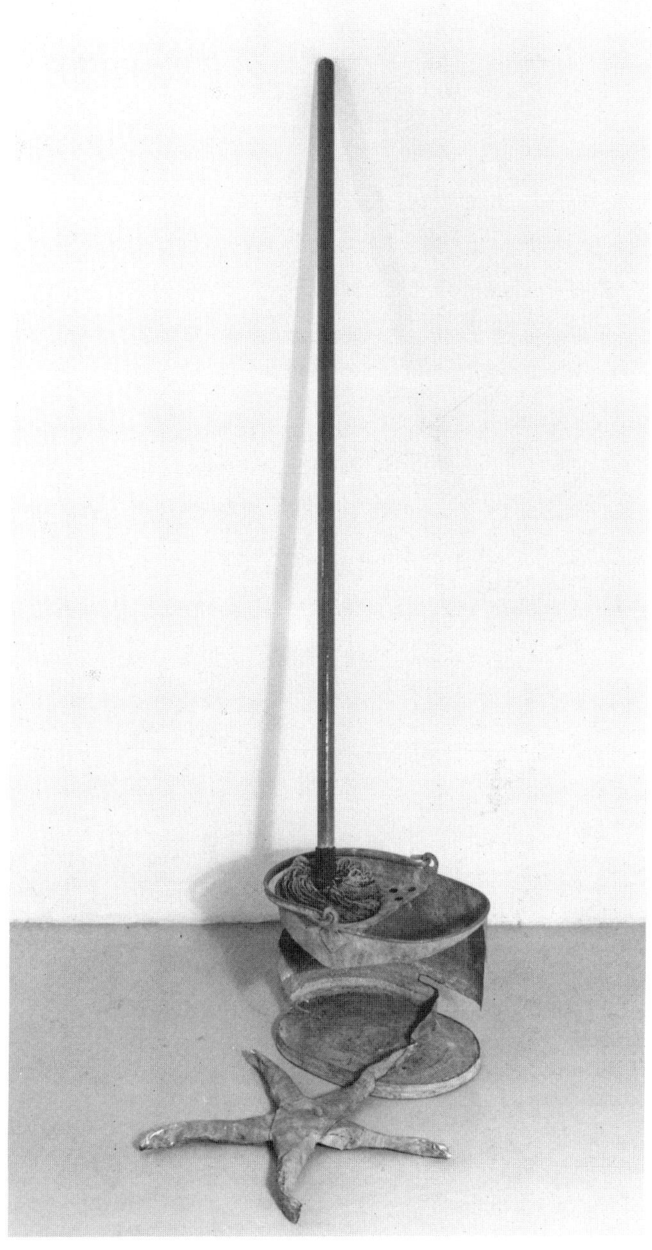

Babylon
1975/76

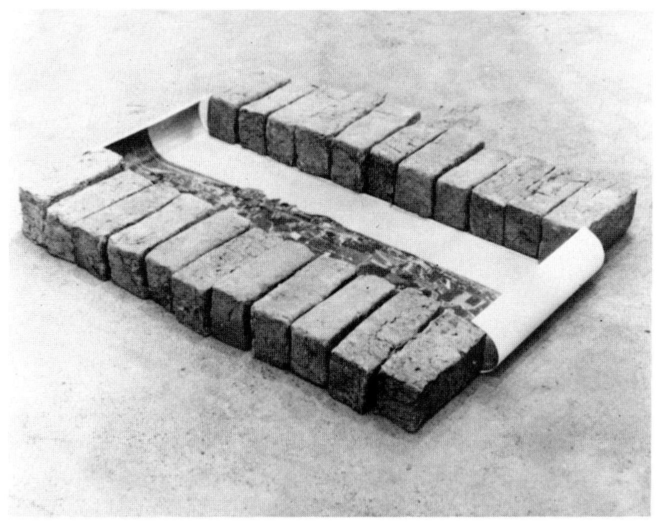

visions of London and all it stands for abandoned, of Paradise and Kingdom Come in Ethiopia. To the sound of Rasta reggae rather than the Salvation Army, Woodrow goes round looking for useable material in junkshops, scrapyards and in the streets of Brixton. He selects from builders' skips and from the gutter, considers the possibilities and, when the time comes, operates on the bucket, the sofa, the broken paraffin stove, the fractured umbrella. He's the surgeon, with gloves and cutters, the deliverer fulfilling dreams, exploiting debased resources.

To begin with, in 1980 Woodrow tended to deconstruct, taking slices out of lined up appliances or dismantling bicycles so as to show how far all the pieces, put end to end, would stretch. He set out all the components of a vacuum cleaner ready for inspection and the obvious disposal method: the Hoover hoovered. The idea of born-again sculpture manifested itself first with the guitar created, like Eve from Adam's rib, out of the side of a washing machine. With that the potential of consumer durables became apparent. Almost anything in the hardware or furnishing departments could, he realised, become something else.

Since 1980 Woodrow has become something of a globetrotter. In New York a panther sprang from the bodywork of a Yellow Taxicab. In Brittany a fearsome black bird flew from three car bonnets grasping a two-way radio in its claw. In Genoa the foliage printed on olive oil cans was made to sprout from a wizened tin-plate tree. In Hamburg, Brisbane, Sao Paulo, Venice, Liverpool, Amsterdam, Toronto and elsewhere Woodrow has demonstrated his omnicompetence. It's the universality of the *National Geographic*, with Oxfam overtones, a bringing together of items advertised (the world's most superior cars, most impressive TVs) and colourful editorial matter (native artefacts, threatened species); it's the re-routing of ideas through unusual channels to incongruous outlets.

In Woodrow's *Lost World* an elephant browses at a
waterhole composed of ten car-doors. The huge
butterfly ears are classroom maps of Africa and
Latin America cut to shape. The trunk embraces a
sub-machine gun. Held by an elephant a gun is no
more use than a swizzle stick. Woodrow tinkers with
our mental images, relying on common knowledge
to augment the hints. Washing machines need only
a coat of black paint to become the banked
amplifiers used in live concerts. Where Duchamp
nominated and Schwitters redeemed the ordinary
and the discarded and thereby created high art, Bill
Woodrow sets up analogies and chain reactions. A
crow, made from one black umbrella, pecks at the
corpse of another.

In his most recent work the artifice is more
pronounced. Blue skies and yellow beaches are
painted on the wide expanses of the indispensible
car. A black ship-of-fools, pieced together from a
load of umbrellas, almost founders in the trough of
a Hokusai wave formed by an old VW boot lid. An
armchair, raised in triumph, shoulder high is
bombarded with forks. The sat-upon becomes the
victimised sitter.

Hoping to make his two-volume *Wonders of Geology*
more convincing, Dr Gideon Mantell asked the
visionary artist and part-time inventor John Martin to
provide a frontispiece showing the Lost World of
prehistory reconstructed in the light of his
discoveries. Martin's 'Country of the Iguanodon' is
classical terrain overrun with stupendous reptiles,
hissing on every headland, obsessively devouring
one another. Milton's Paradise, the Garden of the
Hesperides and the Proceedings of the Zoological
Society were rolled into one for this, the first ever,
artist's impression of dinosaurs in the flesh.

Ransacking the debris of present-day civilisation,
Bill Woodrow fabricates comparable apparitions. His
sculpture is proverbial, fabulous. Cherishing the
outlandish, rejoicing in the jump cut and the shock
decision, he makes dry bones live.

William Feaver

L'Origine du Tatouage
1983

3 car bonnets
220 x 450 x 300cms
photo credit: Lisson Gallery, London

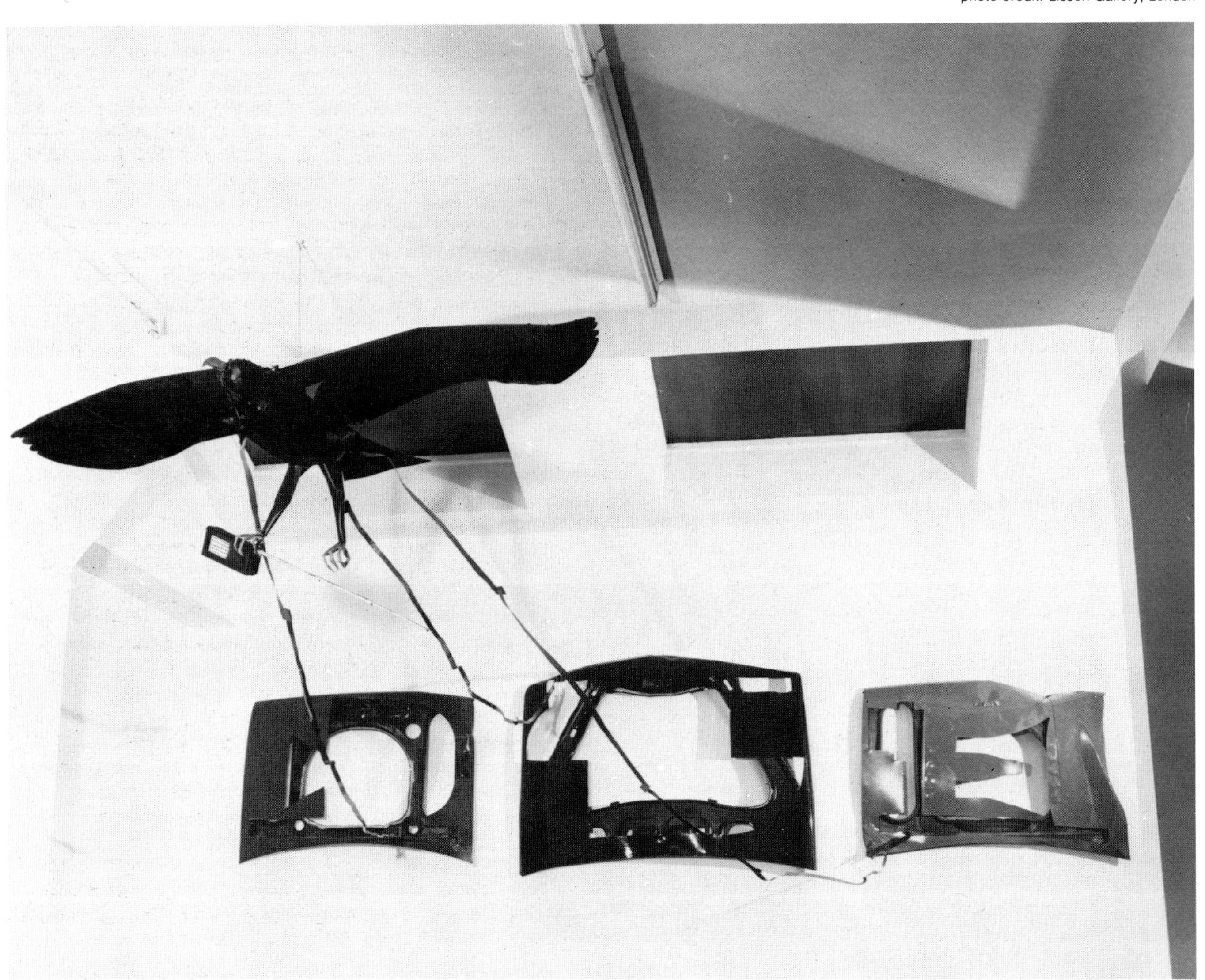

PREFIGURED MOMENTS

If you asked people in and around the British art world whether there was much in the way of performance going on at the moment, you would tend to be answered in the negative. We can identify two main reasons why such an answer would be given. Firstly, and to be quite matter of fact about it, what activity is being carried out in the name of performance tends to take place under the auspices of a small number of organising bodies, the majority of whom are either outside the capital or at one remove from its mainstream art venues, such as South Hill Park, Bracknell, and the Basement Group, Newcastle. Performance per se is no longer centre stage either geographically or art politically. Secondly, and more importantly, it has to be said that you get the 'wrong answer' because you have asked the wrong question. As far as the institutions of art have been concerned — educational establishments, funding bodies, galleries and so on — it is true to say that performance or, speaking more generally, time-based work, has only been able to exist as a category distinct from the traditionally media-defined areas of painting and sculpture. Yet the stake for which time-based work has made play is nothing short of a radical alteration in the ground of our aesthetic understanding, and the exploration of such a possibility has involved an approach which is, in establishment terms, interdisciplinary. It has worked to disrupt the coherence of dominant notions of art. To take just two examples from this present company, in the past eighteen months alone, Bruce McLean has worked in the fields of painting, sculpture, performance, sound and film, and Rose Garrard's recent travelling show, *Beyond Ourselves*, has required the use of a whole range of skills from the traditional fine art media, through video and sound to others, like pattern-cutting and sewing, usually dismissed either as *mere* craft or on grounds of their gender identification. In other words, the point at which performance, or video, or sound art, or whatever, becomes a category in its own right, is the point at which that activity ceases to make any real contribution to *art* practice at all.

To speak in such a way is not intended as a rejection of the rationale of this show. The logistics of organising a travelling show at such a distance and on such a scale necessitate pragmatic solutions. But it is essential to point out that the concerns which nurtured the appearance of time-based work are evident not only within the closely defined limits of the performance and video sections of this exhibition, but throughout the show as a whole.

The aesthetic shift which time-based work marks is one away from the integrity of the autonomous art product. By declaring the bankruptcy of the paradigm of autonomy, the time-based artist, the artist whose work extends in real time, lays claim to a new community. Or rather, as Stuart Brisley defined it in his recent film on performance, *Being and Doing*, the artist re-enters the community from which he or she had hitherto, by virtue of his or her activity as an artist, been isolated. But at this point, if we choose merely to concentrate upon the phenomenon of performance itself, the critical act becomes problematic. The strengths of a position within the body politic can be read in the symbolic significance of social ritual, but lack of rigour can easily lead to a simple equation of art with life. In this latter, unthought-out instance, deprived of the possibility of any distance from which events might objectively be observed, one's only tool of judgement can be a finely tuned sense of outrage. (Objectivity is, of course, understood as a question of relationship, not of disinterest.) Legitimation would be afforded to all that one is simply prepared to put up with. Naturally, if one is left in this situation it is usually the case that one is watching bad performance, and we are then talking of performance as habitual rather than ritual action. But the stale taste of habit has catalysed a rich diffusion of talent throughout the art world in this country. Indeed, many British artists who are now beginning to produce their mature work, and who made performances in the seventies, have now ceased standing before the crowd altogether. Quite apart from Stuart Brisley, one thinks of others who are not here such as Kevin Atherton, Kerry Trengove, Paul Richards and Marc Chaimowicz. In fact it is interesting that in the performance section of this exhibition there are only two people — Silvia Ziranek and Charlie Hooker — who one could properly call performance artists in the sense that their work consists almost entirely in doing things before an audience in a certain place at a certain time. Brisley, as I have said, has not made a performance for some years now, Rose Finn-Kelcey's work tends to be more in the nature of an installation at which she feels the need to be present, and Bruce McLean, although he continues to stage occasional events, does so only as one part of a very broad approach to art making. From our point of view as an audience, however, this seeming categorial muddiness is neither here nor there. It is unfruitful to search for theoretical definitions which will contain this work apart from the rest of the show, thereby enabling judgements upon whether something is or is not performance to be made. It is unrealistic to expect that performance alone might generate a body of critical concepts around itself (a state of affairs which some in Britain anxiously await!) since the stimulus for the work — the stimulus which still informs those artists mentioned above — continually subverts such comforts. By this token, to return to the critical problem, it is necessary to speak of art within the whole complex of cultural phenomena, and accordingly sculpture, say, is as inconclusive a demarcation as performance.

Like most other blanket terms, 'time-based' is

painfully inadequate as a description of the cultural phenomenon under discussion. It would perhaps be more appropriate to introduce the idea of time consciousness since it is as much as anything a development, in broad social terms, of our sense of space which is under way, a development in which an awareness of time nonetheless plays a crucial role. If we take an image from the first machine age — Delaunay's celebration of the aeroplane and the Eiffel Tower, or Marinetti's hymn of praise to the motor car, for example — there is an understanding that the very form of these objects was able to symbolise the way they functioned within the dynamic of shifting social patterns. It was possible to *picture* concepts like Simultaneity and Futurism. But the mere image of, say, a computer or a video machine cannot act in the same way with respect to an advance in technological capability which is electronic rather than mechanical. These new machines are not now simply the products of a particular society but are themselves the means by which that society reproduces itself. Their form, as it were, bears no relation to their content. It is only through the process of their functioning that they are able to represent the world; and when they do not function they are nothing. Time-based work is about something more than the reference of events to the passing moments, it is the involvement with a culture which can only adequately be represented *through* those passing moments.

The logic of this process whereby the fixity of the art object is challenged is seen in the increasing degree to which exchange value takes precedence over use value. And if we talk in terms of knowledge, in the sense that art might provoke one to an understanding of things, then the kind of thing that a video monitor could provide us with must be characterised more as information, the means to something rather than an end in itself. The terms are not now educational but transactional: art addresses the physiognomy of power. Autonomy has ceased to operate as a paradigm because the space in which art functions has dispersed itself within the social fabric. There is no longer a separate realm capable of acting as a container for the ideal solutions to real problems, no longer a safe distance between the dirt of day-to-day actions and the purity which surrounds ones hopes and aspirations. The two spheres have merged into one complex hyperspace which is as yet incompletely mapped onto our consciousness.

On the level of theory it is the usefulness of the concept of utopia which has been devalued. The extreme pessimism of, for example, the Frankfurt School theorists, and particularly of Marcuse and Adorno, led them to view the realm of aesthetics as the last possible escape route from life. But this solution was radically compromised by their inability to consider art itself as contributing to the means by which a passage could be forged from present conditions to the ideal solutions it embodied. Time-based work is eager to reject this analysis since it sees contemporary, 'post-modern' society not as a chronologically ordered sequence of discrete and fully comprehensible states, each one superceding the last, but as a conjunctural field, the nodes within which are identifiable as moments in the cultural process. Such a view reshapes the relationship

between means and ends, and it is now not so much that the desirability of a goal can be used as justification for whatever means one is forced to use in order to achieve it. It is, rather, that one is not able to concede the reasonableness of any goal which is not consistent with and prefigured by the strategy adopted for its attainment. Reconnecting the two moments of this couple brings rationality, as it were, back into harness. It undercuts the incontinent logic of late capitalism, a theoretical process which, far from interweaving with the real process of history, threatens to end history altogether. In Steve Hawley's videotape, *Bad Reasons*, a series of syllogistic excursions reach absurd conclusions, revealing the seductive charm and dangerous implications of unbridled 'reason':

> All that glitters is not gold.
> Shirley Bassey glitters.
> Therefore Shirley Bassey is not gold.

A crucial concept within the renewed linking of means and ends is that of 'potential'. It is akin to Aristotle's theory of change, the teleological solution to the problem of how something which ostensibly does not exist comes into being. An acorn, let us say, is potentially what an oak tree is actually. Prefiguration concerns much the same process. It is the grasping of possibilities within culture, the recognition of beginnings, the breaking open of systems by identifying constituent and structurally important parts which can be used positively, against the dominant grain. In Britain, certainly, it is still not possible to over-estimate the effect which the women's movement has had in bringing this shift to consciousness. Kate Elwes' work has always been concerned with issues of women's consciousness and male power, and Roberta Graham's tape/slide sequence, here transferred to video, is also relevant. The most potent and complete expression of the strengths of the women's movement remains their peace camp outside the gates of the American air force base at Greenham Common in Berkshire. Tina Keane's tape takes Greenham specifically as its subject, but recent performance by Rose Finn-Kelcey and tape/slide works by Stuart Brisley have engaged more generally in the nuclear debate.

Aside from this overall scenario, there are certain formal issues relating to video work in Britain which it is important to bear in mind. We possess an inscrutably monolithic broadcasting system to which access on any significant level is all but impossible. Professionally speaking, therefore, there exists an extremely unproductive relationship between television and the use of video in art. With the notable exception of a very few opportunities on one channel, artists who work with video are still facing requests from TV producers that programmes be made *about* their work. Eventually, one hopes, things will change and artists will be allowed to 'make television', but until it does, the jealousy with which each side guards its territory has led to a curious situation in which, seemingly, some of the most non-communicative work in Britain is being produced in one of the most transparently communicative media. On a practical level, of course, there are issues of skill involved in the question of media access, issues of encroachment on professionally demarcated areas of competence and operation. But one of the major dangers in current British video work is that the response of artists to these issues might be taken to be singularly uncompromising and impractical. If seen in a positive light, though, this confrontation has produced a body of work which offers a serious critique of the media, and in cases where it seems that content, treatment and the crucial question of narrative, that is of process, have retreated before an oppositional stance which centres on production values alone, what at first might appear as 'unwatchability' can be seen on reflection as a refusal to succumb to the grand illusion. On this point, the work in the show which has come out of the Basement in Newcastle is particularly pertinent.

The legacy of time-based activity is a contemporary practice which brings thoughtful and critical interest to bear on matters of cultural significance. In this, British work has a character quite distinct from the more celebratory and spectacular work being done across the Atlantic. The difference is perhaps the mark of our 'natural reserve', but it is, nonetheless, most encouraging.

Michael Archer

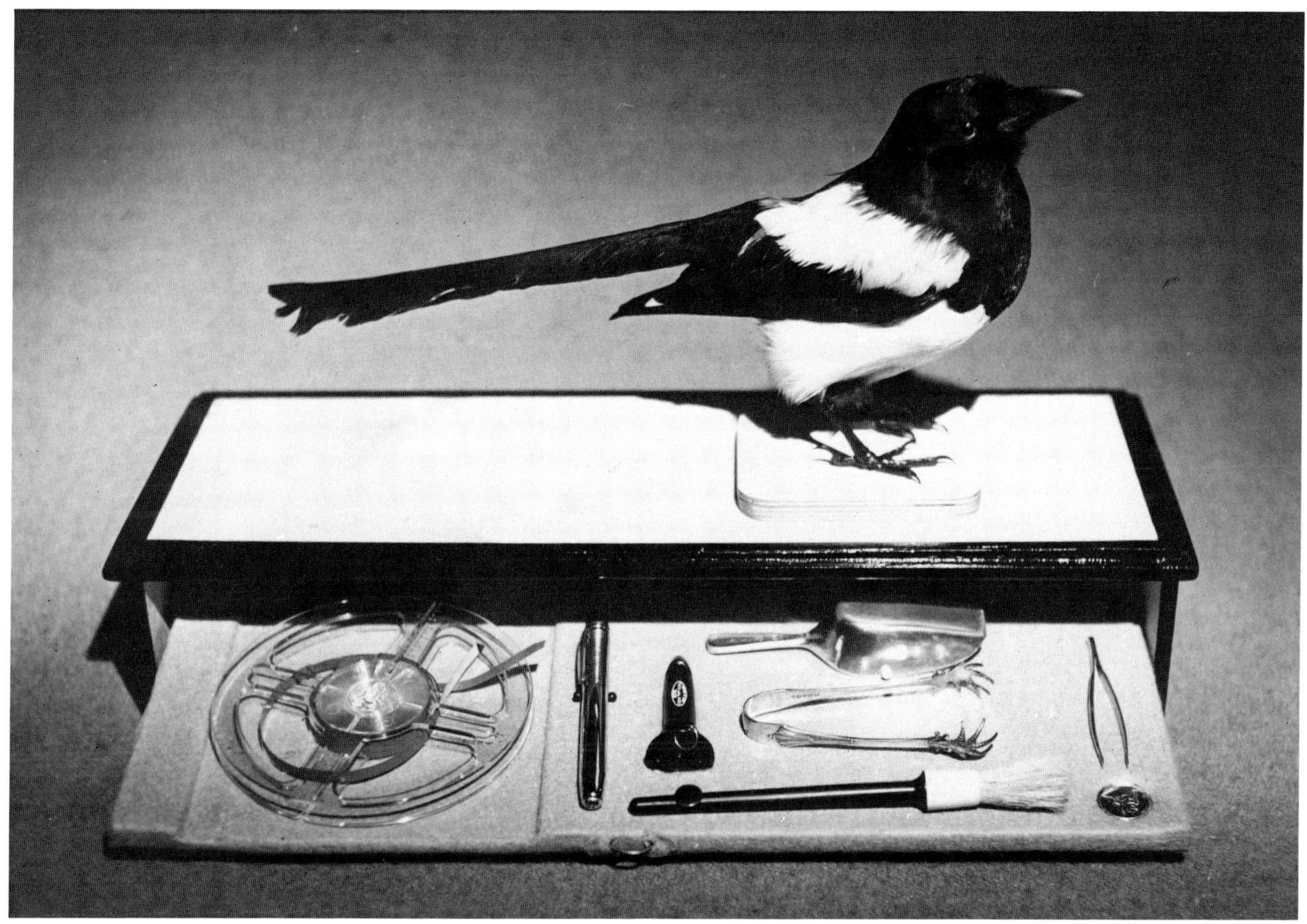

ROSE FINN-KELCEY

Over the last few years Rose Finn-Kelcey has increasingly questioned the very role of the artist in performance. In contrast to many other artists, who see the dialogues between the performer and objects and audience as ends in themselves, she has been concerned that as a live element she can interfere with the public's experience of the performance.

"At the time, I wanted to be both inside the work and yet, as it unfolded, to also be an objective viewer. I didn't want to perform, neither did I wish to direct others and this prompted the notion of surrogate performers and a vacated performance."[1]

Her ambivalent attitude towards appearing was noticeable in *Mind the Gap*, a piece produced for the ICA project "About Time" in 1980. The spectators were carefully positioned amongst the objects used in the performance. A sound tape introduced the audience to the possibility that she may not appear at all. Nevertheless after a period of time she did finally emerge in person. In *May Day* (1981) she introduced the audience to her cast (four radios and one set of speakers). With a candle

flame she then burnt the rope which bound her wrists and fled from the space, leaving her radios, which continued to perform in her place, to broadcast the complex network of sounds.

It is perhaps her determination to translate intensely personal feelings into universal experiences that forces Rose to leave the space. In her absence the spectators are then encouraged to focus on other aspects of the performance to the extent that their own reactions can ultimately become a part of the work as they move into the space she has vacated. The self conscious awkwardness of direct confrontation is avoided. Nevertheless, human qualities and characteristics are reflected in the performance for the spectators either to identify with or to challenge.

Rose Finn-Kelcey in these works is no longer performer but manipulator, no longer puppet but controller. Even without being present, she can animate the objects and create the atmosphere of the performance. Her role as controller is perfectly exemplified in the performance and subsequent video *Glory*. The surrogate performers, cut-out models, are both subject and object of the piece, manoeuvred into position by the red-gloved artist using croupier's sticks and long-handled pincers.

These objects, although recognisable as the characters they portray, become symbols for all people, the table on which the action takes place is analogous to the world, and Rose, the red-gloved controller, represents the powers that be. We are all pawns in their game and the games are played out with that disturbing sense of inevitability that seems to accompany disaster, destruction and war. There is a coolness, a detachment in the manipulation which echoes a character in an earlier work — the button pusher.

The button pusher appeared in *"Live Neutral and Earth"* (1981) and subsequently in *Black and Blue: The Button Pushers Paradise* (1984). The

artist/performer cannot be identified with this character in the same way, for the button pusher is in turn manipulated by unidentified powers. Therein lies the threat — button pushers can be all-powerful but have no ultimate control.

This sense of irony infects a good deal of Rose's work and provides much of the power and subtlety of her performances. The whacky music in *Glory* relieves the tension from an otherwise intensely disturbing work. All other sounds in the piece represent, symbolically or otherwise, the noise of war; the whimsical western tunes distance us immediately from the subject, once again creating neutral territory; that valuable space into which Rose allows her spectators to step.

In that neutral territory we can reflect upon and assimilate the images with which we are

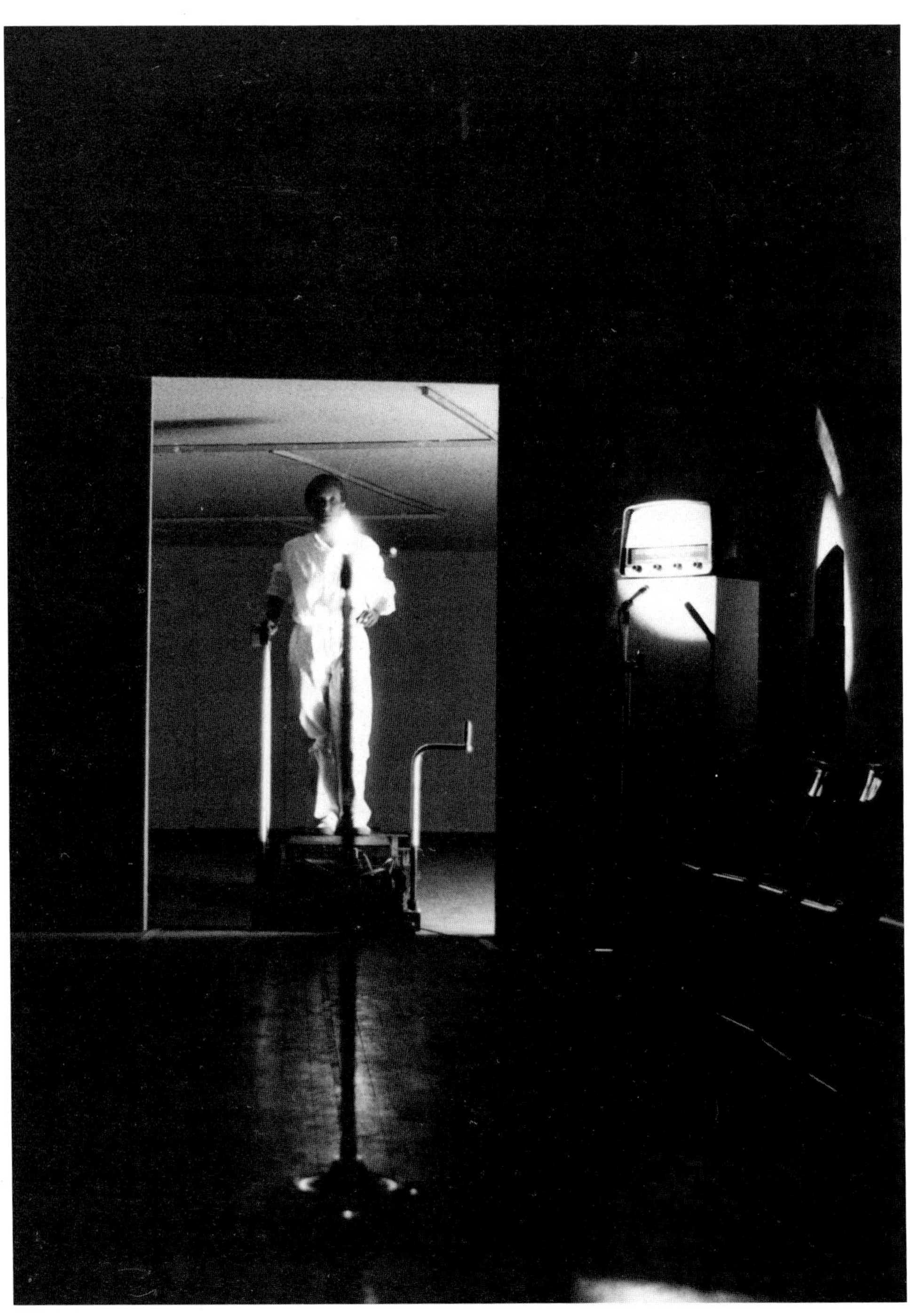

Mind The Gap
1980

I.C.A. Gallery, London

confronted. Heavily symbolic and referential, her work operates on many levels. In *Mind the Gap* the performance itself is an allegory of all performances, referring to the selection of the material and the appearance of the artist: "piece by piece the unrepresented richness of sources came together, drawing painful attention to the gap between intention and realisation."[2]

Much of the imagery in this work emerged from and related to the Frankenstein story from which quotations are read during the performance. In Rose's own words, the story refers to "That kind of creation which occurs at the point of total exhaustion in which the created thing assumes life, as the creator's dwindles." Life and death are represented respectively by the flickering flame and the block of ice. The running track marks the path of life whilst the starter's position, which ends the performance, indicates creation and the beginning.

Symbols of power abound in "*Glory*": the croupier's shovel is equivalent to the faceless robotic arm, the earphones are signals of control, and the artist's red gloves, the only colour in the work, are pulled on as if in preparation for a dirty deed; the spilling of blood. But who is manipulating whom, is it the performer, an unseen instructor or the cut-outs themselves?

In her earlier performances the symbols were perhaps more personal. Magpies in *One for Sorrow Two for Joy* are birds with which the artist identified. Black, blue and silver were the artist's favourite colours: other performances have referred to them symbolically. Rose Finn-Kelcey disliked her own

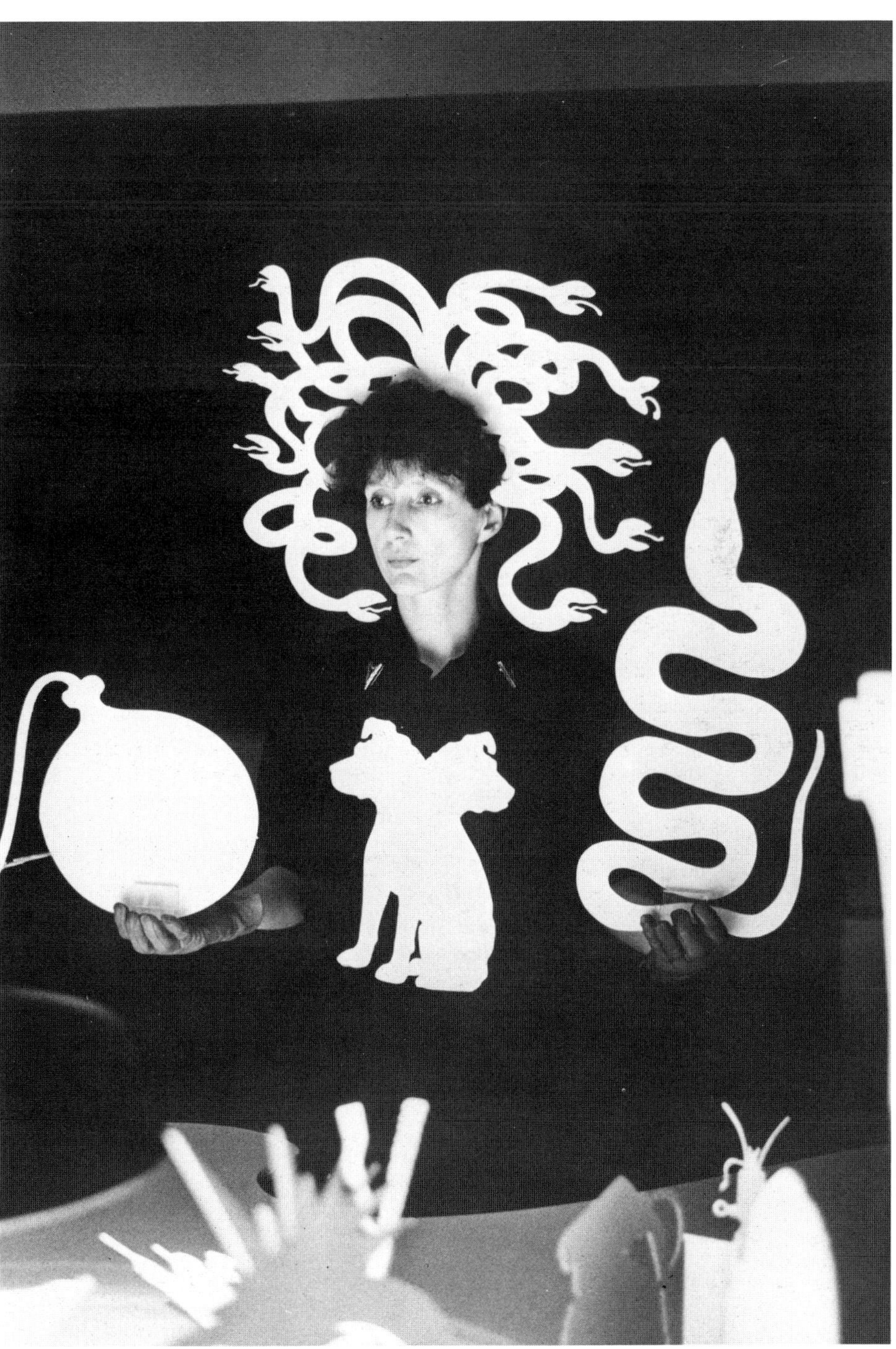

'Glory'
1983

Serpentine Gallery London

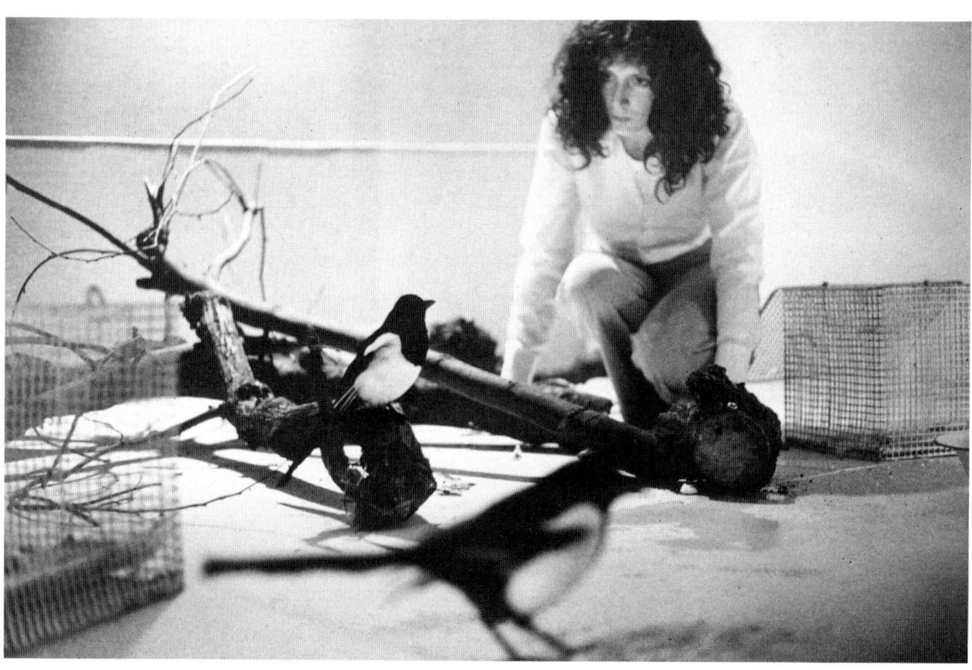

'One For Sorrow
Two For Joy'
1976
Acme Gallery Window

voice and magpies have traditionally been known for their ugly cries. The seventeen songs of the magpie were developed in later work. The cries represented a new form of language: phonetic and evocative, rather than descriptive or illustrative. "I regard working from a codified, though non-verbal text, as analogous to my desire to find an appropriate voice for my expression as a woman artist."[3]

The use of sound, however, is only one way in which Rose manipulates the senses. In many instances she explores the possibility of interaction between the senses, of their ability to fuse with one another or to operate on unexpected levels. In *The Boilermaker's Assistant* (1978), an impossibly technical manual formed the basis of the text which was deposited around the room from four loud speakers, creating a sound tableau which evoked visual counterparts without reference to its content. Sound provides an ironic overlay to *Mind the Gap*. In deliberate contrast to the cool, careful set, props and lighting, the taped muzak allows the audience to stand outside, to detach themselves from the formality of the space.

Over the last eight years Rose's work has moved from the private, personal space into a more public arena. The references are no longer so exclusively autobiographical. The division between the public and the private aspect of a performance such as *One for Sorrow Two for Joy* were evident both physically (by the division of the gallery window) and in its content — a very private experience based on the relationship between performer and magpies. The audience find the piece by chance and come and go as they please. In more recent works the issues are less personal. War and technology are central themes and the spectator is more

specifically controlled, by both the setting and the action. Audiences are placed carefully, often becoming an integral part of the props as in *Mind the Gap*, where they mark the running track.

"For me, the most striking single image in the work was that of the runner. I experienced an immediate identification with its physical vitality and delighted in the image of a woman actively using her body, showing its strength. The pace lacked the more masculine (short lived) drama of the sprinter, but evoked stamina and endurance — the limitations and strengths of the physical female. I caught the irony of running and getting nowhere. Racing oneself, a recurring nightmare but a familiar reality of the artist's struggle with inhibitions, contradictions, disillusionment, political and personal isolation. Each new step, each new possibility inevitably retreats into old solutions and is discarded. But it would be impossible to stop. One has to run the risk in spite of the odds."[4]

Throughout Rose's work there is challenge, both in its formal construction and in the themes she tackles. It attacks our traditional experience of sound, of light and of setting — these are wrenched out of context, re-ordered and returned to a new, subtle but questioning role reflecting her choice of subject. A recurrent issue in her work is the plight of the individual in a highly technological world. However, these works are ultimately optimistic. Although bristling with images of war, aggression, confrontation, there is a sense, achieved through ironic focus, that beyond lies something more hopeful. But first it is necessary to overturn what we have and create the neutral space from which new things shall grow.

Jennifer Walwin

FOOTNOTES

1. Rose Finn-Kelcey, notes for *May Day*, 1981.

2. Harry Walton, notes for *Mind the Gap*, 1980.

3. Rose Finn-Kelcey, notes for *"One for Sorrow, Two for Joy"*, 1976.

4. Catherine Elwes, *Primary Sources*, Christmas 1980.

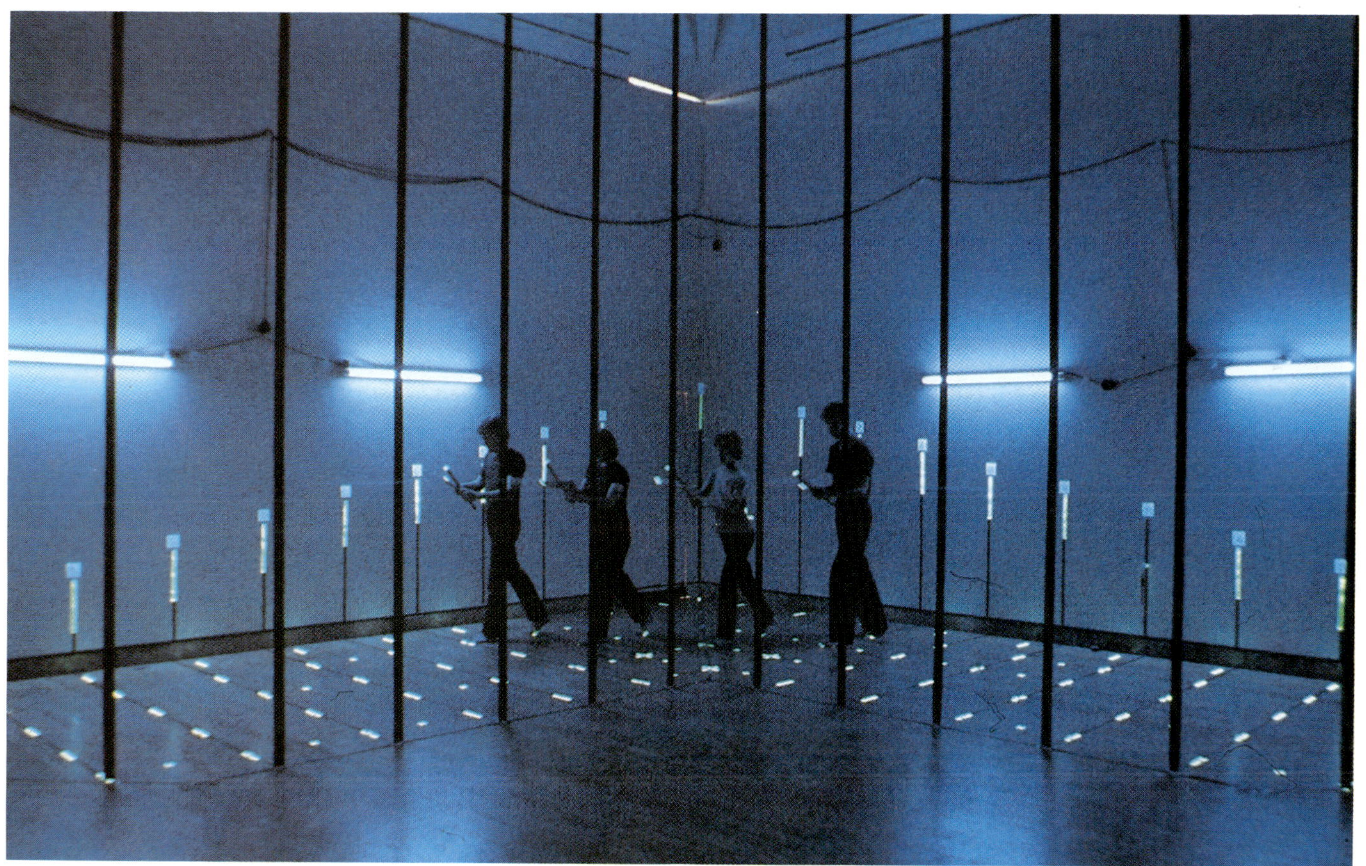

CHARLIE HOOKER

A Charlie Hooker performance has become a systemic interplay of light, music, movement and drawing. These elements and their rules of combination are deployed to make a work specifically in tune with the total ambience of its location, from which it takes its affective cue.

There are many constants in a Hooker performance, wherever its site, that are indicative of his structural concerns and their expressive development. Its structure is made visible by lines and notational markings across a floor and along a wall, which trace the work's spatial limits and become both the route and score for his "walkers" to follow as they traverse the space with percussive wood blocks or chime bars. The performers rhythmic pacing is complemented by their playing and, in recent years, is augmented by additional but stationary wind and string instrumentation (*Transitions 1983*, *Closedown 1984*) playing an obbligato to the movement. As a piece builds, it steps in and out of phase, whilst Hooker alters the regulative framework and its notation throughout, in ways that are not wholly preconceived and which lead precisely to its conclusion. Often (*Mainbeam 1983*, *Closedown 1984*) the spatial limits contract until no further movement is possible; a dialogue between freedom and control is seen, like a process, to have run its course.

The work is an audience-related form which Hooker firmly believes should communicate its purpose.

Accordingly he makes eloquent analogue drawings and maquettes available at the performance. He also holds workshops with students and other young people, partially as a means of making a living as an artist but more pertinently to explain and develop his ideas through working with others inside and out of what might usually be thought of as a 'performance art audience'.

In contrast to other British artists working out of confrontational and narrative modes in performance, from Bruce McLean to Silvia Ziranek, Hooker seemingly builds upon the contemplative 'minimal' or 'systems' music and dance associated with such composers as Philip Glass, Steve Reich, Terry Riley and Le Monte Young. Their superficial similarity notwithstanding, Hooker rejects any such 'influences' and stresses the particularity of the impasse he had reached with painting whilst a student and its subsequent resolution. As his involvement in the lengthy process of conception held his interest more than the painting of his highly structured imagistic works, he searched for a way of working that would include the processes of making (ideational as well as practical) in the work itself. His interest and previous training in percussion, the informal British art school alliance with rock music and a general emphasis upon logical form in the early 1970's, combined to enable Hooker to articulate his intentions through sound sculptures. His mathematical progressions for grand

piano and similar tape works established the
methodology but lacked the synthetic intensity of
the later live group performances. Hooker recalls
when his unique manner of achieving his non-
Wagnerian '*gesamtkunstwerk*' first occurred to him:

> "I was walking home, after working late at
> college, thinking about how to tie in the three
> elements of dance, music and visuals. A friend of
> mine had just given me a pair of big boots with
> studs in the heel and as I walked I was clicking
> my heels, doing little rhythms. Looking down at
> the pavement and the gaps between the paving
> stones, I realised that you could use the cracks
> like a bar [in music] and that I could work out a
> system using grids that people could move
> over."[1]

This idea, of a grid laid out like a vast sheet of
music over which dancer-musicians moved as they
played, was an elegant solution to his problem of
making a multi-dimensional process visible. An idea
moreover that he recognises as indebted to Sol Le
Witt; whose Wall Drawings sanctioned the
possibility of the student Hooker's 'floor drawings'.
Both Le Witt and Hooker issue instructions to others
to realise a work, modified by its space and manner
of execution, the significance of which lies in the
recognition of the systematic procedure that is the
work. Hooker, unintentionally, has returned Le Witt's
device to its inspiration in the time-lapse
photographic studies of movement by Eadweard
Muybridge and reformulated it through performance.

On graduating, Hooker immediately enjoyed critical
and public success when his performance at the
Robert Self Gallery in London led to further
invitations at Self's London and Newcastle galleries.
This *Percussion Walk* period consolidated his ideas
for establishing a system that would generate the
sound of its structure. These essentially simple, self-
enclosed, self-regulating constructs became
increasingly elaborate and, departing from the
rectilinear, embraced other regular forms such as
the spiral within concentric circles of *Spiral Walk
1979-80* (London and Amsterdam).

Increased complexity required the assistance of
professional dancers to maintain the rhythm and
consequently reduced the chance element of the
work. Hooker's collaborations with the pianist
Vincent Brown (1980-81) reintroduced the stochastic
with improvised piano and extended the melodic
range of the works.[2] With the accurately entitled
Behind Bars 1981 (Tate Gallery), Hooker reached
what he describes as a "turning point". "At the
Tate I became interested in creating atmospheres
and each work since then has had various ideas,
environmental, political ideas as an undercurrent
and mood." Indeed, *Behind Bars*, whilst a typical
Hooker word play, connotes the numbing
oppression and closure that resonates through this
and so much of his remorselessly exhilarating work.
This tension found its fullest expression in
Mainbeam 1983 (Gateshead), where he turned the
opportunity (afforded by Newcastle's Basement
Group) for a multi-story carpark work, into a
vigorous movement and sound piece for four
rhythmically driven cars with CB radios and four
grid bound "walkers" beating metal rods, that
entirely eclipsed the moment of its site.

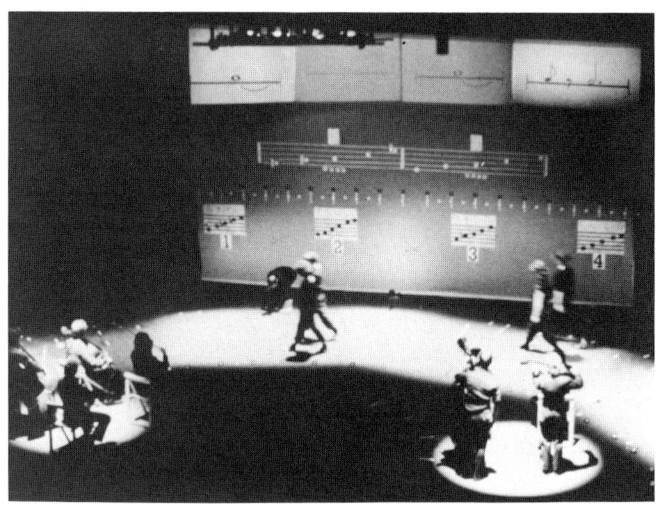

Transitions I
photo credit: Keith Buchan

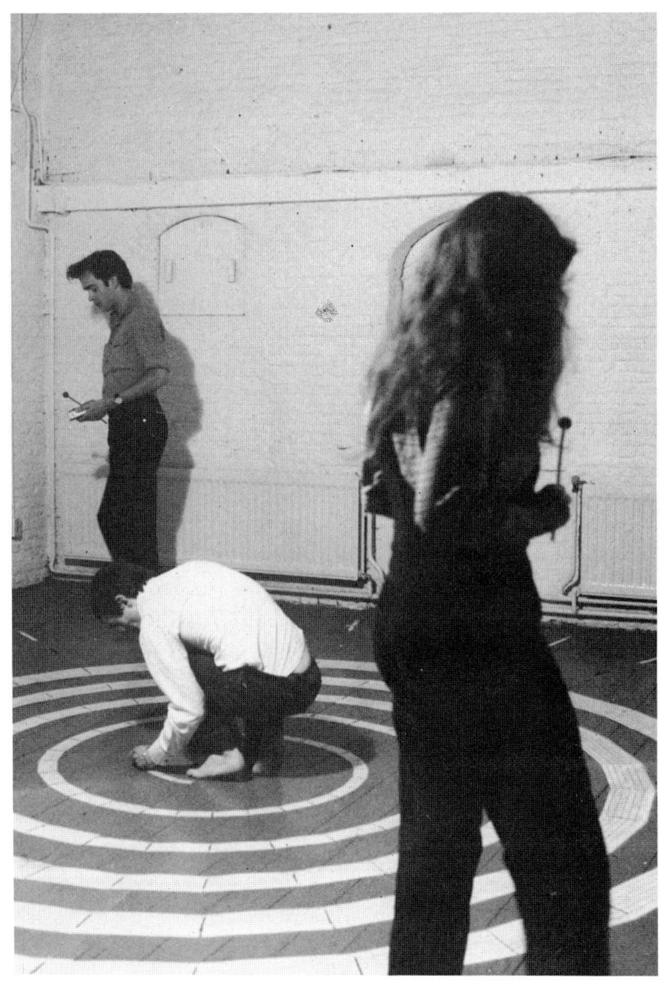

Spiral Walk 2
photo credit: Josine von Drofferlaar

140

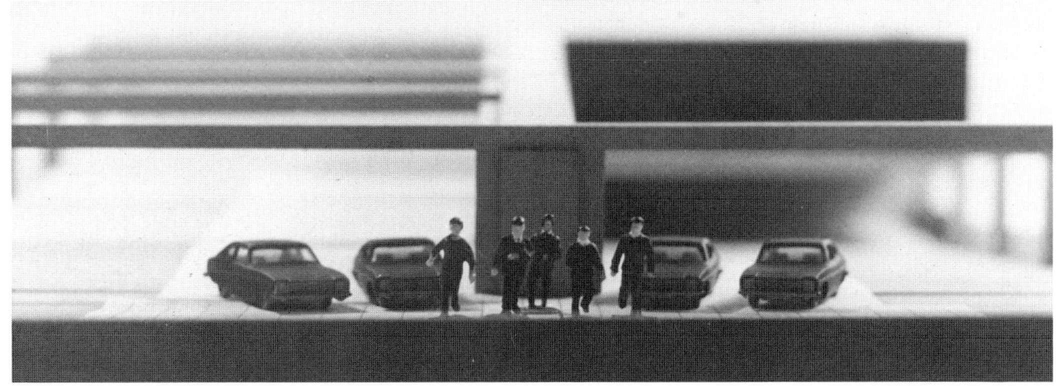

Mainbeam - Maquette
photo credit: Charlie Hooker

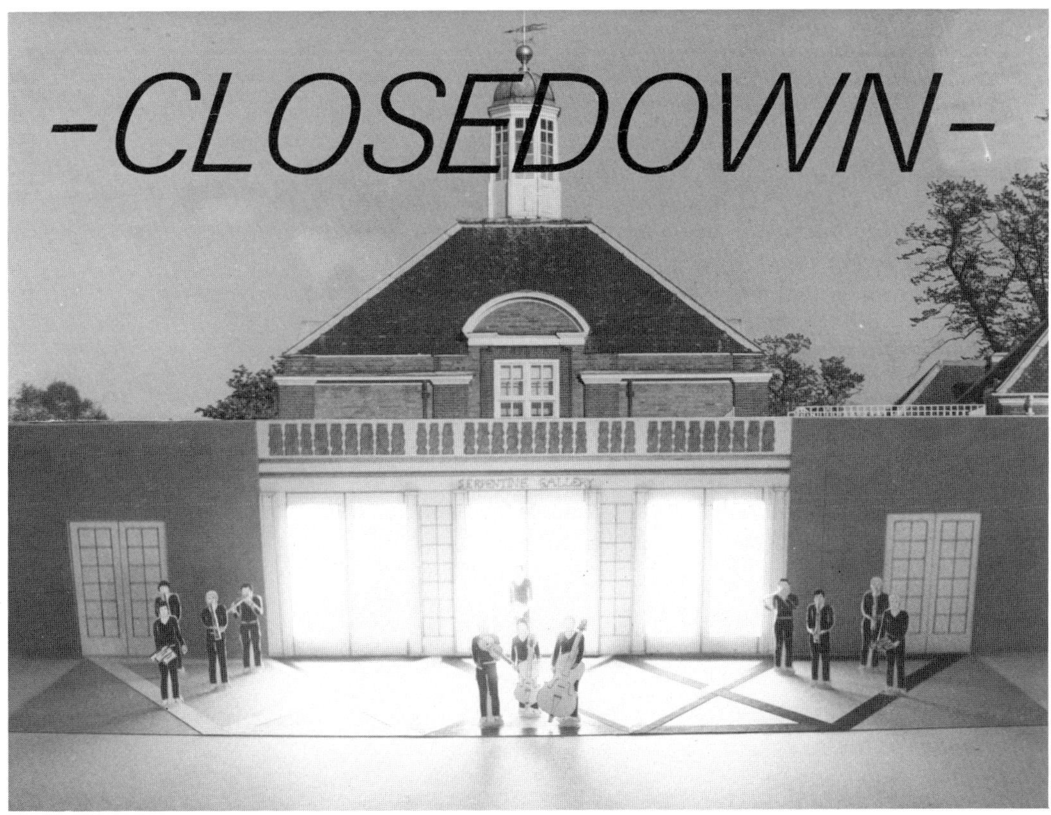

Closedown - Maquette
photo credit: Charlie Hooker

The more tranquil but no less sombre *Transitions 1 1983* (Riverside Studios, London) had two groups of four string players either side of an arc of score for four "walkers", wearing heavy and light tap-dancing shoes which they later discarded for bare feet and percussive wood blocks. A backdrop of musical notation carried changing projections of coloured rhythmic instructions. Hooker fired clash bulbs to punctuate modulation and altered the score's fluorescent tapes, progressing the layering of sound, as the lights dimmed. The natural transition from dusk to dark provided the setting and motif for the open air variation *Closedown 1984* (Serpentine Gallery, London). Three groups of wind and string players were incorporated in the triangular facets of the "walker's" score, their notation affixed and removed from the glazed wall of the gallery, through which projectors, triggered by the "walker's" feet, shone coloured light. The phasing of human and natural orders was obliquely conjured and dissolved into white light and final darkness.

These works are to be considered, within a suitably extended category, as 'visual art' by virtue of the character and provenance of Hooker's ideas. A proposition which runs contrary to the current valorisation of 'oil on canvas' as the privileged medium and signals Hooker's stance as ideological; albeit one that eschews sloganising, as it is grounded in and through the lived act of its production on our frameworks of difference.

Richard Chapman

NOTES:

1. All quotes are from an unpublished conversation with the author, recorded 18th August 1984.

2. *Walk On By,* (Battersea Arts Centre, London.)

Performance Through Two Colours, 1980 (Oval House, London.)
Airpiece, 1980 (Air Gallery, London.)
Three pieces, 1981 (Tower Arts Centre, Winchester.)
Nottingham Workshop, 1981 (Midland Group Gallery, Nottingham.)

Silvia C. Ziranek
A DELIBERATE CASE OF PARTICULARS

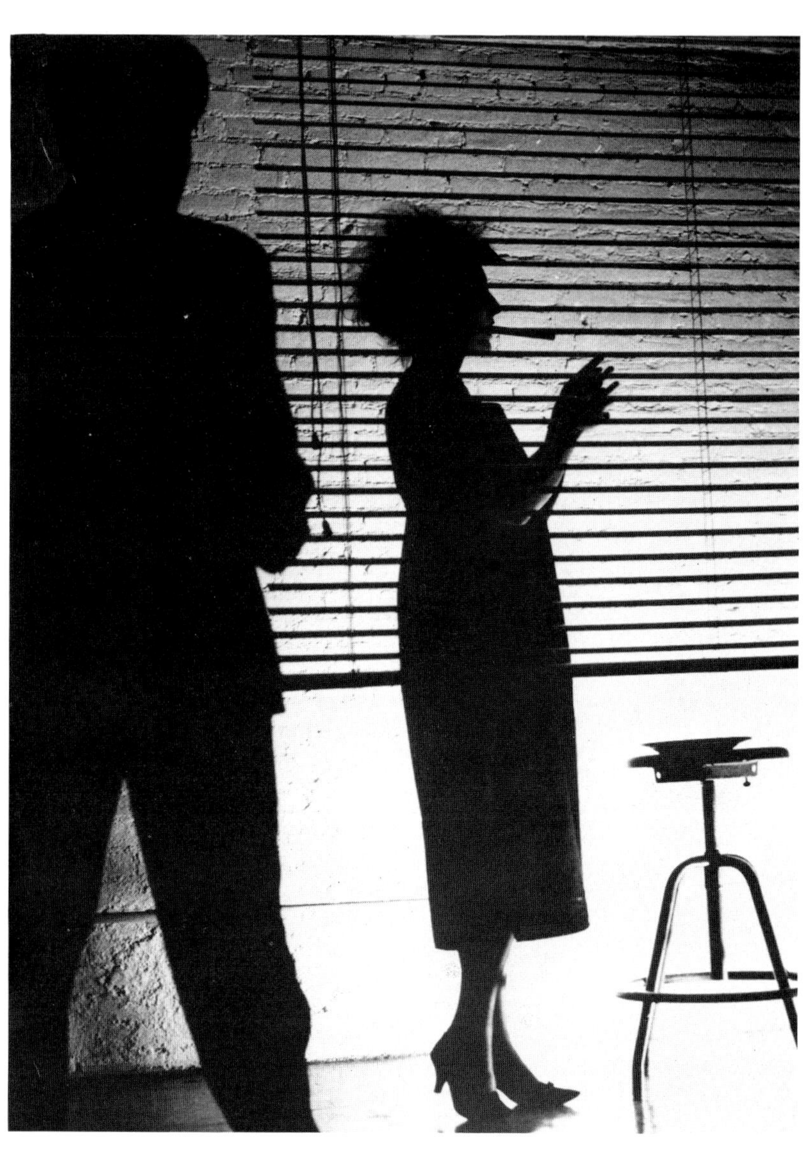

Silvia C. Ziranek
RUBBERGLOVERAMA,
DRAMA
photo credit: A. Whittuck

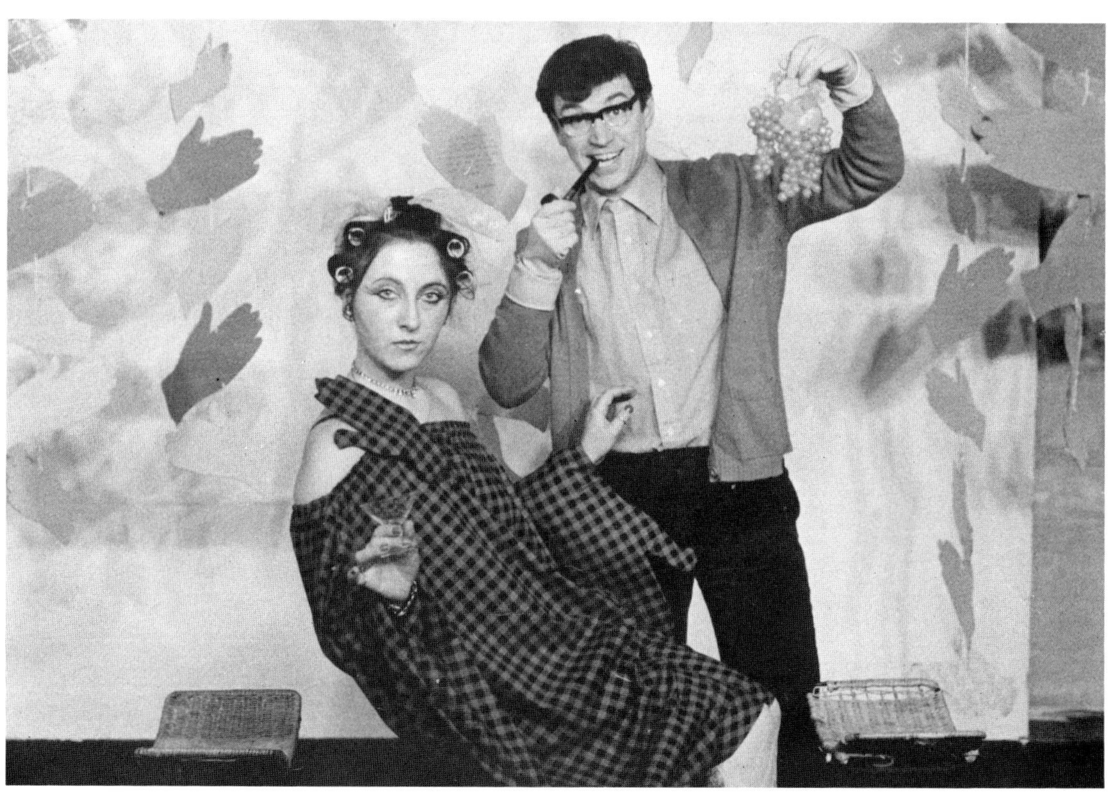

142

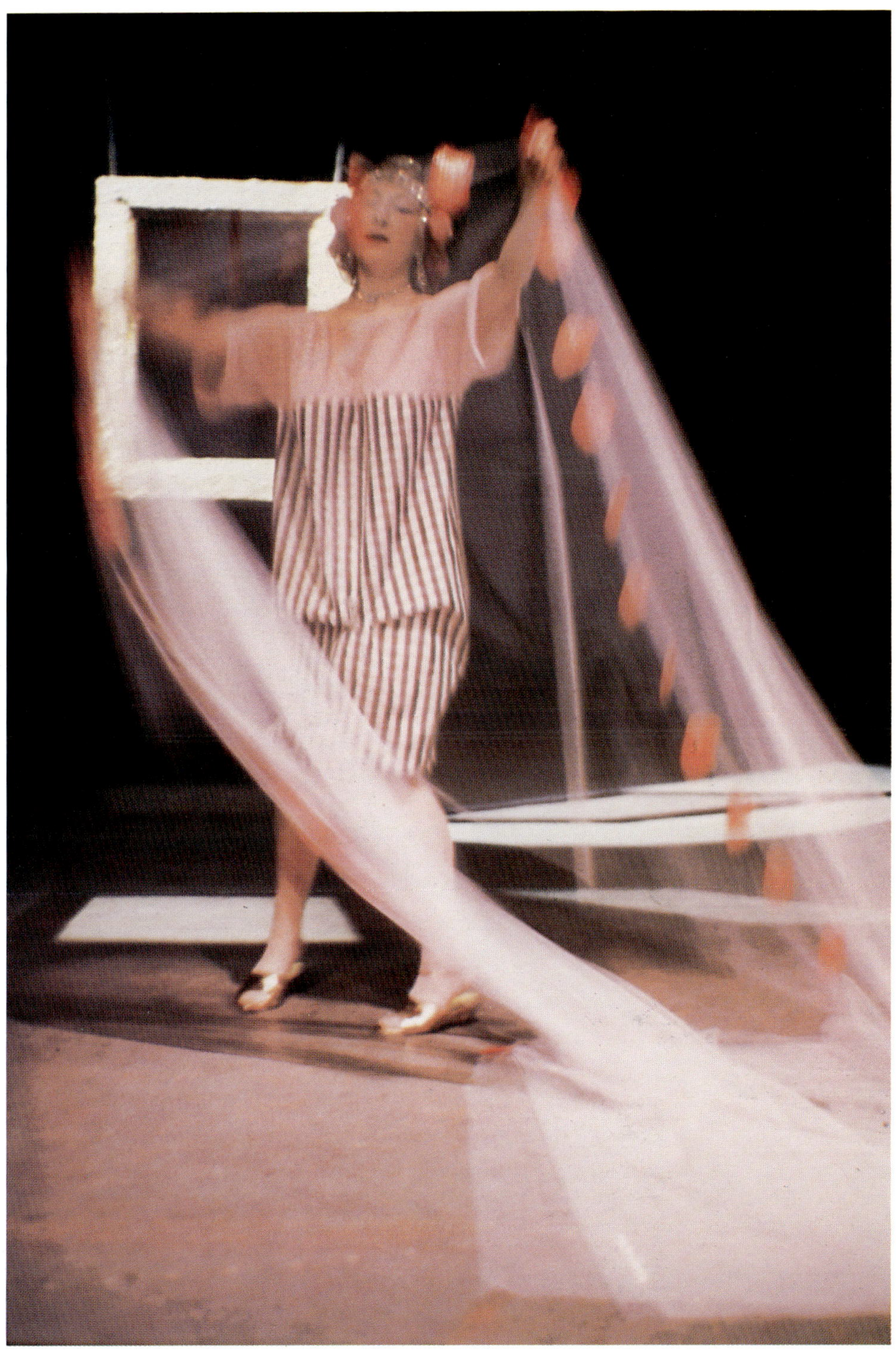

SILVIA C ZIRANEK:

AS AN EXPERIENCE, I SUIT MY PURPOSE

The strength of the performance idiom, whatever resources and techniques the individual artist may employ, depends, surely, on its capacity to present the subject matter directly without intermediaries. It is less constrained by the conventions and traditions of working in a specific medium and more open to the exploration of any methods that might be available to act as a vehicle for expression. In

practice, perhaps in part due to a perceived need to establish a defined status for performance, many artists have shied away from this enviable freedom, working within a self-imposed straight-jacket shunning the world of theatre, entertainment and the spoken word as alien to the purity of their particular brand of visual communication. (There are those, of course, whose achievements within the

143

'acceptable' limits have been very considerable). In recent years there has been a welcome relaxation of these ideals, but, while the creative boundaries are now less well-defined, it still remains largely true that penance, pain and puritanism are the bywords of 'serious' performance art. Silvia Ziranek is an artist for whom such strictures are as inconvenient as they are invalid. Painful — even puritan — subject matter may be discovered amongst her works, but usually alongside a full panoply of alternative content. A Ziranek performance is visual, verbal, stylish, dramatic *and* entertaining, but one should not be seduced into thinking that it is safe.

Ziranek lives in an environment of gold, black and pink, especially pink; washable plastics, tricel and artificial lace; inflatable dolphinettes, boudoir screens and musical door-chimes. She is a natural connoisseuse of the peculiar style of the kitsch (not a term she would use herself), the throwaway, the hybrid, the gaudy, the synthetic, and has a remarkable talent for exposing their inherent splendour. She knows instinctively that there is ample room in her expectations for the castle, yacht and diamonds to come, but until they inevitably arrive, her practical imagination is able to conjure compatible exoticism out of the shunned accessories of popular consumer culture. Technological wizardry holds little fascination for her.

Ziranek is an inspired designer, coaxing a stunning wardrobe with equal panache out of yards of synthetics or silks, worn with a handsome grace that ensures she is a focus of visual attention even within a society competing desperately for the most stylish, outrageous or simply noticeable. Matching this is the originality of her use of language, her sharp wit, keen perceptions and extraordinary talent

for mimicry. Ziranek is fully conscious of her potential and she exploits and exposes it with merciless confidence.

Ziranek has maintained and developed this devastating presence in her art since her days as a student under Bruce McLean. With him, she shares a knowledge of the perfectly judged pose, a gift for spontaneous and accurate deflation of pretension and a fearless determination to leave nothing sacrosanct. Her first public appearance was in collaboration with McLean — with *Nice Style* at Tooth's Gallery in 1973 — and subsequently she has appeared with him on several occasions including *Sorry: A Minimal Musical in Parts* (Battersea Arts Centre, 1977), *ABC* (ARC, Paris 1979), *Un Morceau de Gateau* (RCA, London, 1979) and at the 1979 *Hayward Annual*. On the latter occasion she also presented her work CHILI CON CARDBOARD in three sections: HOTEL REELAXAY, RON ET DELIA, and CHINESE HARDWARE but it was perhaps with RUBBERGLOVERAMA, DRAMA at the ICA in 1980 that she consolidated her unique position. This lengthy piece, a parable of the questionable delights of suburban bliss, released a torrent of double-entendres, metaphor, pun and purloined cliche, verbal and visual, upon a mesmerised audience:

HE KNEW HOW AFTERSHAVE COULD CHANGE THE ONE YOU LOVE TO THE ONE YOU LIVE WITH/TELL ME, CAN PACIFISM ALTERNATE WITH PATE DE FOIE?/I CONSERVE MY PRESERVES WITH A PENCHANT FOR PATIOS/DO YOU DECAFFEINATE THE ONE YOU LOVE?/MODEST AMBITIONS ARE SO INTENTIONAL/HANDCUFFED TO HOPE BUT DESTINED FOR DETERGENT/. . . Love, sex, the neighbours, the kitchen, possessions and pastimes in an undulating scenario that left no-one's pretensions untouched.

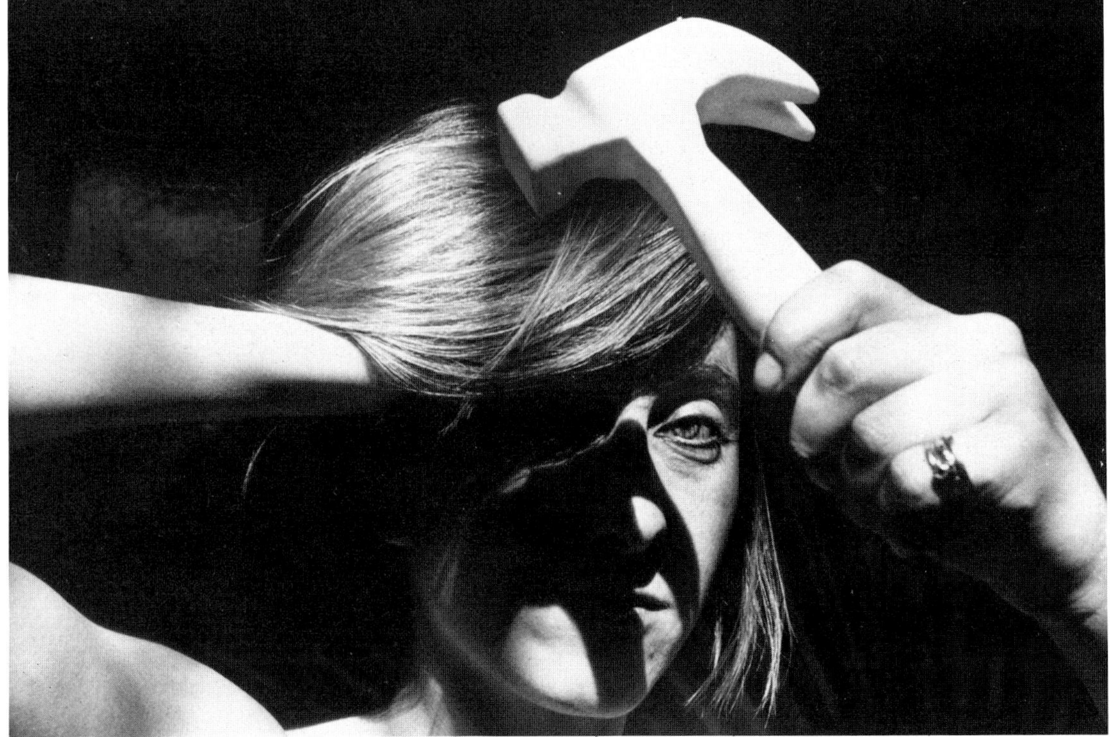

H(AMM)ER (HO)USE
photo credit: R. Wilson

Scenario is one of the more apt terms with which to describe a Ziranek performance for, while there will on different occasions be elements of narrative, culinary instructions and specific episodes, it is in the translation of a mood or attitude — a life-style — to the public stage that we find the key to her work. A piece first executed for the benefit of a New York audience in 1983 illustrates this well: A DELIBERATE CASE OF PARTICULARS/THE INTEMPERATE HEART/I ATE ART has all the ingredients of a Chandler thriller, with a comparable line in wry characterisation (HIS HAIR, SEDUCTIVE AS PASTA IN BRODO, BILLOWED IN AMOROUS TUFTS REMINISCENT OF WHIPPED SCREAMS/HIS EYES WERE COLD AS JELLY, HER LIPS WERE HOT AS CHIPS) but in the end it is a damning recreation of a destructive personal relationship — one the artist knew only too well — in an atmosphere inducing uneasy smiles and shudders of recognition. The theme and subject matter of Ziranek's performances are her own experiences. To a starry-eyed audience, the glamour and articulacy may be dazzling, but there is no element of fantasy; it is the reality of her existence, suitably focussed. As the opening lines of FROM A CONSIDERABLE AMOUNT OF HEIGHT (1979) have it: WELCOME TO CHEZ MOI/THERE IS NO NEED FOR DISGUISE WHEN ALONE, AVEC SOI-MÊME.

It is difficult to find a precise parallel for Ziranek. Cindy Sherman, Gilbert and George even Bruce McLean in their different ways are adopting roles or placing themselves in a particular, artificial position in relation to convention. Ziranek goes one stage further in that what we may at first see as role playing, is actually revealed as the truth. We are forced to the conclusion that our conditioned distinctions between reality and artifice are invalid. Her use of language reinforces this as, despite the unlikely verbal juxtapositions and the confusions of accepted syntax, it makes undeniable sense.

Faced with the precision of her delivery, timing (I NEVER MISS THE POINT WITH MY PETIT POIS), movements and sense of theatre, it is extraordinary to discover that, after the initial concept, the evolution of the words and the gathering of assorted properties, Ziranek never rehearses, never knows exactly what she is going to do until she does it, rarely learns any lines ("I secrete my words in obvious places") and that no performance is the same twice. But then that is the way it is in any social situation.

Whether contained within an intimate gallery or large theatre stage, the space for a Ziranek performance is requisitioned by a masterful arrangement of curious appurtenances, each so *particular*, the whole so *right*; and once the artist has entered, touched the decor with her elegance, made her first pointed pronouncement, we are left in no doubt as to whose salon, whose life, we have been invited to share. Thus deliciously ensnared in a web of EXISTENTIALISATIONALISM, PLUS 10% PHILOSOPHY, we are exposed to A SHOW OF WORDS, A WORLD OF WAYS, PARADE OF PINK, A DOOR TO OR.

Anthony Reynolds

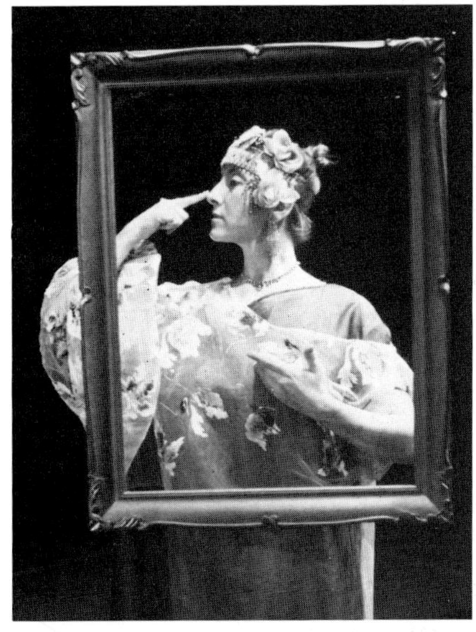

COSTA DEL TEARDROP

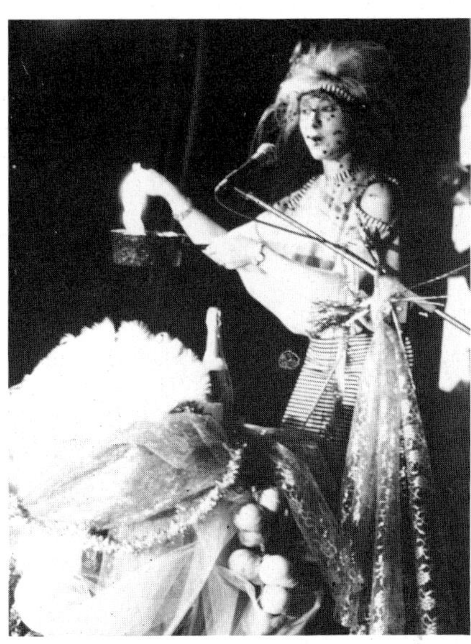

**FROM A CONSIDERABLE
AMOUNT OF HEIGHT**

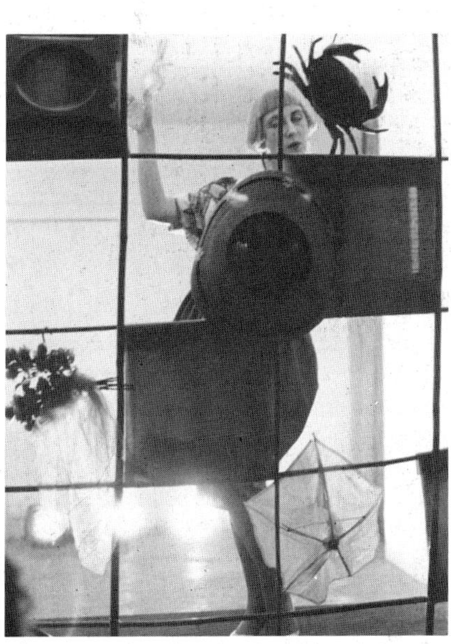

PHOTOS. AND OTHER FEMALES
photo credit: J. Agee

Soundscore for Audio
Arts/Orchard Gallery LP
1984

(part 1)
69 x 102cms
photo credit: Bill Furlong
Drawings for the Soundscore of the LP record parts 1-4

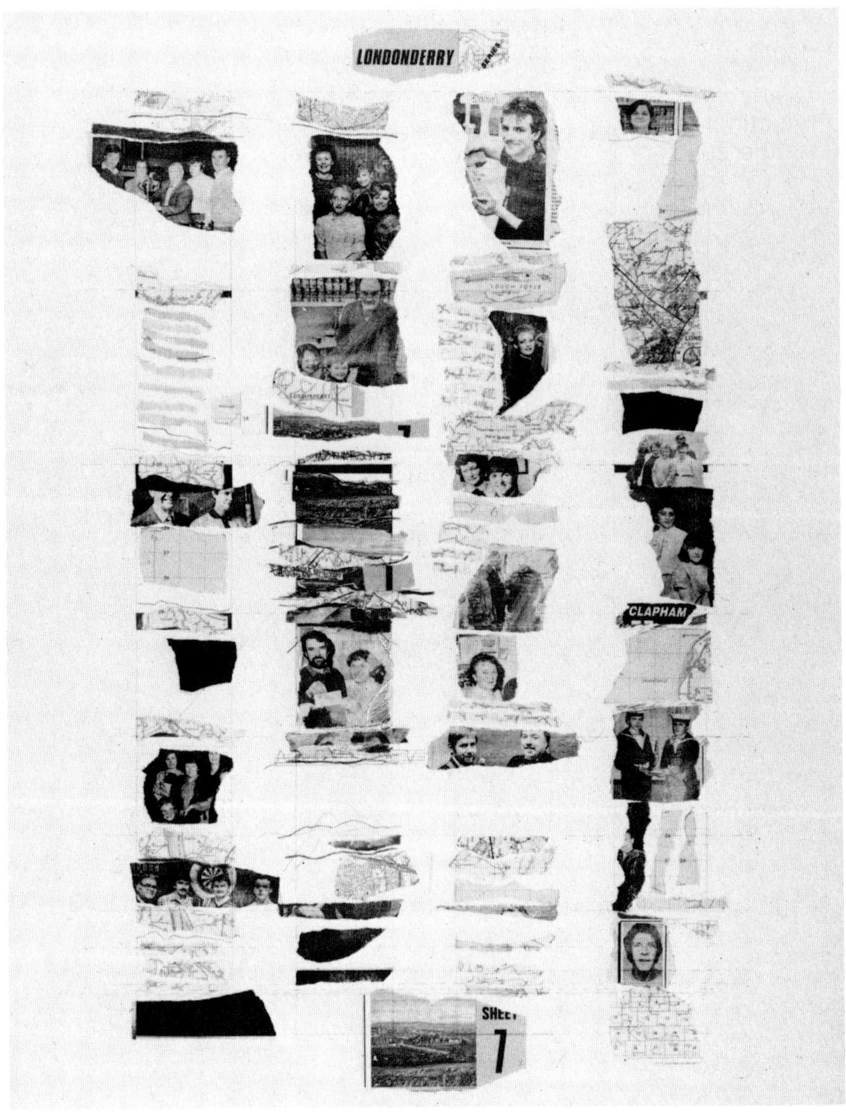

AN INEVITABLE COLLABORATION: THE AUDIO ARTS/ORCHARD GALLERY

The Orchard Gallery opened in Derry in October 1978. In November of that year Bill Furlong, the founder/editor of the London-based Audio Arts, visited the gallery and gave a lecture about the concept of this unique magazine on cassette and its parallel work collaborating with artists. It was the Orchard's first direct, working contact with a key enterprise in contemporary art which emphasised the importance of (notionally) secondary media operating as primary media.

Audio Arts set out to extend the language of art by extending the exhibition possibilities available to artists. Despite the fact that 'product' rather than process has come to dominate the international art market in the eighties, Audio Arts has held to its original course with admirable tenacity. It is the tendency of that market to define as marginal anything that occurs, geographically or spiritually, outside its limits. The activities of Audio Arts and the Orchard Gallery have been informed by a belief that it is possible to operate beyond the limits of the market; this L.P. is a manifestation of that conviction.

Within a few years of opening, the Orchard Gallery seriously began producing and distributing printed material, such as monographs, artist's books, cards which were conceived as extending the exhibition possibilities available through the gallery. These publications related to, but essentially were independent of the exhibitions and events taking place in the gallery itself. A parallel 'space' for bringing people into contact with art was then created. The means used were always determined by the nature of the art to be 'housed' and the audience reached could have been on the other side of the world to that of Derry. Indeed that *was* the idea.

In early 1983 Bill Furlong and I met to discuss what form the inevitable collaboration between Audio Arts and the Orchard should take. We decided to produce a publication which drew on the capabilities of both organisations but which would go beyond their usual formats. An L.P. record, the ubiquitous 12'' black vinyl disc, was the medium chosen to engage in a dialogue between the inhabitants of two distinct locations, Clapham in London, the home of Audio Arts, and Derry, the home of the Orchard Gallery.

Interviews were recorded with random passersby involving a series of set questions about their everyday lives. The sounds, speech, rhythms of thought, the cadences of two realities were then

edited together to form a collage of clues and
triggers about location, culture and ideologies.

Like any successful art, every level of this
production is a manifestation of the central idea,
from the splicing of sounds, accents, phrases in
separate tracks to the use of spliced maps and
texts on the record cover and sleeve as well as the
announcement card and poster. It is clear from the
response of the community in Derry, from the
people who bought the L.P. and saw the installation
of projected maps and texts in the gallery, that this
sound piece succeeds, not only because it is
concerned with the languages of art but because it
transcends those languages to deal with the
realities of human beings.

Finally for me it is the way in which the L.P. echoes
and remakes, almost subliminally, the long historical
relationship between London and Derry, the centre
and the edge, which makes each hearing amount to
a personal epiphany.

Declan McGonagle
Ex Director of Orchard Gallery in Derry
and presently Director of Exhibition at the
Institute of Contemporary Arts in London.

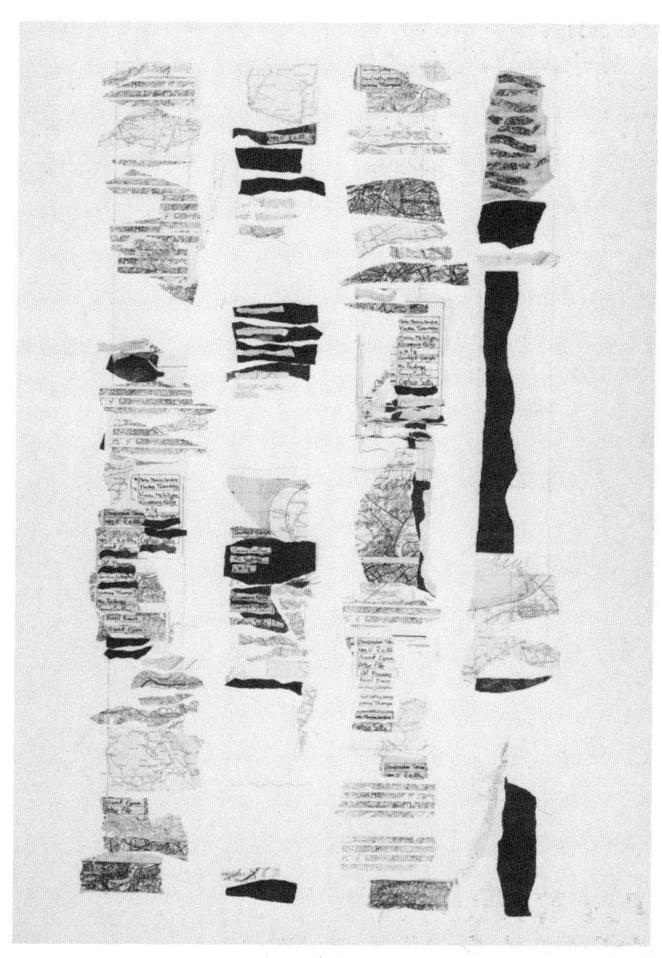

Soundscore for Audio Arts/Orchard Gallery LP
1984

(part 2)
69 x 102cms

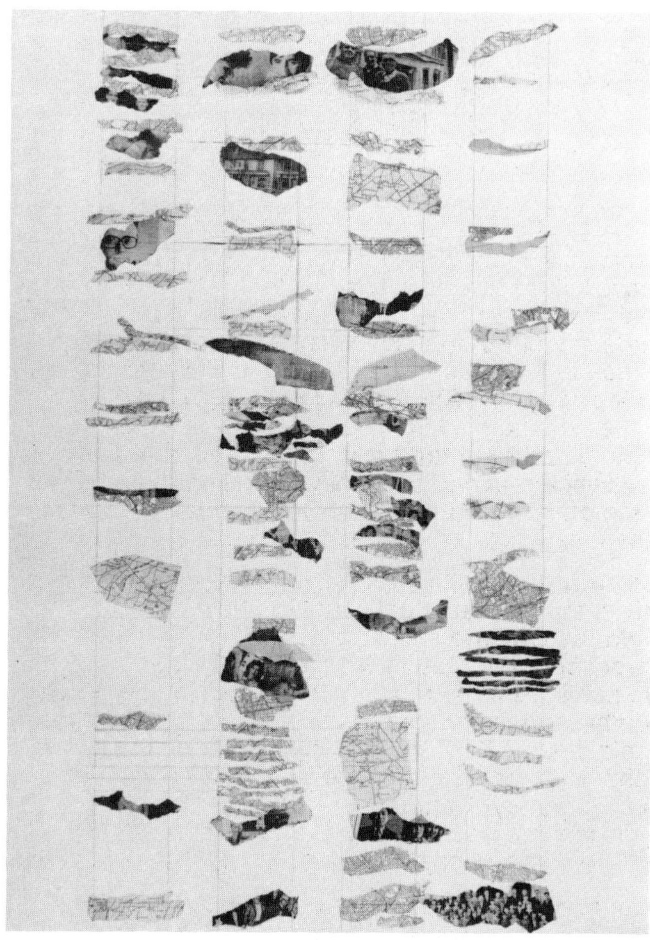

Soundscore for Audio Arts/Orchard Gallery LP
1984   (part 3) 69 x 102cms

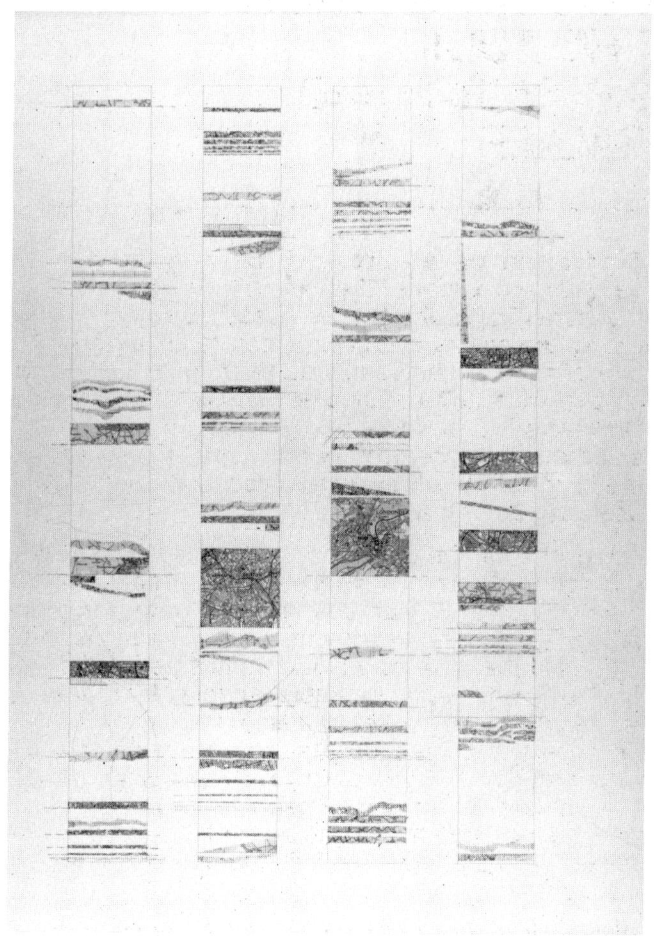

Soundscore for Audio Arts/Orchard Gallery LP
1984   (part 4) 69 x 102cms

The videotapes in this
exhibition were selected
by Ken Gill of Projects UK
and Tony Bond & Bill Wright
of the Art Gallery of NSW.

The commentaries were
written by Ken Gill
with additional
material from the artists
where indicated.

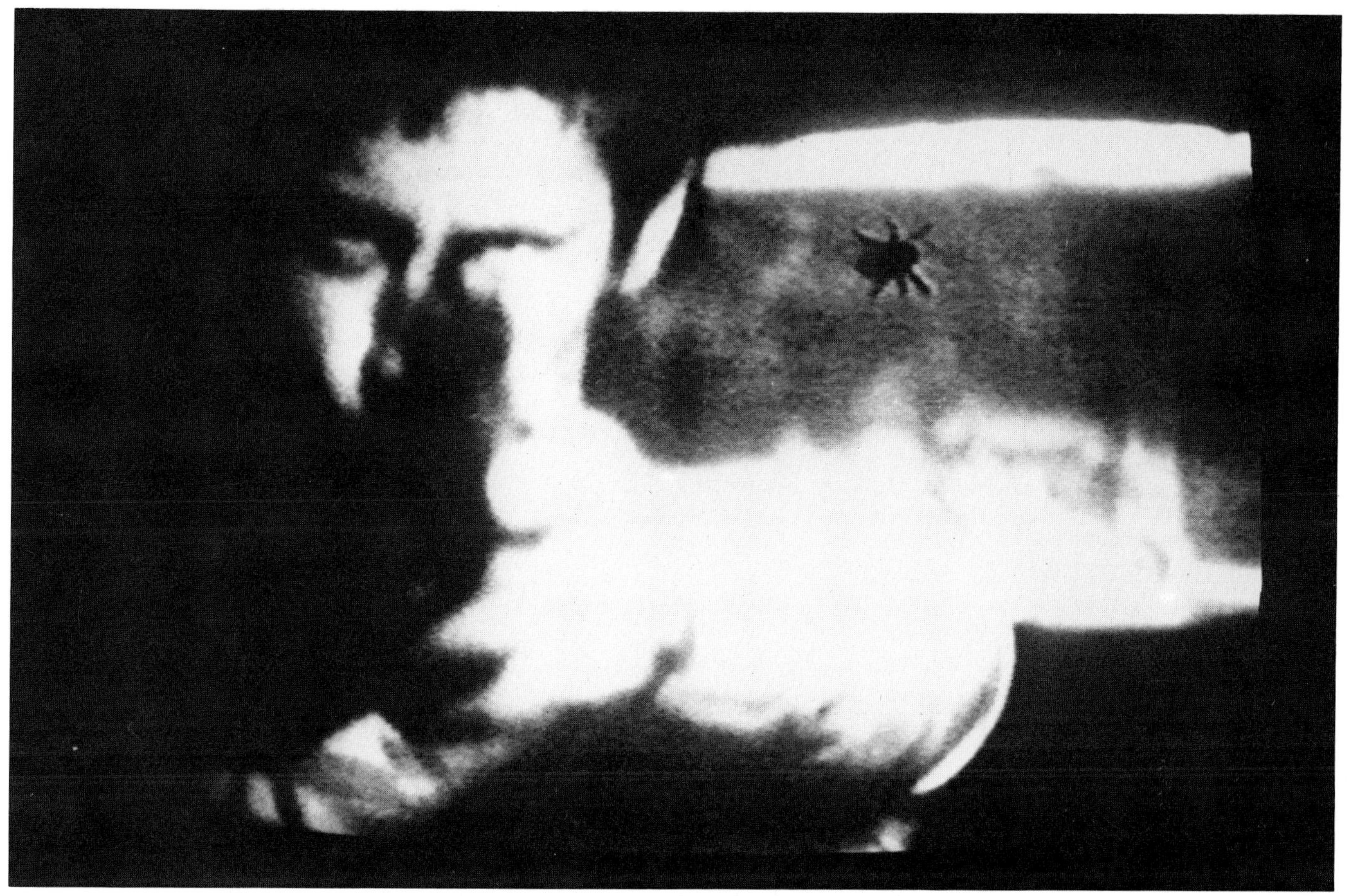

John Adams
'Sensible Shoes'
Video

JOHN ADAMS

"SENSIBLE SHOES"
10 minutes

Born 1953 in Wakefield, England.
Studied at Newcastle Polytechnic department of
Fine Art, where he now lectures in video.
Member of The Basement Group from 1979 until its
dissolution in 1984, with whom he showed widely.
He has received four awards from the Arts Council
of Great Britain and will make a commissioned work
for the City of Boston, USA in 1985.

Recent Shows:
1983: Arnolfini Gallery, Bristol
      LVA/LFMC, London
      Worldwide Video Festival, Kijkhuis, Den
      Haag, Holland
      San Sebastian International Video Festival,
      Spain (prize winner)
      Festivale Internationale Audio-Visuale
      D'Europe, Sicily
      Recent British Video, The Kitchen, New York
      Video Culture Festival, Toronto, Canada
1984: Videographia, Barcelona, Spain
      Rennes Semaine de Video, France
      4th Video Festival, Bracknell
      Arco '84, Madrid, Spain
      Irish Festival of Living Art, Dublin, Eire
      Recent Acquisitions, MOMA, New York
      Festival International du Nouveau Cinema,
      Montreal, Canada

National Video Festival, AFI, Los Angeles,
USA
Hong Kong Arts Centre

Commentary

Sensible Shoes is a multi-layered work which deals
simultaneously with many issues relating to the
content of television in the 1980s, its preoccupations and assumptions, the form of TV, and
the benign attitude encouraged in and adopted by
viewers to what they see.

Principally, Sensible Shoes experiments with
narrative, neatly utilising off-air material to coincide,
suggest links with or comment ironically upon the
main narrated story, that of the relationship of a
woman to two men.

The pace of Sensible Shoes is such that the
narrative weaves between layers of meaning with
an uncanny and arresting ease, encouraging the
viewer to make the choice between passively
consuming the chaotic imagery, or unravelling the
several plots at play, and therefore confronting the
real issues in the work, those relating to the
assumptions made by many television programme
makers, which could be termed 'sexist', 'racist' or
'stereotyped'.

The density of information within Sensible Shoes
makes repeated viewings both profitable and
revealing, as new meanings in the ambiguities of
the visual and spoken narrative, form.

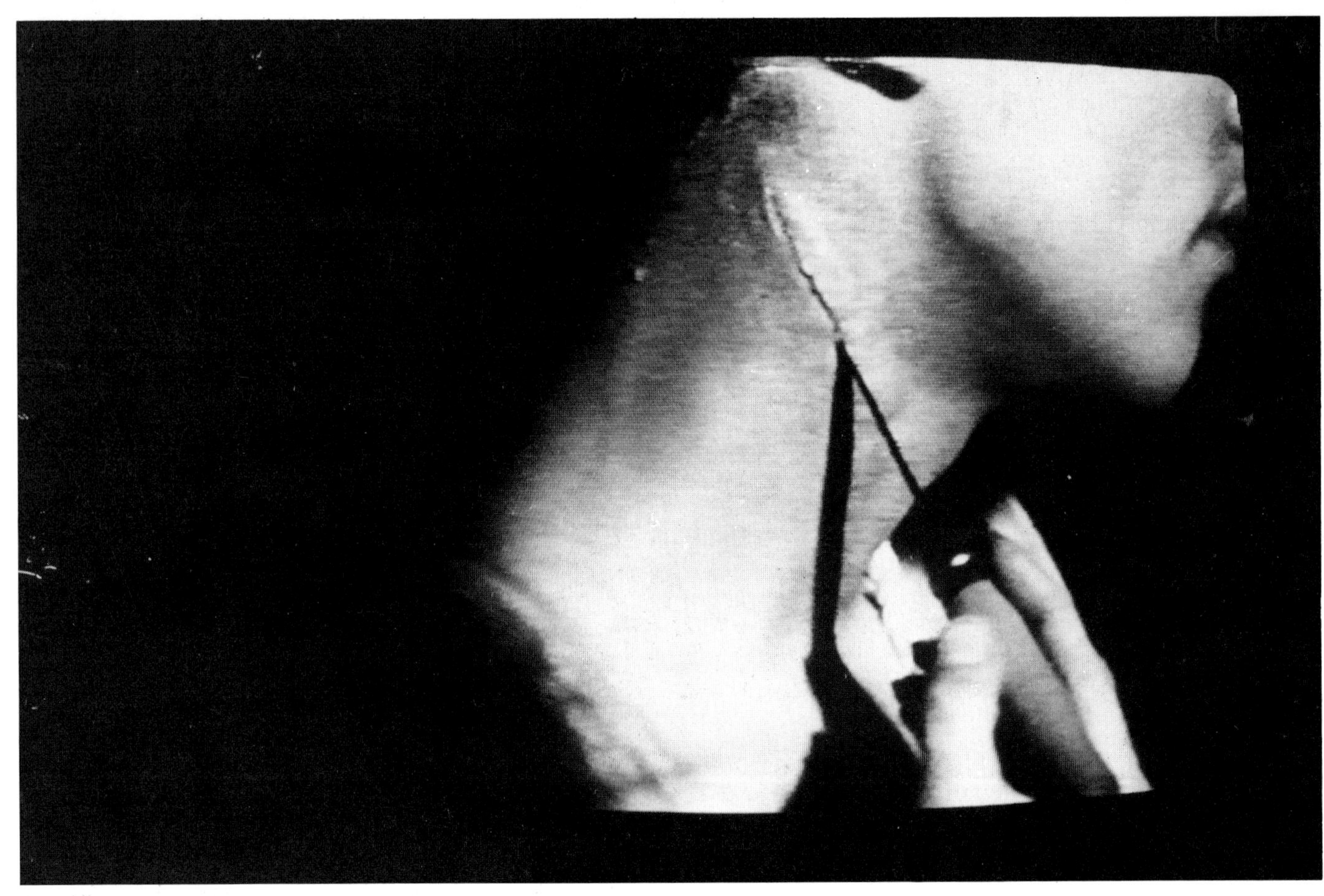

Catherine Elwes
'Kensington Gore'
Video

CATHERINE ELWES

"KENSINGTON GORE"
15 minutes

Born 1952 in St Maixent, France.
Studied at The Slade School of Art and Royal College, London.
Co-curated 'Women's Images of Men' and 'About Time' which toured extensively in Britain in 1980.
She makes regular contributions to Time Out, Undercut, Art Monthly, Feminist Art News, Aspects and Performance magazines.
She is a visiting lecturer at NE London Polytechnic.

Recent Shows:
1982: Women Live, Newcastle & London
National Independent Video Festival, ICA, London
Midland Group, Nottingham
Air Gallery, London
1983: Video Roma, Italy
ICA, London
Recent British Video, The Kitchen, New York
1984: Hong Kong Arts Centre
Rennes Semaine De Video, France
Berlin Film Festival
British/Canadian Video Exchange, Toronto

Commentary
The formal references of Kensington Gore are to a structuralist tradition which dominated British Independent Video in the late 1970s, but through the particular subject matter used, a telescoping of the distancing effect of analytical viewing is achieved.

The tape's strength is the way in which a harrowing story, used as the voice over, is played off against the imagery to successfully manipulate audience reactions, repeatedly drawing the viewer in, only to repel them again with dis-orientation techniques used in the editing of narrative voice over and picture.

The voice over describes the true story of a nasty accident on a film set, as a make up artist prepared a number of gory wounds on the extras. On screen we see lengthy cosmetic preparations on a man's neck, a menacing knife cutting through a wax area to simulate a slashed throat. This trompe l'oeil, coupled with the story, holds the tape's fascination, that of the power of a recorded or intermediate medium, such as television or theatre, to amplify any action.
". . .watching a painstaking, but painless simulation of a slit throat is apparently uncomfortable, and most people (in Britain at least) are relieved to laugh at the slap-stick that punctuates the spectacle, and happily shift into structural interpretations of the distancing devices I use . . .Should we, rather, see the viewers reactions as deeply ingrained credulity — years of subtle indoctrination passing off the hidden ideologies of TV and high culture as irrefutable truth?'' — Catherine Elwes

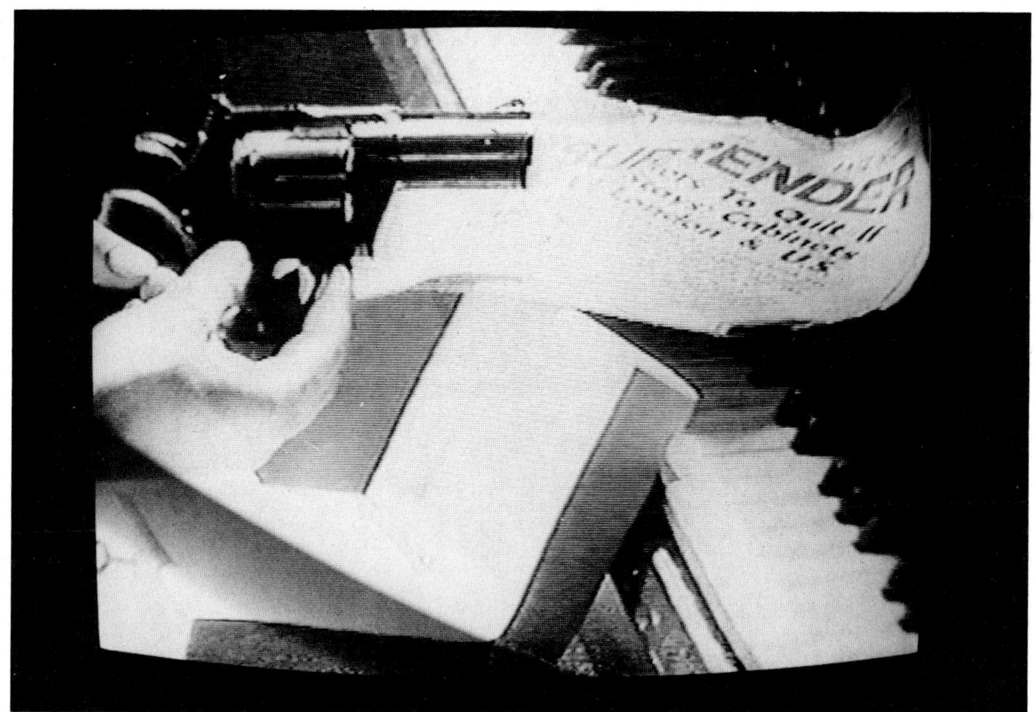

Rose Garrard
"Between The Lines"
Video

ROSE GARRARD

"BETWEEN THE LINES"
25 minutes

Rose Garrard works in painting, sculpture, performance installation and video.
Recent works for broadcast television include 'Pandora the Bringer of Gifts' for TV South West, and 'Tumbled Frame' for Channel 4 Independent television 1984.

Recent Shows:
1977: Incidents In A Garden, Acme Gallery, London
1978: Hayward Annual, London
   Art for Society, Whitechapel Gallery, London
1980: Symposium International de Performance, Lyon, France
   Lives, Hayward Gallery, London
   About Time, ICA, London
1981: Artists For Nuclear Disarmament, Acme Gallery, London
1982: Women Live, Arnolfini, Bristol & Basement, Newcastle
1983: Live To Air, Tate Gallery, London
   Frameworks, Lewis Jonstone Gallery, London
   Frames Of Mind, Kettles Yard, Cambridge
1984: Recent British Video, Toronto, Canada
   Venice Bienale, Italy
   Locarno Video Festival, Switzerland
   'Between Ourselves' — Installation. Touring: Birmingham, City Art Gallery; ICA, London; Arnolfini, Bristol; Bluecoat, Liverpool

Commentary

Like all Rose Garrard's work, "Between The Lines" poses many questions about the roles and routes mapped out for people, especially women, and the role of Art and the Artist.

A school, 'Central Foundation School for Girls' in Whitechapel, London, provides the starting point and main thread of the work. Using this biographical narrative; old school photographs, remembrances of old scholars of the school, who attended between the wars, Garrard is able to inject her own memories of what schooling, after the Second World War, meant for her. Hence, the imagery of piano practice, writing 'lines', etc.

Garrard's iconography is consistent throughout all her work, and the story of Pandora and her box features as a box containing a gun and newspaper exclaiming 'surrender'. Also in the work is the plaster facsimile of a woman, and with the use of a 'Frame Grab', which gives the jerky slow motion effect to the tape throughout, a real inter-meshing of artist and model occurs. This visual effect enhances the dreamlike quality which ingeniously disguises the radical ideas of the tape, which could have been expressed in a very didactic way. By using a more softly-softly approach, Garrard must be avoiding the alienation of an audience from ideas about power which are really very frightening.

"...the repetition is comforting...inside the deserted institution...empty corridors...closed doors...sounds and smells anticipated from an earlier time...memories of childhood games stilled silence with a glance...conformity...Sensing something beyond conditioning...the repetition...endless repetition...endless formal lines...rigid rows before the camera...unsmiling faces...posed for history...uniform...for King and country...in God's name...for those who died...laid down her life in service to...endless lines...focussing on the chair, centre stage...there is always a chair, the power symbol, waiting for an occupant...the chair remains the same...its position changes daily...reading between the lines the repetition is terrifying...."

— Rose Garrard

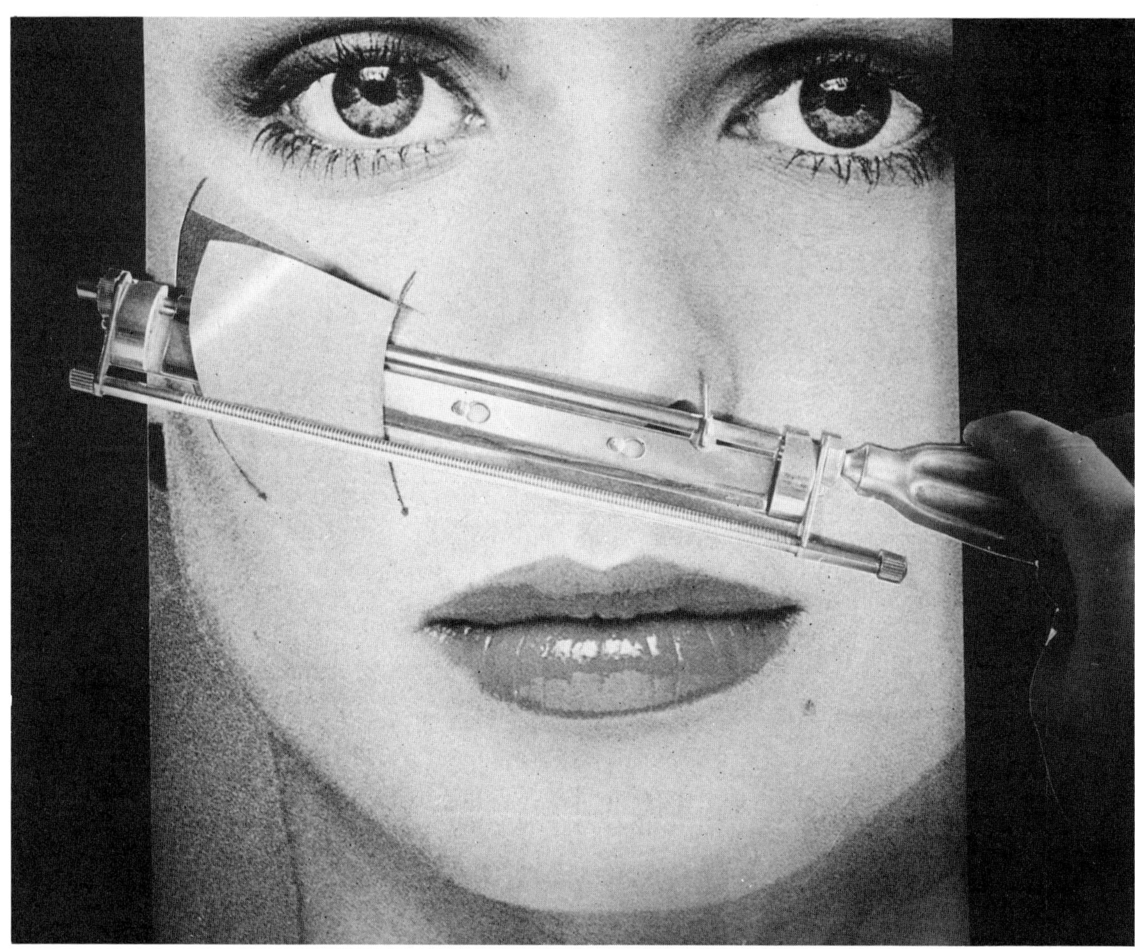

ROBERTA GRAHAM

"SHORT CUTS TO SHARP LOOKS"
40 minutes

Born 1954 in L'Derry, N Ireland.
Studied at West Surrey College of Art & NE London Polytechnic.
Work in the collection of the Arts Council of Great Britain.

Recent Shows:
1982: B2 Gallery, London
Tate Gallery, London
1983: Rochdale Art Gallery
Serpentine Summer Show 1, London
Foto Gallery, Cardiff
Chapter Art Centre, Cardiff
NMW, Newcastle
Arnolfini, Bristol
Orchard Gallery, L'Derry, N Ireland
1984: Perfo 2, Rotterdam, Holland
Fribourg Performance Festival, Switzerland
Violent Silence, Bloomsbury Theatre, London
Midland Group, Nottingham

Commentary
The subject matter of Short Cuts to Sharp Looks is cunning in giving the cool method of image construction (montage) a chilling power: the unblinking expressionless eyes of a magazine advert model, as a grafting tool slices through the cheek is an image which can only compound a sense of confrontation within the viewer.

"...the issues raised are not specifically concerned with the female image. It is an attempt to question how we evaluate the concept of 'beauty' in our own particular culture and our relationships to its antithesis — that of scarification and ethnic deformations, as alternative cosmetic treatments"
— Roberta Graham

Roberta Graham's work addresses taboo subject matter almost always referring to a belief in the fragility of life, it is obsessive in its search for an edge where confrontation between our conscious and subconscious selves must take place, where the veneer of protection built up to anaesthetise, is stripped away.

Graham's work aims at catharsis, a breaking down of those taboos. Given the often lurid subject matter of her work, it would be very easy to become sensational or titillating. The power of the work is its honesty, and the results are surprising. The subjects of other pieces have been The Kray twins, The Yorkshire Ripper, and the media coverage thereof, and light boxes which revealed images of the artist stripping away here skin to reveal the organs beneath. Her work's dark obsessions operate internally in the viewer, playing on their psyche, their own doubts, fears and prejudices.

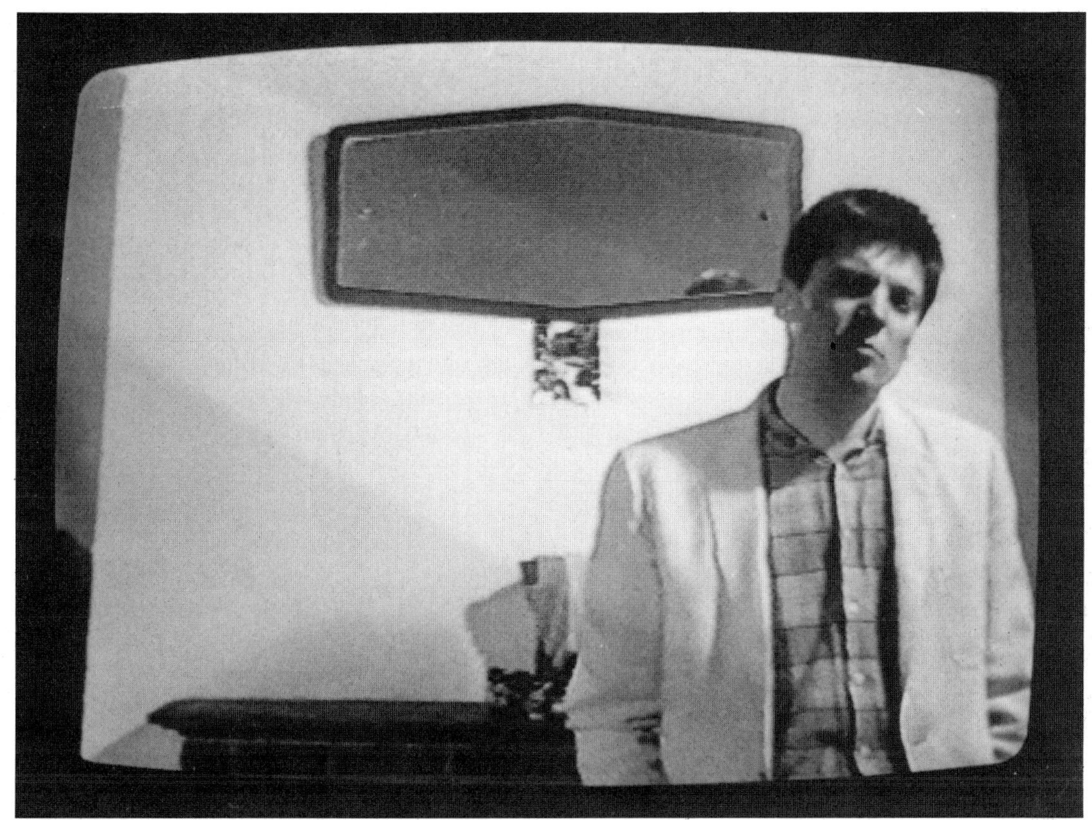

Steve Hawley
'Bad Reasons'
Video

STEVE HAWLEY

"BAD REASONS"
20 minutes

Born 1952 in Wakefield, England.
Studied at Brighton Polytechnic Department of Fine Art.
Visiting lecturer at Brighton Polytechnic, Trent Polytechnic and NE London Polytechnic, where he was Arts Council Video Fellow in 1983.

Recent Shows:
1982: Art For Boxes, Tate Gallery, London
Video Art & Technology, Serpentine Gallery, London
1983: ICA, London
Video Installation Show, Air Gallery, London
3 Video Installations, NMW, Newcastle
Recent British Video, The Kitchen, New York
1984: SAW gallery, Ottawa, Canada
Ljubljana Video Festival, Jugoslavia
Berlin Film Festival
Film Accademy, Zagreb, Jugoslavia
Rennes Semaine De Video, France
Festival International d'Art Video, Locarno, Switzerland

Commentary
Bad Reasons is an attempt to come to grips with the power of language and the inadequacies of reason. The piece is in three parts.

In the first part, 'The undistributed middle and other fallacies in the home', a man walks around his room obsessively constructing syllogisms, but keeps getting them wrong. In the confusion of logic and emotion he resembles Star Trek's Mr Spock, in whom either the Venusian half predominates ("logically speaking Captain, your fear of death is completely irrational"), or the human half ("Mr Scott, I am in love"). The fallacious arguments are preceded by titles couched in the forbidding, yet poetic, language of formal logic — 'The Fallacy of Illicit Process of the Major Term' — and lead to conclusions which are not susceptible to reasoned proof in any case.

The second part, 'We Have Fun Drawing Conclusions', takes as it source material a series of images from children's learn-to-read books. The stereotypes and idealised attitudes are the premises, if you like, on the basis of which the conclusions of our adult lives are reached. Bad Premises make for bad conclusions. However, in another sense the images project a plausible view of childhood, which is separated from actuality by a huge gulf, on the other side of which all farmers are kind, all good girls help their mummies, all skies are sunny and we all have fun.

In the final section, 'Divers, Divers, Can I Have Your Attention Please', two sequences — one of a man constructing logical arguments and the other of a swimming pool — are restructured and finally combined by editing. The rigid order of the man's formal language is chopped up and reformed firstly into a rhyming sequence, then into a rhythmical conclusion in which intellectual meaning is drained out of the words to be replaced by a different kind of understanding, in a similar way, the chaos of the swimming pool has an order imposed upon it.

— Steve Hawley

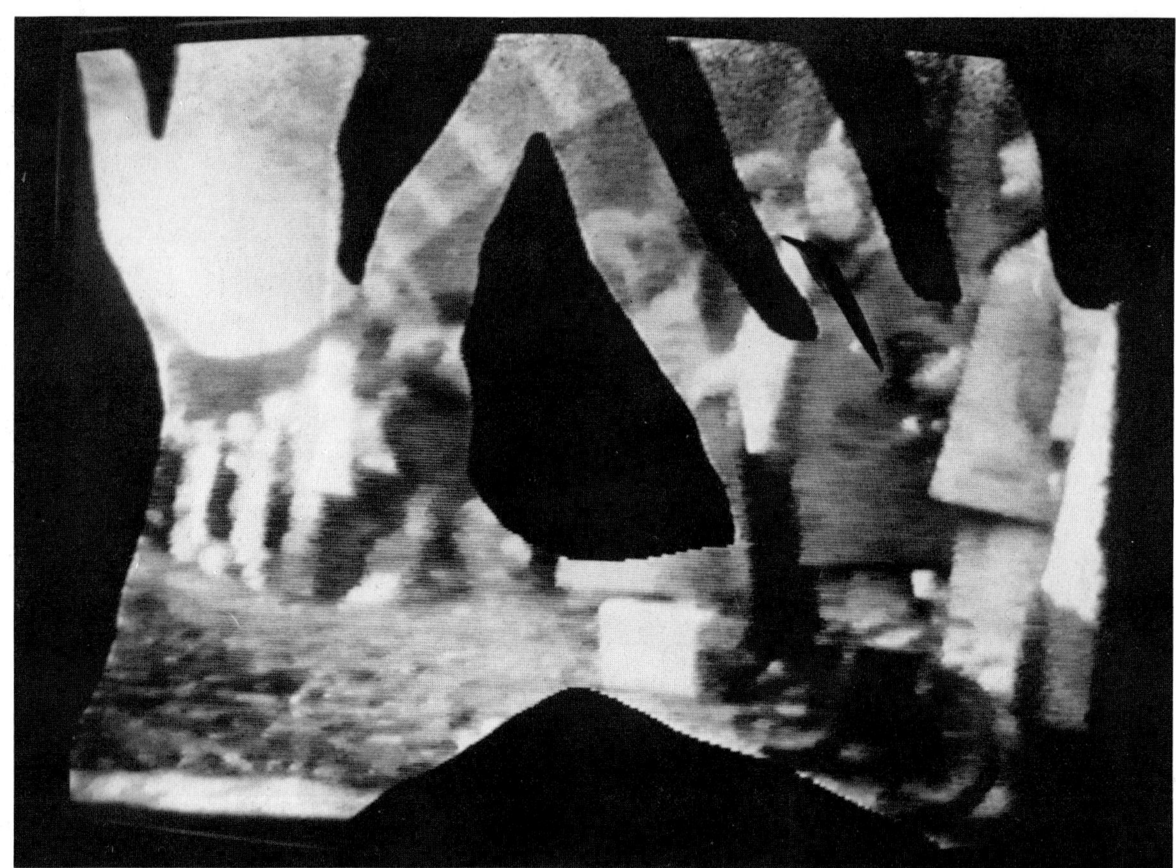

Tina Keane
'In Our Hands: Greenham'
Video

TINA KEANE

"IN OUR HANDS: GREENHAM"
39 minutes

Member of Circles women's work in distribution
Teaches at St Martin's School of Art, Slade School
and Byam Shaw School.
She has received several awards from Arts Council
of Great Britain.

Recent Shows:
1982: Third Eye Centre, Glasgow
      Women Live, LFMC, London
      & Arnolfini, Bristol
      Tate Gallery, London
      Edinburgh Film Festival
      Tyneside Film Festival, Newcastle
      Midland Group, Nottingham
      Slow Dance Film Collective, Liverpool
      Women's Film Festival, Norwich
1983: Video Installation Show, Air Gallery, London
      3 Installations, NMW, Newcastle
      St Pauls Gallery, Leeds
      Recent British Video, The Kitchen, New York
1984: Installation, British/Canadian Exchange,
      A Space, Toronto

Commentary
"The symbol most closely connected with the
women's peace movement is the weaving of webs.
Each link in a web is fragile, but woven together
creates a strong and coherent whole"
— 'Greenham Women Everywhere': Alice Cook and
Gwyn Kirk

"The video images are of an expressive nature, of
pattern woven visuals of personal documentary
material, of actions and rituals at Greenham
Common, filtered through the outline of a woman's
hands. The sound track is a collage of interviews,
songs and music. The video through metaphor,
indicates women's strength, involvement and
struggle against nuclear weapons, taking the future
into our own hands.

Dedicated to the women at Greenham Common
Peace Camp"

— Tina Keane

The Women's Peace Camp at Greenham Common
US Air Base, in Berkshire, has been in existence
since September 1981. Four years on there is still a
hardcore at the base whose numbers are in
hundreds rather than tens. This is regularly
supplemented by thousands during days or weeks of
action.

Greenham Common is specifically important
because it is one of the European sites for US
nuclear Cruise missiles. This is just one of the
reasons for the profound importance of the Peace
Camp as one focus for the Peace movement in
Britain. The non-violent methods, interlaced with the
extensive use of symbolic actions, has not only won
the blockade support throughout much of the world,
but has — through more or less constant press
coverage — kept the issues at stake in sharp public
focus.

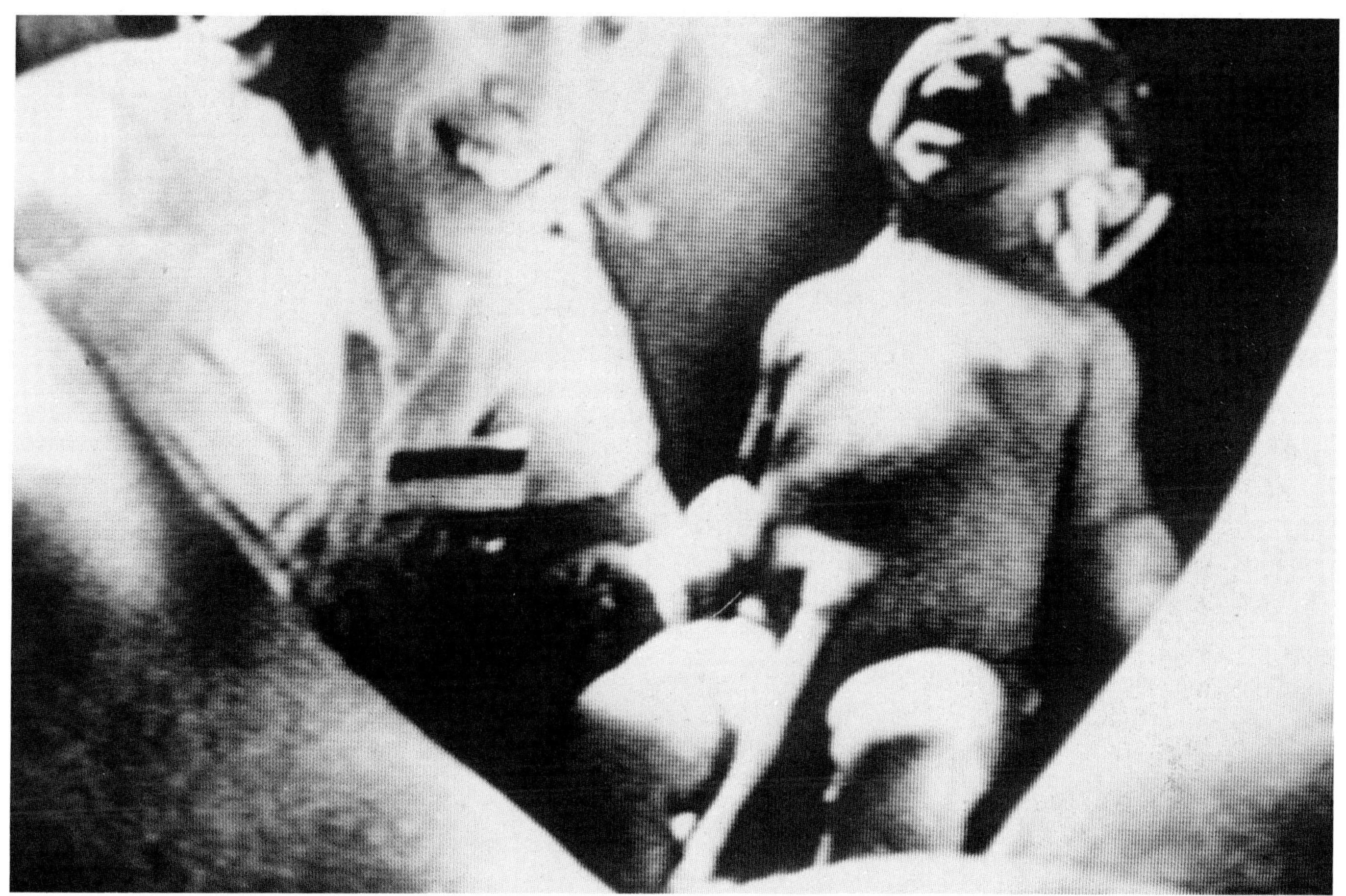

BELINDA WILLIAMS

"THE WAY WE ARE"
12 minutes

Born 1952, Yorkshire, England.
Studied at Brighton Polytechnic Department of Fine Art.
Member of 2B Butlers Wharf in the mid 1970s, and was a member of and administrator for The Basement Group, Newcastle and is now employed at Trade Films, Newcastle establishing the Northern Film & TV archive.
She has received 5 awards from Arts Council of Great Britian, Northern Arts and The British Council.

Recent Shows:
1982: Sheffield Expanded Media Show
LVA, London
Women Live, Newcastle & London
Bienale De Paris, France
4 Days of Performance Art, Midland Group, Nottingham
Cairn, Paris
Nouveau Mixage, Caen, Normandy, France
Photographic Exhibition, NMW, Newcastle
1983: Arnolfini, Bristol
Maison De La Culture, Rennes, France (British rep)
Orchard Gallery, L'Derry, N Ireland
Crescent Centre, Belfast, N Ireland
Het Apollohuis, Eindhoven, Holland

Rochdale Art Gallery, Lancashire
1984: Gruppo Ricerce Materialistica, Turin, Italy

Commentary
The Way We Are traces the development of people from birth to old age examining, in an ironically humorous way, the conditioning which people undergo throughout their lives.

It is illustrated visually by a smoothly melded stream of still images taken from a variety of sources including magazine advertisements, TV, real life and staged situations. The sound, which is taken from an equally broad set of sources, counterpoints with the visuals to magnify and exaggerate upon the scenes depicted, giving the whole work a sense of dull absurdity and pathos.

The function of the material is straightforward in illustrating the determination of male and female roles as they exist in British society. This is a common enough theme not only in Belinda William's work, but in many artists' work, especially that of women, but what really underscores the whole tape is a sense that we have a responsibility to do something to alter this apparently cyclical system of living, not only for ourselves but more importantly for our children. As a mother of two, the pre-occupation with children is always at the fore in William's work, usually coupled with a number of questions related to motherhood, and the great loss of freedom associated with it.

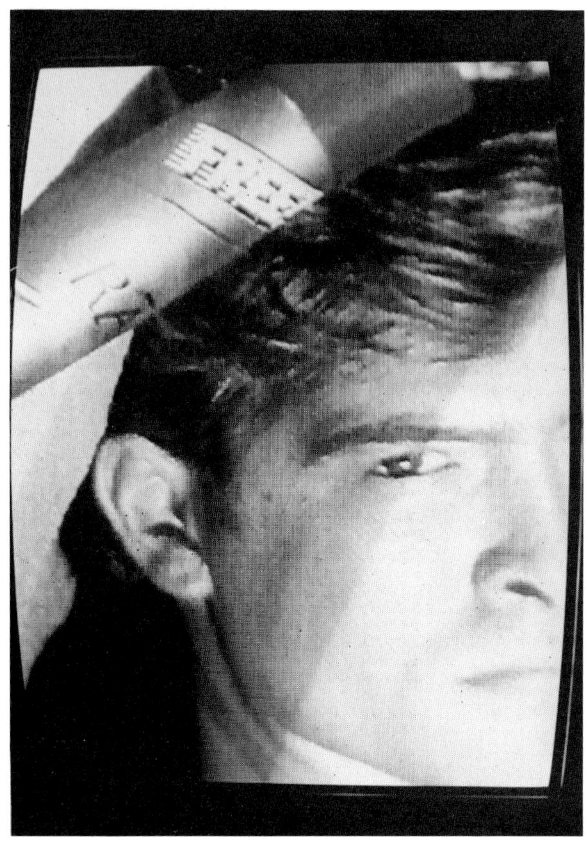

Mike Stubbs
'Ra ads' from 'Pieces'
Video

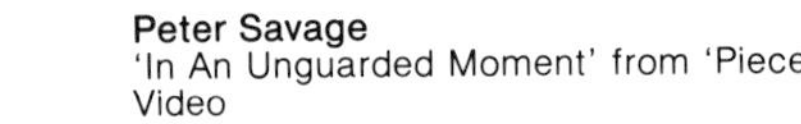

Peter Savage
'In An Unguarded Moment' from 'Pieces'
Video

VARIOUS ARTISTS

"PIECES"
55 minutes

Compiled by Projects UK, 'Pieces' is a compilation of 11 short works in videotape which range in length from 30 seconds to 6 minutes. Essentially, it is a collection of 'little ideas' which point to more general trends in British video art in the 1980s.

'Drawing Conclusions: The science mix' — Steve Hawley & Tony Steyger
Using 2 advertisements, one from the early 1960s and the other from the 1980s, the use of science as a magic selling agent is examined, with surprising results.

'In An Unguarded Moment' — Peter Savage
It's in our blood streams, in the air we breathe, so that we imagine we have adapted to it. It has evolved in us like five fingers, and consequently is assumed to be natural. Theory is one thing . . .

'I Really' — Steve Littman
The tape is concerned with story telling, and experiments with relationships between image and sound, with the use of a wide range of imagery and video techniques.

'Clone Video' — Neil Armstrong
A self promotion tape: the artist as merchandise, jumping through hoops in order to legitimise the activity.

'Passion Ration' — Zoe Redman
This is the story of her passion and his words, not the conventional once-upon-a-time, or a fairy tale, love at first sight and all that balony. Who knows if they lived happily ever after?

'Dance/Slap for Africa' — Nigel Rolfe
This tape was originally part of a large multi media work executed by Nigel Rolfe. The process aspect of this piece is a typical Rolfe pre-occupation, which is always brought to the fore in his work.

'So This Is How You Spend Your Time?' — Richard Layzell
A fragmented narrative of several short sequences is held together by the underlying theme of shifts in the commonplace, through sound, picture and time.

'Definitions' — Jon Bewley
Body Language is the pun, but it is the theory of expression of our real selves through how we gesticulate as well as how we speak, which informs 'Definitions'.

'The Jugo Beat' — Jeremy Welsh
Three spoken accounts of a difficult journey from England to Jugoslavia combine to form the words of a song.

'Around Enfield' — Val Timmis
Using Chromakey, conventions of television are hilariously exploded as the journey from home to work is mixed with the process of videomaking.

'Ra ads' — Mike Stubbs
Ra: the shampoo of the pharoahs.
Four 30 second advertisements extol the virtues of the spray-on shampoo that "preserves hair: prolongs life"

FRANK AUERBACH

Born Berlin, 1931. Arrived in England 1939. Borough Polytechnic, St. Martin's School of Art, Royal College of Art. Individual exhibitions since 1956 in London, New York, Sydney, Melbourne, Essex, Milan, Zurich. Hayward Gallery Retrospective, 1978.
Principal Group Exhibitions in Los Angeles County Museum, Hayward Gallery, Royal Academy, Kunstlerhaus Bregenz, Austria, Galerie des Beaux-Arts, Bordeaux, Walker Art Gallery, Liverpool, Art Gallery of Western Australia, Perth, Museen der Stadt, Cologne, Yale Center for British Art, New Haven, Connecticut, Santa Barbara Museum of Art, Neue Galerie Sammlung Ludwig, Aachen, Sydney Biennale, Metropolitan Museum, Tokyo, Tate Gallery, Lala Kalit Akademi, Delhi.

J.Y.M. Seated II
1981
oil on canvas
55.9 x 50.8 cms
Private Collection, London
Photo credit: Prudence Cuming Associates, London

To The Studios II
1982
oil on panel
122 x 137.2 cms
S.A. McLean, Ireland
Photo credit: Prudence Cuming Associates, London

Head of Debbie Ratcliff
1983-1984
oil on canvas
45.7 x 40.6 x 5.8 cms
Richard Salmon Ltd, London
Photo credit: Prudence Cuming Associates, London

Primrose Hill — Autumn
1984
oil on canvas
120 x 120 cms
Marlborough Fine Art, London

STUART BRISLEY

Born Surrey 1933. Guildford School of Art, Royal College of Art. Akademie der Bildende Kunst Munich, Florida State University.
Solo events and performances at Goethe Institute London, Serpentine Gallery, Henie-Onstad Foundation Oslo, Palazzo Reale, Milan, Biennale of Sydney, Documenta 6 Kassel, Bregenz, Austria, Vienna Performance Festival, Musee D'Art Moderne de la Ville de Paris.

Leaching Out at the Intersection
1981-1984
slide tape

Minus One
1983-1984
slide tape

Being & Doing
1979-1984
16 mm film
Brisley/McMullen in association with the Arts Council of Great Britain

STEPHEN COX

Born Bristol 1946. West of England College of Art, Loughborough College of Art, Central School of Art. Individual exhibitions in London, Amsterdam, Bari, Milan, Rome, Spoleto Festival, Florence, Valdarno, Geneva. Group exhibitions include Biennale de Paris, Hayward Annual, Palais des Beaux Arts, Brussels, Milan Triennale, University of Rome, Venice Biennale, Kunstmuseum Lucerne, 'The Sculpture Show' Hayward and Serpentine Galleries, 'New Art' Tate Gallery, Royal Academy of Arts, International Garden Festival Liverpool, 'An International Survey of Recent Painting and Sculpture' Museum of Modern Art New York.

Landscape with Ruins
1982
aquabianca marble stained with rust and copper

sulphate and Rosso Collemandina
4.7 x 3.36 x 0.85 meters
Made with the patronage of I.M.E.G., Massarosa (Lucca) and exhibited at the 25th Festival dei Due Mondi, Spoleto Italy. Nigel Greenwood Inc. London.

TONY CRAGG

Born Liverpool 1949. Gloucestershire College, Wimbledon School of Art, Royal College of Art. Individual exhibitions from 1979 in London, Hamburg, Bristol, Dusseldorf, Paris, Milan, Munich, Lyon, Karlsruhe, Tokyo, New York, Naples, Amsterdam, Bern, Toronto. Principal group exhibitions include Nuova Immagine Milan, Perspective Basle, Biennale of Venice, 'Objects & Sculpture' Arnolfini Gallery Bristol, 'British Sculpture in the 20th century' Whitechapel Art Gallery, Documenta - Kassel, 'Aspects of British Art Today', Japan, Indian Triennale, XVII Sao Paolo Biennale, 'The Sculpture Show' Hayward and Serpentine Galleries, 'New Art' Tate Gallery, Biennale of Sydney, Museum of Modern Art, New York.

New Stones — Newton's Tones
1978
found plastic objects
366 x 244 cms
Arts Council of Great Britain
Photo credit: Lisson Gallery, London

Palette
1982
mixed material
224 x 252 cms
Lisson Gallery, London
Photo credit: Lisson Gallery, London

Drawn on Objects — Object Poses
1983
mixed materials with crayon
approx. 300 x 300 x 450 cms
Lisson Gallery, London
Photo credit: Lisson Gallery, London

JOHN DAVIES

Born Cheshire, 1946. Hull and Manchester Colleges of Art, Slade School, Sculpture fellowship, Gloucestershire College of Art.
Numerous individual exhibitions at Whitechapel Art Gallery, Marlborough Fine Art, Kunstverein, Hamburg.
Included in many group exhibitions such as Venice Biennale, 'Documenta 6', Kassel, '4th Indian Triennale', 'Europaische Realistische Plastik', Kunsthalle, Bremen, 'British Sculpture since 1900', Whitechapel Art Gallery, 'Aspects of British Art Today', Metropolitan Museum Tokyo, 'The Hard Won Image' Tate Gallery.

Head (white with lines)
1983-1984
paint on fibreglass cast
108.2 cms
Queensland Art Gallery

For the Last Time
1972
fibreglass, wax, paint, clothing and shoes
4 life size figures
James Kirkman, London
Photo credit: Richard Sacks

Drawing of D.Y.
1984
111 x 147.3 cms
pencil and pastel
Marlborough Fine Art (London) Ltd
Photo credit: Jonathon Youens London

RICHARD DEACON

Born Wales, 1949. Somerset College of Art, St Martin's School of Art, Royal College of Art.
Individual shows at the Sheffield Polytechnic, Lisson Gallery, Riverside Studios, Chapter Gallery, Cardiff, Fruitmarket Gallery, Edinburgh.
Group exhibitions in Bristol, Kunstmuseum Lucerne, Hayward and Serpentine Galleries, Tate

Gallery, Margam Castle, Wales, Sao Paolo Biennale, Kunstmuseum Basle.

Art for Other People No. 5
1982
laminated wood
108 x 106 x 182 cms
The Saatchi Collection, London
Photo credit: Lisson Gallery, London

Art for Other People No. 6
1983
leather and brass
30 x 30 x 60 cms
Lisson Gallery, London
Photo credit: Lisson Gallery, London

Art for Other People No. 8
1983
brass and lino
18 x 35 x 35 cms
Lisson Gallery, London
Photo credit: Lisson Gallery, London

Art for Other People No. 9
1983
galvanised steel
53 x 34 x 11 cms
The Saatchi Collection, London
Photo credit: Lisson Gallery, London

Between the Two of Us
1984
Galvanised steel, canvas & rivets
214 x 396 x 31 cms
Lisson Gallery, London
Photo credit: Kurt Wyss, Basle, Switzerland

BARRY FLANAGAN

Born Prestatyn, Wales 1941. St. Martin's School of Art. Individual exhibitions from 1966 at Rowan Gallery, Museum of Modern Art, New York, Museum of Modern Art, Oxford, Art and Project, Amsterdam, Appeldorn Museum, Holland, Arnolfini Gallery, Bristol, Durand-Dessert, Paris, Waddington Galleries, Biennale Di Venezia, Centre Pompidou, Paris, Centro d'Arte Contemporanea, Syracuse, Galerie Karsten Greve, Cologne.
Included in Paris Biennale, Tokyo Biennale, 'Young British Artists', Museum of Modern Art, New York, 'Nine Young Artists', Guggenheim Museum, 'British Avant-Garde' New York Cultural Centre, 'Henry Moore to Gilbert & George' Palais des Beaux Arts, Brussels, 'Within the Decade' Guggenheim Museum, 'Arte Inglese Oggi', Palazzo Reale Milan, 'Made by Sculptors', Stedelijk, Amsterdam, 'Pier and Ocean', Hayward Gallery, 'British Sculpture in the 20th Century' Whitechapel Gallery, 'Aspects of British Art Today', Metropolitan Museum Tokyo, 'Documenta 7', Kassel, 'Zeitgeist', Berlin, 'New Art' Tate Gallery, Liverpool International Garden Festival.

Bye Bye The Elephant
1980
hornton Stone
54.2 x 58.7 x 30.5 cms
Southampton City Art Gallery

Vessel: In Memoriam
1981
bronze, partly gilded
58.4 x 60.9 x 45.7 cms
Museum of Modern Art New York

Soprano
1981
bronze, partly gilded
87 x 48.2 x 71.7 cms
The Pace Gallery, New York
Photo credit: Prudence Cuming Associates Ltd

The Lack of Civility
1982
bronze, edition of seven
67.3 x 80 x 30.5 cms
The artist, courtesy Waddington Galleries London
Photo credit: Prudence Cuming Associates Limited

Untitled (2B x 4)
1982
romano-chiaro marble
29.2 x 60 x 30.5 cms
The British Council Collection, London
Photo credit: Prudence Cuming Associates Limited

LUCIAN FREUD

Born Berlin 1922. Arrived London 1932. Central
School of Art and Goldsmiths College, London.
Many individual exhibitions since 1944 including
Venice Biennale British Pavilion and retrospective
exhibition, Hayward Gallery 1974.
Principal group exhibitions at Leicester Galleries,
Lefevre Gallery, Institute of Contemporary Art,
Vancouver Art Gallery, Galerie Rene Drouin,
Paris, Marlborough Fine Arts, Arts Council Gallery,
Norwich Castle Museum, Royal Academy of Arts,
Tate Gallery, Lala Kalit Akademi, Delhi.

The artist's Mother Resting 1.
1975-1976
oil on canvas
91.4 x 91.4 cms
S.A. McLean, Ireland
Photo credit: Prudence Cuming Associates, London

The Big Man
1976-1977
oil on canvas
91.4 x 91.4 cms
S.A. McLean, Ireland
Photo credit: Prudence Cuming Associates, London

Naked Man with Rat
1977
oil on canvas
91.5 x 91.5 cms
Art Gallery of Western Australia

Naked Girl with Egg
1980-1981
oil on canvas
75 x 60.5 cms
The British Council Collection, London
Photo credit: Prudence Cuming Associates, London

GILBERT AND GEORGE

Gilbert born Dolomites Italy 1943.
George born Devon 1942. They met and studied at
St. Martin's School of Art.
Individual exhibitions since 1968 in, London,
Amsterdam, Dusseldorf, New York, Art Gallery of
New South Wales Sydney, Tokyo, Athens, Bern
Paris, Baltimore, Houston, Florida.
Many group exhibitions at Hayward Gallery,
Palazzo Reale, Milan, The Art Institute, Chicago,
'Documenta (6)', and (7) Kassel, Musee d'Art
Moderne de la Ville, Paris, Bienal de Sao Paulo,
Metropolitan Art Museum, Tokyo, 'Zeitgeist',
Berlin, 'New Art', Tate Gallery, Sydney Biennale,
Yale Center for British Art, New Haven, Hirshhorn
Museum and Sculpture Garden, Washington.
Arts Council film made in 1981.

Flight
1983
photo piece
242 x 303 cms
Courtesy the artists and Anthony D'offay Gallery London
Photo credit: Anthony D'Offay Gallery London

Belief
1983
photo piece
242 x 202 cms
Courtesy the artists and Anthony D'Offay Gallery London
Photo credit: Anthony D'Offay Gallery London

Mouth
1983
photo piece
181.5 x 252.5 cms
Courtesy the artists and Anthony D'Offay Gallery London
Photo credit: Anthony D'Offay Gallery London

ANTONY GORMLEY

Born London 1950. Central School of Art and
Design, Goldsmiths College, University of London,
Slade School of Fine Arts. Individual exhibitions
since 1974 in London and New York. Group
exhibitions in Milan, at Arnolfini Gallery,
Whitechapel Gallery, Venice Biennale, Serpentine
Gallery, Fruitmarket Gallery, Edinburgh, XVII Sao
Paolo Biennale, Tate Gallery, Yorkshire Sculpture
Park, Hayward and Serpentine Galleries, Museum
of Modern Art, New York, Museum of Modern Art,
Tokyo.

Night
1983
lead and fibreglass
79 x 41 x 65 cms
The artist, courtesy Salvatore Ala Gallery, Milan and
New York
Photo credit: David Scott

Rise
1983
lead, fibreglass, clay, wax, plaster
36 x 61 x 207 cms
The artist, courtesy Salvatore Ala Gallery, Milan and
New York.
Photo credit: David Scott

Work
1984
lead, plaster, clay, fibreglass
134 x 190 x 36 cms
The artist, courtesy Salvatore Ala Gallery, Milan and
New York.
Photo credit: David Scott

IAN HAMILTON FINLAY

Born Nassau, 1952.
Individual exhibitions from 1968 including Scottish
National Gallery of Modern Art, National Maritime
Museum, Graeme Murray Gallery, Edinburgh,
Kettle's Yard Gallery, Cambridge, Serpentine
Gallery, University of Strathcylde.
Included in 'The Sculpture Show', Hayward and
Serpentine Galleries, 'The Little Sparta War',
Southampton Art Gallery, 'Skulptur in 20
Jahrhundert', Kunstmuseum, Basle.

Stonypath
1984
20 framed photographs each 40 x 50 cms
David Paterson London

IAN HAMILTON FINLAY with John R Thorpe
Japanese Stacks: Mikuma
1979
sycamore wood, carved
32.5 x 7.5 x 20 cms
Courtesy the artist and Graeme Murray Gallery,
Edinburgh
Photo credit: Antonia Reeve, Edinburgh

Japanese Stacks: Shinano
1979
sycamore wood, carved
20 x 22.5 x 22.5 cms
Courtesy the artist and Graeme Murray Gallery,
Edinburgh
Photo credit: Antonia Reeve, Edinburgh

Japanese Stacks: Yubari
1979
sycamore wood, carved
10 x 57.5 x 25 cms
Courtesy the artist and Graeme Murray Gallery,
Edinburgh
Photo credit: Antonia Reeve, Edinburgh

Japanese Stacks: Akagi
1979
sycamore wood, carved
17.5 x 30 x 12.5 cms
Courtesy the artist and Graeme Murray Gallery
Edinburgh
Photo credit: Antonia Reeve, Edinburgh

Japanese Stacks: Akitsuki
1979
sycamore wood, carved
27.5 x 10 x 60 cms
Courtesy the artist and Graeme Murray Gallery
Edinburgh
Photo credit: Antonia Reeve, Edinburgh

Japanese Stacks: Chokai
1979
sycamore wood, carved
20 x 10 x 22.5 cms
Courtesy the artist and Graeme Murray Gallery
Edinburgh
Photo credit: Antonia Reeve, Edinburgh

IAN HAMILTON FINLAY with Richard Grasby and
Nicholas Sloan
Talismans and Signifiers
1984
No's 3, 5, 7, 11, 18 and 19 of a series of 20
Courtesy the artist and Graeme Murray Gallery
Photo credit: Sean Hudson, Edinburgh

SUSAN HILLER

Born in USA 1942. Smith College Tulane
University. Since 1973 lived in London.
Many individual shows at the University of Sussex,
Museum of Modern Art Oxford, Kettle's Yard
Gallery Cambridge, Gimpels Fils, A Space
Toronto, Ikon Birmingham, Arnolfini Bristol, Andre
Emmerich Zurich, and in Warsaw, New York,
Adelaide, Sydney, Paris,
Included in group exhibitions such as 'British Art
1940-80' Hayward Gallery; 'Landscape: Ritual &
Ephemeral Structures' Tourchstone Gallery New
York, 'Books by artists' National Gallery of
Canada, 'From the traditional to the avant garde'
Rutgers University New Jersey 'Photo (graphic)
Vision' Winchester Gallery, 'Private Lives' Arts
Council of Great Britain, 'Artists Books', Artspace
Sydney & Museum of Contemporary Art Tokyo,
'New Media' Kunsthalle Malmo Sweden, 'Home &
Abroad' Serpentine, 'Demarkation' Richard
Demarco, Edinburgh.

Elan
1982
edition 1/2
C-type photographs handcoloured + 11 minute sound
tape
305 x 143.5 cms
Gimpel Fils, London

SHIRAZEH HOUSHIARY

Born Iran 1955. Chelsea School of Art, Cardiff
College of Art. Individual exhibitions from 1980 in
London, Cardiff, Cambridge, Milan. Principal
group exhibitions include Venice Biennale,
Hayward Annual, Fruitmarket Gallery-Edinburgh,
'Beelden Sculpture' Rotterdam, 'Eros Mythos
Ironie', Neue Galerie Graz, and in Turnin,
Montevideo, Antwerp.

KI
1984
copper
120 x 360 x 75 cms
Lisson Gallery, London
Photo credit: Lisson Gallery, London

Fire is Three
1984
copper
57.5 x 87.5 x 37.5 cms
Private collection, courtesy Lisson Gallery London
Photo credit: Lisson Gallery, London

The Pen and The Ant
1984
copper
150 x 120 x 70 cms
The British Council Collection, London
Photo Credit: Lisson Gallery, London

Front, Back Mirror
1984
aluminium
70 x 70 x 70 cms
Mr & Mrs Brooks Barron, Detroit USA
Photo credit:

ANISH KAPOOR

Born Bombay, India 1954. Arrived in London,
1971. Hornsey College of Art, Chelsea School of
Art.
Numerous individual shows in London, Paris,
Rotterdam, Liverpool, Lyon, New York, Cologne.
Principal group exhibitions from 1974 'Art into
Landscape', Serpentine Gallery, 'New Sculpture',
Midland Group, Nottingham, 'Object and
Sculpture', ICA London, Biennale de Paris, Centro
d'Arte Contemporanea, Syracuse, Rotterdam Arts
Council, 'The Sculpture Show', Hayward Gallery,
'New Art' Tate Gallery, 'Eros Mythos Ironie', Neue
Galerie, Graz, Sao Paolo Biennale XVII, Museum
of Modern Art, New York.

White Sand, Red Millet and Many Flowers
1982
mixed media
101 x 241.5 x 217.4 cms
Arts Council of Great Britain
Photo credit: Prudence Cuming Associates London

Hole and Vessel
1983
mixed media
60 x 150 x 240 cms
Private collection, courtesy Lisson Gallery London

KEN KIFF

Born Essex, 1935. Hornsey School of Art.
Individual exhibitions at the University of Sussex,
Nicola Jacobs Gallery, Talbot Rice Art Centre,
Edinburgh, Edward Thorp Gallery, New York.
Group exhibitions in Bristol, Liverpool, Museum of
Modern Art, New York, Neue Galerie-Sammlung
Ludwig, Aachen, '4th Biennale of Sydney', Musee
Cantini, Marseille, Tate Gallery, Lala Kalit
Akademi, Delhi, Ikon and City Museum
Birmingham, Hirshhorn Museum and Sculpture
Garden, Washington, National Museum of Modern
Art, Tokyo.

Talking with the Psychoanalyst: Night Sky No. 113
1973-1978
acrylic on paper
80 x 132.5 cms
Ed Wolf, London
Photo credit: Prudence Cuming Associates, London

Green Man
1977
oil on board
132.5 x 120 cms
Nicola Jacobs Gallery, London
Photo credit: Prudence Cuming Associates, London

Blue Shadow
1978-1980
oil on board
102 x 82 cms
Nicola Jacobs Gallery, London
Photo credit: Prudence Cuming Associates, London

Triptych: The Cry; Rain on the Sea; The Street
1982-1983
oil and acrylic on board
114 x 266.7 cms
Private Collection New York, courtesy Nicola Jacobs
Gallery, London
Photo credit: Prudence Cuming Associates, London

LEON KOSSOFF

Born London, 1926. St. Martin's School of Art,
Royal College of Art.
Exhibited since 1957 at Beaux Arts Gallery,
Marlborough Fine Art, Whitechapel Art Gallery,
Fischer Fine Art, Museum of Modern Art, Oxford,
Hirschl and Adler, New York. Principal group
exhibitions include 'The Human Clay', Arts
Council of Great Britain 'British Painting
1952-1977', Royal Academy, 'Eight Figurative
Painters', Yale Centre for British Art, New Haven,
'13 Britische Kunstler', Neue Galerie, Aachen,
'The Hard-Won Image', Tate Gallery, 'The Proper
Study', Lala Kalit Akademi, Delhi.

Two Seated Figures No. 1
1980
oil on board
122 x 152.4 cms
Fischer Fine Art Ltd, London
Photo credit: Prudence Cuming Associates, London

From 'Cephalus and Aurora' by Poussin No. 3
1981
oil on board
Art Gallery of New South Wales

Inside Kilburn Underground, Summer 1983
1983
oil on board
137.8 x 168.3 cms
The Saatchi Collection, London
Photo credit: Fischer Fine Art Ltd., London

BOB LAW

Born London 1934. From 1962 exhibited at
Grabowski Gallery, Konrad Fischer, Dusseldorf,
Lisson Gallery, Museum of Modern Art, Oxford,
Rolf Preisig, Basel, Galerie Nancy Gillespie-
Elizabeth De Lange, Paris, Gunnersbury Park,
London. Included in 'Two British Artists', ICA
London, 'Arte Inglese Oggi', Palazzo Reale, Milan,
'British Artists of the 60's, Tate Gallery, 'British
Painting 1952-1977', Royal Academy of Arts, 'Art
Actuel en Belgique et en Grande Bretagne', Palais
des Beaux-Arts, Brussels, 'Malerei Schwarz
Malerei Weiss', Kunstlerhaus, Hamburg, 'British
Sculpture since 1900', Whitechapel Art Gallery,
'Aspects of British Art Today', Metropolitan
Museum, Tokyo, 'ROSC' 84', Dublin, 'St. Ives',
Tate Gallery.

King and Queen
1984
bronze
110.5 x 51.2 x 45 cms (Queen)
104.5 x 53.6 x 43.4 cms (King)
Lisson Gallery, London
Photo credit: Rodney Todd White & Associates, London

The Last Supper
1984
bronze
81.3 x 20.4 x 10 cms (table)
15.3 x 8.3 x 8.1 cms (12 chairs each)
18.5 x 8.9 x 8.4 cms (Christ chair)
Lisson Gallery, London
Photo credit: Rodney Todd White & Associates, London

Christ Chair in Ultramarine
1984
Painted wood
120.3 x 57.5 x 52 cms
Lisson Gallery, London
Photo credit: Rodney Todd White & Associates, London

Cross on Wheels
1984
bronze cast
27 x 87 x 44 cms
Lisson Gallery, London
Photo credit: Lisson Gallery London

A Hole within a Whole on Wheels
1984
bronze
27 x 22.5 x 37.5 cms
Lisson Gallery, London
Photo credit: Lisson Gallery London

CHRISTOPHER LEBRUN

Born Portsmouth 1951. Slade School of Art,
Chelsea School of Art.
Individual exhibitions in London, Paris, New York.
Group exhibitions since 1975 at the Camden Arts
Centre, Milan Triennale, Galleria Civica, Modena,
XIII Festival Internationale de la Peinture, Cagnes-
sur-Mer, Neue Galerie-Sammlung Ludwig,
Aachen, Biennale of Sydney, Venice Biennale,
'Zeitgeist' Berlin, Bonlow Gallery New York,
Galleria d'Arte Moderna, Bologna, Tate Gallery,
Ashmolean Museum, Oxford.

Arion
1981
oil on canvas
213 x 305 cms
Private collection, London, courtesy Nigel Greenwood
Gallery.
Photo credit: Eileen Tweedy, London

Shield
1982-1984
oil on canvas
211 x 213 cms
Courtesy Nigel Greenwood Gallery London
Photo credit: Eileen Tweedy London

Untitled (Wreath) II
1984
oil on canvas
254 x 289.5 cms
Courtesy Nigel Greenwood Gallery London
Photo credit: Eileen Tweedy London

RICHARD LONG

Born Bristol, England, 1945.

Selected Individual Exhibitions:
Konrad Fischer, Dusseldorf, 1968. Stadtisches
Museum Monchengladbach, 1970. Whitechapel
Art Gallery, 1972. Museum of Modern Art, New
York, 1972. Stedelijk Museum, Amsterdam, 1973.
British Pavilion, Venice Biennale, 1976.
Whitechapel Art Gallery, 1977. Kunsthalle, Bern,
1977. Art Gallery of New South Wales, Sydney,
1977. Van Abbemuseum Eindhoven, 1979.
Museum of Modern Art, Oxford, 1979. Fogg Art
Museum, Harvard University, 1980. Centre d'Arts
Plastiques Contemporains, Bordeaux, 1981.
National Gallery of Canada, Ottawa, 1982.
Anthony d'Offay Gallery, 1983.

Principal Group Exhibitions
Galerie Loehr, Frankfurt, 1966. 'When Attitudes
Become Form', Kunsthalle Bern, 1969.
'Information', Museum of Modern Art, New York
1970. 'Guggenheim International', The Solomon
R. Guggenheim Museum, New York, 1971.
'Documenta 5', Kassel, 1972. 'The New Art',
Hayward Gallery, 1972. 'Andre/Le Va/Long',
Corcoran Gallery Washington D.C. 1976. 'Peter
Joseph, David Tremlett, Richard Long at Newlyn',
Newlyn Art Gallery, 1978. 'Matisse, Giacometti,
Judd, Flavin, Andre, Long', Kunsthalle Bern, 1979.
'Andre, Dibbets, Long, Ryman', Louisiana
Museum, Humbleback, Denmark, 1980. 'Pier &
Ocean', Hayward Gallery, 1980. 'Documenta 7',
Kassel, 1982. 'ARS 83', Museum of the Ateneum,
Helsinki, 1983. 'ROSC '84,' Guinness Hop Store,
Dublin, 1984. 'Primitivism in 20th Century Art: An
Affinity of the Tribal and the Modern', Museum of
Modern Art, New York, 1984.

Slate Cairn
1977
slate
600 cms (diameter)
John Kaldor, Sydney

A Straight hundred mile walk in Australia
1977
framed work
John Kaldor, Sydney
Photo credit: Richard Long

River Avon Mud Finger Circles
1984
Mud drawing on paper
180 x 160 cms
The artist, courtesy, Anthony D'Offay Gallery, London

Italy England Planes of Vision
1983
printed work
104 x 155 cms

The artist, courtesy, Anthony D'Offay Gallery, London
Photo credit: Prudence Cuming Associates, London

JULIAN OPIE

Born London 1958. Goldsmith School of Art.
Individual exhibitions at Lisson Gallery,
Kolnischer, Kunstverein, Cologne, Foundation
Cartier, France. Included in 'Young Blood'
Riverside Studios, 'Beelden Sculpture',
Rotterdam, 'Artists for 1990' Paton Gallery,
'Underwater', Plymouth Arts Centre.

Last Stand
1984
oil paint on steel
191 x 158 x 86.5 cms
Lisson Gallery, London
Photo credit: Lisson Gallery London

Abstract Composition with Pilchards
1984
oil paint on steel
100 x 175 x 75 cms
Lisson Gallery, London
Photo credit: Lisson Gallery London

Five Old Masters
1984
oil paint on steel
150 x 120 x 70 cms
Mr & Mrs Archibald Cox Jnr., London
Photo credit: Lisson Gallery London

JOHN WALKER

Born 1939 in Birmingham.
Studies: Birmingham College, Gregory Fellowship
Leeds, Harkness Fellowship USA, Visiting
Professor, Monash University, Melbourne.
Selected Exhibitions: Axiom Gallery London,
Venice Biennale, Kunstverein Hamburg, Museum
Bochum Holland, Museum of Modern Art New
York, Theo Waddington Gallery London and
Phillips Collection Washington.

Oceania My Dilema
1983
triptych oil on canvas
217 x 171 cms each
Courtesy of the Art Gallery of New South Wales

The Red Centre
1984
oil on canvas
213.4 x 167.6 cms

The Silence
1984
oil on canvas
213.4 x 167.6 cms

RICHARD WENTWORTH

Born Samoa 1947. Hornsey College of Art, Royal
College of Art, Mark Rothko Memorial Award
1974.
Individual exhibitions at Lisson Gallery and Galerie
't Venster, Rotterdam.
Group exhibitions at Royal Academy of Art,
Museum of Modern Art Oxford, Realities
Nouvelles, Paris, Whitechapel, Tolly Cobbold
Eastern Arts, South Bank Show, Hayward and
Serpentine Galleries 'Home and Abroad'.

Heist (For S.E.)
1983
linen, duckdown, tinned steel, gilded lead
60 x 90 x 65 cms
The Saatchi Collection, London
Photo credit: The Saatchi Collection

Jetsam
1984
galvanised & enamelled steel, cable
197 x 80 x 80 cms
The Saatchi Collection, London
Photo credit: The Saatchi Collection

Siege
1983-1984
laminated wood, steel, brass lead and cable
Janet and Michael Green, London
Photo credit:

Babar and Fido
1982
Aluminium, gilded and painted, cord floor to ceiling
8 x 19.5 cms (individual parts)
51 cms between cords
Lisson Gallery, London

ALISON WILDING

Born Lancashire 1948. Ravensbourne College of Art & Design, Royal College of Art.
Individual exhibitions at Kettle's Yard Gallery, Cambridge, Salvatore Ala, New York.
Group exhibitions from 1979 include 'New Sculpture' Ikon Gallery Birmingham, 'Eight Women Artists' ACME Gallery, 'Collazione Inglese', Venice, Biennale de Paris, 'The Sculpture Show' Hayward and Serpentine Galleries, XVII Sao Paolo Biennale.

Dark Horse No. 1
1983
portland stone and rubber
24 x 255 x 312.5 cms
The artist, courtesy Salvatore Ala Gallery, Milan and New York
Photo credit: Steven Tucker, New York

Green Rise
1983
slate and copper
58.5 x 10 x 28 cms
The collection of the Contemporary Art Society, London

STEPHEN WILLATS

Born London, 1943. Ealing School of Art, DAAD Fellowship in West Berlin.
Individual exhibitions in London, Eindhoven, East Berlin, West Berlin, Londonderry, Munich, Bristol, Rochdale.
Group exhibitions include Venice Bienale, 'The Sculpture Show', Hayward Gallery, 'The New Art', Tate Gallery, and shows in Milan, Modena, Karlstruhe and Stuttgard.
Projects Works in East and West London 1979-1982.

Pat Purdy and the Glue Sniffers Camp
Jan-Sept 1981
Photographic prints, photographic dye, gouache, Letraset text, felt tip pen, and objects found in the Lurky Place, Hayes London
eight panels 102 x 76.5 cms (each)
plus four panels 66 x 51 cms
Lisson Gallery London
Photo credit: A C Cooper London

Secret Prima Donna
May-October 1983
Photographic prints, photographic dye, pink acrylic paint, Letraset text, felt tip pen, pencil and found objects on paper and card.
two panels 100 x 140 cms (each)
one panel 100 x 102.5 cms plus
two mannequins 85 x 70 cms
Lisson Gallery, London
Photo credit: A C Cooper London

Private Icons
Aug-Dec 1983
three panels 140 x 101 cms (each)
Photographic prints, photographic dye, ink, acrylic paint, Letraset text, felt tip pen, pencil and found objects on paper and card
Lisson Gallery, London
Photo credit: A C Cooper London

BILL WOODROW

Born London 1948. Winchester School of Art, St. Martin's School of Art, Chelsea School of Art.
Individual shows from 1972 in London, Edinburgh, Stuttgart, Paris, Brisbane, Rotterdam, New York, Geneva, Toronto, Toulon.
Numerous group exhibitions at the Museum of Modern Art. Buenos Aires, Museum of Modern Art, Oxford, Whitechapel Art Gallery, Biennale of Sydney, Biennale of Venice, Kunstmuseum Lucerne, Biennale de Paris, Musee d'Ixelles, Brussels, Tate Gallery, XVII Sao Paolo Biennale, Galleria Giorgio Persano Torino, PSI New York.

Car Door, Armchair and Incident
1981
mixed media
200 x 250 x 240 cms
The Artist
Photo credit: Lisson Gallery, London

L'origine du Tatouage
1983
3 car bonnets
220 x 450 x 300 cms
Lisson Gallery, London
Photo credit: Lisson Gallery, London

PERFORMANCE ARTISTS

ROSE FINN-KELCEY

Born in Northampton 1945. Northampton School of Art, Ravensbourne College of Art, Chelsea School of Art. Performances at Midland Gallery and Serpentine Gallery. Since 1973 included in 'Seven from London' Kunsthalle Bern, 'London Calling' Acme Gallery, 'About Time' ICA, 'LA/London' Franklin Furnace New York, Fourth International Symposium of Performance Art Lyon, Timebased Arts Amsterdam.

CHARLIE HOOKER

Born London 1953, Croydon College of Art, Brighton Polytechnic.
Performances since 1975 include Percussions Walks at Robert Self Gallery and Sallyport Towers, Newcastle, Chelsea School of Art, Croydon College of Art. Also De Appel, Amsterdam, The Basement, Newcastle, Brighton Polytechnic, Tower Arts Centre, Winchester, Chisenhale Dance Space, Mainbeam Gateshead Multi Storey carpark, Newcastle, Rochdale Art Gallery, Newcastle Media Workshop.
Took part in 'Hayward Annual, 'Behind Bars', Tate Gallery, 'Sydney Biennale', 'Expanded Media Show', Sheffield Polytechnic, 'Undercurrents' Franklin Furnace Gallery, New York, 'Home and Abroad', Serpentine Gallery.

SILVIA ZIRANEK

SELECTED TITLES, IN CHRONOLOGICAL ORDER 1974-1984

2.83 PRECISELY
A LA RECHERCHE DE PIEDS PERDUS
CHILI CON CARDBOARD
THAT CHARMING VASE
WARM THOUGHTS
RUBBERGLOVERAMA, DRAMA
CHOSEN MOMENTS (WITH SUDS)
TRAGEDY AND CROSSWORDS (PSSST)
THERE'S SOMETHING REAL (ABOUT THE WORLD WE LIVE IN)
SHARE A PLATE WITH THE ONE YOU LOVE
TEETH. AND OTHER EMOTIONS ...
PHOTOS. AND OTHER FEMALES ...
FROM A CONSIDERABLE AMOUNT OF HEIGHT
ACH OUI, GOLDFISH ZUPPA
RARELY TALK/USED AIR
THE RATHER OF WHILE ... TOO MUCH AT ALL
IF YOU THINK IT ENTIRELY NECESSARY, OF COURSE I WILL
A DELIBERATE CASE OF PARTICULARS
AS AN EXPERIENCE I SUIT MY PURPOSE
CHEZ Z (SHE SAID)
COOKING WITH G*D (I (H)ATE SOLITUDE)
COSTA DEL TEARDROP
HUNGER FEEDS THOUGHT
THAT'S THE WAY OF IT
(L)IF(E) HAS A LOT TO DO WITH IT
SOME LIKE THEIR OWN F/ACTS (I'M EXPECTED, YOU SEE)
H(AMM)ER (HO)USE
NOT NECESSARILY S/WORDS

ZIRANEK: POET, PHILOSOPHER, COVERGIRL CUTIE, EXISTENTIAL COOK, HAS WORKED IN NEW YORK, NEWCASTLE, VENICE, ROCHDALE, TORONTO, NOTTINGHAM, PARIS, GLASGOW, ROTTERDAM, ROTHERHITHE, BRISTOL ... AVERSE TO DEFINITION, FINDING DATES CONFINE AMBITION/DEFINE RESTRICTION, THE RA(N)GE OF ST/AGES LEAD INSPIRATION FROM THE BACKYARDS OF SOUTH LONDON, VIA FACE AND FEET AND STANCES INTO LOWER EAST SIDE SPOTLIGHTS, TRANS-ATLANTIC D/ARTS AND HE/ARTACHES STRUCK ME MORE (... THOSE SUPERMARKETS!) THAN SUCH ENDLESS OH BUT DARLING OH BUT GOUACHE MMMMM AHHHHH CHARMING ...... HANDCUFFED TO HOPE — BUT DESTINED FOR DETERGENT, WHO NEEDS LOVE WHEN I HAVE FLOORBOARDS, FUELLED WITH FIRE AND FOOD AND YEARNING, LEANING FAR TOO MUCH ON YIELDING FEELINGS, B/RAISING HOPES AND B/OILING CHANCES, C/HOPPING MOUTHWARE, C/RUSHING F/ACTS ...... THUS THIS STERN BUT HANDSOME BEAUTY D(R)IVES WITH S/WORDS OF TH/OUGHT: THE CO(A)ST OF P/ALMS; THE B/RINK OF (L)IF(E); OR (M)OR(E); OR (W)OR(SE)...... THE V(O)ICE OF E/MOTION, AND EDIBLE P(R)O(BL)EMS, I CAN'T CHANGE THE WORLD — BUT I CAN WASH THE T.V.; I GET ON WITH THINGS THAT COUNT, LIKE CURRIES AND WIRING, I AM NOT A RECIPE, THOUGH I LOOK GOOD WITH A HAMMER: MY UNI/VERSE, MY G(U)ILT, MY ......

VIDEO ARTISTS

JOHN ADAMS

Born 1953 in Wakefield. Studied at Newcastle Polytechnic where he now lectures in video. Member of The Basement Group from 1979 until its dissolution in 1984, he has received four awards from the Arts Council of Great Britain. Recent shows include Worldwide Video Festival, Kijkhuis, Den Haag, Holland San Sebastian International Video Festival, Spain (prize winner) Video Culture Festival, Toronto, Canada Videographia, Barcelona, Spain, Irish Festival of Luving Art, Dublin, Festival International du Nouveau Cinema, Montreal.

CATHERINE ELWES

Born 1952 in St. Maixent, France. Studied at The Slade School of Art and Royal College. She is a visiting lecturer at NE London Polytechnic. Contributed to Women Live, Newcastle & London, National Independent Video Festival, ICA, London, Video Roma, Italy, Recent British Video, The Kitchen, New York, Berlin Film Festival, British/Canadian Video Exchange, Toronto.

ROSE GARRARD

Rose Garrard works in painting, sculpture, performance, installation and video. Recent works for broadcast television, 'Pandora the Bringer of Gifts' and 'Tumbled Frame'. Other shows include Artists for Nuclear Disarmament, Acme Gallery, London, Women Live, Arnolfini, Bristol & Basement, Newcastle and Live to Air, Tate Gallery.

ROBERTA GRAHAM

Born 1954 in L'Derry, N Ireland. Studied at West Surrey College of Art & NE London Polytechnic. Showed at B2 Gallery, London, Tate Gallery, Serpentine Summer Show 1, Perfo 2, Rotterdam, Holland, Fribourg Performance Festival, Switzerland, Violent Silence, Bloomsbury Theatre, London.

STEVE HAWLEY

Born 1952 in Wakefield. Studied at Brighton Polytechnic. Visiting lecturer at Brighton Polytechnic, Trent Polytechnic and NE London Polytechnic, where he was Arts Council Video Fellow. Recent shows: Art for Boxes, Tate Gallery, Recent British Video, The Kitchen, New York, Ljubljana Video Festival, Jugoslavia, Berlin Film Festival, Rennes Semaine de Video, France.

TINA KEANE

Teachers at St. Martin's School of Art, Slade School and Byam Shaw School. She has received several awards from Arts Council of Great Britain. Recent shows include Third Eye Centre, Glasgow, Edinburgh Film Festival, Tyneside Film Festival, Newcastle, Slow Dance Film Collective, Liverpool Women's Film Festival, Norwich, Recent British video, The Kitchen, New York, British/Canadian Exchange, Toronto.

BELINDA WILLIAMS

Born 1952, Yorkshire. Studied at Brighton Polytechnic. Administrator for The Basement Group, Newcastle. Employed at Trade Films, Newcastle. She has received 5 awards from Arts Council of Great Britain, Northern Arts and The British Council. Exhibited in Sheffield Expanded Media Show, Bienale De Paris, Nouveau Mixage, Caen, Normandy, Het Appollohuis, Eindhoven, Holland, Gruppos Ricerce Materialistica, Turin.

Various Artists "Pieces" 55 mins

Steve Hawley & Tony Stegger
Peter Savage
Steve Littman
Neil Armstrong
Zoe Redman
Nigel Rolfe
Richard Layzell
Jon Bewley
Jeremy Welsh
Val Timmis
Mike Stubbs